Baseball's Who's Who
of What Ifs

ALSO BY BILL DEANE

Following The Fugitive: *An Episode Guide and Handbook to the 1960s Television Series* (McFarland, 1996; paperback 2006)

Baseball's Who's Who of What Ifs

Players Derailed en Route to Cooperstown

BILL DEANE

McFarland & Company, Inc., Publishers
Jefferson, North Carolina

LIBRARY OF CONGRESS CATALOGUING-IN-PUBLICATION DATA

Names: Deane, Bill, author.
Title: Baseball's who's who of what ifs : players derailed en route to Cooperstown / Bill Deane.
Description: Jefferson, North Carolina : McFarland & Company, Inc., Publishers, 2021 | Includes bibliographical references and index.
Identifiers: LCCN 2021004693 | ISBN 9781476684796 (paperback : acid free paper) ∞
ISBN 9781476642413 (ebook)
Subjects: LCSH: Baseball players—United States. | Baseball—United States—History. | National Baseball Hall of Fame and Museum.
Classification: LCC GV865.A1 D37192 2021 | DDC 796.357092/2 [B]—dc23
LC record available at https://lccn.loc.gov/2021004693

BRITISH LIBRARY CATALOGUING DATA ARE AVAILABLE

ISBN (print) 978-1-4766-8479-6
ISBN (ebook) 978-1-4766-4241-3

© 2021 Bill Deane. All rights reserved

No part of this book may be reproduced or transmitted in any form or by any means, electronic or mechanical, including photocopying or recording, or by any information storage and retrieval system, without permission in writing from the publisher.

Front cover: Boston Red Stockings infielder Ross Barnes, 1874 (New York Public Library)

Printed in the United States of America

McFarland & Company, Inc., Publishers
  Box 611, Jefferson, North Carolina 28640
    www.mcfarlandpub.com

To Mark,
with whom I learned to love baseball,
and who became a fine man,
no thanks to his older brother.

Table of Contents

Preface 1

The Who's Who of What Ifs 5

Rick Ankiel	5	Buddy Lewis	100
Ross Barnes	10	Jim Maloney	104
Lyman Bostock	15	Carlos May	109
Bill Bradley	20	Austin McHenry	114
Steve Busby	23	Denny McLain	116
Cesar Cedeño	28	Don Newcombe	123
Ray Chapman	34	Dave Orr	131
Tony Conigliaro	39	Mark Prior	134
Jack Coombs	44	Pete Reiser	138
Larry Corcoran	50	J.R. Richard	145
Tommy Davis	53	Al Rosen	153
Charlie Ferguson	58	Herb Score	162
José Fernandez	61	Louis Sockalexis	169
Boo Ferriss	66	Karl Spooner	176
Mark Fidrych	70	Monty Stratton	181
Don Gullett	76	Dickie Thon	185
Ken Hubbs	81	Cecil Travis	192
Bill Hutchison	86	Hal Trosky	198
Charlie Keller	89	Brandon Webb	202
Bill Lange	97	Joe Wood	207

Appendix A: Honorable Mentions 219

Jim Abbott	219	Gene Bearden	221
Harry Agganis	219	Johnny Beazley	222
Moises Alou	220	Albert Belle	225
Lady Baldwin	220	Paul Blair	226

Table of Contents

Steve Blass	227	Charlie Hollocher	255
Vida Blue	228	Dummy Hoy	257
Tiny Bonham	228	LaMarr Hoyt	258
Britt Burns	229	Tex Hughson	258
Chris Carpenter	229	Bo Jackson	259
Rico Carty	229	Joe Jackson	259
Bob Caruthers	230	Jackie Jensen	261
Dean Chance	231	Bill Joyce	261
Spud Chandler	232	Benny Kauff	261
Joe Charboneau	232	Dickey Kerr	262
Ed Cicotte	233	Darryl Kile	264
King Cole	234	Matt Kilroy	264
Hub Collins	235	Silver King	264
Jim Creighton	235	Dave Kingman	265
Hugh Daily	236	Chuck Knoblauch	266
Steve Dalkowski	236	Harry Krause	266
Eric Davis	236	Terry Larkin	267
Willie Davis	237	Frank Lary	267
Paul Dean	237	Sal Maglie	267
Bill Delancey	240	Don Mattingly	268
Jim Devlin	240	Carl Mays	269
Dominic DiMaggio	241	Von McDaniel	269
Mike Donlin	241	Sam McDowell	272
Dave Dravecky	242	Alex McKinnon	273
Fred Dunlap	242	Sadie McMahon	273
Luke Easter	243	Minnie Minoso	273
Jim Eisenreich	244	Justin Morneau	274
Nick Esasky	245	Ed Morris	275
Happy Felsch	245	Mark Mulder	275
Jocko Flynn	246	Thurman Munson	276
Ray Fosse	246	Steve Olin	277
Nomar Garciaparra	247	Tony Oliva	277
Wayne Garland	248	Mel Parnell	279
Dwight Gooden	249	Johnny Pesky	280
Vean Gregg	249	Rico Petrocelli	280
Pedro Guerrero	250	Jimmy Piersall	280
Noodles Hahn	250	Arlie Pond	280
George Hall	252	Bret Saberhagen	281
Josh Hamilton	252	Johan Santana	281
Zaza Harvey	254	Urban Shocker	282
Willard Hershberger	254	Wayne Simpson	283
Bug Holliday	255	Grady Sizemore	284

Dave Stieb	284	Dick Wakefield	287
George Stone	284	Pete Ward	289
Frank Tanana	285	Lefty Williams	290
Oscar Taveras	286	Dontrelle Willis	290
Virgil Trucks	286	Don Wilson	291
Mickey Vernon	286	Jimmy Wood	291
Zoilo Versalles	287	Kerry Wood	292
Eddie Waitkus	287	David Wright	292

APPENDIX B: PLAYERS WHO MADE THE HALL OF FAME DESPITE CAREERS CUT SHORT   293

Roy Campanella	293	Addie Joss	297
Orlando Cepeda	293	Ralph Kiner	298
Roberto Clemente	293	Sandy Koufax	298
Mickey Cochrane	294	Kirby Puckett	298
Dizzy Dean	294	Jackie Robinson	299
Ed Delahanty	296	Amos Rusie	299
Lou Gehrig	296	Ted Williams	299
Hank Greenberg	297	Ross Youngs	300

Bibliography   301

Index   305

Preface

For of all sad words of tongue or pen,
The saddest are these: "It might have been!"
—John Greenleaf Whittier, "Maud Muller," 1856

There has long been a fascination with celebrities who died young: the likes of James Dean, Marilyn Monroe, JFK, Jimi Hendrix, Janis Joplin, and Princess Di became much more famous and beloved after their deaths than they ever were during their lives.

Along the same lines, much has been told and written over the years about athletes who might have become immortals, if only fate hadn't intervened. Unlike participants in other sports, a baseball player has to sustain excellence for a long period of time to qualify for its Hall of Fame. Bill Walton played just 468 NBA games, less than six full seasons' worth, yet was elected to the Naismith Basketball Hall of Fame. Gale Sayers played just 68 NFL games, yet made the Pro Football Hall of Fame. But to qualify for Cooperstown, one must have played in at least 10 major league seasons (if Mike Trout had been killed by COVID-19 before the 2020 season, he wouldn't have been eligible) and, for all practical purposes, excelled for at least a decade. Short-term stars need not apply.

I remember at age 11 or so, reading about Pete Reiser, an outfielder with immense talent who kept running into concrete walls until he was no longer an effective player. Over the years, I heard or read about others with similarly-sad stories, like Monty Stratton, Herb Score, and Ken Hubbs. Then I started living through new examples, such as Tony Conigliaro and J.R. Richard. I thought it was time that someone collected these stories together, in a sort of "Who's Who of What Ifs."

It was important—and difficult—to develop criteria. I was looking for players who realistically might have wound up in the Baseball Hall of Fame, if not for circumstances or tragedy. Thus, rule #1 is that the player can't be in the Hall. Many stars had their careers cut short (see Appendix

B), but made it to Cooperstown anyway, so they don't qualify for this book.

The second rule is that each player must have shown the potential for greatness in the major leagues. I wasn't looking for pretty good players—guys like Steve Blass or Dave Dravecky—whose careers were cut short, though many of them are covered in Appendix A. Most of the players chosen made strong showings in Rookie of the Year, MVP, and/or Cy Young Award voting, were All-Stars or recognized stars. With one exception, each of the players chosen exhibited superstar performance or potential for at least one full season before his career was derailed.

I was disinclined to include players whose downfalls were their own doings. These include men who played long enough to be eligible for the Hall of Fame, and have obvious Cooperstown credentials, but have been shunned by the voters (e.g., Barry Bonds, Roger Clemens), or are not eligible (Pete Rose, Joe Jackson). My hope is that someday they will be reinstated and/or forgiven, and take their rightful places in the Hall, alongside those who committed the same sins but were never caught or accused.

I generally did not include players who had a litany of related or unrelated health problems, as opposed to a single derailing event—men like Rico Carty or Nomar Garciaparra, who were terrific when they played, but just couldn't stay healthy.

I also didn't include 10-year players, like Tony Oliva, who still have a realistic chance of being elected before the ink is dry on this book. Along those lines, I found it particularly difficult to categorize more recent Hall-eligible players like Johan Santana and David Wright.

And I had to be a bit selective about which pitchers to include. Baseball history is littered with examples of hurlers who dominated at an early age, who were overused, and whose arms gave out before they hit what should have been their prime years. As legendary sportswriter Frank Deford wrote, "Pitchers fascinate me because a live arm is such a capricious possession and a dicey thing to depend on."[1] Still, half the players featured in this book are moundsmen.

Appendix A lists the "honorable mentions," including those alluded to in the last few paragraphs: players who had long, distinguished careers despite a disability or derailing event, or had their best years of good but not great careers behind them before fate struck, or have other circumstances preventing their inclusion among the featured 40.

In the end, there is a lot of subjectivity involved, and there are players whom I'd be hard-pressed to explain why they did or didn't make the cut.

One thing you'll see mentioned or alluded to a lot are "similarity

---

1. Deford, Frank. "Confessions of a Sportswriter." *Sports Illustrated*, June 5, 2017, p. 74.

scores." These, developed by Bill James, identify the most similar players to a particular man at a particular age, based on career statistics and position (for a full description, see baseball-reference.com). Especially for position players, these give a pretty good gauge as to someone's career trajectory.

I did not take oft-told stories at face value, but examined them, looking to either pin them down or prove them wrong. Did Reiser really run into 11 walls? Was a rule change the reason Ross Barnes fell from superstardom to mediocrity? When exactly did Smoky Joe Wood hurt his arm? Was Louis Sockalexis as great as he was remembered to be? Along the way, I debunked some myths and corrected the historical record, even on something as recent as Lyman Bostock's death date.

Statistics are chiefly from *The ESPN Baseball Encyclopedia* (New York: Sterling Publishing Co., Inc., 2008) and baseball-reference.com. These include stats which were not officially recorded at the time, such as pre–1913 ERAs. The player files at the National Baseball Library provided most of the other source material; many of the clippings therein are not fully identified, thereby limiting the notes.

Thanks to Cassidy Lent and Matt Rothenberg of the National Baseball Library for their research assistance. Pete Palmer, Wes Parker, Tom Ruane, and Neil Munro also provided help. And special thanks to featured players Steve Busby, Carlos May, Dickie Thon, and the late Boo Ferriss for their cooperation.

The Who's Who of What Ifs

Rick Ankiel

By the time Rick Ankiel joined the 2000 Cardinals' pitching rotation at age 20, the baseball cognoscenti had been awaiting his arrival for several years. Displaying what broadcaster Tim McCarver called "electric stuff," the 6'1", 200-pound southpaw lived up to expectations. He wound up among the league's top 10 in both strikeouts and ERA, and second in both most strikeouts and fewest hits allowed per nine innings. Cards Manager Tony LaRussa picked Ankiel to start Game One of the Division Series against the Braves, and the rookie held a 6–0 lead over future Hall of Famer Greg Maddux after two innings. With a national television audience looking on, it appeared to be the passing of the torch between the great pitcher of one generation to that of the next.

All that changed in the third inning, with the most sudden and public meltdown ever suffered by a baseball player. Rick Ankiel would win only two more big league games.

Richard Alexander Ankiel (pronounced "an-keel") was born July 19, 1979, in Fort Pierce, Florida, son of Richard and Denise Turton Ankiel, joining two half-siblings. Although Rick is listed as a Junior, he says his father's middle name is Patrick, and that young Rick was named after his maternal grandfather, Richard Turton.[1] The elder Richard Ankiel was in and out of trouble with the law; in 2000 his 15th arrest landed him in federal prison for drug smuggling (he and Denise were divorced soon after).[2]

---

1. Ankiel, Rick, and Tim Brown. *The Phenomenon: Pressure, the Yips, and the Pitch That Changed My Life*. New York: Public Affairs, 2017, p. 26.
2. Jordan, Pat. "A Mound of Troubles." *New York Times Magazine*, February 11, 2001, p. 58.

He was a raging drunk and a taskmaster to young Rick, driving him to succeed, barking instructions from the sidelines, and punishing him for mistakes on the field. "I was terribly shy," Rick recalls. "Maybe it was because my dad yelled at me so much."[3]

Rick attended Port St. Lucie High School, where he started attracting scouts' attention as a junior. He had a live arm, a smooth motion, poise beyond his years, and a sharp mind for the game. Ankiel was named *USA TODAY*'s 1997 High School Player of the Year. He made All-American after running up an 11–1 log as a senior, with a 0.47 ERA and 162 strikeouts in 74 innings. He then starred for the bronze medal-winning Team USA in the World Junior Championship, going 3–0 with a 1.82 ERA and 48 K's in 30 innings—not to mention a .387 batting average while playing outfield in games he wasn't on the mound.[4]

Rick Ankiel was ranked as baseball's #18 prospect before he ever threw a professional pitch. He was chosen by the St. Louis Cardinals right out of high school in the second round of the 1997 draft; he undoubtedly would have gone higher except for fear of his agent, Scott Boras. Ankiel wound up signing with the Cards for $2.5 million on August 28, rejecting a scholarship offer by the University of Miami. At the time, that was a record for a player signing with the team which drafted him.

Ankiel began his pro career in 1998 with Peoria in the Class-A Midwest League, and was soon promoted to Prince William of the Carolina League. Between the two, he went 12–6 with a 2.63 ERA and 222 strikeouts (tops in the minors) in 161 innings. He was now ranked as the #2 prospect in the game, behind only outfielder J.D. Drew.

Ankiel kept moving up the pro baseball ladder the following year, going first to Arkansas in the Double-A Texas League, then Memphis in the Triple-A Pacific Coast League. His combined record: 13–3, a 2.36 ERA, and 194 whiffs in 137 innings. Ankiel's minor league stats now showed 298 innings, a 25–9 record, 416 strikeouts, and a 2.51 ERA—almost all as a teenager. *Sports Illustrated*'s Tom Verducci dubbed Ankiel "The Can't-Miss Kid."[5] *Baseball America* named him as its 1999 Minor League Player of the Year, based on not only one's quality of play in the minors, but his potential for success in the majors. He joined the likes of previous honorees Frank Thomas, Manny Ramirez, and Derek Jeter; Ankiel was the first pitcher to win the award since 1988. Cardinals GM Walt Jocketty said, "Although he just turned 20 years old this summer, Rick is a very poised and determined

---

3. *Ibid.*

4. Derewicz, Mark. "Ankiel Wins *Baseball America*'s Minor League Player of the Year Award." *Baseball America* press release, September 15, 1999.

5. Jaffe, Jay. "Rick Ankiel Retires, Closing Out His Fascinating Career." SI.com, March 5, 2014.

young man who we feel will be one of the game's top pitchers entering the next century."[6]

Ankiel was increasingly pampered as he moved inexorably toward the major leagues. A switch-hitter, he was forbidden from batting right-handed, lest he expose his golden left arm to the opposing pitcher. He was put on a pitch-count limit, removed from games even when hurling a no-hitter. Coaches, afraid to tinker with such a valuable commodity, refused to advise him about his mechanics. Ankiel recognized that he was being treated as someone with a special but fragile talent. "If it goes, what do I have to fall back on?," he asked rhetorically. "Really nothing. It's scary."[7]

Ankiel made his big league debut on August 23, 1999, becoming the youngest player in the National League. He pitched five-plus innings against the Montreal Expos, retiring the first eight batters, striking out six, and leaving with a 4–2 lead, though the bullpen blew it. "He's for real," said Expos manager Felipe Alou. "He's going to be something."[8] Ankiel appeared in nine big league games in '99 with a 3.27 ERA (as compared to the league's 4.56 mark), striking out 39 in 33 innings—few enough frames to retain his rookie status for the next season.

Now the #1 prospect, the southpaw made the Cardinals' five-man rotation in 2000, showing a mid-to-high-90s fastball, a curve that Mark McGwire nicknamed "Snapdragon," and an effective changeup. He even displayed eye-opening hitting ability, raking two singles, a triple, and two home runs in his first 12 at bats of the year, before finishing with a .250 season average. Ankiel turned in an impressive freshman season: an 11-7 record, a 3.50 ERA (ninth in the NL), and 194 strikeouts (seventh) in just 175 innings. He broke Dizzy Dean's 68-year-old Cardinals rookie strikeout record. Among NL pitchers, only Randy Johnson had a higher strikeout-per-inning ratio. Ankiel was at his best in the stretch drive, going 4-0 with a 1.97 ERA in September as St. Louis won the Central Division title. Rick would be named *The Sporting News*'s NL Rookie Pitcher of the Year, and finish second behind Braves shortstop Rafael Furcal in BBWAA Rookie of the Year balloting.

With veteran Darryl Kile expected and announced to go, Ankiel was the surprise choice to start Game One of the NLDS on October 3. He escaped trouble in the first two innings as the Cards jumped on Maddux and the Braves for a 6–0 lead. Young Rick Ankiel was at the pinnacle of the baseball world.

But it all came crashing down in the third inning. Ankiel suddenly

---

6. Derewicz, Mark. "Ankiel Wins *Baseball America*'s Minor League Player of the Year Award." *Baseball America* press release, September 15, 1999.
7. Jordan, Pat. "A Mound of Troubles." *New York Times Magazine*, February 11, 2001, p. 60.
8. Beaton, Rod. "Ankiel Bound for Stardom." *USA TODAY*, September 16, 1999, p. 2C.

couldn't throw strikes. He wasn't just missing the strike zone; many of his pitches were sailing 10 feet over the catcher and all the way to the backstop. Ankiel walked four of the eight batters he faced that frame, and uncorked five wild pitches before being yanked. No one could believe what they were seeing. As former pro pitcher Pat Jordan wrote, "His once-classic delivery was riddled with the flaws of a Little Leaguer. He looked like a pitcher who, in a single moment, forgot how to pitch."[9] The Cardinals still managed to win the game and the Series.

Ankiel didn't get the ball again until nine days later, in Game Two of the National League Championship Series against the Mets. It was the same story: he lasted just two-thirds of an inning, giving up three walks and two wild pitches, with five of his 33 pitches going to the backstop, leading to a 6–5 loss. In Game Five, Ankiel entered in relief during a blowout defeat. LaRussa hoped that pitching in a no-pressure situation would enable his young hurler to regain his confidence and command. Nope. Ankiel coughed up two more walks and two more wild pitches, again lasting just two-thirds of an inning. The Cards lost the game and the Series, and their season was over.

During his last two innings of post-season play, spread over three appearances, Ankiel had surrendered nine walks, nine wild pitches, and seven earned runs for a sickening 31.50 ERA. Observers wondered aloud whether he would ever recover from this utter collapse. At age 21, Rick Ankiel had gone from baseball's brightest pitching prospect to a massive question mark. Rick called his father in prison soon after. "You were sorry," the senior Ankiel said disgustedly. "What the heck were you doing?"[10]

Rick underwent counseling over the off-season, but once the 2001 campaign started it was October 2000 all over again. In 24 innings, Ankiel had 25 walks, five wild pitches, and a 7.13 ERA. In his last outing on May 10, he threw five pitches to the backstop.[11] He was sent down to the minor leagues, not to return to The Show for 3½ years. He admits now that he suffered through nightmares and often turned to the bottle for relief.

Ankiel dominated in the low minors in 2001, then missed the '02 season with an elbow strain. After starting out the 2003 campaign 2–6 with a 6.29 ERA in Double-A, Ankiel underwent reconstructive "Tommy John" surgery on July 16 to replace a torn ligament in his left elbow (he would later be named in the Mitchell Report for using HGH during this period[12]).

---

9. Jordan, Pat. "A Mound of Troubles." *New York Times Magazine*, February 11, 2001, p. 58.
10. *Ibid.*, p. 60.
11. Associated Press. "Cards' Ankiel Still a Wild Man." New York *Daily News*, May 11, 2001, p. 32.
12. "Players Listed in the Mitchell Commission Report." ESPN.com, December 13, 2007.

Ankiel returned a year later and even made it back to the Cards briefly at the end of the '04 season. He then pitched in the Puerto Rican winter league and, though he had lost four mph from his fastball, seemed to be getting back on track.

But after another horrendous spring training outing in 2005, Ankiel made a surprising announcement on March 9: he would give up pitching and pursue a career as an outfielder. Following 4½ years of adversity and injury, he was ready to "Turn the page." As LaRussa said, "It wasn't just the frustration of not being able to play because of the recent. It was just the accumulation of work-work-work, rehab-rehab-rehab, and then the pay-off isn't (there). Rick's gone through a lot of tough times. He's been hurt twice. He went through that wildness period. He just wasn't getting the pay-back for going through all that, evidently."[13] Ankiel never pitched in the pros again.

Ankiel now fixes the downfall all on that first erratic pitch on October 3, 2000. "I threw a pitch, it staggered to the backstop, and everything changed," he writes. "My head opened up and filled with uncertainty. My body shut down. Panic thickened my throat. My career stumbled off with a single wayward pitch and took parts of my life with it, parts I loved and parts I hated and parts I'd not even known were there. Anxiety came like a dam break, and then I was wading in it, one sodden step at a time, sloshing about and slowly … slowly … drowning in it."[14] LaRussa reflects on starting Ankiel in Game 1 of the 2000 NLDS as "a decision that perhaps haunts him more than any he has ever made."[15]

Defying the odds, Ankiel did well as a minor league position-player in 2005, collecting 21 homers and 75 RBI in just 85 games. Then came another setback, as he suffered a left knee injury in spring training, 2006, underwent surgery on May 26, and missed the entire season.

But Ankiel rebounded yet again, slamming 32 home runs in 102 Triple-A games in 2007, and earning a call back to the majors. He was given standing ovations to greet his improbable return. Ankiel added 11 homers in 172 at bats with the Cardinals that year, then had a respectable 25 HR, 71 RBI, .264 season for the '08 Cards. Ironically, it was his strong, accurate arm which drew the most attention, as he threw strikes from center field to third base to nab a couple of opposing baserunners in May '08.[16] Ankiel

---

13. Leach, Matthew. "Ankiel to Switch from Mound to Outfield." MLB.com, March 9, 2005.
14. Ankiel, Rick, and Tim Brown. *The Phenomenon: Pressure, the Yips, and the Pitch That Changed My Life.* New York: Public Affairs, 2017, p. 13.
15. Bissinger, Buzz. *Three Nights in August: Strategy, Heartbreak and Joy Inside the Mind of a Manager.* New York: Houghton Mifflin Company, 2006.
16. Dodd, Mike. "Ankiel's Arm Again Drawing Compliments." *USA TODAY*, May 21, 2008.

received five votes for the Gold Glove Award that year.[17] A hernia ended his season in September.

Ankiel kicked around the big leagues for the next five years with the Cardinals, Royals, Braves, Nationals, Astros, and Mets, seeing diminishing success and playing time. He announced his retirement in March 2014. In January 2015, he was named "life skills coordinator" for the Nationals' extended spring training and their Gulf Coast League team. He now serves as a studio analyst for Fox Sports Midwest.

In 2017, Ankiel's memoir was published: *The Phenomenon: Pressure, the Yips, and the Pitch That Changed My Life*. In it, he seems to have come to terms with "The Thing," as he calls the anxiety disorder which unraveled his pitching career. He looks at his 2007 comeback as a victory of redemption. "True, sometimes I wonder what would have come had the Thing never been," he writes. "But not often anymore. See, I feel like I won. Like I found a cure. Not a cure, exactly; a way around it."[18]

Rick lives in Jupiter, Florida, with his wife, Lory (married, December 31, 2006), sons, Declan and Ryker, and his mother. His father is out of the picture.[19]

Ankiel finished his major league career with 76 homers and a .240 average in 653 games—not bad for a converted pitcher, but nothing like the Hall of Fame career he might have carved out from the mound. He was put on the 2019 Hall ballot, but failed to receive a vote.

Year	Team (League)	G	IP	W	L	PCT	SO	BB	H	ERA
1999	St. Louis (NL)	9	33	0	1	.000	39	14	26	3.27
2000		31	175	11	7	.611	194	90	137	3.50
2001		6	24	1	2	.333	27	25	25	7.13
2004		5	10	1	0	1.000	9	1	10	5.40
Totals		51	242	13	10	.565	269	130	198	3.90

17. *Houston Astros 2013 Media Guide*, p. 52.
18. Ankiel, Rick, and Tim Brown. *The Phenomenon: Pressure, the Yips, and the Pitch That Changed My Life*. New York: Public Affairs, 2017, p. 17.
19. Ibid.

Ross Barnes

By age 27, Ross Barnes had already starred on the baseball diamond for over a decade, and was the best hitter and second baseman in the game.

Over the first six years of organized professional league baseball, Barnes had batted a resounding .398, finishing tops in runs scored four times, hits four times, doubles three times, triples twice, and batting three times. Although nobody was keeping track of on-base or slugging percentages in those days, Barnes also had his leagues' best marks in those categories three times each.

But in 1877 a serious illness, along with a rule change, conspired to derail Barnes's career. Ross would play in just 168 more big league games with a pedestrian .269 average, finishing his career short of qualifying for the not-yet-imagined Hall of Fame.

Charles Roscoe Barnes was born May 8, 1850, in Mount Morris, New York, one of at least eight children of Joseph and Mary Weller Barnes.[1] Many sources gave his birth name as Roscoe Conkling Barnes, suggesting he was named after a well-known nineteenth-century U.S. Senator; however, Roscoe Conkling didn't take office until 1867. The Barnes family moved to Rockford, Illinois, when Ross was a teenager.

Barnes began his baseball journey with a Rockford amateur team called the Pioneers, where he was a teammate of another young future star, pitcher Albert Spalding. In 1866, the two 16-year-olds moved up to Rockford's top team, the Forest City club. The pair helped the Forest Citys to become one of the best teams in the country over the next five years, as the sport evolved from amateur to professional. Barnes was not particularly big even for the era, standing 5'8½" and weighing 145–155 pounds at maturity, but he was a strong, graceful, and intelligent ballplayer. He was also known as a natty dresser and a favorite of female fans.

When the National Association, baseball's first pro league, was founded in 1871, Spalding and Barnes were two of the most sought-after players. They joined many former Cincinnati Reds stars on the Boston Red Stockings, leading them to four of the NA's five pennants. Although historians do not yet regard this loosely-organized circuit as a major league, it was comprised of the best baseball players in existence at the time.

In 1871, Barnes played in all 31 of Boston's league games, batting .401 and scoring 66 runs—better than two runs per game, and 15 more than anyone else in the league! He also tied for the lead in total bases, and was one of the top infielders in the league, splitting his time between shortstop and second base. In 1872, Barnes was even better, topping the Association in hits, doubles, batting (.430), slugging, and fielding percentage at second base. He also began a 35-game hitting streak: the last 21 games of that season, and the first 14 of '73.

---

1. "Ross Barnes is Ignored in Mt. Morris." Unidentified clipping in National Baseball Library file, November 2, 1987, p. 1B.

Barnes not only was a deft fielder with either hand (no gloves in those days; he threw right-handed), he revolutionized defensive play at the keystone sack. Until the 1870s, the three basemen planted themselves on their respective sacks; the second baseman stood on second base, ready to accept any throw, but leaving a gaping hole on the right side of the infield. Barnes was the first to expand the role toward what it is today, shifting his position according to the batter and situation.[2] Likewise, Ross was inventive at the bat. A right-handed hitter, he was said to be a pioneer of the sacrifice hit, and was a magician at hitting foul balls. Facing a difficult pitcher, at a time when fouls did not count as strikes, Barnes would deliberately foul off pitch after pitch to wear the hurler down, until he got a serve to his liking.[3] According to the New York *Clipper*, "as a 'scientific batsman'—one who goes in to place a ball advantageously—we never saw Barnes' superior."[4]

Barnes's 1873 campaign, in context of the short season, ranks as one of the best in the annals of the game. Playing in all 60 of Boston's games, Barnes led the league in runs, hits, doubles, triples, total bases, stolen bases, walks, batting (.431), on-base percentage, and slugging. For a 162-game season, his numbers would project to 338 runs, 373 hits, 84 doubles, 30 triples, and 116 steals! For good measure, he also was again the top-fielding second sacker.

Barnes "slumped" to .340 in 1874, a season interrupted by a two-month goodwill tour of Great Britain by the Boston and Philadelphia teams. In 1875 Barnes led the NA in runs, hits, and OBP while batting .364. The National Association was then disbanded (Barnes stands as its all-time leader in runs, doubles, steals, batting, and slugging), replaced by the National League, historically considered the first major circuit. Boston's "Big Four" of Barnes, Spalding, Deacon White, and Cal McVey joined the NL's Chicago White Stockings.

In the circuit's maiden season, Barnes continued to dominate. On May 2, 1876, he drilled the first home run in major league history. On July 26, Barnes lashed out four singles, a double and a triple in one game. Playing in all 66 of Chicago's games, he was tops in the league in runs (126), hits (138), doubles, triples, total bases, walks, batting (.429), OBP, slugging, and fielding. To put his numbers into perspective, no one else in the league had more than 72 runs, 111 hits, or a .366 average. For the fifth straight year, Barnes's team ran away with the league pennant. Nobody could have guessed that Ross Barnes's tenure of dominance was about to come to a screeching halt.

---

2. Bulger, Bozeman. Unidentified clipping in National Baseball Library file.
3. *Ibid.*
4. "The Clipper Prize Winners, No. 4—Roscoe C. Barnes." New York *Clipper*, c. May 1879.

Part of Barnes's success as a hitter was his mastery of the "fair-foul hit." Up to this time, Rule V, Section 11 read, "If the ball from a fair stroke of the bat first touches the ground ... either in front of, or on the foul ball lines, it shall be considered fair."[5] Barnes learned to slap or bunt the ball in such a way that it struck the ground fair, then spun into foul territory, out of reach of the fielders.

The following was added to Section 11 prior to the 1877 season: "All balls batted directly to the ground that bound or roll outside the foul lines between home and first or home and third bases, without first touching the person of a player, shall be considered foul."[6] No one was more responsible for the rule change, nor potentially hurt more by it, than Barnes.

But, contrary to revisionist history, there was far more to Barnes's sudden decline than just a rule change. After all, you don't lead the league in doubles, triples, and slugging by laying down bunts.

According to historian Frank Phelps, "His performance declined sharply in 1877, not because fair foul hits had been outlawed, but due to illness which idled him from mid–May to early September and permanently diminished his muscular strength."[7] Barnes had somehow contracted a malaria-like ailment, possibly the ague, shortly after the 1876 season. He gamely tried to play in '77, and started OK, going 5-for-13 in the first three games. But after his second straight 0-for-4 on May 18, it was clear that he couldn't cut it. The following day's Chicago *Tribune* said that Chicago had "laid off and furloughed their ablest player," who was unable to overcome the effects of "a six months' sickness." Barnes said, "I tell you, this is terrible; to be anxious to do a thing which you know you can do, and yet find that you are bodily unable to do it. I know what I can do, and what I have done, and yet I haven't the strength to do the same again."[8]

Barnes didn't return to the lineup until September 4 and wound up playing just 22 games in 1877 with a .272 average. There was no "disabled list" (or "injured list," as it was renamed in 2019) in those days, and the White Stockings refused to pay Barnes for the time he missed. Afterward, in an unprecedented move, Barnes sued the club in the county courts. He lost, and never played another game for Chicago.

Barnes toiled in the International Association in 1878, then returned to the majors with Cincinnati in 1879 and Boston in 1881, a shadow of his former self, and his career was over at age 31. Even counting his National

---

5. *Constitution and Playing Rules of the National League of Professional Base Ball Clubs.* Chicago: A. G. Spalding & Brothers, 1877, p. 31.
6. *Ibid.*
7. Phelps, Frank V. "Roscoe Conkling Barnes." *Nineteenth Century Stars.* Kansas City, MO: Society for American Baseball Research, 1989, p. 10.
8. Chicago *Tribune*, May 19, 1877, p. 2.

Association service, he falls short of the 10-year minimum required for Hall of Fame consideration.

As time went on and old-timers gave way to a new generation of fans with short memories and no record books, Barnes's heroics were all but forgotten. But not by Hall of Fame player and manager Cap Anson, nor noted writer Sam Crane, who in 1911 did a feature on the 50 greatest players in history. Anson wrote that "Ross Barnes was one of the best ball players that ever wore a shoe, and I would like to have nine men just like him under my management. He was an all-around man, and I do not know of a single man on the diamond at the present time [1900] that I regard as his superior."[9] Ranking him #10 all time, Crane wrote, "Ross Barnes, in the opinion of the players who played on the same clubs with him, and also those who were his opponents, was the best second baseman the game had produced, and (many) still think that Barnes has never been excelled as a guardian of the keystone sack, even by the many stars in the position who have been before the public since."[10]

Other than a one-year stint as umpire in the 1890 Players' League, Barnes spent the rest of his life in white-collar jobs in the Chicago area. Unmarried, he died in Chicago after a brief bout with stomach trouble on February 5, 1915 (though his death date long was mistakenly listed as February 8, the date of his obituary).[11] Most obits were brief and understated. W.E. Phelon of the Cincinnati *Times-Star* decried the lack of notice at Barnes's passing, writing, "Ross Barnes, 40 years ago, was as great as [Ty] Cobb or [Honus] Wagner." *Spalding's Official Base Ball Guide* recalled him as "one of the greatest players who ever lived ... the most expert second baseman who ever played the position."[12] Ironically, Albert Spalding—namesake of that book, and Barnes's long-time teammate—also died at age 64 in 1915.

By the time the first Hall of Fame elections were held in 1936, six decades had passed since Ross Barnes's reign as the best non-pitcher in baseball, and there were few left who had witnessed it. He received just three votes in '36, and a decade later he was made ineligible by the 10-year-minimum rule.

In 2013, SABR named Barnes as an Overlooked 19th Century Baseball Legend. Four years later, it dedicated a monument in his honor at his hometown of Mt. Morris, New York.

---

9. Duxbury, John. "The National League's First Batting Champ." *Baseball Research Journal*. Cooperstown, NY: Society for American Baseball Research, 1976.

10. Crane, Sam. "Sam Crane Writes Series of Stories on Fifty Greatest Ball Players in History: Rouse C. Barnes, No. 10." New York *Journal*, December 26, 1911.

11. "Ross Barnes Dead." *The Sporting Life*, February 13, 1915.

12. Foster, John B., editor. *Spalding's Official Base Ball Guide*. New York: American Sports Publishing Company, 1916, pp. 48–49.

Year	Team (League)	G	AB	R	H	2B	3B	HR	RBI	SB	AVG	OBP	SLG
1871	Boston (NA)	*31	157	*66	63	10	9	0	34	11	.401	.447	.580
1872		45	230	81	*99	*28	2	1	44	12	*.430	.452	*.583
1873		*60	320	*125	*138	*31	*11	2	60	*43	*.431	*.465	*.616
1874		51	259	72	88	12	4	0	39	8	.340	.360	.417
1875		78	393	*115	*143	20	4	1	58	29	.364	*.375	.443
1876	Chicago (NL)	*66	322	*126	*138	*21	*14	1	59		*.429	*.462	*.590
1877		22	92	16	25	1	0	0	5		.272	.323	.283
1879	Cincinnati (NL)	77	323	55	86	9	2	1	30		.266	.301	.316
1881	Boston (NL)	69	295	42	80	14	1	0	17		.271	.309	.325
Totals		499	2391	698	860	146	47	6	346		.360	.388	.468

Lyman Bostock

In November 1977, Lyman Bostock became one of the highest-paid players in baseball history, following a season in which he finished second in the A.L. in batting. Ten months later, he was dead.

Lyman Wesley Bostock, Jr., was born in Birmingham, Alabama, on November 22, 1950. His father had been a first baseman and outfielder in the Negro American League between 1938 and 1949, mostly for the Birmingham Black Barons. Based on extremely limited data, Lyman Sr., batted .352 in league games.[1]

After young Lyman's parents split up, he and his mother, Annie, moved west. "I was seven years old and came to California from Birmingham, Alabama on a bus with my mother," he recalled. "We came with $7 and a prayer."[2] Bostock grew up in Los Angeles, where he often watched the expansion Angels play.

Bostock attended Manual Arts High School in California, where he played basketball and was all-league in baseball. He graduated on June

---

1. Bucek, Jeanine, editorial director. *The Baseball Encyclopedia.* New York: Macmillan, 1996, p. 2778.
2. "Lyman Bostock, Aware and Concerned Citizen." Unidentified clipping in National Baseball Library file.

16, 1968, and went on to California State-Northridge. He led their baseball team to two straight NCAA championships and was team captain in 1972. Bostock was named to the All-League, All-District, All-West Coast, and All-Tournament teams.[3] He finished just 15 credits short of a bachelor's degree.

Bostock was picked by the Twins in the 26th round (595th player selected) of the June 1972 draft. Over the next three years the 6'1", 180-pound lefty swinger moved from Charlotte to Orlando to Tacoma, improving at each stop, and batting .326 in his 291-game minor league career. On January 31, 1974, Lyman married the former Yuovene Brooks.[4]

After an impressive spring training in 1975, Bostock got the call to the parent team, but his big league career got off to a rocky start. He was batting just .219 when he crashed into an outfield fence on a spectacular catch of a drive by Oakland's Bert Campaneris on April 20, suffering a chip fracture of the right ankle, and was put on the disabled list. After surgery, Bostock went to Tacoma for nearly a month before returning to the Twins in late June. He was acting cocky and quarreling with umpires, but not producing. Part of the problem was that he was still favoring his ankle. "I hit off the toes of my front foot, raising the heel into the air instead of pivoting," he recalled.[5] By July 17, as the second half of the season began, Bostock was batting just .195. Nearing his 25th birthday, he was looking more like a suspect than a prospect, and was thinking of quitting the game. He visited an uncle in New York, looking for sympathy, but instead got a lecture.

"He told me to quit arguing with umpires and to shape up," Bostock recalled. "He was right. As long as I argued with umpires, they weren't going to give me a break on anything close to the plate. I figured he might be right on how I was acting off the field, too. So I tried to change. I decided to quit trying to win immediate acceptance. To quit trying to be a star overnight. From then on, I played each game as well as possible and didn't worry about my average."[6]

It paid off. Bostock hit .325 the rest of the way to finish the year with a .282 average in 98 games. Bostock learned a lot about hitting from two all-time greats, his teammates Tony Oliva and Rod Carew, who combined to win 10 AL batting titles between 1964 and 1978. "Tony was the teacher and Rodney was the demonstrator," said Bostock.[7]

---

3. Unidentified clipping in National Baseball Library file.
4. Seeberg, Tom, and Mel Franks, editors. *California Angels 1978 Media Guide*, p. 12.
5. "Bostock Back in Groove." *The Sporting News*, September 11, 1976.
6. Fowler, Bob. *The Sporting News*, July 3, 1976.
7. Miller, Dick. "Lyman's Pie in Sky Proves to Be Angel Food." *The Sporting News*, April 15, 1978, p. 3.

Bostock started as a right fielder, then shifted to center late in his rookie season. "He was an excellent defensive center fielder," wrote Twins beat writer Bob Fowler.[8] Bostock became known for playing shallow and making basket catches. Explaining how he developed his trademark fielding style, Bostock said, "When I was eight years old my mother bought me my first glove, but someone stole it the next day. My mother wasn't about to buy me another one. But a friend of hers at work gave her a replacement. Unfortunately, it was a left-hander's model and I'm right-handed. Since it was the only glove I had, I had to use it." Bostock wore it backwards on his left hand and developed the basket catch. "It was the only way I could catch the ball," he said. "It became a habit, and I still have it."[9] On May 25, 1977, he tied a major league record with 12 putouts in a nine-inning game, and set an A.L. mark with 17 putouts in a doubleheader.

In 1976 Bostock proved his second-half performance of the previous year was not a fluke. On July 24, he hit for the cycle in a 17–2 rout of the White Sox, adding a walk and a sacrifice fly. Despite missing 34 games with hamstring and thumb injuries, he finished fifth in the A.L. in triples and fourth in batting (.323), just 10 points behind league leader George Brett. Manager Gene Mauch was impressed with Bostock's work ethic and progress. "I've never seen a player who was so dedicated to being a star in this game," Mauch said.[10]

Bostock put it all together in 1977. In addition to placing second in the AL batting race with his .336 mark, he finished in the league's top five in runs, hits, doubles, and triples. Though not considered a power-hitter, Bostock contributed 14 homers, 90 RBI, and a .508 slugging percentage. And all at the bargain-basement salary of $20,000!

In context, the average player salary had just surpassed $50,000 the year before, and only a few had reached six figures. But the tide was rapidly turning in the players' favor. They had won the right to free agency by an arbitrator's decision in late 1975, and the first mass free agent draft was held on November 4, 1976. Reggie Jackson was the biggest winner, signing a five-year, $2.9 million contract with the Yankees.

Lyman Bostock was one of the most-attractive commodities as the second free agent draft unfolded. He was drafted by the maximum 13 teams, and offered huge deals by the Yankees and Padres, among others. But Bostock was most impressed by his hometown California Angels, even though their offer was a bit lower. "The Angels showed me more respect in the

---

8. Fowler, Bob. *The Sporting News*, July 3, 1976.
9. Fowler, Bob. "Bostock Bat Brings Out Grind on Twins." *The Sporting News*, April 5, 1975.
10. Fowler, Bob. *The Sporting News*, July 3, 1976.

few hours I spent at Anaheim Stadium before signing than Minnesota did in the six years I was in their organization," Bostock said.[11] He wound up signing a five-year package worth a total of $2,250,000 with California on November 21, 1977, working out to an average of $450,000 per year. At the time only four players, including future Hall of Famers Jackson, Catfish Hunter, and Mike Schmidt, were earning more (though Bostock's agent, Abdul Jalil, claimed that Lyman was #1 in baseball history).[12] In any case, it was a humongous increase over $20,000. "I was in the right place at the right time," Bostock said[13]—words that would be recalled with sad irony less than a year later.

"You have to like Lyman Bostock," said Mauch. "He's the second best hitter I've seen in either league (behind Rod Carew). Without doubt, he'll lead the league in hitting soon."[14]

Bostock felt the pressure of his huge contract, and got off to a wretched 2-for-39 (.051) start with his new team. He was still hitting just .147 at the end of April, and offered to return his first month's salary to the Angels. Owner Gene Autry refused, so Bostock donated the money to charity.

Of course, Bostock eventually began hitting. He batted .318 after April, and with a week left in the season had risen to the top 10 in the AL batting race at .296. Moreover, Bostock had become one of the most well-liked players in the game. He was outgoing and civic-minded, didn't drink or smoke, and was devoted to his wife, Yuovene.[15]

During a road trip to play against the White Sox on September 23, 1978, Bostock visited his uncles, Edward and Thomas Turner, in nearby Gary, Indiana. After dinner with Tom, they stopped to visit two god-daughters of Turner's, Joan Hawkins and Barbara Smith; Bostock had met Hawkins when she was a little girl and asked what had become of her. The women asked if Turner could drop them off at someone else's house, and he obliged. Bostock was sitting in the back seat of Turner's 1976 Buick, next to Smith. Unbeknownst to the four, Barbara's estranged husband, Leonard Smith, was following them. At a stop-light at 10:44 p.m., Smith got out of his car and fired a shotgun into the rear window of the vehicle, apparently trying to kill his wife. Barbara was seriously wounded, but Bostock's wounds—to the left side of his head—were much more grave.[16] He

---

11. "Lyman Bostock, Aware and Concerned Citizen." Unidentified clipping in National Baseball Library file.
12. Ibid.
13. Miller, Dick. "Lyman's Pie in Sky Proves to Be Angel Food." *The Sporting News*, April 15, 1978, p. 3.
14. Seeberg, Tom, and Mel Franks, editors. *California Angels 1978 Media Guide*, p. 13.
15. Miller, Dick. "Bostock Death Stuns Angels." *The Sporting News*, October 7, 1978.
16. Ibid.

died at 1:30 a.m. the next day, so his date of death was September 24, not the 23rd as long listed in "official" sources.[17]

It was the latest in a series of tragedies which had befallen Angels players. Twenty-five-year-old pitcher Dick Wantz died of a cerebral hemorrhage in 1965; relief ace Minnie Rojas was paralyzed in a 1968 car crash that also killed his wife and child; shortstop Chico Ruiz was killed in a 1972 auto accident; pitching prospect Bruce Heinbechner died in a 1973 crash; and 1974 #1 draft pick Mike Miley was killed in yet another auto accident in 1977. The Angels wore black armbands in Bostock's memory for the remainder of the 1978 season.[18] Multiple memorial funds were established in his honor.

Because Bostock had not quite met the four-year service requirement, Yuovene received only a $300 per month widow's benefit from Major League Baseball.[19] More sickening, Leonard Smith never served a day in jail for his crime. The first murder trial ended in a hung jury on July 13, 1979[20]; then, on November 16 of that year, a second jury found him innocent by reason of insanity.[21] On June 20, 1980, less than two years after killing Bostock, Smith was sent home from a state hospital in Logansport, Indiana, after psychiatrists declared him no longer mentally ill.[22]

Could Bostock really have fashioned a Hall of Fame career? After all, he had just 624 career hits at age 27. But at .311, he also had the fourth-highest lifetime batting average among active hitters, and the make-up of a player who would excel for many years to come. Unfortunately, he never had those years.

Year	Team (League)	G	AB	R	H	2B	3B	HR	RBI	SB	AVG	OBP	SLG
1975	Minnesota (AL)	98	369	52	104	21	5	0	29	2	.282	.331	.366
1976		128	474	75	153	21	9	4	60	12	.323	.364	.430
1977		153	593	104	199	36	12	14	90	16	.336	.389	.508
1978	California (AL)	147	568	74	168	24	4	5	71	15	.296	.362	.379
Totals		526	2004	305	624	102	30	23	250	45	.311	.365	.427

---

17. "Baseball's Bostock Slain." UPI, September 25, 1978.
18. "Angels to Don Armbands as a Farewell to Bostock." Associated Press, September 26, 1978.
19. Miller, Dick. "Bostock Death Clouds Angel Future." *The Sporting News*, October 14, 1978.
20. "Mistrial in Bostock Case." *The Sporting News*, July 28, 1979.
21. "Jury Finds Smith Innocent by Insanity." *The Sporting News*, December 1, 1979.
22. "Bostock Defendant Freed." Associated Press, June 21, 1980.

Bill Bradley

Upon Bill Bradley's death in 1954, long-time scribe Ed Bang ranked him—along with Hall of Famers Jimmy Collins and Pie Traynor—as one of the three best third basemen in baseball history. Collins, asked in 1904 who was tops at the hot corner, said, "Well, if I could field and bat like Bradley, I should lay claim to that title myself."[1] But a wayward pitched ball would prove to be Bill's undoing.

William Joseph Bradley was born in Cleveland, Ohio, on February 13, 1878. He grew up playing ball with some future big leaguers, including the Delahanty brothers.[2] After turning down a paltry contract offer from a team in Mobile, Alabama, Bradley began his pro career in Burlington, Iowa, of the Western Association in 1897.

Bradley played for Auburn and Troy of the New York State League the next two seasons, and debuted in the majors with the Chicago Cubs on August 26, 1899. The six-foot, 185-pounder was their regular third baseman through 1900, batting a solid .288. But, after getting a contract offer more than doubling what he made for the Cubs, Bradley jumped to the fledgling American League the next year, joining his hometown team, the Cleveland Bronchos or Blues (now known as the Indians). It should be noted that the AL was probably not quite major league-caliber at this time.

Bill Bradley and "Big Bennie," c. 1909. Library of Congress.

---

1. "Bradley, All-Time Start Third Baseman, Dies." *Cleveland Plain Dealer*, March 13, 1954.
2. Jones, David, editor. *Deadball Stars of the American League*. Dulles, Va.: Potomac Books, Inc., 2006, p. 641.

Bradley revolutionized his position, becoming a pioneer at picking up bunts with his bare hand and throwing in the same motion. Willie Keeler, a master bunter, called him the best hot corner-man he ever faced at fielding those hits. Bradley also attracted notice for his strong arm, his skill in tagging runners, and his personal grounds-keeping, earning the nickname "Pebble Picker." He topped AL third sackers in fielding four times, double plays three times, putouts and range factor twice each, and assists once. Bradley set a league record with seven putouts in a game on September 21, 1901, and again on May 13, 1909; only three AL players matched the record in the 20th century.

Brad, as he was often called, could hit, too. Using his "Big Bennie" bat from the right side of the plate, he hit for extra-base power and batting average. On May 21–24, 1902, he homered in four straight games, and made it six of eight, in the midst of a 29-game hitting streak, May 17–June 17. This was in a year the entire *league* hit just 258 home runs. Bradley wound up that year second in the AL in homers while batting .340. He also finished in the league's top five in runs, hits, doubles, total bases, slugging, and OPS.

Brad continued his excellence over the next two seasons. In 1903, he was second in the AL in runs, triples (22, including an AL record three in one game on July 28, and a cycle on September 24), and slugging, and in the top five in hits, doubles, total bases, batting, and OPS. In 1904, he finished in the top five in runs, hits, doubles, home runs, total bases, RBI, and batting. According to WAR, Bradley ranked second among AL position-players in 1902 and '03, and third in '04. Through age 26, the five most similar players include four Hall of Famers, including Traynor and Frank "Home Run" Baker.

Bradley suffered from a stomach malady in 1905. Though his production was down, he still ranked tenth in WAR among non-pitchers. But, the real turning point of his career came in the second game of a doubleheader vs. New York on July 19, 1906. A fastball was tracking for his head, and he threw up his right arm for protection. "In the third inning Bradley had his right wrist broken by a pitched ball," reported *The Sporting Life*. "This valuable player had his wrist broken by one of [Bill] Hogg's swift shoots."[3]

Bradley, 28, missed the rest of the season, and said the injury hampered his throwing, fielding, and batting the rest of his career. His hitting statistics certainly bear that out: he batted .298 through 1906, a meager .216 with just one homer thereafter. Also contributing to his decline were a bout with typhoid fever in '07, and a torn ligament in his side in '08.

Robbed of his batting prowess, Brad still found ways to help the team. He led the AL in sacrifice hits with 46 in 1907 and 60—the second-highest total ever—in '08. His ninth-inning play on a tough grounder sealed Addie

---

3. *The Sporting Life*, July 28, 1906, p. 3.

Joss's perfect game on October 2, 1908; Bradley named that as the greatest thrill of his career.

Bradley returned to the minor leagues as a player-manager for Toronto in 1911–13, winning the International League pennant in 1912. He nominally returned to the majors in the Federal League, managing (and occasionally pinch-hitting for) Brooklyn in 1914, and playing for Kansas City in 1915. Bradley skippered Erie of the Interstate League in 1916, ending his on-field career.

Bradley wed Anna B. Kellacky on February 8, 1905. They would be married 49 years, and have a son, Norman, and daughter, Anna or "Nan." Norman was reported as a Notre Dame baseball prospect in 1929, but he didn't earn a letter, and there is no evidence he actually played.[4]

In 1928, the Indians signed Bill Bradley as a scout and coach. He scouted for the Tribe for the next quarter-century, except for a one-year stint with the Tigers. According to his obituary, "more than 35 players he discovered made the major leagues."[5]

Bradley died of pneumonia at Ingleside Hospital in Cleveland on March 11, 1954. He received votes in six Hall of Fame elections, and was posthumously elected to the Indians' Hall of Fame in the same class as Bob Feller.

Year	Team (League)	G	AB	R	H	2B	3B	HR	RBI	SB	AVG	OBP	SLG
1899	Chicago (NL)	35	129	26	40	6	1	2	18	4	.310	.378	.419
1900		122	444	63	125	21	8	5	49	14	.282	.330	.399
1901	Cleveland (AL)	133	516	95	151	28	13	1	55	15	.293	.336	.403
1902		*137	550	104	187	39	12	11	77	11	.340	.375	.515
1903		136	536	101	168	36	22	6	68	21	.313	.348	.496
1904		*154	609	94	183	32	8	6	83	23	.300	.334	.409
1905		146	541	63	145	34	6	0	51	22	.268	.321	.353
1906		82	302	32	83	16	2	2	25	13	.275	.324	.361
1907		139	498	48	111	20	1	0	34	20	.223	.286	.267
1908		148	548	70	133	24	7	1	46	18	.243	.297	.318
1909		95	334	30	62	6	3	0	22	8	.186	.236	.222
1910		61	214	12	42	3	0	0	12	6	.196	.236	.210
1914	Brooklyn (FL)	7	6	1	3	1	0	0	3	0	.500	.500	.667
1915	Kansas City (FL)	66	203	15	38	9	1	0	9	6	.187	.225	.241
Totals		1461	5430	754	1471	275	84	34	552	181	.271	.317	.371

4. March 30, 2020 e-mail from Notre Dame baseball expert Cappy Gagnon.
5. "Bradley, All-Time Start Third Baseman, Dies." *Cleveland Plain Dealer*, March 13, 1954.

Steve Busby

In the two years from mid-1973 until mid-1975, Steve Busby won 45 games—tied for second in the majors, and more than future Hall of Famers Nolan Ryan, Fergie Jenkins, Don Sutton, Tom Seaver, Jim Palmer, Steve Carlton, Gaylord Perry, Bert Blyleven, and Phil Niekro, among others. At 25, Busby already owned two no-hitters.

No one could have predicted Busby would win just 18 more big league games.

Steven Lee Busby was born in Burbank, California, on September 29, 1949, the youngest child (following Mike and Susan) of Marvin and Betty Busby. Steve was a fourth cousin of Jim Busby, an All-Star center fielder who would play 13 years in the big leagues (1950–62), but they barely knew each other.[1] Steve starred in football, basketball, and baseball at Fullerton Union High School in California, pitching two no-hitters before graduating in 1967.[2] He was ready to turn pro right out of high school.

"I almost signed with San Francisco in '67," Busby recalled. "Pretty good-sized bonus, too. [Hall of Fame pitcher] Carl Hubbell and some of the other Giants scouts were coming down to watch me play in an American Legion tournament. I was working out the night before, messing around.... I started running, but I didn't have my knee wrapped up, and it gave out on me. I had a knee operation the previous October after hurting it in football." The Giants cut their offer nearly in half, so Busby opted to accept a scholarship from the University of Southern California instead.[3]

Busby majored in business analysis at USC. In 1968, he went 8-3 for their freshman team, also batting .422, to earn the team's MVP award. But he missed the entire '69 season due to an arm injury, requiring surgery to relocate an ulna nerve. Busby returned to go 3-0 in 1970 and 11-2 in '71, leading USC to the College World Series championship. He was named to All-Conference, All-District, and NCAA College All-American first teams. He also played for the Boulder Collegians in 1970, helping them to the Colorado state semi-pro title.[4]

After graduating from USC, Busby was picked by the Kansas City

---

1. Telephone interview with Steve Busby, June 9, 2017.
2. Unidentified clipping in National Baseball Library file.
3. Bordman, Sid. "'I Hope I'm Never Satisfied'—Busby." *The Sporting News*, August 3, 1974.
4. Unidentified clipping in National Baseball Library file.

Royals in the second round of the June 1971 amateur draft. He began his career with San Jose of the Class-A California League. On July 19, in his second pro start, the 6'2", 205-pound right-hander tossed a two-hit shutout against Reno. He finished the season with a 4–1 record, a 0.68 ERA, and 50 strikeouts in 40 innings—not to mention a .333 batting average.

Busby—nicknamed "Buzz"—had a sinking fastball estimated at 92 mph, a nasty slider, and an effective curve. He moved all the way up to AAA in 1972, with Omaha of the American Association. On May 4, Buzz tied a league record by striking out eight straight Tulsa batters. On July 31, he gave up a leadoff single, then retired 21 Oklahoma City batsmen in a row to earn a seven-inning, 7–0 victory. In another game against Evansville, Busby lost a no-hitter in the ninth inning. According to manager Jack McKeon, "I told Steve to quit worrying. I told him, 'You'll pitch a couple no-hitters and it'll be in the big leagues.'"[5]

On August 14, Busby tied another league record by fanning 16 Tulsa hitters. Though his final won-lost record was a mediocre 12–14, Busby had a 3.19 ERA (sixth in the league), and was tops in the AA in games started (30), complete games (17), innings pitched (217), and strikeouts (221). He was voted Minor League Player of the Year by the Southern California Hot Stove League.[6]

Called up to The Show, Busby made his major league debut on September 8. He beat the Twins on a five-hitter, and later added complete-game victories over the Angels and White Sox toward a 3–1 record with a sizzling 1.57 ERA. Buzz even impressed with his bat. On September 20, he hit an apparent grand slam homer against California, but it was nullified because the first base umpire had called "time" as the pitch was being thrown. Called back to the plate, Busby hit a two-run single, and added two more hits later in the game.[7] However, due to the DH rule which started the next year, Busby never batted in the pros after 1972. "I enjoyed hitting," he says. "I felt I had an advantage as a hitter because I could think like a pitcher."[8]

Busby also became one of the best-fielding pitchers in the game, finishing third in Gold Glove voting in 1974, and leading AL pitchers in range factor in 1975.

In spring training, 1973, Busby served notice that he had no-hit stuff. On March 23, he worked the first six innings of a combined no-no against Detroit, and later he tossed seven hitless frames against St. Louis.[9]

---

5. Bordman, Sid. "Steve's Buzz Bomb Act Captures Tigers Again." *The Sporting News*, May 12, 1973, p. 12.
6. Unidentified clipping in National Baseball Library file.
7. *Ibid.*
8. Telephone interview with Steve Busby, June 9, 2017.
9. Bordman, Sid. "'I Hope I'm Never Satisfied'—Busby." *The Sporting News*, August 3, 1974.

Still technically a rookie, Busby was named the Royals' opening day pitcher, but had a rocky start to the season. Entering the April 27 game, he had a 1-2 record and 8.04 ERA, and was suffering shoulder stiffness. But that day, in just his tenth major league appearance, Busby hurled a no-hit game to beat the Tigers, 3-0. Though not exactly a thing of beauty—Busby walked six—it was the first no-no in the AL since 1970.

Other than the no-hitter—and the birth of his and his wife Terri's first child, Melissa, on May 15 (daughters Michelle and Stephanie would follow in 1974 and '79[10])—Busby did not have a good first half of the season. By July 2, his record was 4-9 with a bloated 5.03 ERA. But he went 12-6, 3.60 the rest of the year to finish with a creditable 16-15 log. Busby was named AL Rookie Pitcher of the Year by *The Sporting News*, and finished third in BBWAA Rookie of the Year voting.

On June 19, 1974—just 418 days after his first no-no—Busby struck again. In his 58th career game, Buzz tossed a 2-0 no-hitter over the Brewers. This time, he was in total command, allowing only one baserunner—a second-inning walk to slugger George Scott. Busby retired the last 24 batters of the game to become just the 25th pitcher to hurl two no-hitters, and the first to do so in each of his first two full seasons.[11] He then got out the first nine hitters in his next outing against the White Sox, setting an AL record (since broken) with 33 consecutive batsmen retired, and also contributing to a streak of 54 straight batters faced without allowing a hit. Busby lost his bid for a second straight no-hitter with one out in the sixth inning.[12]

Busby finished the '74 season with 292 innings, 20 complete games, 198 strikeouts, and a 22-14 record—for a team which went just 55-71 in games he didn't get a decision. Only two major leaguers—future Hall of Famers Catfish Hunter and Fergie Jenkins—won more games that year. Busby was unanimously named the Royals' Pitcher of the Year though, curiously, he got no support in Cy Young Award voting.

Despite a rumor that he was ready to quit the team,[13] Busby was on track for his best season yet in 1975. After a 12-inning victory on June 25, he sported an 11-5 record and a nifty 2.42 ERA. That gave Busby 45 wins in a period of less than two years, a total topped by only Hunter:

---

10. Telephone interview with Steve Busby, June 9, 2017.
11. Twyman, Gib. "No-Hit Hurler? 'Not me!' Says Busby." *The Sporting News*, July 6, 1974, p. 13.
12. Bordman, Sid. "'I Hope I'm Never Satisfied'—Busby." *The Sporting News*, August 3, 1974.
13. Associated Press. "KC's Busby Denies Story He's Quitting." May 20, 1975.

Most Wins, July 1, 1973–June 30, 1975

Pitcher	Wins
Catfish Hunter	46
Steve Busby	45
Luis Tiant	45
Nolan Ryan	44
Mike Cuellar	42
Vida Blue	41
Jim Kaat	40
Fergie Jenkins	39
Andy Messersmith	39
Don Sutton	39

Busby was selected to his second straight All-Star team. But, bothered by a "dull sensation in the back of his right shoulder,"[14] he went just 7–7 the rest of the season.

Still troubled by shoulder stiffness, Busby pitched only six times in 1976 before June. He had a 3–1 record and 2.84 ERA through June 12, but things went swiftly downhill from there. He recalls one game around that time where, with ABC-TV cameras trained in on his warm-ups, he "really aired it out and on one particular throw felt a pop in the back."[15] He pitched his last game of the year on July 6, and underwent rotator cuff surgery 13 days later.[16] At that time, it was considered a pioneering surgery and a last resort; Busby thinks that with the advances in sports medicine since then, the problem would have been recognized and addressed earlier. In retrospect, he attributes his arm problems to flawed mechanics.[17]

Despite the loss of their former ace pitcher, the Royals won their first division title in 1976. Busby was reduced to scouting their division rivals, the Oakland A's,[18] then watching the ALCS games from the bench. Kansas City lost a heartbreaker to the Yankees.

Busby's attempt at a comeback in 1977 was a flop. Sent down to Daytona Beach of the Class-A Florida State League, Buzz allowed 11 hits and five runs in three innings of his only game. He then returned to California

---

14. Covitz, Randy. "Busby's Heart Lasted Longer than His Arm." *Kansas City Star*, June 5, 1986.

15. McKenzie, Mike. "Busby, Jones, Leonard … Beat Goes On." *Kansas City Star*, June 24, 1984, p. 1 SPORTS.

16. Bordman, Sid. "Busby Starts Comeback with Royal Good Luck." *The Sporting News*, April 29, 1978, p. 11.

17. Telephone interview with Steve Busby, June 9, 2017.

18. *The Sporting News*, October 2, 1976.

for a rehab program under Dr. Frank Jobe, and had surgery on his left knee.[19]

The following year wasn't much better: a 4–7 record and 4.56 ERA in the minors, and a 7.59 ERA in the majors. For the third straight year, Busby was a spectator as the Royals lost to the Yankees in the ALCS.

Busby went 6–6 with a 3.63 ERA as a spot-starter and reliever for the second-place 1979 Royals, including back-to-back four-hitters in May. He said he was pain-free, though his fastball had slowed down to the 80s, and his control was not there. Busby pitched poorly to start the 1980 season, and was sent down to Omaha for a while (3–2, 2.48). Returning to the bigs, he finally notched his first big league victory of the year, a 7–6 win over Milwaukee on August 26.

It turned out to be the last game of his pro career. On August 29—three days before he would have been eligible for post-season play—the Royals put Busby on waivers.[20] Kansas City went on to win the AL championship, but lose to the Phillies in the World Series.

Given one last chance by his former manager Whitey Herzog, Busby went to spring training with the Cardinals in 1981. But things didn't work out and Buzz announced his retirement on April 7.[21] "I think he did everything possible," Herzog said, "and the arm just wasn't there."[22]

By this time, Busby was going through a divorce and had three daughters to support. He took a job as a Rangers broadcaster in 1982,[23] eventually doing radio and TV for the team through the 2016 season. From 2001–17, Busby also served as a teacher for Athletic Performance Enhancement in Grapevine, Texas, where he lives today with his second wife, Pam. Their 1984 marriage produced Sara and Steven, Jr. Steve now has seven grandchildren, and serves on the board of the Bobby Bragan Youth Foundation in Ft. Worth, Texas.[24]

The heartbreak is not only that Busby's career was cut short just as he should have been reaching his prime, but that he missed the gravy train of skyrocketing salaries and winning teams. The Royals won four division titles between 1976 and 1980, but Busby didn't pitch a single post-season inning. "I'm not one to dwell on what might have been, but that's my

---

19. Bordman, Sid. "Royals Excited by a Buzz-ing in Their Heads." *The Sporting News*, April 1, 1978.
20. Associated Press. "Royals Put Ex-Star Pitcher on Waivers." August 31, 1980.
21. "Busby Gives up Comeback." *New York Times*, April 8, 1981.
22. McKenzie, Mike. "Busby, Jones, Leonard … Beat Goes On." *Kansas City Star*, June 24, 1984, p. 1 SPORTS.
23. *New York Times*, February 11, 1982.
24. Telephone interview with Steve Busby, June 9, 2017.

biggest regret," he says. "I think I could have made a difference in the team's post-season results."[25]

"I always said it doesn't bother me much, that that was part of the game," Busby reflected in 2007. "And that was a bunch of garbage. It bothered me. It hurt. That injury and subsequent injuries stripped me of my identity."[26]

More than a decade later, Busby seems to have come to terms with it all. "The only thing I would change is the outcome," he says. "I would never give a moment of it back."[27]

On May 13, 1986, Busby and Amos Otis became the charter members of the Royals Hall of Fame. "Buzz was outstanding," said Royals owner Ewing Kauffman in announcing the honor. "He's really the best pitcher we ever had.... If it weren't for the injury to Busby, he would have made another (Cooperstown) Hall of Fame."[28]

Year	Team (League)	G	IP	W	L	PCT	SO	BB	H	ERA
1972	Kansas City (AL)	5	40.0	3	1	.750	31	8	28	1.57
1973		37	238.1	16	15	.516	174	105	246	4.23
1974		38	292.1	22	14	.611	198	92	284	3.39
1975		34	260.1	18	12	.600	160	81	233	3.08
1976		13	71.2	3	3	.500	29	49	58	4.40
1978		7	21.1	1	0	1.000	10	15	24	7.59
1979		22	94.1	6	6	.500	45	64	71	3.63
1980		11	42.1	1	3	.250	12	19	59	6.17
Totals		167	1060.2	70	54	.565	659	433	1003	3.72

25. Ibid.
26. Reiter, Bill. "Finding Steve Busby." *Kansas City Star*, April 1, 2007.
27. Telephone interview with Steve Busby, June 9, 2017.
28. Shatel, Tom. "Otis, Busby are First Chosen to Royals Hall of Fame." *Kansas City Times*, May 14, 1986, p. D-3.

Cesar Cedeño

Through age 22, the five most similar players to Cesar Cedeño included Hall of Famers Al Kaline, Ken Griffey, Jr., Mickey Mantle, and Hank Aaron, with Miguel Cabrera and Mike Trout close behind. But something happened that fall which seemingly changed Cedeño forever. By the time he finished his career in 1986, his most similar players were the good-but-not-great Amos Otis, Felipe Alou, and Gary Matthews.

Cesar Eugenito Cedeño was born February 25, 1951, at Santo Domingo in the Dominican Republic. He was the first of Diogene and Juanita (Encarnacion) Cedeño's five children. Diogene wanted his son to help at the grocery store that he ran and, eventually, to become an engineer. But Cesar had other ideas: all he ever wanted to do was play baseball, and he was a prodigy at it. Juanita was the one who encouraged and enabled Cesar in his passion. By age 16, Cesar was playing with grown men for an amateur team sponsored by a local pharmacy. He was already attracting the attention of major league scouts, searching for untapped talent not subject to the draft. Houston Astros scout Pat Gillick—later elected to the Hall of Fame as an executive—signed Cesar for $3,000, just beating out a Cardinals scout.[1] Cesar's Columbia High School days were over.

A 6'2", 175-pound outfielder, Cedeño began his pro career in 1968. He was just 17, far from home and family, and learning a new language. Playing in the Florida State and Appalachian Leagues, the right-handed hitter batted a combined .305. The following year, Cedeño dropped to .274 in the Carolina League, but exhibited a bit more power and speed, to go along with his wide fielding range and strong right arm. He then competed in the Florida Instructional and Dominican Winter Leagues, showing rapid development.

Jumping up to the AAA American Association for 1970, Cedeño really arrived. In just 54 games—the equivalent of one-third of a major league season—he amassed 47 runs, 87 hits, 14 doubles, 9 triples, 14 homers, and 61 RBI, batting .373 with a .691 slugging percentage. The Astros had hoped to bring Cedeño along gradually, but they were struggling and he had nothing more to prove in the minors.

Cedeño debuted with the Astros on June 20, 1970, the youngest player in the majors at age 19. He overcame a slow start to put up some impressive numbers. Despite playing his home games in an extreme pitchers' park, the Astrodome, he batted .310 in 90 games—including a .343 mark with a .519 slugging percentage in road contests.

Cedeño married his childhood sweetheart, Milagros, after his rookie season. But the marriage soon ended in divorce, and Cesar quickly remarried, this time to a Houston gal named Cora.[2]

Cedeño's first full season, 1971, was not much to write home about, though he led the NL with 40 doubles, and topped the Astros in hits and

---

1. Gutman, Bill. *Fisk * Rose * Bonds * Cedeno*. New York: Grosset & Dunlap, Inc., 1974, pp. 115–20.
2. *Ibid.*, pp. 128–29, 144.

RBI. Then, filling out to nearly 200 pounds, he exploded from a prospect into a superstar.

It's hard to overstate how great Cesar Cedeño's 1972 season was, for a youngster in a hitters' graveyard. He was the NL Player of the Month in June, made his first All-Star team, hit for the cycle on August 2, won his first Gold Glove Award in center field, and finished sixth in MVP voting. He joined Lou Brock as just the second man to have 20+ home runs and 50+ stolen bases in the same season. Cedeño finished among the league leaders in runs (fifth), hits (sixth), total bases (second), doubles (first), triples (third), steals (third, 55), batting (fourth, .320), OBP (sixth), slugging (fourth, .537), and OPS (third). He had a .329/.400/.560 slash line on the road. At age 21, Cedeño was ranked as the fourth-best player in the league by the two leading Sabermetric measures, Win Shares and WAR.

And he was just as good in 1973. He actually duplicated his .320 batting average and .537 slugging percentage in the same number of games, with a road slash line of .346/.391/.618. Cedeño posted another 20–50 season, earned his second All-Star selection and second Gold Glove Award (leading the league in range factor), and finished 11th in MVP voting despite playing for a fourth-place team. Though he missed 23 games, he finished second in batting, third in stolen bases (56), fifth in slugging, sixth in doubles and WAR, and seventh in OPS and WS.

The sky was the limit for this wunderkind. Long-time observers, living legends, and star players like Hank Aaron, Stan Musial, Joe DiMaggio, Pete Rose, Joe Morgan, Monte Irvin, Duke Snider, Ralph Kiner, Ted Kluszewski, Leo Durocher, Sparky Anderson, and Harry Walker were touting Cedeño as a potential all-time great, often comparing him with Willie Mays and/or Roberto Clemente. "If I ever saw another Willie Mays, it's Cedeño," said Durocher,[3] who managed both players in their early years. During MLB's winter meetings, managers and general managers were polled as to whom they would add to their rosters, given a choice of any one player. Cedeño was the unanimous choice.[4] Little did they know that Cesar's life was taking a tragic turn almost as they spoke.

On December 11, 1973, while Cora was in their Santo Domino home, Cedeño was in a nearby motel room with 19-year-old Altagracia de la Cruz. According to Cedeño (and substantiated by physical evidence), she was handling his .38-caliber pistol and he was trying to get it back when the gun

---

3. Rumill, Ed. "Durocher Sees a Young Wonder in Cedeno." *Christian Science Monitor*, May 29, 1973.
4. Gutman, Bill. *Fisk * Rose * Bonds * Cedeno*. New York: Grosset & Dunlap, Inc., 1974, p. 146.

went off, striking the girl in the head and killing her.[5] He turned himself in to authorities some eight hours later.

Immediately, it became clear what Cedeño's priorities were. "I was scared," he said. "I saw my baseball career was in danger."[6] Astros brass echoed the sentiment. "Apparently the case hasn't affected him too much, emotionally, and that's what's important," said general manager Spec Richardson, after visiting him in prison.[7]

Cedeño spent 20 days in jail and, on January 15, 1974, was convicted of involuntary manslaughter (roughly the equivalent of second-degree murder in the U.S.) and fined $100.[8] Two civil suits were quickly settled out of court, some say with the help of the Astros' management. The story was swept under the rug after that.

The tone was set in spring training. "He never said anything about it and no one really asked him about it," recalled former teammate Jerry Reuss.[9] "Nobody has said a thing about what happened and nobody on this team will," said teammate Tommy Helms. Approached for an interview, Cedeño said, "That's fine. But only if it's strictly baseball."[10]

Despite the cloud hanging over his head, Cedeño was off to another great season in '74. Batting over .300 well into the summer, he earned his third straight All-Star selection, and was on his way to career highs in homers and RBI. But on July 17, a disturbing phone call was received at the Astros' hotel in Pittsburgh, bringing the '73 tragedy back to the front burner. "I am going to shoot Cedeño just like he did that girl," said the anonymous caller with a Hispanic accent. "I'm going to kill him."[11] Cedeño outwardly shrugged off the threat, but soon went into a season-ending slump. He batted just .188 with a .297 slugging percentage in the last two months of the campaign, dropping him to .269 and .461.

Coincidentally or not, Cedeño was never the same hitter after mid–1974. At a time when he should have been reaching a dominating peak, his numbers instead declined. Though he performed for 12 more seasons as a

---

5. United Press International. "Cedeno Could Get 3 Years in Prison." *San Francisco Examiner*, January 3, 1974.
6. Associated Press. "Cedeno: 'I've Grown Up.'" *San Francisco Chronicle*, January 23, 1974, p. 51.
7. Associated Press. "Cedeno Exonerated, but He's Still in Jail." *San Francisco Examiner*, December 13, 1973.
8. Associated Press. "Cedeno: 'I've Grown Up.'" *San Francisco Chronicle*, January 23, 1974, p. 51.
9. Mendelson, Abby. "Whatever Happened to Cesar Cedeno?" *Baseball Quarterly*, Winter 1978–79, p. 46.
10. Newhan, Ross. "A Contrite Cedeno Tries Hard Not to Be Haunted by the Past." *Los Angeles Times*, March 12, 1974, p. 5.
11. Heiling, Joe. "Cedeno's Life Periled by Pittsburgh Caller." *The Sporting News*, August 3, 1974, p. 7.

quality player, still stealing bases and playing Gold Glove defense, he never again hit as many as 20 homers and just once reached a .300 average. He showed brief bursts of the 1972–73 Cedeño, but couldn't sustain them.

Cedeño's hot temper, which had been an occasional problem before, became more of an issue. Incidents continued throughout and even after his playing career, and alcohol contributed in some cases. Here is a partial rap sheet:

- In 1974, Cedeño threw a helmet which hit a coach.[12]
- On March 12, 1975, he earned a $200 fine for destroying a water cooler in the dugout, with a sliver of glass lodging near a teammate's eye.[13]
- On May 30, 1978, Cedeño smashed his fist into the Plexiglas dugout roof, requiring 17 stitches on his right hand, sidelining him for seven games, and earning him a record $5,000 fine by the Astros.[14]
- On September 8, 1981, he went into the stands to scuffle with an Atlanta heckler, sustaining a $5,000 fine from the NL. Among other things, the heckler was calling Cedeño "killer."[15]
- On May 22, 1983, he stormed off a team flight when he wasn't given one of the nine available first-class seats.[16] After rejoining the team that night, he got into a shouting match with manager Russ Nixon, earning a $100 fine and three-day suspension.[17]
- On January 23, 1985, Cedeño was charged with DWI after driving into a tree, costing him $7,400 in fines and property damage. He said he was arguing with girlfriend Pam Lamon (he was still married to Cora) and lost control of the car. Cedeño had to be handcuffed and bound after attempting to kick his way out of the patrol car.[18] This was less than a year after he had done a stint at the California Institute for Behavioral Medicine.[19] Cedeño pled "no contest" and served two years' probation.
- In June 1987, he smashed a glass into a man's face at a Nassau Bay nightclub.[20]

12. Shattuck, Harry. "Hotheaded Cesar Fined $200 for Cooler Assault." *The Sporting News*, March 29, 1975, p. 53.
13. *Ibid.*
14. Mendelson, Abby. "Whatever Happened to Cesar Cedeno?" *Baseball Quarterly*, Winter 1978–79, p. 45.
15. "Cedeno Goes After a Fan." *San Francisco Chronicle*, September 9, 1981.
16. Associated Press. "No First-Class Plane Seat, No Cesar Cedeno." *Albany (N.Y.) Times-Union*, May 24, 1983.
17. "Cedeno Suspended; Files a Grievance." *The Sporting News*, June 6, 1983.
18. United Press International. "Cedeno Arrested for DWI." *New York Post*, January 24, 1985.
19. Hoard, Greg. "Cedeno Sheds Anger." *Cincinnati Enquirer*, April 24, 1984.
20. Associated Press. "Ex-Astro Cedeno Arrested." *Utica Observer-Dispatch*, May 29, 1988.

- On May 27, 1988, drunk and belligerent, Cedeño beat up Lamon, snatched their baby daughter, and drove away. He then returned, beat Pam some more, and fought with police as he was arrested.[21]

Periodically, reporters or Cedeño himself would declare that he was a new man, ready to resume his Hall of Fame career trajectory. After all, he was still a young player, with all his tools still intact. After he had a torrid second half in 1977, the Astros gave him a record 1-year, $3.5 million contract.[22]

But Cedeño played only 401 games over four more seasons for Houston, averaging just seven homers and 46 RBI per year. He underwent 1978 knee surgery and 1980 ankle surgery, and was traded to Cincinnati after the 1981 season.

After three-plus lackluster seasons with the Reds, Cedeño was dealt to the Cardinals for the 1985 stretch drive, and one last taste of glory. He sparked St. Louis to the NL pennant, batting .434 with big hit after big hit in the final five weeks of the season. Finally getting a chance to play in a World Series, Cedeño went just 2-for-15.

In the midst of the collusion era, St. Louis did not offer free agent Cedeño a contract for 1986. He signed on with the Toronto Blue Jays in March, but they released him three weeks later, just before the season started. He then joined the Dodgers, but got only 78 at bats before being released again on June 5. Cedeño re-signed with the Cardinals in July, but didn't play in the majors for them. He performed briefly in the American Association and Mexican League over the next couple of years, before making one final big league comeback attempt in 1989. Cedeño joined the Astros as a non-roster player in spring training, but was cut in late March.

Cesar Cedeño finished his 17-year career with 2087 hits, 199 homers, 550 stolen bases, and a .285 average. He went on the Hall of Fame ballot in 1992, receiving just two votes. He lives in Houston, and became a minor league hitting coach for the Astros in 2012.

Year	Team (League)	G	AB	R	H	2B	3B	HR	RBI	SB	AVG	OBP	SLG
1970	Houston (NL)	90	355	46	110	21	4	7	42	17	.310	.340	.451
1971		161	611	85	161	*40	6	10	81	20	.264	.293	.398
1972		139	559	103	179	*39	8	22	82	55	.320	.385	.537
1973		139	525	86	168	35	2	25	70	56	.320	.376	.537
1974		160	610	95	164	29	5	26	102	57	.269	.338	.461

21. *Ibid.*
22. Foley, Red. "Astro-Nomical Pact." *Daily News* (New York, N.Y.), February 18, 1978.

Year	Team (League)	G	AB	R	H	2B	3B	HR	RBI	SB	AVG	OBP	SLG
1975	Houston (NL)	131	500	93	144	31	3	13	63	50	.288	.371	.440
1976		150	575	89	171	26	5	18	83	58	.297	.357	.454
1977		141	530	92	148	36	8	14	71	61	.279	.346	.457
1978		50	192	31	54	8	2	7	23	23	.281	.333	.453
1979		132	470	57	123	27	4	6	54	30	.262	.348	.374
1980		137	499	71	154	32	8	10	73	48	.309	.389	.465
1981		82	306	42	83	19	0	5	34	12	.271	.321	.382
1982	Cincinnati (NL)	138	492	52	142	35	1	8	57	16	.289	.346	.413
1983		98	332	40	77	16	0	9	39	13	.232	.302	.361
1984		110	380	59	105	24	2	10	47	19	.276	.321	.429
1985	Cin.-St. L. (NL)	111	296	38	86	16	1	9	49	14	.291	.347	.443
1986	Los Angeles (N)	37	78	5	18	2	1	0	6	1	.231	.294	.282
Totals		2006	7310	1084	2087	436	60	199	976	550	.285	.347	.443

Ray Chapman

It is well-known that the only on-field fatality in major league history occurred in 1920, when Yankees pitcher Carl Mays beaned Indians shortstop Ray Chapman. Many have said that the tragic incident is what has kept Mays out of the Hall of Fame. But few have noted that it may have cost Chapman a place in Cooperstown as well.

Raymond Johnson Chapman was born on his father's family farm in Beaver Dam, Kentucky, on January 15, 1891, the son of Everette and Barbara Johnson Chapman. His family moved to Herrin, Illinois, just after the turn of the century.[1] Chapman began playing semi-pro baseball in 1909 at Mt. Vernon, Illinois, and then played professionally at Springfield, Illinois, Davenport, Iowa, and Toledo, Ohio, over the next three years. He batted .293 with 75 stolen bases for Davenport in 1911, and .310 with 49 steals for Toledo in 1912.

At age 21, Chapman joined Cleveland for the final weeks of the 1912

---

1. Gregory, Corinne Taylor. *Once There Was a Dam*. Beaver Dam, KY, self-published, 1982, p. 121.

season, and hit .312 with 10 stolen bases and 29 runs scored in 31 games. The Indians—then known as the Naps—had their shortstop and leadoff hitter for the foreseeable future. Chapman was 5'10" and 170 pounds, and batted and threw right-handed. He was a natty dresser and an accomplished singer, and had a bubbly personality. He was full of team spirit, and became a popular player throughout the league.

Playing almost all of his career as a defensive specialist in the "Deadball Era," Chapman posted offensive numbers which don't jump off the page at you, but which were very respectable in context. In 1915, he played every game and finished among the American League's top five in runs and triples. In 1917, Chappie again had perfect attendance and was third in runs, fourth in triples, and third in stolen bases (52, a Cleveland record until 1980) while batting .302. In the war-shortened 1918 season, despite service in the U.S. Navy Reserves, Chapman led the league in runs and bases on balls, finishing third in steals. He batted .300 in 1919 and .303 in 1920.

Chapman was one of the fastest men in baseball. On September 27, 1917, as part of a benefit exhibition contest in Boston, he won a loving cup for beating out Ty Cobb and other big league stars by circling the bases in 14 seconds.[2] Representing the Navy in a track meet the following

Ray Chapman (1918), who two years later would become the only man killed by a pitched ball in a big league game. Library of Congress.

---

2. *Ibid.*, p. 122.

year, Chappie won the 100-yard and 220-yard races, the former in 10 seconds flat.³

One of Chapman's chief offensive weapons was the bunt. In an environment where runs were scarce and small-ball strategy prevailed, Chapman set an all-time record with 67 sacrifices in 1917 (note that sacrifice bunts and flies were lumped together in those days). He also topped the AL with 45 in 1913 and 50 in 1919, and had 334 sacs in his brief career, sixth-most ever. Hall of Famer Eddie Collins holds the all-time record with 511 career sacrifices, but played in almost three times as many games as Chapman, 2826 to 1051.

Defensively, Chapman led AL shortstops in putouts three times, assists once, and range factor three times. As is the case with most veteran shortstops, then and now, he was regarded as a field leader.

On October 29, 1919, Chapman married Kathleen Marie Daly in a Cleveland "society wedding." Indians player-manager Tris Speaker served as best man. By the next spring the Chapmans were expecting their first child.⁴

On a drizzly New York day on August 16, 1920, the Indians went up against the Yankees and their ace, Carl Mays. Mays was a top-notch pitcher, but not a well-liked one. A year earlier, he had disgusted the baseball world when he deserted the sinking Red Sox and wound up with the up-and-coming Yanks. Using a deceptive submarine delivery, Mays was not afraid to doctor the ball or pitch inside, and annually ranked among the league leaders in hit batsmen. Chapman was not looking forward to facing his fellow-Kentuckian. "Mays is pitching for the Yankees today," he said to teammates on the train to New York, "so I'll do the fielding and you fellows do the batting."⁵

Chapman led off the fifth inning, crouching over the plate in his usual style. Mays's first pitch, a fastball, sailed inside, and Chapman was unable to get out of its way. Some said he froze, losing the discolored ball in the gray background; others, that he tried to duck under the ball but was too late. In any case, the ball cracked into his left temple and dribbled out into the field. Mays, thinking the ball had hit Chapman's bat, fielded it and threw to first base. Then everyone realized Chapman had collapsed at home plate. Shortly after being helped to his feet, he collapsed again, and was carried to the Indians' clubhouse. He was conscious as he awaited an ambulance, but was unable to speak.⁶

---

3. "Chapman was Gob During World War." Unidentified clipping in National Baseball Library file, August 1920, p. 6.
4. "Ball Player's Widow Was Bride in Society Wedding Last Fall." Unidentified clipping in National Baseball Library file, August 1920, p. 6.
5. Gregory, Corinne Taylor. *Once There Was a Dam*. Beaver Dam, KY, self-published, 1982, p. 134.
6. McAuley, Regis. "Graney Haunted by Memory of Chapman Beaning." Unidentified clipping in National Baseball Library file, 1962.

"He was one of the hardest men to pitch to," said a shaken Mays afterward. "He would crouch over the plate and the only way to get the ball over was to pitch so low to risk it being called a 'ball.' In the fifth inning I pitched him a straight ball inside, just above the waist. I expected that he would drop as [teammate Babe] Ruth does when pitchers swing them in close, but instead Ray ducked and it hit him. I found a rough place on the ball afterward and I believe that made it sail in far more than I intended."[7]

Chapman was rushed to St. Lawrence Hospital in New York, where he underwent emergency surgery for a fractured skull. He died just before five o'clock the next morning. Mays, accompanied by an attorney, gave a statement and was exonerated of any wrongdoing by District Attorney Swann.[8] But Indians outfielder Jack Graney, who later became a pioneering radio broadcaster, was one of many observers who had no doubt about Mays's intent. "People ask me today if I still feel that Mays threw at Chappie," Graney said in 1962. "My answer has always been the same—yes, definitely."[9]

There were immediate outcries to ban Mays from baseball. Quotes from Boston, Detroit, St. Louis, and Washington indicated that those teams would strike if the pitcher were allowed back on the field, and AL President Ban Johnson suggested that Mays might not be. But words from a minister at Chapman's funeral defused the situation. On August 20, the Rev. Dr. Willard Scullen of St. John's Cathedral in Cleveland said that Mays "feels the outcome more deeply than most of us do. The great American game of baseball does not develop a man who would willingly try to injure another participant in the game. And the game would not produce a man capable of killing another man. Chapman, we know, would be the first to decry any thought of revenge if he could but speak."[10] Johnson was so moved that he ordered a transcript of the sermon. "I want it printed and spread wherever baseball is played," said Johnson. "It is the greatest oration I've ever heard, and every baseball player and fan should have a chance to read it."[11] Chapman was laid to rest in Cleveland's Lakeview Cemetery.

In his next outing, August 23, Mays pitched a 10–0 shutout over the Tigers. On a couple of occasions, he yelled "Look out!" as a pitch

---

7. Gregory, Corinne Taylor. *Once There Was a Dam*. Beaver Dam, KY, self-published, 1982, pp. 125–6.
8. "Pitched Ball Kills Chapman; Speaker Exonerates Carl Mays." Unidentified clipping in National Baseball Library file, August 17, 1920.
9. McAuley, Regis. "Graney Haunted by Memory of Chapman Beaning." Unidentified clipping in National Baseball Library file, 1962.
10. Gregory, Corinne Taylor. *Once There Was a Dam*. Beaver Dam, KY, self-published, 1982, pp. 129–30.
11. *Ibid.*, p. 131.

approached inside.[12] Mays finished the year with a 26–11 record, and retired after the 1929 season with a 208–126 career mark. He died in 1971.

After a slump, the 1920 Indians regrouped. Adding future Hall of Famer Joe Sewell to take over at short, they went on to win the AL pennant and their first world championship.

Ray Chapman had reached the .300 mark in three of his last four seasons. With league-wide batting averages leaping up by some 40 points from the 1910s to the 1920s, there is little reason to think he wouldn't have continued to be a .300-hitter for years to come, putting up career numbers comparable to the best shortstops of the pre-integration era. Interestingly, two Hall of Fame shortstops—Dave Bancroft and Rabbit Maranville—were born in 1891, the same year as Chapman—and Ray clearly outshone both players offensively during their time as contemporaries. Following are their comparative statistics through 1920:

Player	*G*	*AB*	*R*	*H*	*2B*	*3B*	*HR*	*RBI*	*SB*	*AVG*
Bancroft	789	2965	410	766	118	27	14	193	71	.258
Maranville	1047	3928	444	986	133	72	21	347	157	.251
Chapman	1051	3785	671	1053	162	81	17	364	238	.278

Kathleen Chapman gave birth to a daughter, Rae-Marie, on February 27, 1921. Sadly, both Ray's widow and daughter would be dead by the end of the decade. Kathleen suffered a nervous breakdown at age 34 and swallowed a poisonous fluid on April 21, 1928. Rae-Marie died in a measles epidemic on April 27, 1929.[13]

Ray Chapman received one mention in Hall of Fame voting, before he was made ineligible by the 10-year rule. He was inducted into the Cleveland Indians Hall of Fame in 2006. A year later, a forgotten 175-pound bronze plaque of Chapman was discovered in a storage crate, refurbished, and put on display at the Indians' new "Heritage Park" museum.[14]

Year	Team (League)	G	AB	R	H	2B	3B	HR	RBI	SB	AVG	OBP	SLG
1912	Cleveland (AL)	31	109	29	34	6	3	0	19	10	.312	.375	.422
1913		141	508	78	131	19	7	3	39	29	.258	.322	.341
1914		106	375	59	103	16	10	2	42	24	.275	.358	.387

---

12. Cleveland *Plain Dealer*, August 23, 1920.
13. Dolgan, Bob. "Fond Memories of a Brother." Cleveland *Plain Dealer*, August 4, 1995, p. 6-D.
14. Withers, Tom. "Chapman Plaque Key to Indians' Success?" Boston *Globe*, October 9, 2007.

Year	Team (League)	G	AB	R	H	2B	3B	HR	RBI	SB	AVG	OBP	SLG
1915	Cleveland (AL)	*154	570	101	154	14	17	3	67	36	.270	.353	.370
1916		109	346	50	80	10	5	0	27	21	.231	.330	.289
1917		*156	563	98	170	28	13	2	36	52	.302	.370	.409
1918		128	446	*84	119	19	8	1	32	35	.267	.390	.352
1919		115	433	75	130	23	10	3	53	18	.300	.351	.420
1920		111	435	97	132	27	8	3	49	13	.303	.380	.423
Totals		1051	3785	671	1053	162	81	17	364	238	.278	.358	.377

Tony Conigliaro

On July 23, 1967, Boston's Tony Conigliaro hit his 100th career home run. At age 22, Conigliaro was the second-youngest player ever to reach that milestone, falling just 65 days short of Mel Ott's all-time record.[1] Ott had gone on to hit more than 500 homers, as had the #3 man on that list, Eddie Mathews. But Tony C would never reach even 200.

Anthony Richard Conigliaro was born January 7, 1945, in Revere, Massachusetts, a suburb of Boston. He was the first of three sons of Salvatore and Theresa Conigliaro in a tight-knit family. Tony's brothers were Billy, who also became a big league player, and Ritchie.

Tony played Little League (where he earned the nickname "Choo Choo," due to his speed), Pony League, American Legion, and sandlot baseball as a youth. He was a three-sport star at St. Mary's High School in Lynn, Massachusetts, earning school MVP honors in football, basketball (setting the school's scoring record), and baseball, where he batted .688 as a junior and .580 as a senior. Upon Conigliaro's graduation, scouts from 14 of the 20 major league baseball teams visited his home on September 10, 1962.[2] Although he had a better offer from the Orioles, Tony signed with his hometown Red Sox.

Conigliaro's pro debut was delayed by about a month in 1963: he suffered a fractured thumb when hit by a pitch thrown by his uncle in practice.[3] But once Tony got on the field, he dominated. Joining the Wellsville

---

1. Deane, Bill. *Baseball Myths*. Lanham, MD: Scarecrow Press, Inc., 2012, p. 156.
2. Boston Red Sox questionnaire completed by Conigliaro on September 20, 1963.
3. Claflin, Larry. "Conigliaro Farewell: Fine, Home Run, Injury." *The Sporting News*, August 8, 1964, p. 23.

Red Sox of the Class-A New York-Pennsylvania League, he played just 83 games, yet smashed a league-leading 42 doubles and added 24 home runs, batting .363 and slugging .730 to earn league MVP honors.

Conigliaro was a 6'3", 200-pound right-handed hitter. He crowded the plate and did not fear any pitcher. A decent fielder, Conigliaro played all three outfield positions, but would find his eventual home in right. In 1965, he would lead AL right fielders in range factor, finishing second in putouts and assists.

The Red Sox were in the midst of a string of sub-.500 seasons in 1964, so they had little to lose in bringing a 19-year-old kid all the way up from Class A to the majors. It didn't hurt that he was talented, home-grown, and good-looking. Tony C or Conig, as he was soon dubbed, was an instant star and fan favorite. On April 17, he hit what proved to be a game-winning home run in his first time up at Fenway Park. On May 24, he suffered a hairline fracture of the left hand when hit by a pitch from Kansas City's Moe Drabowsky, but missed only four games.[4] On July 26, Conigliaro hit his 20th homer of the season to break Ott's all-time record for a teenager. But in the second game of that day's doubleheader against the Indians, Conig suffered a broken right ulna when hit by a Pedro Ramos pitch. "He never saw the ball," said teammate Carl Yastrzemski. "He froze."

The Cleveland team physician predicted Tony was done for the season, but he returned on September 4.[5] Conigliaro finished his rookie campaign with 24 homers (still a record for teenagers), a .290 batting average, and a .530 slugging percentage. Bear in mind that this was the era of the largest strike zone in history (1963–68); the American League batting average was just .240 during this period. Conig fell 58 plate appearances shy of qualifying for the league batting and slugging titles; otherwise, he would have ranked in the top 10 in each.

Capitalizing on his newfound fame, Conigliaro released a rock-and-roll record right after his 20th birthday. In later years, Conig would sing on national TV shows, and also try his hand at acting, even seeking a part in *The Godfather*.

Despite another hit-by-pitch injury—a broken left wrist on July 28 vs. the Athletics' Wes Stock, costing him 22 games—Conigliaro led the AL in homers in 1965. He became the youngest man ever to win a league home run title, and also finished second in the circuit in slugging.

After a slow start in 1966—he was batting just .206 through Memorial Day—Tony C came on strong to lead the Red Sox in homers and RBI. He finished in the AL's top 10 in both categories, along with triples

---

4. *Ibid.*
5. *Ibid.*

and total bases, and led the league in sacrifice flies. Perhaps more significantly, he managed to avoid any serious hit-by-pitch injuries. "Bobby Doerr helped me on that score," Conigliaro said, referring to the Red Sox' first base coach and future Hall of Famer. "He threw hundreds of rubber balls at me in spring training ... and I learned how to get out of the way." The Boston writers overwhelmingly named Conig the team's Most Valuable Player.[6]

In 1967, Conigliaro appeared to be putting it all together at age 22. He was the AL's right fielder in all 15 innings of the All-Star Game, and hit his 100th career homer 12 days later. Entering August, he was among the league's top five in home runs, RBI, and even batting average as the Red Sox—who finished in ninth place out of 10 teams the year before—were battling for the AL pennant. A slump had dropped his batting and slugging averages to .287 and .519, but those would have ranked ninth and fifth, respectively, at the end of the AL season. At this point in his career, according to similarity scores, the 10 most statistically similar players to Conigliaro included Frank Robinson, Miguel Cabrera, Mickey Mantle, Hank Aaron, and Eddie Mathews (not to mention recent MVPs Bryce Harper and Giancarlo Stanton). It seemed that only tragedy could keep Tony Conigliaro from joining these all-time greats.

And then it did.

On August 18, the Red Sox hosted the California Angels. Jack Hamilton, an erratic journeyman right-hander, was pitching for California. Conigliaro stepped to the plate in the third inning, checking the stands to see that his family had made it to the game. The first pitch came in high and tight, and Tony froze. The ball slammed into his left temple—no earflap helmets in those days—and Conigliaro went down in a heap. His cheekbone was broken, his jaw was dislocated, and he could not see. He regained the sight in his right eye after two days, but his left—his batting eye—was swollen shut for a week. When it finally opened, doctors found that he had a perforated retina and 20–300 vision on that side. There was no improvement over the next two months, and Conigliaro could only watch as the Red Sox won the AL pennant, but lost the World Series to the St. Louis Cardinals. After the season, he joined Joe DiMaggio and Jerry Coleman on a tour of Vietnam service hospitals, helping Tony gain some perspective.[7]

Conigliaro went to spring training with the Red Sox in 1968, but after a hopeful start things deteriorated. He experienced blurred vision and headaches. After striking out 22 times, including a stretch of eight K's in 10 at

---

6. Claflin, Larry. "No Arguments—Hub MVP Award Belongs to Tony C." *The Sporting News*, January 14, 1967.
7. Conigliaro, Tony. "Thanks for the Miracle!" *Guideposts*, September, 1969, pp. 2–5.

bats, he returned to Boston for another eye exam, where he was told, "If anything, your sight is getting worse."[8]

Conigliaro remained on the payroll of the Red Sox, but it became clear that no one expected him to be able to come back. He was left unprotected in the AL expansion draft that fall, but neither of the two new league teams—the Kansas City Royals and Seattle Pilots—selected him. He was then left off the 40-man roster as the winter meetings approached, and could have been drafted by any team for $25,000.[9] Nobody bothered.

Down but not out, Tony C came up with a plan to return to baseball—as a right-handed pitcher. He had done some pitching in high school, and hurlers were not expected to hit much. That November, Conigliaro joined the Florida Instructional League. He made four starts, in which his pitching was rocky at best but—with no DH rule—he found that he could hit the ball again. Another eye exam indicated that his eyesight had miraculously returned to normal.[10]

After almost 20 months out of the majors, Conigliaro made it back to the Red Sox in 1969. In his first game back, he hit a dramatic home run in the ninth inning, then scored the winning run in the twelfth. He went on to play 141 games, hit 20 homers, and bat .255—not quite the Tony C of old, but not bad for a man who had been written off less than a year earlier. He was named Comeback Player of the Year by *The Sporting News*, and won the Fred Hutchinson Memorial Award for "character, dedication, and competitive spirit."[11]

Conigliaro went on to have one of his best seasons in 1970. He set career highs in homers (36, fourth in the AL) and RBI (116, second). By then, brother Billy had joined him in the BoSox outfield. But on October 11, Tony was traded to the Angels in a six-player deal. It was all downhill from there.

Conig signed a 1971 contract reported at $80,000 (at a time when only the cream of the crop made six figures), but struggled mightily in the first half of the season. He was hitting in the low .200s with no power. The vision in his left eye had deteriorated again, and he was experiencing headaches and raw nerves. He was frustrated with himself and his teammates, who joked about his lack of production and hinted that he was malingering.[12] On July 9, Conigliaro went 0-for-8 with five strikeouts in a 20-inning, 1–0

---

8. *Ibid.*, pp. 5–6.
9. Claflin, Larry. "Price Tag on Tony C. Slashed Again—to $25,000." *The Sporting News*, November 16, 1968.
10. Conigliaro, Tony. "Thanks for the Miracle!" *Guideposts*, September, 1969, p. 6.
11. Thorn, John, Phil Birnbaum and Bill Deane, editors. *Total Baseball*. Wilmington, DE: SPORT Media Publishing, Inc., 2004, p. 737.
12. Gross, Milton. "'Why Don't They Understand?' Appropriate Song for Tony Conigliaro." Springfield, Mass. *Daily News*, July 13, 1971, p. 43.

loss to Vida Blue and the A's, and was ejected for arguing about the final K. Some 30 hours later, Tony C called a 5 a.m. press conference to announce he was retiring from baseball.[13] "I have lost my sight and am on the edge of losing my mind," Conigliaro said.[14]

Conigliaro dabbled in various business ventures, and he was still a very eligible bachelor. When he was robbed of his All-Star and World Series rings and $6,300 in cash and checks, he was more concerned with the loss of his little black book.[15]

With the introduction of the designated hitter rule, Conigliaro made another comeback attempt in August 1973.[16] It failed, and he was formally released by the Angels six months later, making him a free agent.[17] This paved the way for one final comeback attempt with his original team, and Conigliaro was the opening day DH for the Red Sox in 1975. But after a 4-for-42 skid, he was sent down to the AAA Pawtucket team. He fared little better there, batting .203 with three homers in 37 games, and his playing days were truly over at age 30.

Tony C then embarked on a new career: broadcasting. In September 1975, he started on WJAR-TV in Providence, Rhode Island.[18] A year later, he moved to KGO-TV in San Francisco,[19] where he eventually won an Emmy. On January 9, 1982, two days after his 37th birthday, Conigliaro had a promising audition for his new dream job: to become an analyst for the Red Sox TV crew.

After the interview, brother Billy was driving Tony to Logan Airport when Tony suddenly went into cardiac arrest. By the time Billy could get him to a hospital, Tony had suffered irreversible brain damage.

For the next eight years, Tony C was an invalid, requiring a feeding tube and 'round-the-clock care. He had part of a lung removed in 1983.[20] Benefits were held to raise money, and a 1985 workman's compensation settlement for $225,000 helped for a while.[21] When the money ran out, Tony's parents and brothers took over the care. His father died of a heart attack at

---

13. Charlton, James, editor. *The Baseball Chronology*. New York: Macmillan Publishing Co., 1991, p. 517.
14. "Tony C's Farewell: I'm Ready to Crack." AP release, July 11, 1971.
15. Miller, Dick. "Note to Thieves: Return Tony C's Little Black Book." *The Sporting News*, October 9, 1971.
16. "Tony C. Tries 3rd Baseball Comeback." AP release, August 19, 1973.
17. "Tony Conig Released by Angels." AP release, February, 1974.
18. "Conigliaro Signs Pact to Anchor Sports Show." *The Sporting News*, September 27, 1975.
19. Ron, Bergman. "Tony C's New Career—Bay Area Sportscaster." *The Sporting News*, November 6, 1976.
20. "Tony C Has Surgery; Part of Lung Removed." AP release, 1983.
21. "Tony C Gets Big Settlement." *USA Today*, December 19, 1985.

age 60 in 1987.²² The tragic story of Tony Conigliaro ended on February 24, 1990, when he died at age 45 in Salem, Massachusetts.

But his name lives on. On August 5, 1990, the Red Sox announced the establishment of the Tony Conigliaro Award, to be presented annually by the Boston BBWAA chapter to a major league player who overcomes adversity "through the attributes of spirit, determination, and courage." Through 2019, 32 players—including Dickie Thon (1991)—had been honored.²³ In 2007, the Sox added a 200-seat section on Fenway Park's right field roof, naming it "Conigliaro's Corner."

Year	Team (League)	G	AB	R	H	2B	3B	HR	RBI	SB	AVG	OBP	SLG
1964	Boston (AL)	111	404	69	117	21	2	24	52	2	.290	.354	.530
1965		138	521	82	140	21	5	*32	82	4	.269	.338	.512
1966		150	558	77	148	26	7	28	93	0	.265	.330	.487
1967		95	349	59	100	11	5	20	67	4	.287	.341	.519
1969		141	506	57	129	21	3	20	82	2	.255	.321	.427
1970		146	560	89	149	20	1	36	116	4	.266	.324	.498
1971	California (AL)	74	266	23	59	18	0	4	15	3	.222	.285	.335
1975	Boston (AL)	21	57	8	7	1	0	2	9	1	.123	.221	.246
Totals		876	3221	464	849	139	23	166	516	20	.264	.327	.476

22. *The Sporting News*, August 17, 1987.
23. Nowlin, Bill, and Clayton Trutor, editors. *Overcoming Adversity: Baseball's Tony Conigliaro Award*. Phoenix: Society for American Baseball Research, Inc., 2017, p. 1.

Jack Coombs

Entering the 1913 season, Jack Coombs was among the top pitchers in baseball. He had broken out in 1910 with 31 wins, including 13 shutouts, and capped off the campaign with three World Series triumphs. Coombs added 28 and 21 victories the next two seasons, giving him a three-year total of 80 wins in 1910–12.

But Jack Coombs would have zero wins in 1913–14.

John Wesley Coombs was born November 28, 1882, in Le Grand, Iowa. His family moved to a 116-acre farm outside of Kennebunk, Maine, when

Jack was four.[1] He grew up in Maine, attending Colburn Classical High School in Waterville, and going on to Colby College in the same town. Coombs earned a B.S. in chemistry, and fame as one of the better collegiate pitchers in the northeast. He played semipro ball during the summers. The right-hander was big for the era, topping six feet in height and weighing in at a muscular 185. Coombs was described as "a sidearm hurler who ... threw a fast, heavy ball with plenty on it."[2] Connie Mack signed him for $2,400 to pitch for the Philadelphia Athletics after his graduation.[3] Coombs never played a game in the minor leagues.

Colby Jack made a dazzling debut with the A's on July 5, 1906, shutting out the Washington Senators, 3–0. Less than two months later, he authored one of the great pitching performances of all time. On September 1, Coombs hurled a 24-inning complete game to beat the Red Sox, allowing just one run and striking out 18 (and even stealing two bases!). This earned him the nickname "Iron Man," to go along with "Colby Jack." So, did Mack reward his young pitcher with some well-earned rest? Hardly. Coombs was right back in the box four days later, pitching

Jack Coombs (1914). From July through October 1910, Coombs earned 24 victories, plus three more in the World Series. Library of Congress.

---

1. Lieb, Frederick J. "Jack Coombs Dies at 73; Won 24-Inning Marathon." *The Sporting News*, April 24, 1957, p. 30.
2. "Strong-Armed Jack Coombs Overcame Typhoid Spine." Unidentified clipping in National Baseball Library file, November 21, 1963.
3. Lieb, Frederick J. "Jack Coombs Dies at 73; Won 24-Inning Marathon." *The Sporting News*, April 24, 1957, p. 30.

another complete game, and continued racking up innings the rest of the year. He finished his rookie half-season with 173 innings, 10 wins, and a 2.50 ERA.

Not surprisingly, Coombs's arm was balky the next few years. Coombs had just six wins in 1907 and seven in '08. In fact, with his pitching future in doubt, he spent the first two months of the latter season as the team's starting right fielder, not appearing on the mound until June 11. Coombs wound up batting .255 in 78 games overall. Colby Jack was a good hitting-pitcher, with a .235 career average, plus .333 in World Series play. A switch-hitter, he batted .319 in 1911 with 45 hits, including two extra-inning home runs.[4]

According to Mack, Coombs's transformation into a great pitcher began with the development of a second pitch. "In the middle of the 1909 season, I had Jack finish a game," Mack recalled. "He worked six beautiful innings, and showed a little curve.... I called him aside after the game and said, 'Jack, if you'll pitch that curve and practice it on every occasion, I'll promise you will be a great pitcher.'"[5] Coombs finished the year with a 12–11 record and 2.32 ERA.

The 1910 season didn't start out looking like a special one for Coombs. He lost his first two decisions, was dropped from the rotation for a spell, and didn't earn his first victory until May 14. By July Coombs had a mere seven wins and one shutout.

Then, on a staff which included future Hall of Famers Eddie Plank and Chief Bender, Coombs fulfilled Mack's prophecy and emerged as the ace. He ran off 10 victories in July, five by shutout. On August 4, he locked into a 16-inning scoreless duel with Chicago's Ed Walsh, ended by darkness; Coombs allowed just three hits and struck out 18 in what he later recalled as "the best game I ever pitched."[6] Later that month, he started an 11-game winning streak. From September 5–25, Coombs strung together 53 consecutive scoreless innings, a record at the time. Colby Jack finished the year with a pitching season for the ages: a 31–9 record and 1.30 ERA, leading the league in games (45), wins, and shutouts, and not allowing a home run all season. His 13 whitewashes remain the all-time AL record, and he also had 11 complete games in which he allowed just one run. After hurling 353 innings in the regular season, Coombs labored to earn three complete-game victories in six days, October 18–23, as the A's beat the Cubs in the World Series. He threw 151 pitches to win Game Two on Tuesday, 120

---

4. Jones David, editor. *Deadball Stars of the American League*. Dulles, VA: Potomac Books, Inc., 2006, p. 615.

5. Lieb, Frederick J. "Jack Coombs Dies at 73; Won 24-Inning Marathon." *The Sporting News*, April 24, 1957, p. 30.

6. Coombs, Jack, as told to Frederick G. Lieb. "My Greatest Diamond Thrill." *The Sporting News*, November 2, 1944.

pitches to take Game Three on Thursday, and 120 more to win the clincher on Sunday.[7]

After the 1910 season, Coombs married Mary Elizabeth Russ of Palestine, Texas, starting a union which would last 46 years but produce no children.[8] Jack would see a nephew, Bobby Coombs, pitch briefly in the major leagues.

Not surprisingly (due to the heavy workload, not the marriage), Jack Coombs's effectiveness was down in 1911. He was just 1–3 in April, and his season ERA jumped more than two runs, though part of that was due to the newly-introduced cork-center ball, which helped raise the league ERA from 2.52 to 3.34. But Coombs used his considerable brains as well as his arm, pitching to spots, and learning the tendencies of batters and even umpires. He went 7–0 after August to wind up with a 28–12 record, again leading the AL in wins and the A's to a world championship. In Game Three of the World Series, he came out victorious in an extra-inning pitching duel against Giants immortal Christy Mathewson, allowing just three hits in 11 innings in what he called "my biggest thrill."[9] Coombs was forced out of another extra-inning contest in Game Five. He suffered a groin injury midway through the game, and ruptured it while beating out a bunt in the tenth inning.[10] Though still hampered in 1912—he missed 24 days of action in April–May, and didn't win a game after August 24—Coombs managed to turn in a 21–10 record.

It is not clear what exactly disabled Coombs after the 1912 season, and reading contemporary newspaper articles does little to solve the mystery. There was usually a lumping together of various injuries and illnesses which somehow conspired to break Coombs down. The 1911 World Series injury had necessitated surgery, and he suffered a serious beaning in the Philadelphia City Series on October 7, 1912.[11] Coombs developed a high fever during spring training the following year, and was sent home to recuperate after two aborted appearances on April 10 and 12. He spent weeks in a hospital, and then was strapped to a board in his bed at home, attended by doctors and nurses day and night.[12] Coombs was reportedly battling for

---

7. "Coombs Was the Big Star." Unidentified clipping in National Baseball Library file, October 25, 1910.
8. Jones David, eEditor. *Deadball Stars of the American League*. Dulles, VA: Potomac Books, Inc., 2006, p. 615.
9. Coombs, Jack, as told to Frederick G. Lieb. "My Greatest Diamond Thrill." *The Sporting News*, November 2, 1944.
10. Neft, David S., and Richard M. Cohen. *The World Series*. New York: St. Martin's Press, 1990.
11. "Baseball's Greatest Come Back." Unidentified clipping in National Baseball Library file, July, 1915.
12. "Philadelphia Points." *The Sporting Life*, May, 1913.

his life, and he lost 54 pounds.[13] Among the ailments ascribed to him were enteric fever, ptomaine poisoning, intestinal trouble, tuberculosis, pneumonia, grippe, pleurisy and, most commonly, typhoid fever of the spine. A late-summer comeback attempt failed, and Coombs returned to the hospital from September through November. Coombs didn't pitch again until a couple of brief appearances at the end of the 1914 season. Mack gave him his release on December 9, making him a free agent.[14]

Coombs signed a contract with the Brooklyn Robins, conditional (at his insistence) on his ability to return from two years of virtual inactivity. He soon laid the concerns to rest with a remarkable comeback. Every day, he was fitted with a heavy rubber brace from hip to knees, supplemented by bandages and a metal brace.[15] Though his fastball was gone, Coombs used his guile to post a 15–10 record and 2.58 ERA in 1915, aiding Brooklyn to its first winning season since 1903. A year later, he helped the Robins to the NL pennant with a 13–8, 2.66 log, including a 6–0 mark against John McGraw's Giants (Coombs beat the Giants 11 straight times from 1915 to 1917, plus the 1911 World Series win). He then gave Brooklyn its only World Series win, 4–3 in Game Three. Coombs finished with a 5–0 Fall Classic record.

Colby Jack was no longer effective the next two years, but he was still valuable to the club as an unofficial pitching coach. He retired following a 1–0 loss to the Giants on August 30, 1918.

Coombs had some business interests to fall back on, but couldn't get baseball out of his system. He signed to manage the Phillies in 1919, but resigned on July 8 with the team mired in last place. He joined the Tigers as a coach the following year, and made two mop-up pitching appearances before leaving the big leagues for good.

Coombs then embarked on a long college baseball coaching career, serving for Williams (1921–24), Princeton (1925–28), and Duke (1929–52), where he posted a 381–171 (.686) record, won seven state titles, and produced 21 major league players. Both Duke's and Colby's baseball fields are named after Coombs. He also did some scouting for the A's and ran some baseball clinics during this time. In 1938, he authored the Prentice-Hall textbook, *Baseball: Individual Strategy and Team Play*.[16] Coombs earned enshrinement in the Collegiate Baseball Coaches, Duke Sports, and North Carolina Sports Halls of Fame.[17]

There were many who thought Coombs should be honored by the

---

13. Unidentified clipping in National Baseball Library file.
14. "Jack Coombs Now Made Free Agent." Unidentified clipping in National Baseball Library file, December 9, 1914.
15. "Coombs Wears Harness While He's Pitching." New York *Tribune*, October 15, 1916.
16. "Coombs Writes a Book." *The Sporting News*, August 25, 1938.
17. Jones David, Editor. *Deadball Stars of the American League*. Dulles, VA: Potomac Books, Inc., 2006, p. 617.

National Baseball Hall of Fame as well, comparing his credentials to 1953 inductee Dizzy Dean's. Dean had only 150 career victories, but dominated with an 82–32 record in a three-year stretch (1934–36). Similarly, Coombs had 158 wins, including an 80–31 log in his three-year period of dominance (1910–12). "No better pitcher ever walked out to a mound," said Hall of Famer Frank Baker, Jack's teammate from 1908 to 1914.[18] Coombs received a smattering of Hall of Fame votes from the BBWAA before his candidacy was turned over to the Veterans' Committee in 1953. *The Sporting News* publisher J.G. Taylor Spink, chairman of that committee until 1959, wrote in his resignation letter that, "I am strongly of the opinion that the rules for election of old-time stars need revision in order that more of these outstanding players might gain rightful recognition. As matters now stand, only one or two can be elected every two years, and many of these distinguished old-timers never will gain election under such a system. I have in mind men like Billy Hamilton, Bob Caruthers, Amos Rusie, Tim Keefe, Jack Coombs and others of that character."[19] Hamilton (1961), Rusie (1977), and Keefe (1964) would later be elected to the Hall, but not Coombs.

In his final years, Coombs hoped to be remembered by the Vets' Committee. After they elected outfielder Sam Crawford and manager Joe McCarthy in 1957, Coombs wrote on March 2 that "I had hopes that the committee would give me the honor of joining the other baseball men in the Hall of Fame. However, they made a grand selection in giving Crawford and McCarthy that honor. I shall live in hopes that I can join the group in 1959 when the men who make the selection will again meet. If the honor is going to come to me I hope that I will be alive when it comes for to me it would not be a pleasurable honor to enjoy after I am six feet under the sod. At the age of 75 one can never tell what will happen."[20]

Forty-four days later, on April 15, 1957, Jack Coombs died of a coronary occlusion in Palestine, Texas.

Year	Team (League)	G	IP	W	L	PCT	SO	BB	H	ERA
1906	Philadelphia (AL)	23	173.0	10	10	.500	90	68	144	2.50
1907		23	132.2	6	9	.400	73	64	109	3.12
1908		26	153.0	7	5	.583	80	64	130	2.00
1909		30	205.2	12	11	.522	97	73	156	2.32
1910		*45	353.0	*31	9	.775	224	115	248	1.30
1911		47	336.2	*28	12	.700	185	119	*360	3.53

18. Lieb, Frederick J. "Jack Coombs Dies at 73; Won 24-Inning Marathon." *The Sporting News*, April 24, 1957, p. 30.
19. "Spink Resigns Shrine Post, Stresses Need of Electing More Old-Time Stars." *The Sporting News*, August 5, 1959, p. 6.
20. Coombs, John W. Letter to Lew Slaw, March 2, 1957.

Year	Team (League)	G	IP	W	L	PCT	SO	BB	H	ERA
1912	Philadelphia (AL)	40	262.1	21	10	.677	120	94	227	3.29
1913		2	5.1	0	0	-----	0	6	5	10.13
1914		2	8.0	0	1	.000	1	3	8	4.50
1915	Brooklyn (NL)	29	195.2	15	10	.600	56	91	166	2.58
1916		27	159.0	13	8	.619	47	44	136	2.66
1917		31	141.0	7	11	.389	34	49	147	3.96
1918		27	189.0	8	14	.364	44	49	191	3.81
1920	Detroit (AL)	2	5.2	0	0	-----	1	2	7	3.18
Totals		354	2320.0	158	110	.590	1052	841	2034	2.78

Larry Corcoran

In the five seasons from 1880 to 1884, nobody in baseball won more games (170) or struck out more batters (1076) than Larry Corcoran, though Pud Galvin (168, 1074) and Old Hoss Radbourn (165, 1074) were close behind. At just 25 years of age, Corcoran appeared to be on the same career path as those two future Hall of Famers.

But Corcoran would win just seven more big league games, and live just seven more years.

Lawrence J. Corcoran was born in Brooklyn, New York, on August 10, 1859. Though diminutive in size (5'3" and 127 pounds), the righty was pitching in organized baseball—and attracting attention at it—at age 17. He had just turned 20 and had not yet reached the major leagues when *The New York Clipper*—a weekly newspaper devoted to sport and theater—did a feature on him. "The first time we saw Corcoran play," they wrote, "was in the Spring of 1877, when he pitched for a second-class co-operative team called the Mutuals, on the Capitoline Grounds, Brooklyn.... We remarked his good delivery and (surprising) speed for his size, which soon brought him into notice as a pitcher."[1]

Later in 1877, Corcoran joined the Livingstons of Geneseo, then turned pro with a team in Buffalo. He pitched for Springfield and Holyoke, Massachusetts, in 1878–79, after which the *Clipper* reported, "He has wonderful speed for his strength, and with it a troublesome curve. He also has more than ordinary command of the ball in delivery for so swift a pitcher.

---

1. "Larry Corcoran, Pitcher." *New York Clipper*, September 13, 1879.

He is a good 'headwork' player in the position, and with (a skillful catcher to receive him), it would be difficult to get a base-hit from his pitching. He is reticent in his work, a plucky fielder, has plenty of endurance, and is to be relied upon for faithfulness in his position."[2]

At age 20, Corcoran made it to the majors with the Chicago White Stockings, who had finished in fourth place the year before. With Larry anchoring their two-man pitching staff, Chicago easily won the 1880 NL pennant. He won 43 games—including a 13-game winning streak in June–July, and a no-hitter vs. Boston on August 19—lost just 14, and topped the league with 268 strikeouts.

Corcoran led the White Stockings to another pennant in 1881, going 31–14 to pace the league in victories. In '82, Larry went 27–12, posting the best winning percentage and ERA in the league, enjoying two 10-game winning streaks, and notching his second no-no, vs. Worcester on September 20. He followed with 34 wins in 1883 and 35 in '84.

Corcoran's 1884 work included his third no-hitter—June 27 vs. Providence—a record that wouldn't be broken until 1965. He remains one of just six pitchers to hurl three or more no-nos, joined by Cy Young, Bob Feller, Sandy Koufax, Nolan Ryan, and Justin Verlander. Corcoran's feat is made more impressive by the fact that all three of his were pitched

Larry Corcoran, shown here at the end of the line (1887), pitched three no-hitters before his 25th birthday. Library of Congress.

2. *Ibid.*

at Chicago's White Stocking Park, a band-box with foul lines shorter than 200 feet.

On June 16, the ambidextrous Corcoran pitched alternately right- and left-handed in a loss against Buffalo.[3] On July 15, his brother Michael pitched one game for the White Stockings. When Larry wasn't pitching, he often played outfield or shortstop. A switch-hitter, he batted .223 lifetime.

At age 25, Corcoran already owned a 170–83 career won-lost record. Five of the 10 most similar pitchers at that age are Hall of Famers, including Christy Mathewson and Walter Johnson. But Corcoran had averaged over 450 innings per season, and he paid the price. After winning five of his first seven games in 1885, he was sidelined with a sore shoulder.

The Sporting Life reported in mid-season that Corcoran "has been released at his urgent request and has gone to his home at Newark, N.J. with the hope of building himself up again. It is said that his arm is so sore that there is no possibility of his pitching again this year. It is said that Larry was used very meanly by the club he has served so well, and that during June and July while he was under a doctor's care his pay was stopped."[4] Corcoran resurfaced with New York for three games at the end of the season, earning his final two big league wins.

His arm shot, Corcoran made two unsuccessful appearances with Washington in 1886 and two more with Indianapolis in '87, then went to the minor leagues where he fared no better and wound up as an umpire. Having pitched in parts of just eight major league seasons, he is not eligible for the Hall of Fame.

On October 14, 1891, Larry Corcoran died of "chronic parenchymalous nephritis"[5]—better-known as Bright's disease—at his Newark home on 24 Cherry Street. He was just 32 and left behind his wife, Gertrude, and four young children.[6]

Year	Team (League)	G	IP	W	L	PCT	SO	BB	H	ERA
1880	Chicago (NL)	63	536.1	43	14	.754	*268	*99	404	1.95
1881		45	396.2	*31	14	.689	150	78	380	2.31
1882		39	355.2	27	12	*.692	170	63	281	*1.95
1883		56	473.2	34	20	.630	216	82	483	2.49
1884		60	516.2	35	23	.602	272	116	473	2.40
1885	Chicago-New York (NL)	10	84.1	7	3	.700	20	35	87	3.42

---

3. Michelson, Court. *Michelson's Book of World Baseball Records*. Chicago: Adams Press, 1985, p. 38.
4. *The Sporting Life*, July 22, 1885, p. 5.
5. Death certificate in National Baseball Library file.
6. "A Famous Ball Pitcher Dead." Unidentified clipping in National Baseball Library file.

Year	Team (League)	G	IP	W	L	PCT	SO	BB	H	ERA
1886	Washington (NL)	2	14.0	0	1	.000	3	4	16	5.79
1887	Indianapolis (NL)	2	15.0	0	2	.000	4	19	23	12.60
Totals		277	2392.1	177	89	.665	1103	496	2147	2.36

Tommy Davis

At age 23 in 1962, Tommy Davis had a breakout year. Despite playing half his games in a pitchers' paradise, Davis led the major leagues in hits (230), RBI (153), and batting average (.346). He followed that with another big season, again topping the majors in batting, and helping the Dodgers to the 1963 world championship. Besides hitting for average, Davis had speed—he stole 68 bases in the minors one year—and some power, topping the Dodgers in RBI three straight years.

But a gruesome injury turned him into the prototypical journeyman player.

Herman Thomas Davis, Jr., was born in Brooklyn, New York, on March 21, 1939, an only child (contrary to popular misconception that he was the brother of long-time teammate and roommate Willie Davis). Called "Tommy" to distinguish from his father, he was playing fast-pitch softball at age nine, and was part of a state champion Kiwanis League team at 16.[1] Tommy graduated from Boys High in Brooklyn in 1956, after lettering in basketball and track, in addition to baseball, where he caught and played first base.[2] He was the team's high scorer in hoops, ahead of future Basketball Hall of Famer Lenny Wilkens.[3]

Davis then began his pro baseball career at age 17. The 6'2", 200-pounder with the sweet, level, right-handed swing was wooed by the Yankees, among others. He signed instead with his hometown Dodgers, after a phone call from Jackie Robinson and a $4,000 bonus offer from scout Al Campanis.[4] After batting .325 in the PONY League, Davis moved to Kokomo in the Midwest League (managed by Pete Reiser) for 1957.

---

1. Stewart, Mark, and Paul Hirsch. "Tommy Davis." In SABR's BioProject.
2. Brown, Robert J. "DAVIS, Herman Thomas 'Tommy.'" In *Biographical Dictionary of American Sports: Baseball*, edited by David L. Porter.
3. Cottrol, Bob. "'T. DAVIS, dh.'" *Black Sports*, August 1974, p. 54.
4. Hunter, Bob. "D Stands for Davis, Dodgers—and Dynamite." *The Sporting News*, December 22, 1962, p. 5.

There, Davis paced the team to the top of the standings, leading the league in runs, hits, total bases, stolen bases (a league record 68 in 127 games), and batting (.357). That earned a jump all the way from Class D to AA for '58.

Tommy married Shirley Johnson on February 6, 1957. They would have three daughters and a son: Lauren (born May 18, 1958), Leslie (May 10, 1961), Carlyn (February 11, 1963), and Herman Thomas III (August 31, 1966).[5]

Davis played in the Texas and International Leagues in 1958, topping .300 at both stops. With Spokane in 1959, Davis led the AAA Pacific Coast League in hits, total bases, and batting (.345), and also topped outfielders in putouts and chances accepted. He was voted PCL Rookie of the Year, and finished his 459-game minor league career with a .335 average. Tommy joined the Dodgers for his first at bat in September, and was in the big leagues to stay.

Davis had a rocky beginning to the 1960 season. He was batting a paltry .138 (8-for-58) through May 22, was benched most of June, and didn't hit his first big league home run until July 10. But he came on strong to finish at .276 (including an NL-best 20-game hitting streak) with 11 homers, earning one of the league's 16 Rookie of the Year votes.

Nineteen-sixty-one was just the opposite. Davis was batting .314 with 15 home runs through July, but then was hampered by a serious back problem. He didn't have a homer the rest of the year, nor a hit after September 8. Following the season, Davis was hospitalized for 10 days and put in traction.[6]

Despite the checkered start, future Hall of Famers were already recognizing Tommy's hitting potential. Prior to the 1961 season, teammate Duke Snider predicted that "this kid will lead the league in batting inside of two or three years." A year later, manager Walt Alston said, "For a young player, I think Tommy swings as correctly as any I've seen. He has a nice level stroke and hits the ball where it's pitched, and to any field."[7]

With Davis back in physical shape in 1962, Alston and coach Pete Reiser worked on his mental approach. They felt he was too unassuming and easy-going. Davis certainly didn't go easy on pitchers in 1962, authoring a historic season at the bat.

Healthy all year, Davis slashed hits and drove in runners in bunches. By the end of the season, he had amassed 230 hits, 21 more than anyone else in the majors. His 153 RBI were the most in the NL in a 60-year period: nobody had more since Triple Crown–winner Joe Medwick's 154 in 1937,

---

5. Cottrol, Bob. "'T. DAVIS, dh.'" *Black Sports*, August 1974, p. 58.
6. Hunter, Bob. "D Stands for Davis, Dodgers—and Dynamite." *The Sporting News*, December 22, 1962, p. 5.
7. *Ibid.*, p. 6.

and Tommy's total wouldn't be topped again until Sammy Sosa did so in 1998. In fact, only five players in league history have surpassed 153: Hack Wilson (191, 159), Chuck Klein (170), Sam Thompson (166, 165), Sosa (160, 158), and Medwick.

Davis also finished among the league's top five in runs (120), triples, total bases (356), slugging, and OPS. He was even seventh in stolen bases with 18 in 24 attempts, including a steal of home against Juan Marichal. But the Dodgers lost the pennant in a three-game playoff against the Giants, likely costing Davis in MVP voting. He finished third, behind teammate Maury Wills, who stole a record 104 bases, and the Giants' Willie Mays.

Through age 23, the most similar player to Davis is Mookie Betts, with Duke Snider third. Davis also contributed defensively. As in the previous years, he played wherever the Dodgers needed him, including all three outfield positions and 39 games at third base. He led NL left fielders in range factor, zone runs, and fielding percentage.

The increased strike zone dropped NL batting averages by 16 points in 1963, but Davis was still at the top of the heap at .326. His RBI total dipped to 88 (53 on the road), but that led the pennant-winning Dodgers, and he finished eighth in MVP voting. The team then pulled off a stunning four-game World Series sweep of the Yankees, and Davis was a big reason. In Game Two, he tied Series records with two triples and with six putouts in left. In Game Three, he drove in the game's only run to give Don Drysdale a 1–0 victory. Davis batted a Series-high .400 overall, en route to a .313 career post-season average.

Tommy had an off-year in 1964, especially in the first half. Part of it, as usual, was his home park: he had 11 home runs and 51 RBI on the road, but just three and 35 at home. Yet he finished strong, slugging .600 in September, and leading the Dodgers in RBI for the third consecutive season. The Dodgers dealt Frank Howard away following the season, leaving Davis as the team's only legitimate power threat.

After a slow start to the '65 season, Davis seemed to be getting back on track, with six hits in his last nine at bats as he stood on first base on May 1. Ron Fairly then hit a grounder to the first baseman. Davis lit out for second and went into an awkward slide—even though, as it turned out, there was no play at that base.

"I was undecided whether to slide, so I didn't go down like I should have," Davis explained. "I looked down and my ankle was out in right field." According to *The Sporting News*, "His spikes caught in the cement-hard [Dodger Stadium] base-path, and he rolled over like a fighter who has been hit on the button."[8] Davis suffered torn ligaments, a broken right leg, and

---

8. Hunter, Bob. "Never Rains, Just Pours, Dodgers Find." *The Sporting News*, May 15, 1965.

a dislocated ankle. Team physician Robert Kerlan gave a grim prognosis. "Whatever the Dodgers get out of him henceforth will be a bonus," Kerlan said. "Tommy may play again—and he may not. The bones were completely shattered."[9]

Davis was hospitalized for six weeks and in a cast for 3½ months.[10] Except for a token pinch-hitting appearance on the last day of the season, he was done for the year, including the World Series. A year after the injury, Davis was still a question mark. Playing sparingly, he had just five hits in the Dodgers' first 34 games of 1966 before working his way back into the regular lineup.

Davis would play another 11 seasons, but he had lost much of his speed and power. "He ran with a limp," recalled teammate Wes Parker. "It hurt his fielding, and cost him infield hits and extra-base hits."[11] Though Davis still hit for decent BA, he averaged just six homers per year after 1965, only twice reaching double-figures. "Naturally, it affected my speed," Tommy said, "and subconsciously I didn't put weight on my back foot, which is the way most hitters hit.... I learned to hit off my front foot."[12] Davis didn't even realize that he had changed his hitting style until 1975, when he shifted his weight back to try for more power. "I used to hit like that all the time when I was younger," he said, "but when I tried to do it this time, I noticed that the ankle hurt. That's when I realized it was a style of hitting that I had been away from for 10 years."[13]

The Dodgers traded Davis after the 1966 season, beginning a historically nomadic journey. Over the next decade, he went to the Mets, White Sox, Seattle Pilots, Astros, A's, Cubs, A's again, Cubs again, Orioles, Yankees (he was cut without playing for them), Angels, and Royals, before being released for good on January 17, 1977. Playing for 10 different teams tied a major league record at the time.

Unable to do the job in the field by his mid–30s, Davis got a new lease on life with the designated hitter rule, serving the Orioles in that capacity for the first three seasons of its existence. In 1973, he finished third in the AL in batting and tenth in MVP voting; in '74, he was named the league's DH of the Year.

Davis finished with 2121 career hits, 153 homers, 1052 RBI, and a .294 average, including a record .320 as a pinch-hitter. He estimated that the

---

9. Grieve, Curley. "Bonus for Dodgers if Davis Ever Again Plays." *San Francisco Examiner*, May 12, 1965.
10. Rapoport, Ron. "Tommy Davis Very Bitter Toward Baseball." *Tampa Times*, June 28, 1976, p. 4-C.
11. Telephone interview with Wes Parker, May 17, 2020.
12. *Ibid.*
13. Henneman, Jim. "Old Bat Style Makes T. Davis New Man." *The Sporting News*, August 23, 1975, p. 10.

ankle injury cost him at least 300 hits.[14] That seems conservative; he probably lost nearly that many just in the at bats he missed in 1965–66, never mind what the reduction of power and speed cost him the rest of his career. "He was the best hitter the [Los Angeles] Dodgers ever had,"[15] said Wes Parker, who has been associated with the team for most of the past six decades.

Davis served as a batting instructor for the Angels, Mariners, and Dodgers in the 1980s. He later owned a silkscreen advertising business and a promotional item venture called Tommy Davis Enterprises. His second wife, Carol, gave him a fourth daughter.[16]

Tommy Davis went on the Hall of Fame ballot in 1982, getting just five votes. Could he have done better without the 1965 injury? "I don't know if I would have made the Hall of Fame," Davis said in 2011, but added that "I had better years than some guys who are in."[17]

Year	Team (League)	G	AB	R	H	2B	3B	HR	RBI	SB	AVG	OBP	SLG
1959	Los Angeles (NL)	1	1	0	0	0	0	0	0	0	.000	.000	.000
1960		110	352	43	97	18	1	11	44	6	.276	.302	.426
1961		132	460	60	128	13	2	15	58	10	.278	.325	.413
1962		163	665	120	*230	27	9	27	*153	18	*.346	.374	.535
1963		146	556	69	181	19	3	16	88	15	*.326	.359	.457
1964		152	592	70	163	20	5	14	86	11	.275	.311	.397
1965		17	60	3	15	1	1	0	9	2	.250	.270	.300
1966		100	313	27	98	11	1	3	27	3	.313	.345	.383
1967	New York (NL)	154	577	72	174	32	0	16	73	9	.302	.342	.440
1968	Chicago (AL)	132	456	30	122	5	3	8	50	4	.268	.289	.344
1969	Sea. (A)–Hou. (N)	147	533	54	142	32	1	7	89	20	.266	.318	.370
1970	Hou. (N)–Oak. (A)–Chi. (N)	134	455	45	129	23	3	6	65	10	.284	.308	.387
1971	Oakland (AL)	79	219	26	71	8	1	3	42	7	.324	.363	.411
1972	Chi. (N)–Balt. (A)	41	108	12	28	4	0	0	12	2	.259	.310	.296

---

14. "Tommy Davis Milestones." *The Sporting News*, August 9, 1975.
15. Telephone interview with Wes Parker, May 17, 2020.
16. Stewart, Mark, and Paul Hirsch. "Tommy Davis." In SABR's BioProject.
17. *Ibid.*

Year	Team (League)	G	AB	R	H	2B	3B	HR	RBI	SB	AVG	OBP	SLG
1973	Baltimore (AL)	137	552	53	169	20	3	7	89	11	.306	.341	.391
1974		158	626	67	181	20	1	11	84	6	.289	.325	.377
1975		116	460	43	130	14	1	6	57	2	.283	.315	.357
1976	Cal.–K.C. (AL)	80	238	17	63	5	0	3	26	0	.265	.311	.324
Totals		1999	7223	811	2121	272	35	153	1052	136	.294	.329	.405

Charlie Ferguson

Former NL President John K. Tener said, "With due respect to [Honus] Wagner, [Ty] Cobb, and [Babe] Ruth, I believe [Charlie] Ferguson would have been remembered as king of them all."[1] *The Sporting News* described Ferguson in 1908 as "The one man who stood out clean-cut and away above all the players of his time or of the present as a player without a weakness, who could play and did play every position on the field, and played them all with exceptional ability."[2] Hall of Famers Harry Wright and Wilbert Robinson considered him among the best players they ever saw, Robby ranking him among the top five with Wagner, Ruth, Cobb, and Willie Keeler.[3]

They were describing a man who played his last game at age 24.

Charles J. Ferguson was born April 17, 1863, at Charlottesville, Virginia. He played there in 1882 for the University of Virginia (though he wasn't a student of that school), and the following year pitched and caught for an independent team in Richmond, Virginia. A.J. Reach signed him to hurl for the fledgling Philadelphia Phillies in 1884.[4]

A right-hander, Ferguson stood just under six feet tall and weighed 165 pounds. According to *The Sporting News*, "He was a first-class pitcher,

---

1. Fitzpatrick, Frank. "The Short Life and Tragic Death of a Long-Ago Phillies Phenom." *Philadelphia Inquirer,* February 23, 2003, p. D11.
2. "Without a Weakness." *The Sporting News,* January 30, 1908, p. 8.
3. Wright, Craig R. "The First Superstar of the Phillies." *A Page from Baseball's Past* (BaseballsPast.com).
4. Phelps, Frank V., and Jim Sumner. "Charles J. Ferguson." *Nineteenth Century Stars.* Kansas City, MO: Society for American Baseball Research, 1989, p. 42.

possessing good speed, all the curves and shoots, combined with coolness and strategic skill."[5]

Ferguson's rookie record of 21 wins and 25 losses didn't reflect his true performance. The Phillies had gone a wretched 17–81 in their maiden season of 1883, and didn't do much better (18–48) when Ferguson wasn't pitching in '84. Fergy showed skill with the bat, too, hitting .246 and playing five games in the outfield.

Ferguson improved to 26–20 with a 2.22 ERA in 1885. On August 29, he no-hit the defending champion Providence Grays in a 1–0 victory. Showing even more promise as an all-around player, Ferguson batted .306 and played outfield in 15 games.

Ferguson had his best pitching season in 1886, closing it out with a flourish. On October 9, he became one of the few players ever to pitch two complete-game victories in one day, subduing Detroit, 5–1 and 6–1.[6] That gave him 11 consecutive wins to end the season (and he extended it to 16 straight the following year). Ferguson wound up the '86 campaign with a 30–9 record, finishing second in the NL in winning percentage, ERA, fewest hits allowed per game, and fewest walks allowed per game. He also played 27 games in the outfield, and batted .253 overall.

In 1887, Ferguson had his best all-around season. Though he pitched "just" 37 games, he went 22–10,

Charlie Ferguson, shown at the end of his four-year career (1887), during which he won 99 games. Library of Congress.

5. "Death of Pitcher Ferguson, of the Philadelphia Club." *Philadelphia Public Ledger*, April 30, 1888.
6. Reichler, Joseph L., editor. *The Great All-Time Baseball Record Book.* New York: Macmillan Publishing Co., 1993, p. 257.

finishing second in the league in percentage and third in ERA. He also played second base in many of the games he didn't pitch, and was rated as one of the better keystoners in the league. At bat, Ferguson hit a robust .337 (.413, according to that year's system of counting walks as hits), and drove in 85 runs in just 72 games. And he saved his best for last: Ferguson led the Phillies to 16 wins in their last 17 games of 1887. Not only did he go 7–0 with a 1.75 ERA on the mound during that period, but he batted .361, and fielded a startling .963 (the league average was .924) at second base.[7] Nobody could have guessed those would be the final 17 games of Ferguson's career.

In his last two seasons, Ferguson had some health issues. In 1886, he and some teammates became ill during a western road trip due to "bad water." Ferguson, who had a reputation as a hypochondriac, also complained of a weak arm and general fatigue, but management refused his request for time off. He left anyway, getting a doctor's attestation that he was bedridden at home for 10 days. Unmoved, the team fined and suspended him for the rest of the season. Ferguson returned for the '87 season, but again complained of lameness of arm and exhaustion of body after it was over—not hard to believe of a man who hurled over 1,500 innings in four seasons.[8]

At age 24, Ferguson's career record showed 99 wins, 64 losses (an average record of 25–16), and a 2.67 ERA. In addition to his 183 games on the mound, Fergy played 27 games at second base, 22 in center field, 18 in right field, 13 in left field, and five at third base, batting .288 overall. He was considered a solid fielder and excellent baserunner.

In the spring of 1888, Ferguson contracted "typho malarial fever."[9] According to author Craig Wright, Philadelphia was notorious for its unsanitary water systems in that era, contributing to 27,000 typhoid deaths in that city between 1860 and 1909.[10] By April 29, it was clear that Ferguson would not recover. With most of his teammates present, he died at 10:55 p.m. at his residence (which he apparently shared with team captain Art Irwin) on 2512 North Broad Street, Philadelphia.[11] He left behind his wife of three years, the former Mary Smith, but no children—a daughter had died in infancy the previous June.[12] Charlie Ferguson had just

---

7. Phelps, Frank V. and Jim Sumner. "Charles J. Ferguson." *Nineteenth Century Stars*. Kansas City, MO: Society for American Baseball Research, 1989, p. 42.
8. Casway, Jerrold. "Bacteria Beat the Phillies." *Baseball Research Journal*, Spring 2016, pp. 117–18.
9. Death certificate in National Baseball Library file.
10. Wright, Craig R. "The First Superstar of the Phillies." *A Page from Baseball's Past* (BaseballsPast.com).
11. "Death of Pitcher Ferguson, of the Philadelphia Club." *Philadelphia Public Ledger*, April 30, 1888.
12. Casway, Jerrold. "Bacteria Beat the Phillies." *Baseball Research Journal*, Spring 2016, p. 116, 118.

turned 25 years old. He was buried at Maplewood Cemetery in Charlottesville, Virginia.[13]

Team President Reach and Secretary John Rogers adopted the following resolutions:

Resolved, That in the death of Charles J. Ferguson this club has lost one of its most skillful and gentlemanly players—one who, by his fidelity to duty, his obedience to discipline and his exemplary conduct, has won for him the esteem of the management, the friendship of his companions and the admiration of every lover of the National game.

Resolved, That as a tribute of respect to his memory, the management and players will attend his obsequies in Philadelphia, and a committee will accompany his mortal remains to their final resting place in Virginia. Also, that the flags at our ball park be half-masted and craped, and that the players, while in uniform, wear the usual badge of mourning for a period of 30 days.[14]

Year	Team (League)	G	IP	W	L	PCT.	SO	BB	H	ERA
1884	Philadelphia (NL)	50	416.2	21	25	.457	194	93	443	3.54
1885		48	405.0	26	20	.565	197	81	345	2.22
1886		48	395.2	30	9	.769	212	69	317	1.98
1887		37	297.1	22	10	.688	125	47	297	3.00
Totals		183	1514.2	99	64	.607	728	290	1402	2.67

13. "A Great Player Gone." *The Sporting Life*, May 9, 1888, p. 3.
14. *Ibid.*

José Fernandez

On September 20, 2016, the Marlins' José Fernandez pitched eight shutout innings, striking out 12, walking none, and allowing only three hits, to earn a 1–0 victory over the Washington Nationals. He told a teammate it was the best game he ever pitched.

It was also the last game he ever pitched.

José Delfin Fernandez y Gomez was born July 31, 1992, in Santa Clara, Cuba. Like many people trapped on that communist island, José's family longed to escape to America. His stepfather, Ramon, made it in 2005, settling in Tampa, Florida. Over the next three years, José and his mother, Maritza, made four daring attempts to escape by boat. One resulted in three months of jail time for the teenager. The fourth, in April 2008, included stepsister Yadenis and her mother. Maritza fell overboard at one point; 15-year-old José jumped into the Gulf of Mexico to save her life. After three days, the foursome reached Mexico. From there, they made their ways to Tampa to rejoin Ramon.[1]

Fernandez had already showed talent for baseball, and in Tampa he hooked up with a man named Orlando Chinea. The 51-year-old trainer had been the Cuban national team's pitching coach in the 1990s, and had also coached four years for Japan's Yomiuri Giants. In Cuba, Chinea had tutored future major league stars Jose Contreras and brothers Livan and Orlando "El Duque" Hernandez. Chinea had also escaped from Santa Clara, Cuba in 2008, with future major leaguer Kendrys Morales. He put Fernandez on a strenuous, unorthodox training regimen which he would continue for the rest of his life. It included running while wearing a snorkel, pushing an SUV up to 500 feet, and swinging an axe 400 times per session. Chinea also taught Fernandez the language and customs of his new country.[2] José would become a U.S. citizen in 2015.

Fernandez enrolled in Braulio Alonso High School in Tampa, and made their Ravens baseball team as a sophomore in 2009. By the end of the season, he was hitting 94 mph on the radar gun and leading the Ravens to the state title.[3] The next year, Fernandez was a cocky young athlete, sometimes showing up opposing players and rebelling against authority. It was Chinea who would dispense tough love to get him back on track.

As a senior, Fernandez went 13–1 with two no-hitters and a 1.35 ERA en route to another state title.[4] The Marlins chose him in the first round of the 2011 draft (14th player selected), and he signed with them for a $2 million bonus on August 15. He made one brief appearance each in the Gulf Coast and New York–Penn Leagues before the year was over.

Fernandez was a big right-hander, standing 6'2" and weighing between 215 and 245 pounds. His smooth mechanics produced a monstrous 8½-foot stride, as compared to the five feet averaged by other pitchers. His repertoire included a four-seam fastball, a splitter, a hard curveball, all with electric stuff (occasionally reaching 100 mph), and a change-up.

In 2012, Fernandez pitched 14 games for Greensboro in the South Atlantic League, and 11 with Jupiter in the Florida State League. His combined stats were phenomenal: a 14–1 record and 1.75 ERA, with 158 strikeouts and just 89 hits allowed in 134 innings.

---

1. Chen, Albert. "José Fernandez is Ready for his Second Act." *Sports Illustrated*, February 17, 2014, pp. 40–41.
2. *Ibid.*, p. 38, 40.
3. *Ibid.*, p. 41.
4. Sewell, Marty, et al. *2016 Miami Marlins Media Guide*, pp. 116–19.

José Fernandez

The Marlins figured Fernandez, 20, would start the 2013 season in Double-A. But due to injuries to some of their starters, he made the jump all the way from A-ball to the parent club, becoming the youngest player in the majors. On a team which would finish with a 62–100 record, Fernandez would emerge as a shining hope for the future. He made his big league debut against the Mets on April 7, 2013, allowing just three hits, one walk, and one run in five innings, while fanning eight.

Fernandez continued pitching well, though he didn't have much to show for it in the first half of the season: a 5–5 record despite a fine 2.75 ERA. Nevertheless, he made the NL All-Star team, and pitched a flawless inning at Citi Field on July 15, striking out Dustin Pedroia and Chris Davis, and retiring Miguel Cabrera on an infield pop-up in between.

After the break, Fernandez was lights-out: a 7–1 record with a 1.32 ERA. He recorded 13 strikeouts against Pittsburgh on July 28, and 14 more vs. Cleveland on August 2, becoming the first pitcher since Randy Johnson in 2004 to notch 13+ K's in consecutive starts.[5] After Fernandez reached a team-imposed innings limit on September 11, the Marlins shut him down for the rest of the season.

Fernandez wound up leading the NL with a microscopic .182 opposing batting average (lowest since Pedro Martinez in 2000), or just 5.79 hits allowed per nine innings. José also finished second in ERA (2.19), strikeouts per nine innings (9.75), and adjusted pitcher runs and wins, and third in pitcher WAR (6.3) and WHIP. His 176 ERA+ was the best by any rookie in the 101 years since ERA became an official stat. Fernandez easily won NL Rookie of the Year honors, and finished third in Cy Young Award voting.

Fernandez also showed he could handle a bat, hitting .220—better than the average of batters who faced him—and homering in his final at bat of the season. But when he styled while completing the circuit, he incited a bench-clearing brawl between the Braves and Marlins. Afterward, Miami manager Mike Redmond dressed the rookie down for his disrespectful behavior. "He's a young kid and he's going to be one of the top pitchers in this league for a long time," Redmond said. "You want your pitchers and players to be judged for the way they pitch and the way they compete, not the theatrics."[6]

Fernandez was apologetic, but explained that his heritage played a role: "Baseball in Cuba's a lot more different, a lot more emotion, a lot more passion. At the end of the day it's a game, and you're supposed to have fun, right?"[7]

---

5. *Ibid.*
6. Yahoo Sports staff. "Fernandez: 'I'll Never Show Anybody Up.'" September 12, 2013.
7. Chen, Albert. "José Fernandez is Ready for his Second Act." *Sports Illustrated*, February 17, 2014, p. 44.

This was an example of the different sides of Fernandez's personality. Adjectives used to describe him included charismatic, guileless, child-like, energetic, confident, joyful, hard-working, and intense—yet there was often a "but" attached. "There were two Joses, the combustible child and the hardest worker they've ever seen," explained one feature article, saying he was "capable of greatness, yes, but also self-destruction." As his former high school principal, Loui Diaz, said, "He can be an idiot. He can be stupid. But at heart he's a good kid, capable of great humility."[8]

Fernandez picked up in 2014 right where he left off the previous year. He had nine strikeouts and zero walks on Opening Day, joining Hall of Famers Cy Young, Walter Johnson, Bob Gibson, Fergie Jenkins, and Steve Carlton as the only pitchers to do that, according to the Associated Press. Fernandez was named NL Pitcher of the Month for April, after going 4–1 with a 1.59 ERA. He was leading the major leagues in strikeouts through May 9, when something went wrong in a game against San Diego. His fastball velocity dropped from 95 to 91 mph in the fifth inning, and he was shelled for four runs with none out in the sixth before being removed. Afterward, the team doctor found a "significant tear" in Fernandez's pitching elbow, recommending Tommy John surgery.[9] Fernandez went under the knife at the Kerlan-Jobe Clinic in Los Angeles on May 16.[10]

True to his nature, Fernandez worked his tail off to make it back. After five minor league rehab appearances, he returned to the Marlins on July 2, 2015. Fernandez had another setback when he suffered a right biceps strain on August 7, missing five weeks. He wound up pitching only 65 innings in the majors that year, though he went 6–1.

Fernandez had a rocky start to the 2016 season, giving up five runs in five-and-two-thirds innings (despite 13 strikeouts) on April 6 to pick up the first home loss of his career. Fernandez had been 17–0 with a 1.40 ERA in 26 starts at Miami through 2015, setting a post–1900 record for most consecutive home wins to start a career.[11] José was 1–2, 4.37 through April 23, but then reeled off eight wins in a row. His average velocity of 95.3 mph was even faster than before his surgery.[12] José Fernandez was all the way back.

Fernandez pitched in his second All-Star Game on July 12 at Petco Park, going an inning-and-a-third, including a strikeout of Mike Trout. Six days later, José notched his 500th career strikeout in his 400th inning, setting a major league record for fastest to reach that milestone.[13] Among the

---

8. *Ibid.*, p. 38, 44.
9. ESPN.com. "Jose Fernandez Has Torn UCL." May 13, 2014.
10. Sewell, Marty, et al. *2016 Miami Marlins Media Guide*, pp. 116–19.
11. *Ibid.*
12. Davis, Craig. "No Holding Back." *Baseball Digest*, Nov./Dec. 2016, p. 48.
13. *Ibid.*

six most similar pitchers at the same age are Tom Seaver, Addie Joss, and Roger Clemens.

At about 3:35 p.m. on September 25, 2016 (the same day that golf legend Arnold Palmer died), the U.S. Coast Guard discovered the capsized wreckage of a 32-foot Sea Vee motorboat named "Kaught Looking" off Miami Beach. The boat had slammed into a stone jetty at 66 mph, ejecting and killing all three passengers, none of whom was wearing a life vest.[14] One of them was José Fernandez, the owner and pilot of the boat. It was later revealed that Fernandez had cocaine and alcohol—twice the legal limit—in his system. Had he survived, he would have faced criminal charges.[15]

The baseball world mourned. The Marlins cancelled their game that day and retired his #16, and the rest of the season players around the majors sported formal and informal tributes to the likeable, talented young pitcher with the .691 career win percentage and 2.58 ERA. Among Fernandez's survivors were his girlfriend, Maria Arias, expecting their first child (Penelope Jo Fernandez was born February 24, 2017). Maria had texted one of the passengers that night, saying that the couple had been arguing. "He's been drinking and is not in the best state of mind," she warned.[16]

Fernandez finished his final season leading the NL with 12.88 strikeouts per nine innings. He was also second in strikeouts, fifth in wins, and seventh in ERA, earning 18 points in Cy Young Award voting—and following Lyman Bostock as the only men to receive votes for a major award after their deaths. In a rude irony, Fernandez also received the 2016 Players' Choice Award for NL Comeback Player of the Year.

More irony came from a 2015 tweet by Fernandez, recalled soon after the accident: "If you were given a book with the story of your life, would you read the end?"

Year	Team (League)	G	IP	W	L	PCT	SO	BB	H	ERA
2013	Miami (NL)	28	172.2	12	6	.667	187	58	111	2.19
2014		8	51.2	4	2	.667	70	13	36	2.44
2015		11	64.2	6	1	.857	79	14	61	2.92
2016		29	182.1	16	8	.667	253	55	149	2.86
Totals		76	471.1	38	17	.691	589	140	357	2.58

---

14. Alvarez, Lizette, and Niraj Chokshi. "Marlins Pitcher Jose Fernandez is Killed in a Boating Accident." *New York Times*, September 26, 2016.

15. Associated Press. "Report: Fernandez Likely Piloted Boat During Fatal Crash." *Daily Star* (Oneonta, NY), March 17, 2017.

16. *Ibid.*

Boo Ferriss

Boo Ferriss's career featured one of the most blazing starts ever—and one of the most abrupt ends.

David Meadow Ferriss was born December 5, 1921, at Shaw, Mississippi, the second of three children of cotton plantation owners William D. and Lellie Ferriss. Dave got the nickname "Boo" from his family at a very young age, from his attempt to say "brother."[1] A star athlete, Boo played football and basketball in addition to baseball, in which he was good enough to join the Shaw High School team at age 12. However, he suffered a broken right wrist in a collision at second base that year. While anxiously waiting for it to heal, Boo learned to throw left-handed. Obviously, his right arm recovered, but Ferriss was able to play as a left-handed first baseman between pitching appearances in his college years.[2]

Ferriss enrolled at Mississippi State College, their first student ever to receive a full baseball scholarship.[3] He also played semi-pro baseball in 1940, leading his team to the Mississippi-Louisiana title, and pitching in the National Semi-Pro Tournament in Wichita, Kansas.[4] The following summer he pitched for the Brattleboro, Vermont, club in the independent Northern League, going 4–4 according to partial records. After his junior year at Mississippi State, Ferriss joined organized baseball at age 20 in 1942, toiling for the Greensboro Red Sox of the Class-B Piedmont League. He posted a 2.22 ERA over 21 games, though his record was a modest 7–7. He then went 3–0 in playoff competition as Greensboro won the league championship.[5] Ferriss was named MVP of the playoffs.[6]

Ferriss's pitching and college career then were put on hold due to World War II (he would later resume his college studies in the off-seasons, earning a Bachelor of Science in the spring of 1948). Ferriss became a corporal of physical training in the U.S. Army Air Force. Pitching for a service team, he went 8–2 in 1943 and 20–8 in 1944—and even batted .417.[7] In early

---

1. Telephone interview with Dave "Boo" Ferriss, June 13, 2015.
2. King, Joe. "Ferriss Is a Rightie, All Right; Injury as Kid Made Him Lefty, Too." *New York World Telegram*, June 9, 1945.
3. "Coach Dave 'Boo' Ferriss to be Conferred with Honorary Degree at Delta State's Spring Commencement." Delta State University press release, January 6, 2009.
4. Letter from Dave "Boo" Ferriss, June 25, 2015.
5. King, Joe. "Ferriss Is a Rightie, All Right; Injury as Kid Made Him Lefty, Too." *New York World Telegram*, June 9, 1945.
6. Letter from Dave "Boo" Ferriss, June 25, 2015.
7. "No Flash in the Pan." Unidentified clipping in National Baseball Library file, May 10, 1945.

1945, after spending four months in the hospital, Ferriss received a medical discharge due to chronic asthma.

Ferriss went to spring training with the Louisville Colonels of the American Association (AA, the highest minor classification at the time), then was called up by the parent Boston Red Sox in late April.[8] At 6'2" and 208 pounds, the right-hander was big for his era. He exhibited a deceptive fastball, a curve thrown anywhere from over-hand to side-arm, and poise belying his youth.[9] He was also a good fielder and hitter, and would bat .250 in his big league career. Off the field, Ferriss was an easy-going, big-hearted guy, popular wherever he went.

Ferriss made his major league debut on April 29, and shut out the Philadelphia Athletics, 2–0. A week later he whitewashed the powerful New York Yankees, 5–0. Boo became only the fourth pitcher ever to begin his career with two straight shutouts, but he wasn't done. On May 13, while beating Detroit, he extended his scoreless streak to 22 innings, an AL record for the start of one's career which stood until 2008. Then came complete-game wins over the White Sox, Browns, White Sox again (a one-hitter), Indians, and A's, giving him an 8–0 record with four shutouts to start his career. He was the talk of the baseball world—and he didn't even have a locker yet!

The 1945 All-Star Game, scheduled at Fenway Park for July 10, was cancelled due to wartime travel restrictions. In its stead, the Red Sox played an exhibition game against the cross-town Boston Braves, raising $73,000 for the American Red Cross and National War Fund. Ferriss announced plans to pitch both right- and left-handed in the game, but wound up sticking with his right as the Sox subdued the Braves, 8–1.[10]

Despite pitching for a sub-.500 team in a great hitters' park, Ferriss continued to dominate. By July 22, he had racked up a 17–2 record with a 1.90 ERA. Then, with the hot weather exacerbating his asthma and hay fever, Ferriss began to struggle. Before the summer was over, it was announced that his meteoric career might be finished. "A specialist reportedly has given Ferriss the choice of undergoing an operation in the hope of relieving an asthmatic condition, or giving up baseball for good," said a September 5 article.[11] But Ferriss finished the season, winding up with a 21–10 record for a team which went only 71–83. He was second in the league in victories, complete games (26), innings pitched, and shutouts

---

8. Letter from Dave "Boo" Ferriss, June 25, 2015.
9. Daniel, Dan. "Hub Find Drives Experts to Record Books." Unidentified clipping in National Baseball Library file, May 7, 1945.
10. Deane, Bill. "The Year the All-Star Game Was Cancelled." *Information Please Sports Almanac*. Houghton-Mifflin, 1995.
11. "Asthma May End Pitching Career of Ferriss." Unidentified clipping in National Baseball Library file, September 5, 1945.

(5). On September 23, the Red Sox honored him with "Ferriss Day" at Fenway Park.[12] In the forerunner of the Rookie of the Year Award, the Chicago chapter of the BBWAA named Ferriss as baseball's top first-year player.[13] Perhaps more impressively, he finished fourth in AL MVP voting.

Despite his spectacular freshman season, there were a lot of question marks about Ferriss entering the following campaign. Would he be able to overcome his health problems and poor finish of the year before? Would he be as successful now that all the stars were back from military service? It didn't take long for Boo to answer the questions.

All Ferriss did in 1946 was win his first 10 decisions, make the All-Star team, and lead the Red Sox to the AL pennant with a sensational 25–6 record. He topped the league in winning percentage (.806) while joining Hall of Famers Hal Newhouser and Bob Feller in the top three in wins, complete games (26), and shutouts (6) en route to a seventh-place finish in MVP voting. He then shut the Cardinals out, 4–0, in Game Three of the World Series, before taking a no-decision in Game Seven, which the BoSox lost.

Ferriss signed a reported $22,000 contract for 1947,[14] but was not as effective as in his first two seasons. He alternated wins and losses pretty much the whole season. At some point, he suffered what proved to be a career-altering arm injury. "Happened in Cleveland," recalled Ferriss in 1981. "I was in a tight game with Red Embree. It was a cold rainy night and the Indians had the bases loaded. I reached back for something extra and I felt a snap or a pop in my shoulder. I retired the batter and Bobby Doerr won the game for me with a homer and I didn't think much about it until the next day in Chicago. I started to throw a ball and couldn't do it."[15]

Ferriss's details don't quite jibe with any 1947 game, but the closest match is July 14. Embree didn't pitch, and the Indians never loaded the bases, but Ferriss beat them, 1–0, on a ninth-inning Doerr homer, giving Boo an 8–7 record and 3.62 ERA for the season. He was right back in the box on the 18th, but was blasted out in the fourth inning, and went just 4–4, 4.96 the rest of the year. His only prolonged absence was between August 24–September 11, but that was due to a badly-cut toe suffered during a pregame workout.[16]

Ferriss finished the year with a disappointing 12–11 record and 4.04

---

12. "Ferriss Day in Boston." *New York World Telegram*, September, 1945.
13. Deane, Bill. *Award Voting*. Kansas City, MO: Society for American Baseball Research, 1988, p. 56.
14. United Press release, February 11, 1947.
15. Burnes, Robert L. "The Phenom of '45: His 8–0 Start Was Matched by Fernando." Unidentified clipping in National Baseball Library file, 1981.
16. Malaney, Jack. "Sidelining of Two Aces Speeds Red Sox' Foldup." *The Sporting News*, September 17, 1947, p. 10.

ERA, and totally lost his effectiveness after that. In 1948, he was hammered for a 5.23 ERA, though he somehow finished 7–3—the final wins of his big league career. But he did have one last highlight. On October 3, the final scheduled game of the regular season, Ferriss pitched two-and-two-thirds scoreless innings to save a 10–5 win over the Yankees, enabling the Red Sox to tie the Indians for first place. Boston lost a one-game playoff the next day.

His shoulder not responding to treatment from the club physician, Ferriss faced only 29 batters in 1949 and six in '50, then was sent to the minors. His final major league pitching record shows 65 wins and just 30 losses for a .684 percentage.

Ferriss went 10–7 with a 3.66 ERA for Class-A Birmingham in 1950, then his contract was sold to Louisville. After going 7–7, 5.25 and 7–5, 4.71 in 1951–52, his pro pitching career was over at age 31.

Ferriss described his 1947 arm injury as a torn labrum, costing him the power behind his money pitch, the sinking fastball. He said in 2015 that "they didn't know how to treat it," but with modern medical advances, "Nowadays I would be back on the mound in six months." Did the ambidextrous Ferriss think about trying to come back as a southpaw? "I was just concentrating on trying to get my right arm back in shape," he said. "It just didn't work out."[17]

Dave Ferriss married Miriam Izard on November 28, 1948.[18] The couple had two children, David and Margaret.

Ferriss served as pitching coach for the Red Sox, 1955–59, then went on to a long college coaching career. In 1959 he joined Delta State University in Cleveland, Mississippi, as athletic director and baseball coach. He later was instrumental in starting Fellowship of Christian Athletes chapters there and in other Mississippi colleges and high schools.[19] In 1967–68 Ferriss spent 18 months as assistant athletic director of his alma mater, Mississippi State, then returned to Delta State as Executive Director of their development foundation. He returned to the coaching lines from 1970 to 1988, guiding Delta State to a 639–387 record, four conference championships, and three NCAA Division 2 College World Series appearances. Upon his retirement, his accomplishments were recognized in the Mississippi Senate on October 5, 1988.[20]

Ferriss was inducted into the Mississippi Sports Hall of Fame in 1965.[21] He later was inducted into the Halls of Fame of Mississippi State University Sports, Semi-Pro Baseball, the American Baseball Coaches Association,

---

17. Telephone interview with Dave "Boo" Ferriss, June 13, 2015.
18. David M. Ferriss player questionnaire in National Baseball Library files.
19. Letter from Dave "Boo" Ferriss, June 25, 2015.
20. *Ibid.*
21. "Ferriss, Passeau Honored." *The Sporting News*, April 10, 1965.

the Boston Red Sox, and Mississippi Semi-Pro Baseball. Ferriss received an honorary Doctor of Public Service degree from Delta State in 2009,[22] and the first Rubenstein Award from the Mississippi Sports Hall of Fame in 2012.[23] Delta State's baseball field is named after Boo Ferriss, as is the award given to Mississippi's top college baseball player each year.[24]

Until he died on November 24, 2016, Ferriss still lived in Cleveland, Mississippi (proudly listed in the phone book as "Ferriss, Boo") with his wife of 68 years. He followed baseball closely, and was still sharp of mind and strong of pen. When I sent him the draft of this chapter in 2015, he wrote back with three pages of handwritten clarifications.

Did Boo Ferriss think he might have made it to the Baseball Hall of Fame if not for his arm injury?

"I don't know about that," he says. "I was just fortunate to have two good years in the major leagues, and set some records. The injury just changed things for me. I am thankful I could continue my career by coaching college baseball for 26 years, a most enjoyable and rewarding experience."[25]

Year	Team (League)	G	IP	W	L	PCT	SO	BB	H	ERA
1945	Boston (AL)	35	264.2	21	10	.677	94	85	263	2.96
1946		40	274.0	25	6	*.806	106	71	274	3.25
1947		33	218.1	12	11	.522	64	92	241	4.04
1948		31	115.1	7	3	.700	30	61	127	5.23
1949		4	6.2	0	0	-----	1	4	7	4.05
1950		1	1.0	0	0	-----	1	1	2	18.00
Totals		144	880.0	65	30	.684	296	314	914	3.64

---

22. "Coach Dave 'Boo' Ferriss to be Conferred with Honorary Degree at Delta State's Spring Commencement." Delta State University press release, January 6, 2009.
23. Associated Press. "Boo Ferriss Named First Rubenstein Award Winner." BostonHerald.com, July 17, 2012.
24. "Coach Dave 'Boo' Ferriss to be Conferred with Honorary Degree at Delta State's Spring Commencement." Delta State University press release, January 6, 2009.
25. Telephone interview with Dave "Boo" Ferriss, June 13, 2015.

Mark Fidrych

Rarely if ever has a single player lit up the baseball world the way Mark Fidrych did in 1976. The Bird flew in from nowhere, soared to great heights, and flew off almost as suddenly as he came.

Mark Steven Fidrych was born August 14, 1954, in Worcester,

Massachusetts, the second of four children (the rest girls, Paula, Carol Ann, and Lorie Jean) of Paul and Virginia Fidrych in a religious family.[1] Paul was a Polish-American schoolteacher, while Virginia was of Danish ancestry.[2] Mark grew up in nearby Northborough, where he played Little League baseball. A hyperactive and none-too-studious child, Mark was held back in both first and second grade, resulting in his being nearly 20 years old by the time he finished high school.[3] He did well in football and basketball as well as baseball, but lost his sports eligibility due to his age. Mark then transferred from Algonquin Regional High in Northborough to the private Worcester Academy for his senior year, with his father taking out a loan to pay the tuition.[4] Though he was a good pitcher, no one could have predicted that Mark would be a major league star two years later.

Unbeknownst to Mark, he had been scouted by the Tigers in high school. Joe Kusick liked not only what he saw on the field—good speed and excellent control—but the right-handed pitcher's long, lanky (6'3", 175 pounds) body.[5] So Fidrych was totally surprised when Detroit picked him in the tenth round (232nd player selected) of the June 5, 1974, amateur draft. He was pumping gas at the Pierca Gas and Oil Station in Northborough when he got the news.[6] Upon hearing that he had been drafted, his first thought was that he would be off to military service. Fidrych signed for a $3,000 bonus and joined the Bristol, Virginia Tigers of the Appalachian (rookie) League, where he was put in the bullpen. It was there that coach Jeff Hogan nicknamed the gangly, beak-nosed, curly-locked blonde "Big Bird," for his resemblance to the *Sesame Street* character.[7] Fidrych turned in a 3–0 record with seven saves and a 2.38 ERA in 23 appearances.

Fidrych's most dramatic (but unpublicized) saves that year took place off the field. There was a car wreck outside the trailer Fidrych shared with a teammate. The Bird went outside to see the car on fire, and hear two small children crying from the back seat. He went through the car window in the dark and pulled both kids out of the car to safety.[8]

---

1. Braunstein, Bill. "The Bird in a Gilded Cage." *Cleveland Plain Dealer Magazine*, May 11, 1980, p. 16.
2. Furlong, William Barry. "Will Success Spoil The Bird?" *The New York Times Magazine*, August 22, 1976, p. 80.
3. Braunstein, Bill. "The Bird in a Gilded Cage." *Cleveland Plain Dealer Magazine*, May 11, 1980, p. 16.
4. Marsh, Dave. "The Tale of the Bird." *Rolling Stone*, May 5, 1977, p. 45.
5. *Ibid.*
6. Furlong, William Barry. "Will Success Spoil The Bird?" *The New York Times Magazine*, August 22, 1976, p. 13.
7. Braunstein, Bill. "The Bird in a Gilded Cage." *Cleveland Plain Dealer Magazine*, May 11, 1980, p. 17.
8. Fenech, Anthony. "Q&A with Doug Wilson, Author of 'The Bird: The Life and Legacy of Mark Fidrych.'" *Detroit Free Press*, March 24, 2013.

Fidrych made a rapid rise through the Tigers' system in 1975, improving at each stop. He started with Lakeland of the Class-A Florida State League, posting a less-than-imposing 5–9 record and 3.77 ERA. Nonetheless, he moved up to Montgomery of the AA Southern League, where he went 2–0 with four saves and a 3.21 ERA in 14 relief appearances. Fidrych's final stop was with AAA Evansville, where he logged a 4–1 record and 1.58 ERA, adding a 12-inning victory in the American Association championship game.

Fidrych went to spring training with the Tigers as a non-roster invitee in 1976. He mostly pitched batting practice, and had little success in his few innings of game action. But manager Ralph Houk had seen him in the winter instructional league and liked his "fantastic concentration."[9] Fidrych made the team as its tenth pitcher, signing for the minimum salary of $16,500.[10] Topps did not issue a baseball card for him that year, and the flaky Fidrych did not even hook up a telephone, rhetorically asking, "Who would I call?"[11]

Pitching for the Tigers would be a challenge. Detroit had finished with the worst record in baseball in 1975 at 57–102, drawing barely a million fans. They scored the fewest runs in the AL, and ranked near the bottom of the league in defense as well. Moreover, the city of Detroit was "a disaster—almost a battle ground—where it is no longer safe to walk the streets," according to famed Detroit sportswriter Joe Falls.[12] Baseball, too, was in dire straits, suffering in popularity and attendance due to labor upheavals and other factors. It was not a promising environment for a rookie pitcher.

Fidrych, wearing uniform #20, made two brief relief appearances, facing just six batters in the first 37 days of the 1976 season. He finally got a chance to start a game on May 15, due to the illness of scheduled starter Joe Coleman. Fidrych made it count. He had a no-hitter for six innings, and finished with a two-hit victory over Cleveland. Despite taking a 2–0 loss in his next spot-start against Boston 10 days later, Fidrych pitched well and earned a place in the Tigers' regular rotation. He displayed a 93 mph fastball and a sinking slider with pinpoint control, consistently locating his pitches just above the knees. He became the fastest-working pitcher in the AL, averaging just two hours, 11 minutes per start, according to Bill James.

Fidrych proceeded to run off six straight wins, and was gathering buzz

---

9. Furlong, William Barry. "Will Success Spoil The Bird?" *The New York Times Magazine*, August 22, 1976, p. 81.
10. Braunstein, Bill. "The Bird in a Gilded Cage." *Cleveland Plain Dealer Magazine*, May 11, 1980, p. 17.
11. Furlong, William Barry. "Will Success Spoil The Bird?" *The New York Times Magazine*, August 22, 1976, p. 80.
12. Falls, Joe. "'F' as in Fidrych and Fright." *The Sporting News*, September 11, 1976.

in Detroit as an eccentric character as well as an outstanding pitcher. The media was entertained by his malapropisms, guileless modesty, and casual profanity in explaining his success and his offbeat antics. The Bird would get on his hands and knees to landscape the pitcher's mound, stop to shake hands with teammates who made good plays behind him, and seemingly talk to the ball before he threw it. "I'm not so much talking to the ball as addressing myself," Fidrych explained. "It's my way of keeping myself in the ball game.... (I)t's necessary for a pitcher because when you lose your mind, the ball is lost."[13] The Detroit fans loved him. According to long-time broadcaster Ernie Harwell, Fidrych became the "first big leaguer to take curtain calls on a regular basis."

This was long before the days of ESPN or MLB Network, so Fidrych's success was just a rumor to most fans. That was about to change.

On June 28, Fidrych faced the Yankees—on their way to the AL pennant—in a nationally-televised *ABC Monday Night Baseball* game. Going through his usual antics, Fidrych pitched a complete game, 5–1 victory. The Bird instantly went from a Detroit curiosity to a national phenomenon. After the game, the Yankees' star Thurman Munson—en route to the 1976 AL MVP Award—snorted that Fidrych was a "fly-by-night" and a "showboat." Asked to respond to the remarks, Fidrych said, "Who's Thurman Munson?"[14]

Fidrych was named the AL Player of the Month for June. Chosen for the AL All-Star team, he was picked to start the 1976 Midsummer Classic. "I guess this is my biggest thrill since I got a mini-bike when I was 14," said The Bird.[15]

In his 29 starts, the Tigers drew an average of 31,077 fans per game—about 20,000 more than they drew in other games.[16] His newfound fame created all kinds of unusual offers and opportunities. The Michigan State Legislature made a resolution, recommending a pay-raise for Fidrych.[17] He met President Gerald Ford and entertainers Frank Sinatra and Elton John. He was offered a basketball scholarship by the University of Detroit's Dick Vitale. Fidrych made commercials, and was talked about as a potential movie star. A Detroit disk jockey led a movement to change the state bird from a robin to a Fidrych.[18]

Nevertheless, The Bird realized that fame can be fleeting. "This could

---

13. Unidentified clipping in National Baseball Library file, October 3, 1976.
14. Rushin, Steve. "Where Are They Now? Mark Fidrych." *Sports Illustrated*, July 2, 2001.
15. Foley, Red. "Bird Talks to Press, Too." *New York Daily News*, July 12, 1976.
16. Braunstein, Bill. "The Bird in a Gilded Cage." *Cleveland Plain Dealer Magazine*, May 11, 1980, p. 12.
17. Rushin, Steve. "Where Are They Now? Mark Fidrych." *Sports Illustrated*, July 2, 2001.
18. Furlong, William Barry. "Will Success Spoil The Bird?" *The New York Times Magazine*, August 22, 1976, p. 13.

burn out," he said late in the season. "It's like a bubble now—it's still rising. But it could explode."[19]

Fidrych continued his outstanding mound-work in the second half of the season, and wound up with a 19–9 record for team that was otherwise 55–78. He completed 24 of his 29 starts, five of them extra-inning games, averaging 8.6 innings per start. He led the American League in complete games and ERA (2.34). He also excelled defensively, topping the league in assists (59), range factor, and total chances without an error (78). By modern measures, he is identified as the best overall pitcher in baseball in 1976 by Win Shares (27), Total Pitching Wins (4.4), and WAR (9.6).

Fidrych easily won the AL Rookie of the Year Award, finished second behind Jim Palmer in Cy Young Award balloting, and ranked 11th in MVP voting. *The Sporting News* named him AL Rookie Pitcher of the Year. The New York chapter of the BBWAA gave Fidrych the Sid Mercer Award as "the baseball player of the year."[20] The Detroit chapter named him Tiger of the Year,[21] and Detroit's United Foundation tabbed him as Sportsman of the Year.[22]

With help from his father, Fidrych negotiated a three-year contract which gave him a retroactive raise and bonus for 1976, and would pay him a reported $50,000 in 1977, $75,000 in '78, and $100,000 in '79.[23] The salaries would pale in comparison with other stars and even non-stars of that era, but Fidrych wanted to make sure he reached four years of big league service to qualify for a pension.

Fidrych's career path went off-course in spring training of 1977. On March 21, he was needlessly shagging fly balls in the outfield. He leapt for one ball and landed hard on his left leg. Ten days later, Fidrych underwent surgery to repair torn meniscus cartilage in his knee. But with the Tigers struggling for wins and fans, he was back on the mound just eight weeks later.

After dropping his first two decisions, Fidrych resumed his status as one of the best pitchers in the game. He reeled off six straight victories in June to enter July with a 6–2 record, seven complete games in eight starts, and a 1.83 ERA—similar to his record (8–1, 2.05) entering July '76. The Bird was picked to the AL All-Star team for the second straight year. But the bubble was about to explode.

---

19. Furlong, William Barry. "It's a Bird! It's a Flake! It's Mark Fidrych!" *TV Guide*, September 11, 1976, p. 16.
20. Durso, Joseph. "Baseball Writers' Dinner: Satire, Song and Fidrych." *New York Times*, January 31, 1977, p. 39.
21. "Tiger Tales." *The Sporting News*, November 20, 1976.
22. Unidentified clipping in National Baseball Library file, December 4, 1976.
23. Braunstein, Bill. "The Bird in a Gilded Cage." *Cleveland Plain Dealer Magazine*, May 11, 1980, p. 14.

Pitching against Baltimore on July 4, Fidrych had a 2–0 lead in the sixth inning when his arm started "feeling weird," and the O's erupted for six runs. After two more aborted outings on July 8 and 12, Fidrych was shut down for the season.[24] He was diagnosed with tendonitis, but in reality he had suffered a rotator cuff injury. No doubt the heavy workload at ages 21–22, and coming back too soon from knee surgery, were key factors.

Fidrych returned to become the Tigers' opening day pitcher on April 7, 1978, and started the season with two complete-game wins. But he came out after just four innings in his third start on April 17, complaining of shoulder pain. He would not win another big league game for 28 months.

The rest of the Bird's pitching in 1978 consisted of just 13 innings for the Lakeland Tigers. After a year of rehab, he attempted a comeback with Detroit in May 1979, but was torched for a 10.43 ERA in in four starts before being shelved for another year. Doctors put Fidrych on a regimen of massage, manipulation, weight-lifting, and ice treatment which they hoped would get him back on the mound the following year.[25]

Fidrych signed a $130,000 contract for 1980,[26] but after being lit up in spring training, he was sent down to Evansville. He pitched creditably enough (3.12 ERA in 117 innings) to earn one last call to the majors. Fidrych struggled to a 5.68 ERA in nine games with Detroit. In his final outing, October 1, he was credited with an 11–7 victory against Toronto. His big league career was over at age 26.

Fidrych toiled for Evansville in 1981 (5.75 ERA in 83 innings) before being released by the Tigers on October 5. "It's one of the most difficult things I've ever had to do," said Tigers GM Jim Campbell.[27] Signed by the Red Sox as a free agent on February 25, 1982, Fidrych joined the AAA Pawtucket club, where he fared no better. After going 6–8 with a 4.98 ERA in 1982 and 2–5, 9.68 the following season, Fidrych retired from baseball on June 29, 1983. By the time his torn rotator cuff was diagnosed and operated on two years later, he felt it was too late for another baseball comeback attempt.

Fidrych married waitress Ann Pantanzis in 1986, and they had a daughter, Jessica, the following year. Mark adored them both. With the money he made in baseball, he had bought a 123-acre farm in Northborough, and later a 10-wheel dump truck, which he used for hauling asphalt and gravel for local firms.[28] He expressed no regret at the way his baseball

---

24. Meyer, Paul. "Don't Feel Sorry for Mark Fidrych." Cox News Service, July 20, 1981.
25. Braunstein, Bill. "The Bird in a Gilded Cage." *Cleveland Plain Dealer Magazine*, May 11, 1980, p. 13.
26. Ibid.
27. Gage, Tom. "Tiger Tales." *The Sporting News*, October 24, 1981.
28. Rushin, Steve. "Where Are They Now? Mark Fidrych." *Sports Illustrated*, July 2, 2001.

career turned out, only gratitude at having enjoyed some success at the top, paving the way for a contented post-baseball career. He was happy that people remembered him, and refused to charge for his autograph.

Like so many of the players featured in this book, Fidrych's story had a tragic ending. On April 13, 2009, he was found dead under his truck on his property. Authorities said that he was working on the truck when his clothes became entangled in its spinning power takeoff shaft, strangling him.[29] Mark Fidrych was 54.

Year	Team (League)	G	IP	W	L	PCT	SO	BB	H	ERA
1976	Detroit (AL)	31	250.1	19	9	.679	97	53	217	*2.34
1977		11	81.0	6	4	.600	42	12	82	2.89
1978		3	22.0	2	0	1.000	10	5	17	2.45
1979		4	14.2	0	3	.000	5	9	23	10.43
1980		9	44.1	2	3	.400	16	20	58	5.68
Totals		58	412.1	29	19	.604	170	99	397	3.10

29. "Examiner: Fidrych Suffocated to Death." ESPN.com, April 16, 2009.

Don Gullett

When he was healthy, Don Gullett won baseball games. The problem was, he wasn't often healthy.

Donald Edward Gullett was born in Lynn, Kentucky (population 67, according to a 1977 article[1]), about 110 miles east of Cincinnati, on January 6, 1951. He was one of eight children—three boys and five girls—of Buford (a construction digger) and Lettie Gullett in a close-knit, religious family. Don became a football, basketball, and baseball star at Southshore McKell High School in Lynn, making All-State in all three sports in 1968–69. In football, he scored 248 points in 13 games, including an incredible 72 in one day. In basketball, he averaged 25 points a contest, with a high of 46. In baseball, Don tossed several no-hitters, including a perfect game in which he struck out 20 of 21 batters.[2] He had 120 K's in 52 innings as a

1. Hirshey, Dave. "Farmer Gullett's New Kentucky Home." *New York Sunday News Magazine*, April 3, 1977, p. 13.
2. Unidentified clipping in National Baseball Library file.

senior. Don graduated fifth in his class and married his childhood sweetheart, cheerleader Cathy Holcomb, on January 23, 1970.[3] Children Don, Jr., and Tracy would follow.[4]

"I had 35 offers to play college football, schools like UK [Kentucky], Tennessee, Notre Dame, and a few [17] for basketball" recalled Gullett. "But baseball was always my first love."[5] The Cincinnati Reds chose him in the first round (14th player selected) of the June 5, 1969, amateur draft, and sent him to Sioux Falls, South Dakota, of the Class-A Northern League. The six-foot, 190-pound southpaw went 7–2 with 87 strikeouts in 78 innings, and a league-leading 1.96 ERA.

Gullett made the Reds at age 19 the following spring, making him the youngest player in the league. On April 16, Reds star pitcher Jim Maloney suffered a leg injury while running the bases, and Gullett was rushed into the game. It became the changing of the guard between the Reds' ace pitcher of the 1960s and their ace pitcher of the 1970s. The rookie pitched five scoreless innings (also collecting a triple, walk, and stolen base on offense) to earn his first big league win; Maloney would never win another.

Working mostly out of the bullpen in 1970, Gullett wound up nearly duplicating his minor league stats: a 5–2 record, 76 strikeouts in 78 innings, and a 2.43 ERA. On August 23, he tied an NL record by striking out six straight batters in relief. Gullett also had six saves, and added two more in the NLCS against the Pirates. In post-season play that year, he appeared in five games with a 0.87 ERA. The Reds wanted Gullett to pitch winter ball in Puerto Rico, but he refused, and the team then announced the winter vacation as if it were their idea.[6]

Gullett joined the Reds' rotation at age 20 in 1971, and became their best pitcher. Although the team slipped to 79–83, Gullett went 16–6, leading the NL in win percentage and finishing sixth in ERA. In one of the earliest uses of a pitch-count, manager Sparky Anderson limited him to 100 pitches per game.[7]

Plagued by illness all season, Gullett slipped to 9–10 in 1972—his only year in the pros with a win percentage under .600. "I'd go out there and feel tired," he recalled. "My appetite left me and I lost weight.... (A)fter the first six or eight weeks of the season, I just told (the team) that something

---

3. Vecsey, George. "Don Gullett is Supposed to Go Straight from the Holler to the Hall of Fame." *SPORT*, April 1976, p. 38.
4. *77 New York Yankees Press, TV, Radio Guide*, p. 68.
5. Hirshey, Dave. "Farmer Gullett's New Kentucky Home." *New York Sunday News Magazine*, April 3, 1977, p. 14.
6. *The Sporting News*, November 14, 1970.
7. Vecsey, George. "Don Gullett is Supposed to Go Straight from the Holler to the Hall of Fame." *SPORT*, April 1976, p. 42.

wasn't right with me. So they did a bunch of tests and it turned out I had hepatitis."[8]

Still weakened, Gullett started slowly in '73, but recovered to have a sensational second half. Adding a forkball to go with his blazing fastball, hard slider, and curve,[9] Gullett went 9–0 after July 14. He wound finishing fourth in the league in wins and a close second in win percentage (.692 to Tommy John's .696), helping the Reds to their third division title in four years. He even led pitchers with a perfect 1.000 fielding percentage.

Despite chronic back spasms, Gullett had another solid season in 1974. He was the NL Player of the Month in July after going 6–1 with a 1.83 ERA, and wound up among the league leaders in wins and strikeouts. Gullett was named the left-handed pitcher on *The Sporting News* NL All-Star team.[10] At age 23, he already had 65 career wins. "[B]arring an injury," said Sparky Anderson, "he's almost sure of making the Hall of Fame.... [Y]ou know he's going to win at least 250 games with the start he has."[11]

Gullett was putting it all together in 1975. Through June 16, he was 9–3 with a 2.09 ERA. But he suffered a broken thumb stabbing at a Larvell Blanks line drive that day, and was disabled until August 18. Gullett came back strong to finish the year 15–4, 2.42, despite having missed more than one-third of the season. He led the NL in win percentage, and had the league's fourth-best ERA, though he was two innings short of qualifying for the title.

Gullett capped off the year with "the greatest day in my life in baseball."[12] On October 4, 1975, in the opening game of the NLCS, he pitched the Reds to an 8–3 victory and hit a single and a home run, good for three RBI. Gullett was a decent hitter throughout his career (.194 average in regular-season play, .292 in post-season), but had never hit a homer before. He added a win in Game Five of the World Series as the Reds won the world championship.

The injury bug stung again in 1976. Beset by a pinched nerve in his neck and shoulder problems, Gullett was out of action between May 20–June 5, June 20–July 6, and July 30–August 30. In between, he racked up an 11–3 (.786) record and 3.00 ERA. He again added wins in the NLCS and World Series as the Reds won their second straight world title, this time over the Yankees. But true to form, Gullett suffered an injury—a dislocated

---

8. Ballew, Bill. "Don Gullett: Ex-Fireballer Now Teaching in the Minors." *Sports Collectors Digest*, July 19, 1991, p. 151.
9. Lawson, Earl. "Forkball Gullett's New Payoff Pitch." *The Sporting News*, August 25, 1973.
10. Unidentified clipping in National Baseball Library file.
11. Lawson, Earl. "Sparky Calls Gullett and Bench Hall of Famers after Cubs Fall." Unidentified clipping in National Baseball Library file, July 22, 1974.
12. Associated Press. "Bucs Beaten 8–3." October 5, 1975.

right ankle and torn tendon—while pitching in the eighth inning of the opener, and was in a cast for weeks afterward.

Baseball's first mass free agent re-entry draft was held 13 days after the World Series ended and, despite his injury history, Don Gullett was among the most prized players in it. He wound up signing a six-year, $2 million deal with the Yankees on November 18. Comparing him to a Hall of Fame Yankees southpaw with a .690 career winning percentage, Yanks President Gabe Paul said, "We feel Gullett is a modern Whitey Ford."[13]

In 1977, as usual, Gullett missed a lot of action but won when he pitched. He reportedly injured his shoulder before the season even started, while competing in the ABC TV show, *Superstars*.[14] Gullett was sidelined between July 30 and September 4, and had three other gaps of more than 10 days. Still, he went 14–4 to help the Yankees to their first world championship since 1964, and his third in a row. Gullett was listed as leading the league in winning percentage (.778) by some sources, though he fell short of the 15-win minimum.

Through 1977, Gullett's career record was 105–48 for a sizzling .686 win percentage. The most similar pitchers through age 26 were Hall of Famers Lefty Gomez and Jim Palmer, with Roger Clemens, and Cy Young also in the top 10.

Suffering shoulder tightness, Gullett didn't pitch his first game of the 1978 season until June 4. He then won his first four decisions, and had a 4–1 record and 2.86 ERA entering the game of July 9. But, pitching on three days' rest, he was shelled for four earned runs in two-thirds of an inning that day. "My shoulder felt a little funny in my warm-ups," Gullett recalled, "but that had happened before. I didn't think anything of it. Then, I couldn't get anybody out."[15]

Don Gullett, 27, would never pitch another professional game.

Diagnosed with a double rotator cuff tear, Gullett had surgery performed by Dr. Frank Jobe on September 29.[16] The Yankees went on to win another world title and voted Gullett a full share of post-season money.[17]

Gullett remained on the Yankees' payroll, suiting up every day for the next two seasons. There were occasional reports of an impending comeback throughout 1979 and '80, and he was working on a submarine delivery to reduce the strain on his shoulder. But his fastball, formerly in the low- to mid–90s, struggled to reach 80 mph, and he remained out of the arena. "It

13. Chass, Murray. "Pact Worth a Reported $2 Million." *New York Times*, November 19, 1976, p. A19.
14. Young, Dick. "Young Ideas." *The Sporting News*, April 9, 1977.
15. Salvatore, Ernie. "Gullett May Never Pitch, but He Can't Afford to Quit." Unidentified clipping in National Baseball Library file, February, 1980.
16. Associated Press. "Gullett's Comeback: A Long, Lonely Road." September 17, 1980.
17. Associated Press. "Yankees Cheapskates? Ask Gullett!" October 15, 1978.

eats my heart out not being able to participate," Gullett said.[18] The Yankees finally released him on October 24, 1980.

Gullett returned to his wife and children and his 75-acre Maloneton, Kentucky, farm, two miles from his birthplace. He tried playing some local softball, but kept reinjuring his shoulder. Gullett avoided watching or talking about baseball, smoked like a chimney, and put on weight. On January 31, 1986, he suffered a heart attack at age 35.[19] Four years later, he underwent triple bypass surgery.[20]

In 1990, Gullett returned to baseball as pitching coach for the Reds' AA team, the Chattanooga Lookouts. He moved up to AAA Nashville the following year,[21] then made it back to the majors, serving as Reds pitching coach from 1993 until 2005.[22] He now lives in South Shore, Kentucky.

Year	Team (League)	G	IP	W	L	PCT	SO	BB	H	ERA
1970	Cincinnati (NL)	44	77.2	5	2	.714	76	44	54	2.43
1971		35	217.2	16	6	*.727	107	64	196	2.65
1972		31	134.2	9	10	.474	96	43	127	3.94
1973		45	228.1	18	8	.692	153	69	198	3.51
1974		36	243.0	17	11	.607	183	88	201	3.04
1975		22	159.2	15	4	*.789	98	56	127	2.42
1976		23	126.0	11	3	.786	64	48	119	3.00
1977	New York (AL)	22	158.1	14	4	.778	116	69	137	3.58
1978		8	44.2	4	2	.667	28	20	46	3.64
Totals		266	1390.0	109	50	.686	921	501	1205	3.11

The Cincinnati Chucker Curse

Particularly between the 1960s and 1990s, star Cincinnati Reds pitchers seemed to be snake-bitten—call it the Cincinnati Chucker Curse. And we're not talking just about flashes in the pan—these were, by and large, pitchers who were, or seemed on the verge of ranking, among the most dominating in the game, but were finished by age 30. Among those, Don Gullett, Jim Maloney, and Wayne Simpson are featured in this book. Others:

---

18. Whiteside, Larry. "Gullett Gets Hope with New Delivery." *Boston Globe*, September 26, 1980.
19. Lupica, Mike. "At 35, Gullett is Too Young to be Old." *New York Daily News*, February 6, 1986.
20. "Gullett, 39, is Glad to be Alive after Heart Surgery." *The National Sports Daily*, June 21, 1990, p. 18.
21. Ballew, Bill. "Don Gullett: Ex-Fireballer Now Teaching in the Minors." *Sports Collectors Digest*, July 19, 1991, p. 152.
22. Rosencrans, C. Trent. "Lack of Progress Doomed Gullett." *Cincinnati Post*, June, 2005.

Gary Nolan—He debuted as an 18-year-old fireballer in 1967, and went 14–8 with a 2.58 ERA and 206 strikeouts, one of the best pitching seasons ever by a teenager. He was 9–4, 2.40 before his arm gave out in 1968. He reinvented himself as a control pitcher, with intermittent success while continuing to battle arm, shoulder, and neck problems. Nolan was 110–67 lifetime when the Reds traded him in 1977, just after his 29th birthday. He never won another game.

Mario Soto—He joined the Reds just past his 21st birthday in 1977, and was their ace in some of their most wretched years. In 1982 Soto earned his first of three straight All-Star picks, going 14–13 for a team that went 61–101, striking out 274, and posting a 2.79 ERA. The next year he was 17–13, 2.70 with 242 K's for a 74–88 team. In 1984, Soto was 18–7 for a 70–92 club, his seventh straight winning season. When the Reds finally started turning things around in '85, Soto dropped to 12–15. It was all downhill from there, as arm problems took hold and he went just 11–19 over three seasons before his release at age 32.

Jose Rijo—He had gone 19–30 over four seasons in the AL after an ill-advised call-up at age 18, but he joined the Reds at 22 and became one of the best pitchers in the league. Rijo had eight straight winning seasons and six straight sub-three ERAs for Cincinnati, winning a strikeout title and a World Series MVP. But he went on the DL a month after his 30th birthday in 1995 and, except for a 94-inning comeback attempt in 2001–02, was finished.

Then, there was Jim O'Toole ... and Sammy Ellis ... and Mel Queen ... and Jim Merritt ... and Tom Browning....

Ken Hubbs

One thing most baseball observers agreed on was that Ken Hubbs would be a long-time big leaguer. "He plays second base and probably will do so for the next decade," predicted *Chicago Daily News* writer Bob Smith when Hubbs made the Cubs.[1] "He figures to be with us for a long spell," wrote *Pittsburgh Press* Sports Editor Chester Smith.[2] "He'll be a major leaguer for many, many more years," said Cubs skipper Bob Kennedy.[3]

1. Smith, Bob. "Hubbs Gains Stature." *Chicago Daily News*, May 15, 1962.
2. Smith, Chester L. "Plenty of Ground Covered by Hubbs in Errorless String." *Pittsburgh Press*, August 17, 1962.
3. Holtzman, Jerome. "'Luck Will Change,' Claims Soph Hubbs, Battling Plate Skid." *The Sporting News*, July 13, 1963.

"[H]e'll be around for a long time," said Pirates manager Danny Murtaugh.[4] "I would like to stay 20 years," said Hubbs himself.[5]

They all proved tragically wrong.

Kenneth Douglas Hubbs was born December 23, 1941, in Riverside, California, the second son of Eulis and Dorothy Hubbs in an athletic, devoutly Mormon family. Ken grew up in nearby Colton, about 50 miles east of Los Angeles. Eulis was stricken with polio when Ken was an infant, and spent the rest of his life in a wheelchair, yet continued his career as an insurance salesman, and fathered three more sons (Gary, Kirk, and Kraig joining Keith and Ken).[6]

In the spring of 1942, young Kenny suffered a ruptured hernia. Too young for restorative surgery, he wore a truss for the next five years before growing out of the hernia.[7] Fully recovered, he soon became a star athlete in boxing, football, basketball, and track, in addition to baseball.

Ken first got national attention as a baseball player at age 12. He led the Colton team to the 1954 Little League World Series, broadcast on TV with Mel Allen at the mike. The right-handed Hubbs pitched his team to an 8–1 win over Melrose Park in the semifinal game; then, Colton lost the championship contest to Schenectady, 7–5, despite Ken's long home run and sparkling defensive play at shortstop.[8] The team would hold an annual reunion thereafter, with Ken attending the tenth one just 19 days before his death.[9]

Ken continued his athletic prowess at Colton Union High School, becoming the nation's first athlete ever to make All-American at two sports in the same year: football (quarterback) and basketball (forward). He won the *Los Angeles Examiner* trophy as the "Best All-Around Athlete in Southern California" in 1959.[10] Hubbs was also an excellent pupil, and student body president—the quintessential all-American boy.

On June 3, 1959, Hubbs participated in a high school All-American basketball tournament. He was given a card to fill out, asking him to complete the sentence, "My goal in life is…." Hubbs wrote, "To become a major league baseball player within the next 3 years."[11]

---

4. Biederman, Les. "No Flubs for Cubs' Hubbs—That's Theme after 71-Game Streak." *Pittsburgh Press*, August 30, 1962.

5. Smith, Bob. "Hubbs' Seven-Week Climb to Majors." *Chicago Daily News*, April 14, 1962.

6. "Kenny Hubbs, the All-American Boy." Anonymous manuscript in National Baseball Library file.

7. *Ibid.*

8. *Ibid.*

9. "Kid Teammates Join Hubbs in Happy Reunion." *The Sporting News*, February 8, 1964.

10. Unidentified clipping in National Baseball Library file.

11. "Kenny Hubbs, the All-American Boy." Anonymous manuscript in National Baseball Library file.

After weighing various college athletic scholarship offers, Hubbs signed with the Chicago Cubs on June 19, 1959, as soon as he graduated from high school. Cubs scout Gene Handley spent much of the day with the Hubbs family before convincing Ken to sign. The amount of Hubbs's bonus has been reported as between $15,000 and $60,000, but the lower number is probably closer.

Hubbs began his career as a 17-year-old shortstop-outfielder with the Morristown, Tennessee Cubs of the Class-D Appalachian League. He batted a solid .298 with a .480 slugging percentage, knocking in 50 runs and scoring 52 in 56 games to help the team to the league title. Hubbs finished the year with four games for the Ft. Worth Cats of the AAA American Association.

Hubbs played for San Antonio (Texas League, AA) and Lancaster (Eastern League, A) in 1960, slipping to a combined .217 batting average. But he rebounded to hit .286 for Wenatchee, Washington (Northwest League, B) in '61, switching to second base in mid-season, and earning his first major league cup of coffee. Hubbs played 10 games with the Cubs at age 19, then went to the Arizona Instructional League after the season. There he batted .340 and worked hard on his second base play.[12]

Hubbs made the Cubs and started the 1962 season with a salary of $7,000. The 6'2", 175-pound second sacker immediately impressed both at bat (including 5-for-5 games on April 17 and May 20; on the latter date, he had eight hits in a doubleheader) and in the field. Despite being a 20-year-old rookie at a new position, Hubbs went practically all summer without making an error.

Hubbs's errorless streak gained national attention and set new records. Between June 13 and September 5, he went 78 consecutive games, and 418 fielding chances, without a miscue. He broke records held by Hall of Famers Red Schoendienst (NL marks of 57 games and 320 chances in 1950) and Bobby Doerr (major league standards of 73 and 414, respectively, in 1948). Hubbs's records would survive until 1978. On the last day of the season, Hubbs started a triple play against the Mets. In the midst of the errorless streak, the Cubs tore up Hubbs's contract on August 21 and increased the amount to $12,000, also signing him to a '63 contract at an estimated at $15,000.[13]

Hubbs acquitted himself pretty well offensively, too. In a lineup featuring future Hall of Famers Ernie Banks, Billy Williams, Ron Santo, and Lou Brock, Hubbs finished second on the team in runs and hits, and led the Cubs in three-baggers. He batted a respectable .260 and finished among

---

12. "Greenies with Golden Touch." *The Sporting News*, December 15, 1962.
13. Kuenster, John. "Hubbs Earns, Then Learns." *Chicago Daily News*, September 1, 1962.

the NL leaders in singles, triples, and sacrifice hits. On the negative side, he topped the league in strikeouts and grounding into double plays.

After the season, Hubbs was overwhelmingly named NL Rookie of the Year, receiving 19 of a possible 20 votes. Perhaps more impressively, he also won the NL Gold Glove Award at second base. With voting done by the league's players, Hubbs beat out all-time defensive great Bill Mazeroski for the honor, 141–81. It was the first time a rookie had won a Gold Glove, and turned out to be the only time between 1960 and 1967 that Maz didn't win the award.

After the 1962 and '63 seasons, Ken took courses at San Bernardino Valley College in California. He had attended Brigham Young University after the '59 season.

Called a victim of the "Sophomore Jinx," Hubbs saw his batting average sink to .235 in 1963. Part of that was because of the enlargement of the strike zone that year, precipitating a 16-point league-wide drop in BA. And, considering that no NL second baseman had more than 10 homers or 52 RBI, Hubbs (8, 47) was holding his own, offensively. "It isn't that I'm not hitting the ball good," Hubbs said in mid-season. "I've already hit more homers than I did last year and I'm satisfied that I'm getting good wood. I've cut down on my strikeouts, too.... (Last year the) balls were dropping in. This year, nothing drops."[14] Bob Kennedy, the Cubs' Head Coach (closest thing to a manager in their experimental "College of Coaches" scheme), predicted Hubbs would bounce back strong in 1964. "Next year, I believe Kenny will start back up," Kennedy said. "I'm confident that he'll improve with each passing year until he reaches solid stardom."[15]

Hubbs's fielding was arguably better in 1963 than '62, though he finished a distant second to Mazeroski in Gold Glove voting. Hubbs's range factor improved from 5.50 to 5.64 chances handled per nine innings, as compared to the league average of 5.21.

Hubbs had many hobbies. He was an avid golfer, hunter, and horseback rider, and was even learning to play the bagpipes. He had a special love of flying, and often joined pilots in the cockpit during team charter flights. Hubbs began taking flying lessons, and in November 1963, bought his own Cessna 172 airplane. He got his pilot's license in January 1964.

Two weeks later, Hubbs took his close friend Dennis Doyle—an orphan who grew up in the Hubbs home—on a plane ride from Colton to surprise Doyle's wife and baby, who were visiting her parents in Provo,

---

14. Holtzman, Jerome. "'Luck Will Change,' Claims Soph Hubbs, Battling Plate Skid." *The Sporting News*, July 13, 1963.
15. Munzel, Edgar. "Soph Flop Hubbs Still Ranks as Cubs' Fixture for '64." *The Sporting News*, October 5, 1963.

Utah. The two wound up staying the night, planning to return to Colton the next day. The sky was clear, so Hubbs took off at 10 a.m. on February 13. About 65 miles southwest in Delta, Utah, he encountered an unexpected, blinding snowstorm. Hubbs turned the plane around and headed back toward Provo, flying low due to the poor visibility. Four miles short of the airport, caught in a turbulent, desolate spot between two mountains, the plane crashed into the ice-covered Utah Lake. It wasn't until the following day that anyone realized the two men were missing, and on February 15 the shattered plane and two lifeless bodies were discovered.[16]

In a bitter irony, on February 14—not knowing that Hubbs already lay dead in Utah—the Cubs' brass discussed grounding him. "We decided that we would have Kennedy talk to him when Ken arrived in camp [10 days later] and tell him that he would have to give up piloting his plane until the end of the season," said Cubs Vice-President John Holland.

More than 2,000 people attended Hubbs's funeral, with Banks and Santo among the six teammates serving as pallbearers. On May 4, the Dodgers and Cubs donated $5,000 game proceeds to start a Ken Hubbs Memorial Youth Center.[17] After the season, the Chicago BBWAA chapter instituted an annual award in Hubbs's name, "for excellence and exemplary conduct on and off the field."[18] Banks was the first winner. Decades later, Hubbs was still remembered fondly in Chicago. On June 26, 2002, the Cubs held Ken Hubbs Memorial Night at Wrigley Field.

Some might dispute that Hubbs might have fashioned a Hall of Fame career; even playing half his games in the friendly confines of Wrigley Field, Ken batted just .247. But remember, he had just turned 22, an age at which most players haven't even reached the majors. Through age 20, the five most similar players to Hubbs include Hall of Famers Roberto Alomar, Mazeroski, and Bobby Doerr. Cubs broadcaster Lou Boudreau said, "I definitely felt he was on his way to a Hall of Fame career. His bat hadn't come around, but it would have."[19] A researcher working on a book about Hubbs said that several former players, including Banks, told him that Hubbs would have been a Hall of Famer.[20] Another Hall of Fame teammate, Santo, agreed. "I think Kenny would have been one of the best second basemen ever," said Santo decades later. "He was a Ryne Sandberg type at that age, with a little

---

16. Munzel, Edgar. "Hubbs Took Off with Sky Clear, His Dad Reveals." *The Sporting News*, March 28, 1964.
17. Hunter, Bob. "Dodgers Put $5,000 into Hubbs Fund." *The Sporting News*, May 16, 1964, p. 27.
18. "Exemplary Conduct Award to Honor Hubbs' Memory." *The Sporting News*, November 28, 1964.
19. Stone, Larry. "Flameouts." *Baseball Digest*, November/December 2013, p. 31.
20. Brown, Mark. "Where Were You When the Hope of the Cubs Died?" *Chicago Sun-Times*, July 9, 2003.

power at the plate. He could run and he could field. We'll never know how good he would have been."[21]

Year	Team (League)	G	AB	R	H	2B	3B	HR	RBI	SB	AVG	OBP	SLG
1961	Chicago (NL)	10	28	4	5	1	1	1	2	0	.179	.179	.393
1962		160	661	90	172	24	9	5	49	3	.260	.299	.346
1963		154	566	54	133	19	3	8	47	8	.235	.285	.322
Totals		324	1255	148	310	44	13	14	98	11	.247	.290	.336

21. Claire, Fred. "Lidle Tragedy Stirs Memories of Hubbs." MLB.com, October 16, 2006.

Bill Hutchison

A rules change helped turn Bill Hutchison from the best pitcher in baseball, into just another pitcher out of baseball.

William Forrest Hutchison (often spelled as "Hutchinson") was born December 17, 1859, in New Haven, Connecticut, the son of Helen Seabold and the Rev. William Hutchison, a widely-known minister. Following in the footsteps of his grandfather, father, and several other relatives, young Bill attended Yale University. He was shortstop on the University baseball team for three years, serving as captain in 1880. Hutchison graduated that year with a B.A., then took a special engineering course at Sheffield Scientific School.[1]

Hutchison went to Biddeford, Maine, to learn the cotton manufacturing business, but had to give it up due to ill health. He then went into the railroad and lumber business in Kansas City, Missouri, and Cedar Rapids, Iowa.[2] In between he continued playing amateur baseball, taking up pitching, and earning two brief pro stops, including one in the 1884 Union Association, a league dubiously considered major. Following some business setbacks, Hutchison returned to pro ball in 1887, soon becoming the highest-paid player and—though in his late 20s—one of the most sought-after pitching prospects in the minor leagues. He went 26–10 and 23–10 (in half-a-season) for Des Moines in 1887–88, then joined Cap Anson's Chicago White Stockings as a 29-year-old rookie in 1889.[3]

1. *Obituary Record of Yale Graduates, 1925–1926.*
2. Ibid.
3. Dellinger, Harold A. "William Forrest Hutchinson." *Nineteenth Century Stars.* Kansas City, MO: Society for American Baseball Research, 1989, p. 66.

Hutchison was a 5'9", 175-pound right-hander with blazing speed but erratic control, earning him the nickname Wild Bill. Reporters marveled at Hutchison, a baseball player who actually trained during the off-season.

From 1890-92—in a circuit which included future Hall of Famers Cy Young, Kid Nichols, Tim Keefe, John Clarkson, and Amos Rusie—Hutchison led the National League in games pitched, games started, innings, and victories each year. He amassed 121 wins in those three seasons—more than half of his team's total—and topped the league in strikeouts in 1892.

Despite his late start, Hutchison was on an impressive career path. Through age 32, the seven most similar pitchers include Hall of Famers Warren Spahn, Joe McGinnity, Stan Coveleski, and Bob Gibson.

In 1893, the pitcher's box was moved back to the current 60'6". According to the *Reach Official Base Ball Guide*, "The object of the change in distance was to increase the batting, handicap the pitcher and add to the interest of the sport.... As a generality the pitchers were astoundingly handicapped by the extra five feet. Indeed, the added distance in many notable instances drove pitchers out of the business, or so weakened their former effectiveness as to make them of little or no worth to their respective clubs."[4]

Some pitchers were affected more by this change than others, but evidently none more than Wild Bill. His ERAs nearly doubled, he walked almost twice as many batters as he struck out, and he struggled through three losing seasons with the White Stockings before returning to the minor leagues.

Hutchison was a decent hitter, batting .216 lifetime with 12 home runs. While the lengthened pitching distance hurt his mound-work, it helped his hitting: he batted .309 with six homers in 1894.

Wild Bill had one last hurrah in the minors, going 38–14 for Minneapolis in the Western League in 1896. That earned him a final shot in the majors, but he went 1–4 with the 1897 Cardinals and returned to Minneapolis. By the end of the century, he was back in the railroad business, though he continued to play semi-pro ball until he was almost 50.[5]

Hutchison, who was unmarried, died March 19, 1926, at Kansas City, Missouri. He was buried in the family plot in Norwich, Connecticut.[6]

---

4. *Reach's Official Base Ball Guide for 1894*. Philadelphia: A. J. Reach Co., 1894, p. 10.
5. Dellinger, Harold A. "William Forrest Hutchinson." *Nineteenth Century Stars*. Kansas City, MO: Society for American Baseball Research, 1989, p. 66.
6. *Obituary Record of Yale Graduates, 1925–1926*.

Year	Team (League)	G	IP	W	L	PCT	SO	BB	H	ERA
1884	Kansas City (UA)	2	17.0	1	1	.500	5	1	14	2.65
1889	Chicago (NL)	37	318.0	16	17	.485	136	117	306	3.54
1890		*71	*603.0	*41	25	.621	289	199	505	2.70
1891		*66	*561.0	*44	19	.698	261	178	508	2.81
1892		*75	*622.0	*36	36	.500	*314	190	571	2.76
1893		44	348.1	16	24	.400	80	156	420	4.75
1894		37	279.0	14	16	.467	60	140	374	6.03
1895		38	291.0	13	21	.382	85	129	371	4.73
1897	St. Louis (NL)	6	40.0	1	4	.200	5	22	55	6.07
Totals		376	3079.1	182	163	.528	1235	1132	3124	3.59

How Much Farther Was It?

Though baseball histories say that the pitching distance was increased from 50 feet to 60½ feet in 1893, that's not really true. Prior to 1893, the pertinent rules read as follow:

> RULE 5. The Pitcher's Lines must be … five and one half feet long by four feet wide, distant fifty feet from the center of the Home Base….
> RULE 18. The pitcher shall take his position facing the batsman with both feet square on the ground, one foot on the rear line of the "box."

In other words, while the front of the pitcher's box was 50 feet away from home plate, the back of the box—where the pitcher had to start his delivery, and where the current distance is measured from—was 55'6" away. And, since home plate at that time was a one-foot-square base within the diamond, much like first and third, the center of the base was about 8½ inches closer than the rear point—the point from which the 60'6" distance is measured.

So, the pre-1893 pitcher was beginning his delivery about 56'2½" away from the back of home plate. Instead of a 21 percent leap in the pitching distance in 1893, the increase was a relatively modest 7.6 percent.[7]

---

7. Deane, Bill. *Baseball Myths*. Lanham, MD: Scarecrow Press, 2012, pp. 9–10.

Charlie Keller

Though he was overshadowed by teammate Joe DiMaggio, Charlie "King Kong" Keller was one of the AL's top sluggers until a congenital back problem derailed his career. How good was he? Among post-1900 left fielders (players with at least 1000 games, the majority in left), Keller ranks third in WAR per game, behind only Barry Bonds and Ted Williams. Let that sink in.

Charles Ernest Keller II was born September 12, 1916, at the German-American family's 140-acre dairy farm in Middletown, Maryland. He was followed by brothers Hugh, Frank, and Hal. (Hal would play 25 games as a Senators catcher, 1949–52, and serve as a farm director for the new Senators in the 1960s.) Starting at age seven, Charlie was doing daily chores like milking cows, chopping wood, and plowing, helping build his prodigious strength.

Charlie graduated from Middletown High School in 1934 and went on to the University of Maryland. Joining the National Youth Association, a WPA program, he did painting and ditch-digging work around the university, 50 hours per month for $15, to help pay his way.[1] Keller still found time to play college football, basketball, and baseball. In the latter, he started as a catcher before finding a home in the outfield, and batted .470, .506, and .494 in his varsity years.[2] He eventually earned a Bachelor of Science degree in agricultural economics.

Keller also played for Kinston, North Carolina, of the independent, semi-pro Coastal Plain League in 1935–36, leading the circuit in batting (.385, .466) both seasons.[3]

There are conflicting stories about what Yankees scout signed Keller, and what his bonus was. Amounts range from $2,500 to $12,000. Some say that the team paid off the mortgage on the Keller family farm, some that Keller paid it himself with his bonus, and still others that the farm was lost in the Depression before Keller even signed, and the money went toward his college tuition. By all accounts, though, Keller was a prized prospect being sought by many teams before the Yankees won out. He insisted that they let him complete college first, and start with their highest farm team, the Newark Bears of the International League. Hall of Fame executive

---

1. Edwards, Henry P. American League Service Bureau press release, January 14, 1940.
2. Segar, Charles. "Keller, Hero in the First World's Series He Ever Saw." *The Sporting News*, January 4, 1940.
3. Patterson, Arthur E. "Keller Promises to Make Grade." Unidentified clipping in National Baseball Library file, January 26, 1939.

George Weiss, who worked for the Yankees from 1932 to 1960, recalled reeling in Keller as his "greatest satisfaction."[4]

Keller was not particularly large at 5'10" and about 185 pounds, but he was a beast of a man. As Milton Gross wrote, "His black beetle-browed eyes, his muscled blacksmith arms, his thick neck and hogshead of a chest were of wrestler's proportions."[5] "Keller wasn't scouted," famously quipped teammate Lefty Gomez, "he was trapped." With a swarthy complexion and long arms, Keller got the nickname "King Kong," after the 1933 movie ape. As Jim Murray wrote decades later, "They used to call him King Kong because he looked like something that could swat airplanes or come to work by vine."[6] Keller credited Reds catcher Willard Hershberger with the moniker, picked up by the print media, but not by on-field personnel. Not surprisingly, Keller hated the nickname, and probably the others bestowed on him by the press, including Gargantua, The Beast, Scrap-Iron, and Killer Keller.

Keller swung a 38-ounce, 38-inch bat from the left side, had a keen eye, and could hit the ball a long way, but he preferred to use the whole field and shoot the gaps. Despite his stocky build, Keller had excellent speed. He would average 11 triples per year in his five full big league seasons, and in 1942 and again in '46, he would tie a league record by grounding into only five double plays in 150+ games. In a war benefit event on July 28, 1943, Keller was matched in a 60-yard-dash against several Indians and Yankees speedsters. Included was George "Snuffy" Stirnweiss, a 24-year-old rookie who had stolen 73 bases in the minors the year before, and who would lead the AL in that category in 1944 and '45. Keller beat them all, finishing the race in seven seconds flat.[7]

Keller left college early to begin his pro career, and would have to finish his degree requirements the following year. He was starting his journey on what historians consider the greatest minor league team of all time—and he became the best player on it. The 1937 Newark Bears went 109–43 (.717), winning the International League pennant by 25½ games. They then went 12–3 in three rounds of playoffs, including a triumph in the "Little World Series" vs. Columbus, the American Association champion.

Keller finished the 1937 season with a .353 batting average and .541 slugging percentage, leading the league in runs (120), hits (189), triples (14), total bases, and batting. He was said to be the youngest player and the first pro rookie to win a batting title at the highest level of the minors. In the Little World Series, Keller batted .478. *The Sporting News* named him

---

4. King, Joe. "Weiss Calls Find of Keller Best Move." Unidentified clipping in National Baseball Library file, January 28, 1953.
5. Gross, Milton. "Charlie Keller's Comeback." *Sportfolio*, September, 1948, p. 14.
6. Murray, Jim. "Murray's Best." *The Sporting News*, December 27, 1969, p. 38.
7. "Keller Convinces Snuffy He's Snappy Sprinter." *The Sporting News*, August 5, 1943.

"Outstanding Minor League Player of 1937," giving him a framed scroll on June 2, 1938.[8] For most players, that would have landed him in the majors in '38 or before, but Keller wasn't even invited to spring training. The Yankees had just won their second of four straight world championships with a 102–52 record, and were in no hurry to replace anyone.

Keller's 1938 numbers for Newark were even better: 149 runs, 211 hits, 22 homers, a .365 batting average, and a .569 slugging percentage. He again led the league in runs and hits, set a club record with 131 RBI, and lost the batting title only on an administrative decision. League officials, having no formal rule for the crown, awarded it to Newark teammate Buddy Rosar, who batted .387 but had only 91 games and 323 at bats. The Yankees finally purchased Keller's contract for the parent team in October (though they promptly tried to trade him for Indians rookie star Jeff Heath).[9] "I should have been in the major leagues two years earlier than I was," Keller recalled.[10]

Charlie married college sweetheart Martha Lee Williamson on January 22, 1938. Martha had been a sports standout herself, playing lacrosse, hockey, basketball, and tennis at Bryn Mawr.[11] Charles E. Keller III came along on August 5, 1939, followed soon after by Donald L. and Martha Jean.

Slowed by a spring training groin and/or thigh injury, Keller made his big league debut on April 22, 1939 (at age 22 years, 222 days). After playing regularly into early June, he was benched for most of the next two months. Through August 1, he had just 176 at bats and two homers (he lost another to a rainout on May 22). But from then through the end of the season, Keller hung up a .356/.464/.563 slash line to finish a fine rookie year. His .334 batting average ranked fifth in the league, and he earned seven MVP points. In later years, Keller liked to remind people that he and Ted Williams debuted in the same year, and he outhit Ted (.327). "With his power and speed," said Williams, "there's no reason why he shouldn't be an outstanding hitter for a long time."[12]

Keller then put on a one-man show in the World Series against the Reds. In Game One, he tripled to the right-center field fence in the bottom of the ninth, and scored on a single to give the Yankees a 2–1 walk-off win. In Game Two, he singled and doubled, scoring a run and driving in another in a 4–0 victory. In Game Three, Keller belted two two-run homers, powering a 7–3 triumph. The Yanks completed the sweep the next

---

8. Gaven, Michael F. "'Greatest Day in My Life,' Says Keller, Receiving The Sporting News Scroll As 'Outstanding Minor.'" *The Sporting News*, June 9, 1938.
9. Daniel, Dan. "Daniel's Dope." *New York World Telegram*, October 11, 1939.
10. Madden, Bill. "'King Kong' Keller Dies." *New York Daily News*, May 24, 1990.
11. "Meet the Missus." *The Sporting News*, November 23, 1939.
12. Knight, Fred. "Keller Admits His Ambition." Unidentified clipping in National Baseball Library file, September 5, 1941.

day in 10 innings. Keller broke a scoreless tie with another homer in the seventh, singled and scored in the ninth, and tallied his third run in the tenth, knocking catcher Ernie Lombardi out of commission (though he claimed he didn't touch Lombardi) and allowing Joe DiMaggio to score behind him for a 7–4 win. Keller finished the Series leading all players in runs (8), hits (7), triples, homers (3), batting (.438), and slugging (1.188). The rest of the Yankees hit just .174. Keller returned to Maryland to a hero's welcome.

The rangy, strong-armed Keller was moved from right field to left in 1940. With today's homogenous ballparks that might be considered a demotion, but at that time and place it was quite the opposite. "The reason for the shift is obvious," wrote noted scribe Dan Daniel. "In Yankee Stadium, left field is by far the bigger terrain. In addition, it is the sun field."[13] Keller went on to lead AL left fielders in putouts in 1941, '42, '43, and '46, in range factor in 1942 and '46, and in fielding percentage in 1942 and '43. With Keller in left, DiMaggio in center, and Tommy Henrich in right, the Yankees' trio was often touted as "Baseball's greatest outfield." In 1941 they became the first outfield tandem to each hit 30+ homers in the same season.

Keller also made a shift in his batting strategy in '40, at the request of management. They wanted to take advantage of his strength and Yankee Stadium's short porch. Noted writer Arthur Daley later estimated that Keller "sacrificed some fifty points a year on his batting average by switching from a straight away hitter to all fields and becoming a pull hitter with dead aim on the right field stands."[14] "My best value to the team is in extra-base-hits and runs batted in," Keller agreed.[15] Charlie had some difficulty adapting to the new style, batting just .231 through May 20. But he lifted it to .286 by season's end, earning his first All-Star selection, leading the AL in walks, finishing second in triples (15), seventh in OPS, and tenth in WAR. He almost doubled his home run total to 21 although, ironically, only seven were hit at home.

On April 22, 1941, Keller hit a homer in Philadelphia estimated at over 500 feet. "He is the strong man of the Yankees, perhaps of the league," wrote one reporter in 1942. "He is built like Gargantua, has a fine eye, and there is neither hitch nor any other ailment in his swing."[16] Notwithstanding that blast, Keller again started slowly in 1941, and was hitting a mere

---

13. Daniel, Dan. "McCarthy Plans to Shift Selkirk Back to Right Field." *New York World-Telegram*, March 11, 1940.
14. Daley, Arthur. "His Majesty, King Kong." *New York Times*, September, 1948
15. Frank, Stanley. "Muscles in His Sweat." *Baseball Digest*, 1943.
16. "The * of the Week." Unidentified clipping in National Baseball Library file, August, 1942.

.244 through June 6. Then he tore up the league over the next three months, earning another All-Star nod. By September 11, he was at .302, leading the league in RBI by 10, and just one behind Williams for the lead in homers. But on that day, favoring a muscle or tendon pull in his left thigh, Keller made an awkward slide into second base and suffered a chip fracture at his right ankle. He was put in a cast and expected to be out the rest of the year, but he vowed to be back in time for the World Series. Keller missed 12 games, costing him the RBI crown. He returned for the last two regular-season contests, but went 0-for-7 to drop his average below .300. Nevertheless, he finished among the AL's top five in homers (second), RBI (third), walks, slugging, OPS, and WAR, and was ranked fifth in MVP voting.

Despite his injury, Keller again came up huge in the World Series, this time against the Brooklyn Dodgers. He scored two runs in a 3–2 victory in Game One, had two hits, a run, and an RBI in a 3–2 loss the next day, singled in what proved to be the winning run in a 2–1 win in Game Three, and collected four hits in Game Four. His two-run double off the right field wall was the big blow as the Yanks scored four with two out in the ninth (following Mickey Owen's infamous passed ball) to pull out a 7–4 win in that contest; Charlie recalled that hit as his biggest thrill in baseball. New York went on to take the Fall Classic the next day, and Keller batted .389 in the Series, leading all performers in runs (5), hits (7), doubles (2), and RBI (5).

For the fourth straight year, Keller was slow to get untracked in 1942. He was hitting just .242 through June 29, but lifted his average 50 points by the end of the season. He wound up in the league's top three in homers, total bases, RBI, walks, slugging, OPS, and WAR. Though Keller batted just .200 as the Yankees lost the 1942 World Series to the Cardinals in five games, he led all players with two homers and five RBI. He would finish his Fall Classic career the next year with five homers, a .306 batting average, and a .611 slugging percentage in 19 games.

Keller held out prior to the 1943 season, before signing for a modest $2,000 raise to $18,000 (his peak would be $27,500 in 1948). He missed 13 contests and the All-Star Game, July 2–16, due to a deep spike wound in his left knee, and was hitting just .247 at that point. As usual, he picked up the pace in the second half, finishing among the league leaders in many categories. Keller topped the AL in walks, OPS, adjusted batting runs and wins, offensive win percentage, and win probability added (WPA). He was second in runs, homers, and slugging, third in triples and total bases, fifth in WAR, and sixth in RBI. A *Saturday Evening Post* article that year called him "the Yankees' Second Gehrig." After the Yankees beat the Cardinals in the World Series, Keller was among a group of stars (including

Bill Dickey, Joe Gordon, Bobby Doerr, Luke Appling, Joe Medwick, and Stan Musial) selected to play an exhibition series for U.S. soldiers in the Pacific Theater.[17]

Despite being married with three small children, Keller—working in a defense plant at the time—was classified "1-A" for the military draft in November 1943. He joined the Merchant Marines on December 21 and became Ensign Charles Keller. He would first serve as a fitness officer in Florida, then a transporter and purser aboard ship, and played no baseball during his 20 months of military service.

Keller returned to the diamond late in the 1945 season. He made his season debut on August 19, and naturally showed some rust, batting just .222 with two RBI over his first two weeks. But he went on a tear from then on, amassing eight homers, 32 RBI, and a .339 average over the last 29 games.

After batting just once over the first five games of 1946, Keller didn't miss a game the rest of the season. In a change of pattern, he had a strong first half, batting .326 with 18 homers and 55 RBI to earn his fourth All-Star selection (he homered in the game). But his back began bothering him, and his performance declined. He still finished in the league's top five in runs, triples, homers, total bases, RBI, walks, slugging, and OPS. With the Yankees not in the World Series for a change, Keller then signed on for a 27-game post-season barnstorming tour with Bob Feller, Phil Rizzuto, and other big league stars.[18]

Despite ongoing back problems treated by Novocain shots, Keller got off to a strong start in the power department in 1947. Through June 5, 43 games into the season, he was leading the AL in home runs (13) and RBI (36), on pace for 47 and 129. As of June 1, Keller trailed only Rudy York in homers, 173–164, among major leaguers in the 1940s. Charlie earned his fifth All-Star pick, though he wound up declining it.

But Keller left the June 5 game in the fifth inning after aggravating his back, and was essentially done for the season—and, at just 30, as a star player. He had only two fruitless pinch-hit appearances before going under the knife "for removal of a cartilage 'washer' between vertebrae"[19] on July 17, and was hospitalized until August 5. The operation by Dr. Thomas L. Hoen and its aftermath left Keller with his right leg two inches shorter than his right,[20] and the reduced flexibility would put strain on all his muscles. "I

---

17. King, Joe. "Chandler, Keller, Dickey, Gordon on A.L. Squad." *New York World Telegram*, September, 1943.
18. United Press. "Feller's Team to Play 27 Games." September 18, 1946.
19. Daniel, Dan. "Keller May Return Before World Series." *New York World Telegram*, July 19, 1947.
20. Daniel, Dan. "Yankees May Have to Train in Cuba." *New York World Telegram*, October 15, 1947.

was done for all intents and purposes," recalled Keller. "Atrophy on my right side took away all my power."[21]

Keller was reduced to a spectator at the 1947 World Series, and there was doubt he would ever play again. It was said that no player had ever come back from such surgery. But Keller was determined to return to the field in 1948, and signed a provisional contract. He had a setback in February, when he was involved in a bad auto accident when someone ran a red light. He suffered an ankle injury in May, and missed 45 games, June 2–July 21, after fracturing two bones in his left hand while trying to make a shoestring catch. He wound up playing only 83 games in 1948, with but six homers.

Tearing a muscle in his right side with a swing just before opening day in '49, Keller was stuck on the bench. The team debated whether to put him on the disabled list; in those days it required a player to remain on it for 60 days. Having to bring its roster down to 25 by May 18, the Yankees gave Keller the ultimate slap in the face, demoting him back to the Newark Bears on that date. He played in just eight games there (going 4-for-18) before returning to the Yanks, and finally made his 1949 big league debut on June 16, having missed the first 52 games. But Keller became just a bit player, and the writing was on the wall. On September 23, the Yankees held "Charlie Keller Day" at Yankee Stadium. He agreed to it only under the condition that the proceeds be used to create two scholarships for New York youths going to his alma mater. The first recipient was Jack Scarbath, who became a College Football Hall of Famer and NFL quarterback.[22]

The Yankees granted Keller his outright release on December 19, making him a free agent. The New York baseball writers feted him at Toots Shor's restaurant on January 23, 1950.

On December 27, 1949, the Tigers, managed by Keller's former teammate Red Rolfe, signed Charlie as a pinch-hitter—and for his presence. "I signed Keller to give my ball club some class," said Rolfe.[23] Keller was a quiet, private man, but known as a great teammate. "Charlie would slap a fellow on the back when he had a good day," recalled DiMaggio. "But the ones he went looking for in the clubhouse after a game were the fellows who had a bad day.... Charlie would sit down with a fellow who was in the dumps and talk to him and cheer him up."[24]

Keller was used almost exclusively off the bench over the next two

---

21. Mann, Jack. "'King Kong' Keller Becomes a Harness Racing Kingpin." *Washington Star*, December 17, 1978.
22. Steadman, John. "Hometown Celebrates Keller, Who Batted 1.000 for Humanity." *Baltimore Sun*, September 27, 1998.
23. Graham, Frank. "Night to Remember." *The Sporting News*, January 1950.
24. *Ibid.*

seasons, and did creditably in that role. In a rare start, he had his last big game on September 19, 1950, going 4-for-5 with two homers and five RBI. Keller wound up leading the AL in pinch-hits in 1951, but didn't play after August and was released on November 9.

Keller spent the 1952 season coaching his sons in Little League (the boys would lead their team to the state championship a year later). Then, the Yankees re-signed Charlie for one last fling on September 4. But he made only two appearances, striking out as a pinch-hitter on September 13, and replacing Mickey Mantle in the field in the ninth inning the next day, and wound up watching another World Series from the bench. The Yankees gave Keller his unconditional release on October 13. He finished his abbreviated career with a .410 OBP and .518 slugging percentage. Said teammate Tommy Byrne, "If he wouldn't have had the back problem, he'd have been one of the top five Yankees of all time, with Ruth, Gehrig, DiMaggio and Mantle."[25]

Keller returned to the Yankees as a coach for a couple of brief terms, filling in for the ailing Bill Dickey in 1957, and the injured Ralph Houk in 1959.

Charlie's two sons were signed by the Yankees in October 1958, and both showed promise before the same back problems ended their careers. Don, a third baseman, played from 1959 to 1961, batting .283 with a .423 OBP in 276 games. Charlie, Jr. ("Son of Kong") really looked like he had the stuff. An outfielder-first baseman, he had a .310/.424/.541 slash line in 447 games, 1959–62, winning the Eastern League batting title with .349 in '61. A brother and two cousins of Charlie, Sr., also required back surgery.[26]

For a player with just 3790 career at bats, Charlie Keller, Sr., did fairly well in Hall of Fame balloting. He received votes in 11 elections, finishing at 6.1 percent in 1972—ahead of Richie Ashburn, among others. Keller was enshrined in the Maryland Athletic Hall of Fame on December 14, 1957, and the Maryland Baseball Shrine of Immortals on August 17, 1962.

In 1955, Keller used his baseball earnings to buy a 100-acre farm six miles from his birthplace. He named it Yankeeland Farm and raised Standardbred trotting horses, all bestowed with Yankee names. Starting small, it eventually moved into the top 10 in North America in producing money-winning harness horses; in 1970, his Fresh Yankee was named

---

25. Steadman, John. "Hometown Celebrates Keller, Who Batted 1.000 for Humanity." *Baltimore Sun*, September 27, 1998.

26. Krupinsle, Joe. "Son of Kong Wants to Make It on His Own." *Newsday*, September 1, 1961.

Horse of the Year.[27] The farm would remain in the family until sold at auction for $3.7 million in 2006.[28]

After a long bout with colon cancer, Charlie Keller died at his home on May 23, 1990. He was survived by his wife of 52 years, his three children, six grandchildren, and three great-grandchildren, all living in the Frederick area.[29]

Year	Team (League)	G	AB	R	H	2B	3B	HR	RBI	SB	AVG	OBP	SLG
1939	New York (AL)	111	398	87	133	21	6	11	83	6	.334	.447	.500
1940		138	500	102	143	18	15	21	93	8	.286	.411	.508
1941		140	507	102	151	24	10	33	122	6	.298	.416	.580
1942		152	544	106	159	24	9	26	108	14	.292	.417	.513
1943		141	512	97	139	15	11	31	86	7	.271	.396	.525
1945		44	163	26	49	7	4	10	34	0	.301	.412	.577
1946		150	538	98	148	29	10	30	101	1	.275	.405	.533
1947		45	151	36	36	6	1	13	36	0	.238	.404	.550
1948		83	247	41	66	15	2	6	44	1	.267	.372	.417
1949		60	116	17	29	4	1	3	16	2	.250	.392	.379
1950	Detroit (AL)	50	51	7	16	1	3	2	16	0	.314	.453	.569
1951		54	62	6	16	2	0	3	21	0	.258	.370	.435
1952	New York (AL)	2	1	0	0	0	0	0	0	0	.000	.000	.000
Totals		1170	3790	725	1085	166	72	189	760	45	.286	.410	.518

27. Associated Press. "Charlie Keller, 73, Baseball Player, Breeder of Harness Race Horses." *Philadelphia Inquirer*, May 25, 1990.
28. Dunkel, Tom. "End of the Race for Family Farm." *Baltimore Sun*, November 26, 2006.
29. Unidentified clipping in National Baseball Library file, May 24, 1990.

Bill Lange

At age 28, Bill Lange had already amassed 400 stolen bases and a .330 batting average. The 10 most similar players at that age include Hall of Famers Elmer Flick, Honus Wagner, and Edd Roush. Although the Hall wasn't thought of yet, Lange seemed surely on track to join it.

But he gave it all up for love.

William Alexander Lange was born June 6, 1871, in San Francisco, California, the seventh of eight children of Mary Kortz and Charles Lange, a career Army man. Bill became a big man for the era, growing to 6'1½" and 215 pounds. He became well-known as an amateur and semi-pro ballplayer on the west coast, and turned pro just after his 20th birthday. A right-handed batter and thrower, Lange played for Seattle and Oakland in 1891–92, performing at pitcher, catcher, infield, and outfield,[1] and batting a combined .294 with 75 stolen bases and 113 runs in 146 games.

Big Bill Lange joined the Chicago White Stockings in 1893. He soon drew attention as a fan favorite, and an all-around player who could fill in at any position, hit for good average and power, and traverse the bases like a runaway train. Lange finished fifth in the league in stolen bases as a sophomore, then ranked second in both 1895 and '96 and first in '97, amassing 290 steals in that four-year span (though players could get credit for SB by taking extra bases on teammates' hits).

Lange had his best all-around season in 1895, batting a hefty .389, and finishing in the league's top five in home runs, slugging and on-base percentage. (He would have had another homer, except for a curious scoring practice of the time. On August 27, Lange hit a ball out of the park for a walk-off victory, but since the winning run scored from third base, he was credited with only a single.[2]) Lange helped Chicago to its first winning record since 1891. From 1895–97, he scored 353 runs in 363 games, batting .352 with 46 triples.

Finding his home in center field, Lange was rated as an excellent defender, often ranking among the league leaders in range factor and double plays. One play in particular was talked about for decades afterward. With Chicago clinging to a 6–5 lead, Washington put two men on base with one out in the bottom of the ninth inning. Kip Selbach then drove a ball to the deepest part of the park. Lange raced back at full speed, speared the ball, and crashed through the fence, yet was able to throw the ball in and double off baserunner Jake Boyd, spectacularly ending the Chicago victory. Though some "scholarly" sources dismiss this tale as apocryphal, it appears to have occurred on July 28, 1895. An unidentified contemporary account of the "recent" event says, "Lange gave one glance, whirled and sprinted for the fence, head down and racing as only he could. At the last instant as the ball was going over his head Lange leaped, stuck up both hands and clutched the ball. In the effort he turned a complete somersault and his 210 pounds of bone and muscle crashed upside down against the fence. One entire panel was (torn) down, and Lange rolled out

---

1. "W. A. Lange." *New York Clipper*, March 24, 1894.
2. Bucek, Jeanine, editorial director. *The Baseball Encyclopedia*. New York: Macmillan, 1996, p. 3020.

of the park."³ According to *The Sporting Life*, "A low throw from centre by Lange, doubling up Boyd at third, closed the game and was a great piece of fielding."⁴

Somewhere along the line, Lange picked up the nickname "Little Eva," presumably based on a character in *Uncle Tom's Cabin* and a subsequent children's book. The nickname possibly referred to Lange's graceful play and/or his strutting persona.

Upon the departure of Cap Anson after the 1897 season, Lange was tabbed as team captain, with Tom Burns taking over as manager. But Lange's leadership tenure was short-lived, as he suffered through an injury-plagued season featuring training violations and disputes with management.

At his San Francisco home during the winter of 1898–99, Lange fell in love with 21-year-old Grace Anna Giselman, the only daughter of a wealthy German-born insurance and real estate tycoon. William Giselman had no respect for Lange's profession, but offered to put Big Bill into his business. As that was the only way he could secure Grace's hand in marriage, Lange agreed to retire from baseball after the 1899 season. Lange then became a businessman, and married Grace on April 15, 1900. At 28, his baseball playing career was over.

Lange wound up having played just 813 big league games. Granted, it was during a heavy-hitting era, but consider these 162-game averages: 138 runs, 210 hits, 16 triples, and 80 stolen bases, to go along with his .330 batting average and .400 OBP.

While remaining in the real estate and insurance business (despite severe setbacks caused by the great 1906 San Francisco earthquake), Lange did some west coast scouting for the Reds in 1909–11, and later did the same for the White Sox and Giants.⁵ Among his recommendations were for future MVP Roger Peckinpaugh and future Hall of Famer George Kelly. Lange had the inside track on Kelly, since George was Bill's nephew, son of his sister, Mary.

Unfortunately, Lange's story-book romance ended in divorce in 1915. A second marriage, to Mona Vircum in 1919, was even shorter. Bill finally connected on the 0–2 pitch, marrying Sarah Griffith on September 14, 1924. He became a father for the first time at age 56 when William, Jr., was born on May 23, 1928.⁶ Sarah died in 1948, but Bill, Sr., lived long enough to see his son to join him in the real estate business.⁷

---

3. Unidentified clipping in National Baseball Library file.
4. *The Sporting Life*, August 3, 1895, p. 4.
5. "Is Proud Parent." *The Sporting News*, 1928.
6. *Ibid.*
7. "Big Bill Lange Dies at 79; Swiped 100 Bases in '96." *The Sporting News*, 1950.

The first Hall of Fame elections were held in 1936, including a poll of 78 old-time baseball experts entrusted to choose from among the best nineteenth-century players. But their votes were scattered among 57 players, and no one was named more than 40 times. Lange received six votes, which was good enough to rank tied for 14th. Twelve of the 13 ahead of him eventually made the Hall of Fame, as did 15 of those behind him, including John Clarkson, Hugh Duffy, Kid Nichols, and Dan Brouthers. A decade later, Lange was made ineligible by the 10-year rule, though one could argue that his credentials are better than his Hall of Fame nephew's.

Lange died in San Francisco on July 23, 1950. "I have seen all the other great outfielders—[Tris] Speaker, [Ty] Cobb, [Joe] DiMaggio," said Hall of Famer Clark Griffith, who had been in pro baseball since 1888. "I consider Bill Lange the equal of, if not better than, all outfielders of all time. There wasn't anything he couldn't do."[8]

Year	Team (League)	G	AB	R	H	2B	3B	HR	RBI	SB	AVG	OBP	SLG
1893	Chicago (NL)	117	469	92	132	8	7	8	88	47	.281	.358	.380
1894		113	449	86	146	17	9	6	91	66	.325	.401	.443
1895		123	478	120	186	27	16	10	98	67	.389	.456	.575
1896		122	469	114	153	21	16	4	92	84	.326	.414	.465
1897		118	479	119	163	24	14	5	83	*73	.340	.406	.480
1898		113	442	79	141	16	11	5	69	22	.319	.377	.439
1899		107	416	81	135	21	7	1	58	41	.325	.382	.416
Totals		813	3202	691	1056	134	80	39	579	400	.330	.400	.458

8. Ibid.

Buddy Lewis

On June 2, 1941, the Senators' Buddy Lewis notched his one thousandth major league hit. He became just the fourth player ever to reach that milestone before his 25th birthday, joining Ty Cobb, Fred Lindstrom, and Mel Ott. In the three-quarters of a century since, only Al Kaline and Robin Yount have been added to the list:

Youngest Players to Get 1000 Hits, 1876–2020

Player	Date of Birth	Date of Hit	Age (Yr.-Mo.)
Ty Cobb	12/18/1886	5/13/1911	24-4
Mel Ott	3/2/1909	8/4/1933	24-5
Al Kaline	12/19/1934	8/11/1959	24-7
Fred Lindstrom	11/21/1905	7/31/1930	24-8
Buddy Lewis	8/10/1916	6/2/1941	24-9
Robin Yount	9/16/1955	8/16/1980	24-11

Of the six players, only Lewis did not make it to the Baseball Hall of Fame.

John Kelly Lewis, Jr., was born August 10, 1916, in Gastonia, North Carolina, the fifth of six children, and the only boy of the bunch. John, Sr., was a "truck farmer."[1]

Johnny earned his athletic reputation in American Legion baseball starting in 1929. In 1932 and '33, he led his team to the North Carolina state championship. In the latter year Lewis caught the attention of a friend of Bill Terry's, who recommended the youngster to the Giants' player-manager. Lewis wound up spending several weeks working out with the Giants in 1934, and promised Terry he would sign with the team if they would pay for his college. Terry turned him down.[2]

Upon graduating from Lowell (North Carolina) High School, Lewis passed the entrance exam for West Point, but opted to go to college instead.[3] He spent a year at Wake Forest, then turned pro with the Chattanooga Lookouts, a Washington Senators farm team in the strong Southern Association. Lewis batted .333 in 10 games in 1934, and .303 with 60 extra-base hits in 154 games the following year. Though he had just turned 19, he earned a call-up to the big leagues on September 10. Lewis got into eight games, and would never return to the minors.

Lewis, a 6'1", 175-pound third baseman, had the misfortune of joining a mediocre team in a cavernous ballpark. In his 11 seasons with the Senators, only twice would they win as many games as they lost. Washington's Griffith Stadium was a poor hitters' park; while Lewis would post a solid .452 career slugging percentage in road stadiums, he would slug just .387 with but 17 of his 71 home runs in Washington.

Called "Buddy," supposedly after his mentor, Senators veteran infielder

---

1. Cunningham, Bill. "Local Boy Makes Good." *Collier's*, September 12, 1936, p. 16.
2. Edwards, Henry P. American League Service Bureau press release, December 27, 1936.
3. Cobbledick, Gordon. "Lewis Threatens to Join Long List of Nats' Stars Bought at Bargain Prices." Unidentified news clipping, May 21, 1936.

Buddy Myer[4] (though there is evidence he was called that before he even made the majors), Lewis was a teen-aged sensation in his first full season. Six weeks into the campaign, he was batting .388, and noted writer Shirley Povich proclaimed him as "bracketed with the Yankees' Joe DiMaggio as the prize rookie of the 1936 season."[5] Lewis naturally cooled off, yet finished the year at .291 with 100 runs scored—impressive for a kid not old enough to vote, playing in a pitchers' park.

Over the following years, Lewis settled in as the Senators' #2 or #3 hitter. Between 1937–40, he averaged 104 runs, 191 hits, 32 doubles, 10 triples, and a .311 average each season. Buddy received MVP votes in 1937 and '38, was an All-Star in '38, and led the AL with 16 triples in '39. He also became known as the best bunter in the league.

A lefty batter and righty thrower, Lewis was not regarded as a great-fielding third sacker, as he led the league in errors in 1936 and '38. But he had above-average range factors, topping the AL in that category, along with assists and double plays, in 1938. Nevertheless, he was converted into an outfielder in 1940 at the order of team owner Clark Griffith.[6] A year later, management planned to return Lewis to third base, but he declined, saying he thought his staying in the garden was best for himself and the team.[7] Buddy became one of the best in the league at his new position, leading AL right fielders in assists in each of his four full seasons there, and in range factor twice.

Lewis turned 25 late in the 1941 season. While he was already a very good player, he was on track to become a great one as he entered his prime athletic years. At the same age, the two most similar players to Lewis are Hall of Famers George Davis and Fred Lindstrom, with Al Kaline and Sam Crawford also in the top 10.

But world events took Lewis on a different path. In the spring of 1941, with the country's entrance into World War II appearing imminent, and his being classified as A1 for the draft, Lewis secretly began flying lessons under the name John Kelly.[8] After getting two deferments from the draft (as sole support of his parents) during the season, Lewis applied for the U.S. Army Air Corps. He was inducted on November 17, 1941, and passed examinations for a flying cadetship two months later, becoming the first major leaguer to become a military flier.

Unlike many prominent players in military service at that time, Lewis

---

4. Schudel, Matt. "Baseball Star of '30s and '40s Also Served as WWII Pilot." *Washington Post*, February 27, 2011, p. C7.
5. Povich, Shirley. "This Morning..." *Washington Post*, May 20, 1936.
6. Smith, Jack. "Lewis, Forced into OF, Takes Liking to Job." *New York Daily News*, April 21, 1940.
7. Daniel, Dan. "Daniel's Dope." *New York World Telegram*, January 30, 1941.
8. Povich, Shirley. "This Morning." *Washington Post*, January 23, 1945, p. 10.

did not seek or receive a cushy stateside position of playing ball to entertain the troops. He became a prolific pilot, completing 368 missions in a C-47 plane over "The Hump," a treacherous journey above the Himalayas and enemy territory between China, Burma, and India, to transport troops and supplies. Lewis was promoted from corporal to first lieutenant to captain. He earned the Distinguished Flying Cross in 1944, along with the Air Medal with Oak Leaf Cluster and a unit citation. Lewis spent nearly four years in the service, not returning to the Senators' lineup until July 27, 1945. He was approaching his 29th birthday, but looked and seemed older. Lewis had put on 15 pounds and his hair color had turned. As noted scribe Dan Daniel wrote, "He came back into baseball an old man, gray and wizened."[9]

"When I came back from the war," Lewis recalled decades later, "my whole philosophy of life was completely different. I had changed so much that baseball didn't mean as much to me as it did before the war.... It changed me."[10]

Lewis hit .333 in 69 games in 1945, had a solid season in '46, and enjoyed a good first half in '47, batting over .300 into the summer and earning selection to the All-Star team. But slowed by a hip injury on the field and distracted by business problems off it, he sunk to .261 by season's end. "[T]here were complications in my auto business," Lewis explained. "I had to buy out my partner, and found myself the sole owner of the agency. I couldn't keep my mind on baseball."[11] Lewis voluntarily retired from the game on March 26, 1948, devoting full-time to the prosperous auto dealership in his hometown of Gastonia. He had exactly 1500 hits in 5004 at bats at that point, giving him a rounded-off .300 average.

After a year away from the field, Lewis attempted a comeback. He was reinstated on December 29, 1948, and signed a $16,000 contract with the Senators.[12] But Buddy had a disappointing season, dropping his career average below .300, and was offered a pay-cut to $10,000 for the following year. Instead, he retired for good on February 25, 1950. "One of the reasons I quit was because of night baseball," Lewis said about baseball's growing trend. "The damp night air gave me breathing problems."[13]

Lewis returned to his auto business, and married Frances Oates in 1951. They would have three children, daughters Kelly and Carol Lee, and son John Michael. Buddy returned to his American Legion roots, serving

---

9. Daniel, Dan. "Daniel's Dope." *New York World Telegram*, March 4, 1948.
10. Van Blair, Rick. "Buddy Lewis: His Dream Came True, but War Cut it Short." *Sports Collectors Digest*, July 31, 1992, p. 202.
11. Povich, Shirley. "Can Buddy Lewis Come Back?" *Baseball Digest*, April 1949, p. 51.
12. Associated Press. "Lewis Wants to Show Nats He's a Bargain at $16,000." March 30, 1949.
13. Van Blair, Rick. "Buddy Lewis: His Dream Came True, but War Cut it Short." *Sports Collectors Digest*, July 31, 1992, p. 201.

as coach and athletic officer in the program.[14] He was elected to the North Carolina American Legion Baseball Hall of Fame in 1967, and the North Carolina Sports Hall of Fame in 1976.[15]

Buddy Lewis died of cancer at age 94 on February 18, 2011.

Year	Team (League)	G	AB	R	H	2B	3B	HR	RBI	SB	AVG	OBP	SLG
1935	Washington (AL)	8	28	0	3	0	0	0	2	0	.107	.107	.107
1936		143	601	100	175	21	13	6	67	6	.291	.347	.399
1937		156	668	107	210	32	6	10	79	11	.314	.367	.425
1938		151	656	122	194	35	9	12	91	17	.296	.354	.431
1939		140	536	87	171	23	*16	10	75	10	.319	.402	.478
1940		148	600	101	190	38	10	6	63	15	.317	.393	.443
1941		149	569	97	169	29	11	9	72	10	.297	.386	.434
1945		69	258	42	86	14	7	2	37	1	.333	.423	.465
1946		150	582	82	170	28	13	7	45	5	.292	.359	.421
1947		140	506	67	132	15	4	6	48	6	.261	.330	.342
1949		95	257	25	63	14	4	3	28	2	.245	.355	.366
Totals		1349	5261	830	1563	249	93	71	607	83	.297	.368	.420

---

14. Patrick, Neale. "Player-to-Coach Road with Lewis." *The Sporting News*, July 20, 1963.
15. Rosen, Byron. "Penny for Your Thoughts Can Help Olympic Program." *Washington Post*, February 21, 1976.

Jim Maloney

Entering the 1970 season at age 29, Jim Maloney had a career record of 134–80 (.626) with a 3.08 ERA and 1585 strikeouts in 1802 innings. The most similar pitcher at the same age was Sandy Koufax, with fellow-Cooperstonians Steve Carlton, Fergie Jenkins, Greg Maddux, and Jim Palmer also among the 10 closest comps.

But Maloney would not win another major league game.

James William Maloney was born June 2, 1940, at Fresno, California, the first child of Earl and Marjorie Kickashear Maloney. Daughter Jeanne would follow. Jim attended Heaton Grammar and Hamilton Junior High School in Fresno.[1] He played Little League and American Legion baseball,

---

1. Player questionnaire on file at National Baseball Library.

and starred for the Fresno High School Warriors for three years. Mostly playing shortstop—future big leaguer Dick Ellsworth was the team's star pitcher—Maloney batted .500 and slugged .927 in 96 at bats as a senior. During two of his rare pitching appearances, Maloney struck out 25 batters in a nine-inning game and 16 in a seven-inning contest.[2]

After graduating from Fresno High (where he also played football and basketball) in 1958, Maloney started on an athletic scholarship at the University of California at Berkeley, then transferred to Fresno City College at mid-term. Joining the baseball team there, he hurled 19 consecutive hitless, scoreless innings. Soon after, Cincinnati Reds scout Bobby Mattick—who had previously inked Frank Robinson and Vada Pinson—signed Maloney to a bonus contract reported at $100,000. The *Fresno Bee* claimed that Maloney had "been hounded by major league scouts from the 16 teams in the National and American Leagues for two years." Said Mattick, "Without a doubt, Jim is the finest pitching prospect on the west coast."[3]

Maloney began his pro career in 1959 with Topeka of the Class-B Three-I League. Using a blazing fastball and little else, he was just 6–7 with a 4.50 ERA, but struck out 131 in 124 innings. Moving up to the AA Southern Association the next year, Jim went 14–5 with a 2.79 ERA for Nashville, leading the league in win percentage (.737) for a team which was 51–77 otherwise. The Reds called up the 20-year-old, and he made his big league debut on July 27.

Maloney struggled against big league hitters in 1960 and '61 (4.49 ERA). He made a brief appearance in the 1961 World Series, but was pounded there, too. A week later, on October 15, Jim married Carolyn Ruth Dougherty, whom he had met on a blind date in Topeka.[4] They would have two daughters, Jami and Sharon, and a son, Jason.[5]

Maloney was sent back down to the minors in 1962, but after going 4–1 with a 2.20 ERA in Triple-A (San Diego, Pacific Coast League), he earned his way back to The Show. He pitched respectably for the Reds for the rest of the year.

Showing an effective breaking ball and much-improved control, Maloney burst into stardom in 1963: a sizzling 23–7 record, a 2.77 ERA, and 265 strikeouts in 250 innings. He led the NL in strikeouts per nine innings, and was second behind only Sandy Koufax in total K's. On May 21, Maloney tied a major league record with eight consecutive whiffs, part of a 16-K

---

2. Meehan, Tom. "Jim Maloney Signs Cincinnati Pact for Reported $100,000." *Fresno Bee*, 1959, p. 18-A.
3. *Ibid.*
4. McHugh, Roy. "Square Deal Maloney of the Reds." *SPORT*, December 1963, p. 68.
5. Hertzel, Bob. "Maloney on Walker: 'Let Him Talk.'" *Cincinnati Enquirer*, May 2, 1969, p. 33.

performance (just two shy of the modern record at that time) against the Braves. But despite his expanding pitch selection, it was his speed which had people talking. "He was faster than anyone I've seen this season," said Hank Aaron. "Faster than Sandy Koufax."[6] Koufax later agreed, calling Maloney "consistently the hardest thrower in the National League."[7] The 6'2", 210-pound right-hander was clocked at 99.5 mph at one point. If that doesn't impress in comparison with some of today's flamethrowers, consider this: before the 1970s, only three pitchers ever were officially timed at more than 95.5 mph; Hall of Famers Walter Johnson (99.7) and Bob Feller (98.6) were the other two.[8]

On September 2, Maloney notched his 20th victory of the season—on the same day that his former high school teammate, Dick Ellsworth, did the same for the Cubs. The two were inducted into the Fresno County Athletic Hall of Fame on November 13.[9]

Maloney pitched even better in 1964, though his record didn't quite show it (at one point, he was 3–7 despite a 2.41 ERA). While the league ERA went up by .25 runs, his dropped to 2.71. Then came arguably his best season. In 1965, Maloney posted his lowest ERA (2.54) while pitching his most innings (255), won 20 for the second time, earned All-Star selection, and authored two of the most remarkable single-game pitching performances of all time.

On June 14, Maloney pitched no-hit, no-run ball against the Mets for nine innings. Unfortunately, his teammates didn't score, either. The tenth inning was the same story; by this time, Maloney had retired 27 straight batters. Finally, the Mets broke through with two hits, including a solo home run, in the eleventh to win, 1–0. Maloney finished with 18 strikeouts, one walk, and a heartbreaking loss.

Barely two months later, on August 19 against the Cubs, Maloney again pitched no-hit ball for 10 innings. This time he emerged a 1–0 winner, fanning 12, walking 10, and throwing 187 pitches.[10] As with the first gem, this one earned Jim a $1,000 raise on the spot.[11] Maloney was long listed as one of just five pitchers to throw two no-hitters in one season, until a 1991 "statistical accuracy committee" threw out the first one on the grounds that it didn't wind up as a no-hitter.

---

6. Lawson, Earl. "Maloney Masters Bender, Rates as Red Ace." *The Sporting News*, June 8, 1963, p. 7.
7. "Sandy Tabs Maloney Fastest." *The Sporting News*, August 28, 1965.
8. Reichler, Joseph, editor. *The Great All-Time Baseball Record Book*. New York: Macmillan 1981, p. 232.
9. "Fresno Honors Maloney and Ellsworth." *The Sporting News*, November 30, 1963.
10. Lawson, Earl. "Life's a Comedy to Reds' No-Hit Flash Maloney." *The Sporting News*, September 4, 1965, p. 5.
11. Associated Press. "No-Hitter by Maloney Brings 2d $1,000 Raise." August 20, 1965.

Maloney set a goal to reach a $100,000 salary but, despite frequent holdouts, never came close. Maloney's salary was reported at $32,000 in 1965, $46,000 in '66, and $60,000 in '67 and '68, and his contract squabbles did not enamor him with Reds management or even their fans.

From 1966–68, Maloney battled chronic shoulder pain (a 1969 article said he had suffered from "an on-and-off sore arm since 1961"[12]) and some leg woes. Though his numbers were down a bit, he finished in the league's top 10 in wins each year, and tied for the NL lead in shutouts in '66.

On April 30, 1969, Maloney hurled another no-hit game, fanning 13 in a 10–0 shutout of the Astros. His no-nos were not flukes. In five of his seven qualifying seasons, he finished among the NL's top five in fewest hits allowed per nine innings, and his lifetime rate of 7.39 ranks 29th all-time. Besides the three no-hitters, Maloney tossed five complete one-hit games and nine two-hitters.[13] His NL record for low-hit games (complete games allowing fewer than two hits) still stood into the 21st century. Jim also had two games (April 18, 1964, and August 16, 1967) in which he was replaced in the seventh inning without having surrendered a hit. "Jim Maloney was virtually unhittable," said the Dodgers' Wes Parker. "Stuff-wise, he was right up there with anybody you could talk about."[14]

But Maloney's arm troubles were getting worse, sidelining him for much of May through July, and limiting him to just 179 innings for the season. "He's too muscular," said Reds trainer Bill Cooper. "Instead of stretching his muscles when he pitches, he rips them. That was okay when he was younger, and the muscles healed quickly. But at 29–30 they don't heal so fast anymore."[15]

Maloney did well when he pitched (.706 win percentage, 2.77 ERA), but he didn't pitch enough to satisfy management. "Listen," said manager Dave Bristol, "if a guy's arm is really sore he won't even be able to throw the ball. Right? If he can throw it up to the plate and get somebody out, then it can't be that sore, so he's gotta stay in there."[16] Sheldon Bender, Reds director of player personnel, said, "We have to get some way to get him out to the mound and make him realize he's going to have to pitch with pain."[17] According to Maloney, Reds GM "Bob Howsam said my pain threshold was low, and that Bob Gibson would pitch on one leg if he had to."[18] Practically

---

12. Jordan, Pat. "The Trials of Jim Maloney." *SPORT*, November 1969, p. 38.
13. Associated Press. "Reds Trade Maloney to Angels for Garrett." December 15, 1970.
14. Telephone interview with Wes Parker, May 17, 2020.
15. Jordan, Pat. "The Trials of Jim Maloney." *SPORT*, November 1969, p. 39.
16. *Ibid.*, p. 41.
17. "Maloney Spurns Reds." Unidentified clipping in National Baseball Library file, February 24, 1970.
18. Ford, Bill. "Former Red Maloney Longs for Return to Baseball." *Cincinnati Enquirer*, December 13, 1986.

shamed into playing, Maloney returned to the rotation and underwent regular cortisone shots to numb the pain. His reward? A pay-cut for 1970.

In the seven seasons from 1963 to 1969, Maloney had a 117–60 record (.661), 1375 strikeouts, and a 2.90 ERA. Over that span, he was third in the major leagues in wins and win percentage, and sixth in strikeouts. Unfortunately, Maloney was overshadowed by three all-time greats whose best years coincided with his, and who also pitched in the National League: Hall of Famers Sandy Koufax, Juan Marichal, and Bob Gibson.

On April 16, 1970—in his second start of the season—Maloney batted in the bottom of the third inning against the Dodgers. He was a decent hitter throughout his career, batting .201 with seven home runs. This time, Maloney grounded to the shortstop, but never made it to first base. As he broke from the batters' box, he heard something pop in his left ankle, and had to be helped from the field. The next day, Maloney underwent surgery for a ruptured Achilles tendon.[19] The Reds wound up winning the game, 12–2. Ironically, it was the first career victory for Don Gullett, featured in another chapter of this book.

It was not the first time Maloney had trouble with the lower half of his body, nor would it be the last. He suffered a puffed right knee in 1966, and later developed a problem with his left heel.[20] In 1969, he injured his groin running the bases during his no-hitter.[21]

Maloney was out of action until September, and unable to get anyone out when he returned. The Reds went to the World Series, but he was not on the post-season roster. Maloney was traded to the California Angels on December 15, 1970, but pitched just 30 ineffective innings for them in 1971 between injuries, including a rib cage problem and pulls of both hamstring muscles.[22] Ironically, after the constant arm problems, it turned out to be leg woes which effectively ended his career.

The Angels unconditionally released Maloney on January 3, 1972, and he signed with the St. Louis Cardinals the next day.[23] But the Cards also released him, on April 4—just before the season started.[24]

Maloney hooked on with Phoenix of the Pacific Coast League. He seemed to be getting back on track, posting a 5–1 record and 2.61 ERA. But when the trading deadline came and went with no call back to the

---

19. Associated Press. "Surgery Puts Maloney Out at Least 8 Weeks." April 17, 1970.
20. Ford, Bill. "Former Red Maloney Longs for Return to Baseball." *Cincinnati Enquirer*, December 13, 1986.
21. Hertzel, Bob. "Maloney on Walker: 'Let Him Talk.'" *Cincinnati Enquirer*, May 2, 1969, p. 33.
22. Lovelace, Jerry. St. Louis National Baseball Club press release, January 4, 1972.
23. *Ibid.*
24. Lovelace, Jerry. St. Louis National Baseball Club press release, April 4, 1972.

majors, Maloney announced his retirement on June 15.[25] He had just turned 32.

Maloney joined his father in the used-car business in his hometown. Jim returned to baseball in 1981 as pitching coach for the Giants' Fresno franchise in the California League, then managed the team to a last-place finish the following year before being replaced.[26] At 42, he even pitched one game for the team, but was knocked out in the second inning. Maloney went through alcoholism and divorce before getting his life back together. He now lives in Fresno with his second wife, Lyn.

In 1973, Maloney was elected to the Cincinnati Reds' Hall of Fame on his first try.[27] His attempts at the National Baseball Hall of Fame were not as successful. Maloney got two votes each in 1978 and '79 before being dropped from the ballot.

Year	Team (League)	G	IP	W	L	PCT	SO	BB	H	ERA
1960	Cincinnati (NL)	11	63.2	2	6	.250	48	37	61	4.66
1961		27	94.2	6	7	.462	57	59	86	4.37
1962		22	115.1	9	7	.563	105	66	90	3.51
1963		33	250.1	23	7	.767	265	88	183	2.77
1964		31	216.0	15	10	.600	214	83	175	2.71
1965		33	255.1	20	9	.690	244	110	189	2.54
1966		32	224.2	16	8	.667	216	90	174	2.80
1967		30	196.1	15	11	.577	153	72	181	3.25
1968		33	207.0	16	10	.615	181	80	183	3.61
1969		30	178.2	12	5	.706	102	86	135	2.77
1970		7	16.2	0	1	.000	7	15	26	11.34
1971	California (AL)	13	30.1	0	3	.000	13	24	35	5.04
Totals		302	1949.0	134	84	.615	1605	810	1518	3.19

---

25. "Phoenix—End of the Line for Maloney, McCormick." *The Sporting News*, July 1, 1972.
26. Ford, Bill. "Former Red Maloney Longs for Return to Baseball." *Cincinnati Enquirer*, December 13, 1986.
27. Ferguson, Jim. "Maloney in Reds' Hall of Fame." Cincinnati Reds News Release, August 2, 1973.

Carlos May

Carlos May was having a great rookie season. Through August 8, 1969, May had played in 100 games with 18 home runs and 62 runs batted in.

Projected for 162 games, that would be 29 homers and 100 RBI—good for any first-year-player, but even more impressive because May played his home games in cavernous old Comiskey Park. In the team's 68-year history, no White Sox *player*, let alone rookie, had ever hit more than 29 home runs in a season.

But May's dreams of the Rookie of the Year Award, and a long successful career, were literally shot down.

Carlos May was born May 17, 1948, in Birmingham, Alabama, the son of Tommy and Mildred May. They had four children, but one died at birth and another in early childhood. Tommy left the family when Carlos was little and was not a factor in his life.[1]

Carlos's brother, Lee—older by five years—would become a top-flight power-hitter in the major leagues, yet Carlos seemed destine to outshine Lee in the athletic department. Overcoming rheumatic fever which caused a heart murmur,[2] Carlos starred in football and baseball at A.H. Parker High School in Birmingham, including a .735 batting average as a sophomore.[3] He had just turned 18 when he was picked by the Chicago White Sox in the very first round of the 1966 amateur draft.

May—among his odd nicknames was Wally Gator[4]—began his pro career that year with the Sarasota White Sox of the Gulf Coast (Rookie) League. After batting .426 in 16 games, he finished the season with the Winter Haven Sun Sox of the Class-A Florida State League, slipping to .153 in 37 games. After the season, he briefly attended Southern University.[5]

May really showed his hitting talent over the next two seasons in the minors. Displaying good strike zone judgment and hitting line drives to all fields, the lefty swinger batted .338 for the Appleton Foxes of the Midwest League in 1967, and .330 for the Lynchburg White Sox of the Carolina League in '68 (with slugging percentages of .589 and .516). May won the circuit's batting title in the latter season, and had the highest mark in his league in '67 as well, although he fell short of the plate-appearance requirement, missing the last month of the season due to service in the U.S. Marine Corps.[6] Though he was still just in A-ball, the White Sox called him up to the majors for a trial in September 1968. He never returned to the minors.

On February 8, 1969, May married Margaret Hubbard, a gal he had

---

1. Telephone interview with Carlos May, November 21, 2015.
2. *The Sporting News*, June 29, 1974.
3. Munzel, Edgar. "Boycott Opened Chisox Door for Rookie Picker May." *The Sporting News*, March 8, 1969.
4. Player questionnaire on file at National Baseball Library.
5. *Ibid*.
6. Holtzman, Jerome. "Carlos Could be Big Kick in Chisox Future." *The Sporting News*, November 4, 1967.

met in Lynchburg.⁷ The two would adopt a 25-day-old boy, Luis, on August 26, 1970.⁸ They would later have a daughter, Elizabeth, who was born with brain damage and died at age three on August 10, 1976.⁹ The Mays would divorce in 1975.

Carlos made the White Sox' opening day lineup in 1969, and quickly proved he had a big league bat. The muscular outfielder had two two-homer games in his first five contests of the season. Besides power, May showed plate discipline, hustle, and speed, despite his stocky (six feet, 215 pounds) build. White Sox' manager Don Gutteridge said, "He really loves to hit. In that respect he reminds me of Ted Williams." Coach Tony Cuccinello added that "He walks up there swinging and he has power in any direction. A little more experience and he'll stand up there with the best of them."[10]

By July 16, May had 18 round-trippers and seemed a good bet to break the team record of 29 held by Gus Zernial and Eddie Robinson. May made the All-Star team—as did his brother, Lee of the Reds. Though Lee was five years older, he was just two years removed from his rookie season, and 1969 marked his first All-Star selection, too.

Through August 8, Carlos was batting .281 for the season. More impressively, he had an on-base percentage of .385 and a slugging mark of .488 (compared to the AL averages of .246, .321, and .369, respectively). But, those turned out to be his final numbers for the season.

May went to Camp Pendleton, California, for a short stint with the Marine Corps reserves. During maneuvers at 1:45 p.m. on August 11, he was using a five-foot-long tool to swab the tube of an 81 mm mortar, which he mistakenly assumed to be unloaded. The device pushed the unexploded shell into the firing pin, ejecting the tool with such force that the top half of May's right thumb was ripped off.[11] The missing digit from his throwing hand was never found. May also suffered lacerations of his left thumb and minor powder burns on his face.[12] The Marines officially ruled the loss a 50 percent disability, and early reports speculated that May's baseball career was over.[13] "The thumb is by far the most important finger on a person's hand," explained Dr. Claude Lambert, professor of orthopedic surgery at

---

7. Munzel, Edgar. "Boycott Opened Chisox Door for Rookie Picker May." *The Sporting News*, March 8, 1969.
8. *The Sporting News*, September 12, 1970.
9. *The Sporting News*, August 7, 1976, p. 49.
10. Rumill, Ed. "'He Reminds Me of Ted Williams.'" *Christian Science Monitor*, June 18, 1969.
11. Holtzman, Jerome. "Injured May Seen Resuming Career." *The Sporting News*, August 30, 1969.
12. "White Sox Rookie May Hurt in Marine Training." *The Sporting News*, August 23, 1969.
13. Munzel, Edgar. "May Tests Thumb, Eyeing Chisox First Base Job." *The Sporting News*, February 13, 1971.

the University of Illinois Medical School. Lambert suggested that two artificial thumbs, one for batting and one for throwing, might be the only hope for May to resume his pro career.[14] "It's a tragic blow because this boy had such a bright future," said Sox' manager Gutteridge. "Mainly, though, we should be thankful that he's alive."[15]

May quickly dismissed such talk. "I'll be playing baseball again," he said at an August 14 press conference. "I love the game. I figure I'll have to cut down on my stroke a little bit. And I will have to change my grip to control throws. But I'll play again."[16]

Missing the last eight weeks of the season cost May the AL Rookie of the Year Award. The Royals' Lou Piniella (135 games, 11 homers, 68 RBI, .282) took the honor with nine of a possible 24 votes, outpolling Red Sox' pitcher Mike Nagy (6), May (5), and Angels reliever Ken Tatum (4). May did win *The Sporting News*'s Rookie Player of the Year Award, though, matching brother Lee's 1967 honor.[17]

May's second surgery was on November 5, a 3½-hour skin graft procedure at the Veterans' Hospital in Long Beach, California. More skin graft operations followed over the next year. In between, May practiced swinging and throwing, helped by his wife.[18]

Against all odds, May joined the White Sox for spring training in 1970. On his first swing of the bat, he ripped his stub of a thumb open. Keeping the digit bandaged, he tore it again and again until the skin toughened, but showed he could still play.[19] Amazingly, May wound up leading the White Sox with 150 games played in '70. He also gained some trivia immortality by taking uniform #17. With his surname above the numeral on his home uni, Carlos had his birthday on his back: MAY 17.

Due to the handicap, May says "I had to change my game."[20] Instead of a slugger, he became more of a spray-hitter, batting for good average but not much power. New White Sox' manager Chuck Tanner predicted that May would win a batting title. Carlos came close, finishing seventh in the league in batting in 1971, and fourth—just 10 points behind champion Rod Carew—in '72. May earned his second All-Star selection that year, posting the

---

14. Nightingale, Dave. "Surgeon Sees a Possibility of Artificial Thumbs for May." *Springfield* (Mass.) *Daily News*, August 20, 1969, p. 55.
15. "Carlos' Only Chance: Go Lefty." *Binghamton* (N.Y.) *Evening Press*, August 12, 1969, p. 2-B.
16. Holtzman, Jerome. "Injured May Seen Resuming Career." *The Sporting News*, August 30, 1969.
17. Henkey, Ben. "Prize-Winning Rookies: May and Nagy in A.L.—Griffin, Laboy in N.L." *The Sporting News*, November 8, 1969, p.34.
18. Holtzman, Jerome. "No Maybes about Carlos, He's Okay." *The Sporting News*, November 22, 1969.
19. Associated Press. "Chisox' May Tests Blasted Thumb." February 24, 1970.
20. Telephone interview with Carlos May, November 21, 2015.

second-best on-base percentage (.405) in the AL, and also finishing among the league's top 10 in runs, hits, total bases, walks, and even stolen bases.

But the positions he played—left field, first base and, later, designated hitter—are generally reserved for power-hitters, and May no longer fit the bill: he averaged just nine home runs per season over the last eight years of his career. As May's batting averages fell over the subsequent years, he no longer was perceived to have much value as a major league player, and saw less and less playing time. "I was put on the shelf," he says.[21]

Meanwhile, brother Lee kept rolling on, becoming one of the majors' premier sluggers. From 1969–77, he averaged 29 home runs and 100 RBI per year; only Hall of Famer Johnny Bench topped him in both categories over that span. Lee finished his 18-year career in 1982, having amassed 354 homers.

Carlos was traded to the New York Yankees on May 18, 1976, enabling him to get his only taste of post-season play that fall. He was sold to the California Angels on September 16, 1977, and finished that season with just 47 hits. Though May had not yet reached his 30th birthday, it was clear that his big league days were drawing to a close.

May signed a $100,000-per-year contract with the Nanshai Hawks on February 2, 1978,[22] and wound up playing four seasons in Japan. In 415 games, he batted .308 with 70 home runs, so he evidently still had something left in the tank.

May returned to the United States and embarked on a 29-year career with the U.S. Postal Service. He lives near Chicago in Matteson, Illinois, with his wife of more than 40 years, the former Rosemary Brussard.[23] His great-nephew, Jacob May—Lee's grandson—played with the White Sox in 2017.

It seems obvious that May's 1969 injury not only altered his career, but shortened it. Besides losing grip strength and bat control due to the missing thumb, he acknowledges that he experienced numbness in the hand. Is it possible that Carlos would have enjoyed as long and successful career as brother Lee—or even better—if not for the injury? "I don't know about *that*," Carlos modestly says.[24]

Year	Team (League)	G	AB	R	H	2B	3B	HR	RBI	SB	AVG	OBP	SLG
1968	Chicago (AL)	17	67	4	12	1	0	0	1	0	.179	.214	.194
1969		100	367	62	103	18	2	18	62	1	.281	.385	.488

---

21. *Ibid.*
22. Associated Press. "Carlos May Signs with Japan Club." February 3, 1978.
23. Telephone interview with Carlos May, November 21, 2015.
24. *Ibid.*

Year	Team (League)	G	AB	R	H	2B	3B	HR	RBI	SB	AVG	OBP	SLG
1970	Chicago (AL)	150	555	83	158	18	4	12	68	12	.285	.373	.414
1971		141	500	64	147	21	7	7	70	16	.294	.375	.406
1972		148	523	83	161	26	3	12	68	23	.308	.405	.438
1973		149	553	62	148	20	0	20	96	8	.268	.334	.412
1974		149	551	66	137	19	2	8	58	8	.249	.306	.334
1975		128	454	55	123	19	2	8	53	12	.271	.373	.374
1976	Chi.-N.Y. (AL)	107	351	45	91	13	2	3	43	5	.259	.344	.333
1977	N.Y.-Calif. (AL)	76	199	21	47	7	1	2	17	0	.236	.311	.312
Totals		1165	4120	545	1127	172	23	90	536	85	.274	.357	.392

Austin McHenry

In early 1922, *The Sporting News* was calling 26-year-old Austin McHenry "one of the game's greatest hitters." But by the end of that year, they were reporting his death.

Austin Bush McHenry was born September 22, 1895, in or near Wrightsville (contemporary sources say Stout), Ohio, the first of two children (daughter Alice followed) of Dr. Oscar E. and Hannah M. Jones McHenry.[1]

Austin began his pro baseball career with Portsmouth of the Ohio State League in 1915. After batting .301 in parts of two seasons, the 5'11", 165-pound outfielder was sold to Milwaukee of the American Association on July 10, 1916, thus moving from the lowest level of the minor leagues to the highest. On July 24, 1917, McHenry was optioned to Peoria.[2] It was there that he suffered an injury which contemporary observers believed led to his early demise. "McHenry was beaned in a game in Peoria," said one report. "[T]hat blow eventually led to his death and cut short one of the most brilliant careers in the history of baseball. A tumor developed from the blow and ended in the sad death of the hard-hitting outfielder."[3]

At one point, McHenry's contract was sold to the Cincinnati Reds, but

---

1. Certificate of Death, Austin B. McHenry.
2. Unidentified clipping in National Baseball Library file, 1921.
3. Unidentified clipping in National Baseball Library file, 1934.

after suffering a broken nose before the 1918 season started, he was returned to Milwaukee. Batting .306 for Milwaukee with a league-leading five home runs in the first 44 games of the campaign, McHenry was traded to the St. Louis Cardinals for three players on June 3,[4] and made his big league debut 19 days later. From then on, he was the team's regular left fielder.

McHenry showed improvement each year, and his team followed suit. In 1920, his 10 home runs were good enough for fourth place in the National League. The Reds and Giants reportedly made offers for his services.

McHenry blossomed at age 25 in 1921, ranking third in the league in batting (.350), second in slugging, fifth in hits and doubles, fourth in home runs, and third in total bases and RBI. The right-handed batter and thrower also excelled in the field, topping NL left fielders in putouts and range factor. Though he was overshadowed by teammate Rogers Hornsby, the game's experts recognized the youngster's value. "McHenry is without question one of the game's greatest outfielders," reported *The Sporting News*. "And he is one of the game's greatest hitters.... (H)e is one of the longest drivers in baseball."[5]

An anonymous St. Louis newspaper, discussing the top NL players, was even more glowing: "[W]hile all admitted the superiority, presently, of Rogers Hornsby, Austin McHenry was the unanimous runner-up choice for 1922.... He is always in top shape. A veritable ballhawk in the field, and a terror at bat, 'Mac,' because of his clean life, seems destined to enjoy many more years of activity in the Big League.... Add to his mechanical ability a wonderfully even disposition and a real love of the game, a popularity with his teammates exceeded by none, and you have in 'Ole Aus' McHenry, one of the most valuable players in the National League, or any other league."[6]

Though the Cardinals played in hitter-friendly Sportsman's Park starting in July 1920, McHenry hit 21 of his 34 career home runs in road parks. He also batted .308 and slugged .461 on the road, as compared to .296 and .434 at home.

McHenry seemed to be on his way to another strong season in 1922. He was batting .326 and slugging .495 in mid–June, but started to slump both at bat and in the field. Something was wrong. *The Sporting News* said he was suffering "complications following the flu."[7] Cardinals manager Branch Rickey recalled McHenry having trouble with fly balls, and asking the outfielder if he felt well. "Yes, I feel all right," responded McHenry, "but I can't see. I don't know what it is. Maybe I'm going blind."[8] McHenry played

---

4. Unidentified clipping in National Baseball Library file, 1921.
5. "Dimmed by Others' Glare." *The Sporting News*, January 14, 1922.
6. "Interesting Facts about Interesting People..." Unidentified clipping in National Baseball Library file, 1965.
7. *The Sporting News*, August 3, 1922, p. 9.
8. "Rickey Tells Pitiful Story about M'Henry." *The Sporting News*, December 7, 1922.

only two games after June 26, finishing the season with a .303 average. The Cardinals, leading the pennant race in mid-summer, wound up tied for third place. Discussing the factors which led to this outcome, Rickey said, "McHenry's absence I think was the most disastrous."

Doctors were at first baffled, but surgery in Cincinnati revealed glioma of the brain.[9] McHenry died at his Jefferson Township, Ohio, home on November 27, 1922, with his wife Ethel, five-year-old daughter Leone, and three-year-old son, Bush, Jr., at his bedside.[10]

Year	Team (League)	G	AB	R	H	2B	3B	HR	RBI	SB	AVG	OBP	SLG
1918	St. Louis (NL)	80	272	32	71	12	6	1	29	8	.261	.319	.360
1919		110	371	41	106	19	11	1	47	7	.286	.322	.404
1920		137	504	66	142	19	11	10	65	8	.282	.316	.423
1921		152	574	92	201	37	8	17	102	10	.350	.393	.531
1922		64	238	31	72	18	3	5	43	2	.303	.344	.466
Totals		543	1959	262	592	105	39	34	286	35	.302	.343	.448

9. Certificate of Death, Austin B. McHenry.
10. "Rickey Tells Pitiful Story about M'Henry." *The Sporting News*, December 7, 1922.

Denny McLain

At age 25, Denny McLain already owned a 114–57 career won-lost record, including an incredible 55–15 mark in the previous two seasons. But he would go just 17–34 the rest of his career.

Dennis Dale McLain was born March 29, 1944, in Chicago, Illinois, the son of Tom and Betty McLain. Brother Timothy followed in 1946. The family lived in the Chicago suburb of Markham. Denny idolized his father, an insurance adjuster, a drunk, and a harsh disciplinarian who started him in baseball and organ-playing. When Tom had a fatal heart attack two days after his 37th birthday, 15-year-old Denny was devastated, and his strained relationship with his mother (a Polish Jew who remarried just seven months later) grew worse.[1] Tom's death also contributed to a fatalistic out-

1. Condon, David. "The Day Denny McLain Pitched His $100,000 Game." *Chicago Tribune Magazine*, October 27, 1968, p. 29.

look for Denny. "My grandfather died young," he would say in 1968. "My dad died young. I will die young. I haven't much time to make my mark."[2]

Denny became a pitching prodigy at a young age, starring in scholastic and league (Little, Connie Mack, Babe Ruth, and various other organized leagues) baseball. After going 38–7 as a scholarship student for Mt. Carmel High School in Chicago, he eschewed college scholarship offers to sign for a bonus estimated between $17,000 and $25,000 with his hometown White Sox on June 11, 1962.[3] Denny started his pro career with Harlan, Kentucky, of the Class-D Appalachian League.

McLain didn't wait long to make a splash. In his first professional game on June 28, he fired a no-hitter and struck out 17 to beat Salem, 3–0. His next time out, the 6'1", 190-pound, bespectacled righty fanned 15 but lost on two unearned runs. McLain then moved to the Midwest League, where he struck out 93 in 91 innings but posted a mediocre 4–7 won-lost record. More concerning to the White Sox was that McLain thought he was above club rules, often disappearing from the team for days at a time.

In the spring of 1963, the White Sox were ordered by Commissioner Ford Frick to part with one of their bonus pitchers. They matched McLain against Bruce Howard in an intra-squad game to determine which of the two would stay. Howard's team won, 2–1, and McLain wound up going to the Tigers for the $8,000 waiver price.[4] Howard would go on to post a 26–31 lifetime record in the majors.

Joining the Class-A Northern League, McLain went 13–2 to lead the league in winning percentage (.867). Moving up to AA in the South Atlantic League, he recorded a 5–4 log, leading to his first taste of the major leagues at age 19. McLain started three of the Tigers' last eight games of the season, going 2–1 for a season-long pro record of 20–7 with 261 strikeouts.

McLain homered in his major league debut on September 21, but it proved to be a fluke. He would never hit another four-bagger in his 616-at bat career, batting just .133, though he would lead the AL in sacrifice hits in 1968 and '69. McLain would become a decent fielder, however, topping AL pitchers in fielding percentage in 1966 and '71, and in putouts in 1968 and '71, and starting a triple play on September 1, 1968.[5]

On October 5, 1963, McLain eloped to New Buffalo, Michigan, with Sharon (who spelled her name "Sharyn" for much of her life) Alice Boudreau, daughter of former AL MVP and future Hall of Famer Lou

---

2. Dexter, Dave, Jr. *Playback* (c. 1972), p. 203.
3. Unidentified clipping in National Baseball Library file.
4. Condon, David. "The Day Denny McLain Pitched His $100,000 Game." *Chicago Tribune Magazine*, October 27, 1968, p. 29, 31.
5. "Just Instinct, Says McLain of His Role in Triple Play." *The Sporting News*, September 14, 1968.

Boudreau.[6] There are various colorful stories about how the two met, but the consensus is that they had known each other throughout their teen years. They would have a daughter, Kristin, in 1965, followed by two miscarriages which the McLains attributed to the strain of watching Denny play.[7] They then would adopt two children, Dennis Louis and Timothy Edward, before daughter Michelle joined the family in 1972.

After he went 3-1 with a 1.53 ERA for the AAA Syracuse Chiefs in 1964, Denny was called up to the Tigers to stay. He served as a spot starter that year and for the first part of the next season. After a slow start (1-3, 4.35 through June 11, 1965), McLain arrived. On June 15, he struck out 14 batters—including a record-tying seven straight—in a six-plus inning relief appearance. He joined the team's regular rotation and wound up 16-6, finishing among the league leaders in wins, percentage, strikeouts, and ERA (2.61). McLain had reached the majors with little more than a blazing fastball, but by then Tigers manager Chuck Dressen had taught him an effective curve and coach Johnny Sain had added a slider. Still, McLain preferred to challenge hitters with fast ones thrown at different angles, making him prone to the long-ball; he would lead the AL in homers allowed in three straight seasons.

Denny's brother, also a right-handed pitcher, made his pro debut in 1965. But Tim's career would be over the following year, even though he went 7-2 with a 1.77 ERA. He later became an assistant manager in one of Denny's various enterprises.[8]

McLain started the 1966 All-Star Game, pitching three perfect innings and striking out future Hall of Famers Willie Mays, Hank Aaron, and Joe Torre. Despite a rocky second half (including a 229-pitch outing on August 29), Denny notched his first 20-win season, finishing second in the league. He was well on his way to another in '67, winning his 17th game on August 29, but—as the Tigers battled unsuccessfully for the pennant—was winless in five starts thereafter, also missing 12 days in September with a mysterious injury. McLain suffered two dislocated toes in what he claimed was a household accident. Teammates thought he suffered the injury kicking a water cooler after getting knocked out of the box; later, rumors surfaced that the injury was caused by gamblers to whom he owed money.

McLain's ability to win ballgames caused team officials to overlook his personal failings and eccentricities. Denny was cocky, often rude, earning the nickname "Mighty Mouth." He was known to blast management and

---

6. Condon, David. "The Day Denny McLain Pitched His $100,000 Game." *Chicago Tribune Magazine*, October 27, 1968, p. 29.

7. Associated Press. "McLain to Quit Baseball if his Wife Loses Child." July 26, 1969.

8. McWhirter, Glenna. "McLain a Very Big Man in Market Place, Too." *The Sporting News*, August 23, 1969.

fans, even the city of Detroit. McLain gambled heavily on sports, drank up to a case of Pepsi Cola a day, and bowled hundreds of games a week in the off-season (he said it made his legs and pitching arm stronger). He took up flying, and played the electric organ at Las Vegas nightclubs. McLain participated in various questionable business ventures and get-rich-quick schemes, spending money faster than he earned it, yet not always paying his bills. "When you can do it out there between the white lines, you can live any way you want to," said McLain. "I like to travel fast and always go first class."[9]

"The problem was that for Denny, having it made was never good enough," recalled publicist Mert Silbar, who briefly represented McLain. "He had to have more, whether more was good stuff or bad stuff."[10] Teammate Mickey Lolich later reflected of McLain, "He was always trying to make a fast buck. He thought he was a high roller. He liked to buy things; the only trouble was he always forgot to pay for them."[11]

McLain entered the 1968 season with new contact lenses, and a new attitude. "I just know I'll have a good year," he said. "I can feel it. I've got to prove something to some people."[12]

After starting the campaign with two no-decisions, McLain earned his first win on April 21, and kept winning from there. By mid-season he had racked up a 15–2 record and there was talk of his becoming the first 30-game winner in the major leagues since Dizzy Dean in 1934. McLain kept rolling along, winning his 20th game on July 27 and his 25th (against just three losses) on August 16.

"I've seen the great ones," said Tigers teammate Eddie Mathews, who played with Warren Spahn for 13 seasons, and batted for years against the likes of Bob Gibson, Juan Marichal, and Sandy Koufax. "But no one pitches as effortlessly as Denny."[13] Pitching coach Sain agreed. "With his easy pitching motion, I don't know why he can't be a good pitcher forever," Sain said.[14]

But no matter how easy one's motion, pitching 336 innings at age 24 is bound to strain his body. "I've got a torn muscle in back of my shoulder and that's giving me a lotta pain," said McLain in mid–August.[15] No one paid

---

9. McLain, Denny, with Eli Zaret. *I Told You I Wasn't Perfect*. Chicago: Triumph Books, 2007, p. 91.
10. *Chicago Tribune*, July 12, 1985, Section 4, p. 1.
11. Kram, Mark. "The Dark Side of a Loser." *Inside Sports*, October 1984.
12. Spoelstra, Watson. "Contact Lenses Give Denny Rose-Color View of '68 Tigers." *The Sporting News*, February 10, 1968.
13. Condon, David. "The Day Denny McLain Pitched His $100,000 Game." *Chicago Tribune Magazine*, October 27, 1968, p. 31.
14. Daley, Arthur. "The Play's the Thing." Baseball Writers' Association of America program, February 2, 1969, p. 63.
15. United Press International. "McLain Has Torn Shoulder Muscle." *Pittsburgh Press*, August 20, 1968.

much attention. He endured 15 cortisone shots for pain in 1968, and would have 24 more in 1969.[16] There were other remedies, too. "[I]n some cases red, white, blue, purple and green pills" were offered by the team, McLain recalls. "And the pills were laying on the training (tables). And to think that doctors were handing them out, (regardless of) all odds and safety; the theme was WIN FOR THE GIPPER."[17]

After suffering two straight losses, McLain started another winning streak. On September 14, with Dean in attendance, Denny won #30 against Oakland. #31 came against the Yankees five days later, despite a grooved pitch to Mickey Mantle for the Hall of Famer's next-to-last career homer. Although he had a loss and no-decision in his final two starts, McLain finished an amazing 31–6 with 280 strikeouts and a 1.96 ERA, leading the AL in innings, wins (no one else in the league had more than 22), and percentage. Denny struggled in the World Series, losing his first two starts against the Cardinals' Bob Gibson, but won Game Six on two days' rest to help the Tigers to the world championship.

After the season, McLain was heaped with honors. He won the AL Cy Young Award unanimously. He also won the AL MVP Award unanimously, the first pitcher to do so. McLain was named the Associated Press's Male Athlete of the Year, *The Sporting News*'s Man of the Year, and winner of the Sid Mercer and Walter Johnson Awards, among others. McLain's salary increased to $72,000 (he also would receive over $62,000 in endorsements and other income).[18] To put that into perspective, at the time only seven major leaguers earned as much as $100,000 per year.[19]

After the season, dubbed the "Year of the Pitcher," rules-makers made some changes to lessen the advantages of hurlers. The strike zone was shrunk vertically by about eight inches, and the mound was lowered from 15 inches high to 10. McLain predicted the latter change would particularly affect his job. "If they lower the mound, they'll shorten the careers of pitchers quite a bit," he said.[20] A 1985 article indicates that this prediction came true for McLain: "Shifting much of the drive for his pitches from legs to arm, he soon was straining, pulling and finally severing tendons. Today, he has little range of arm motion above his shoulder."[21]

The new rules had the desired effect: the AL ERA leapt from 2.98 to

---

16. Coffey, Wayne. "Breakfast at Denny's." *New York Daily News*, April 6, 2008, p. 83.
17. Denny McLain Facebook post, August 8, 2014.
18. Popa, Robert A. "Plea of Bankruptcy is Filed by McLain." *New York Daily News*, June 10, 1970.
19. Spoelstra, Watson. "Denny Nabs $65,000 Pact; Says, It's What I Wanted.'" *The Sporting News*, December 14, 1968.
20. Ogle, Jim. "Lowering Mound Would Cut Careers, McLain Contends." *The Sporting News*, December 14, 1968.
21. *Chicago Tribune*, July 12, 1985, Section 4, p. 1.

3.62 in 1969. But McLain was still at the top of the heap, going 24–9 for a team 19 games out of first place, and again leading the league in games started, innings (325), and victories, along with shutouts (9). He and Baltimore's Mike Cuellar tied for the league's Cy Young Award. At the end of the season, McLain signed a reported $100,000 contract for 1970, beating out 17-year veteran Al Kaline as the first Tiger ever to reach that milestone.[22] The seven most similar pitchers to McLain through age 25 include Hall of Famers Dean, Bob Feller, and Don Drysdale (but also disappointments featured in this book: Dwight Gooden, Joe Wood, Vida Blue, and Don Gullett). Denny McLain was on top of the baseball world.

But not for long.

Following an investigation, on February 19, 1970, Commissioner Bowie Kuhn suspended McLain from all organized baseball activities. It was due to his admitted 1967 involvement in a Flint, Michigan, sports bookmaking operation. Kuhn said McLain's "conduct was not in the best interests of baseball." He would not be paid during the suspension, was not to return to the diamond before July, and could not even work out with the team.[23] Then, on June 9, McLain filed for bankruptcy, listing more than $400,000 in debts, but barely $400 in liquid assets.[24]

McLain returned to high expectations on July 1, but he just didn't have it. By the time the season ended, he had earned two more suspensions and gone just 3–5 with a 4.63 ERA. "My concentration was destroyed by the suspensions," McLain said years later. "It never came back."[25] On October 9, after a psychiatric report recommended a "change of location," McLain was traded to the Washington Senators in an eight-player deal.[26] Expressing happiness with the change, McLain signed another $100,000 pact on January 26, 1971.[27]

But Denny endured a horrid 22-loss season, and was dealt to the Oakland A's for two minor league pitchers on March 4, 1972. Faring no better there, he was sent down to Birmingham of the AA Southern League in May, after he refused Oakland owner Charlie Finley's $25,000 buy-out offer.[28] On June 29, McLain went to the Braves in a convoluted swap for another downtrodden former MVP, Orlando Cepeda. By the end of the year, McLain had posted a woeful 6.37 ERA in the majors and 6.32 in the minors.

---

22. Spoelstra, Watson. "McLain First Tiger 100-Grand Player." *The Sporting News*, October 18, 1969.
23. Durso, Joseph. "For McLains—a Reprieve and a Lesson." *New York Times*, April 2, 1970.
24. Popa, Robert A. "Plea of Bankruptcy is Filed by McLain." *New York Daily News*, June 10, 1970.
25. *Chicago Tribune*, July 12, 1985, Section 4, p. 1.
26. Lipsyte, Robert. "In a Nutshell." *New York Times*, October 10, 1970.
27. Associated Press. "McLain Signs Pact with the Senators at $100,000 Salary." January 26, 1971.
28. *The Sporting News*, August 5, 1972.

McLain signed with the Iowa Oaks (American Association) on April 23, 1973, claiming he was pain-free and ready to work his way back to the majors, but he still had nothing. "There is no comparison to what he was in his prime with Detroit," said Indianapolis Indians slugger Andy Kosco, who had played in the AL between 1965 and 1968. "He's just throwing it up there, right across."[29] McLain said, "I probably throw just as hard as always. The ball just doesn't go as fast."[30] On July 9, McLain was sent down to the AA Texas League. For the year, he struggled to a 5.20 ERA over 116 innings, and his pro baseball career was over at age 29.

While McLain and others offered all kinds of explanations for his precipitous fall from glory, the overriding factor was that his arm was overused at a young age and paid the price. "I believe I had a partially torn rotator cuff for several years, but there was no surgery available for it," McLain reflected in 2007. "Besides the cortisone every few weeks, it was rubdowns, pills for pain, greenies, and Contac. By '68, there was never a time I pitched without some pain."[31] McLain filed a worker's compensation suit against the Tigers and other former teams, claiming they damaged his pitching arm beyond repair. In 1977, he was awarded a mere $31,500 in an out-of-court settlement.

McLain became an Iowa Oaks play-by-play announcer for KBAB radio in 1975, then signed on later that year as vice president and general manager of the Memphis Blues of the International League. Both jobs ended badly and by September 1976 he was out of baseball entirely. McLain resumed bouncing around from one questionable enterprise and short-lived job to another, getting sued by someone just about every year, with many personal setbacks along the way. In 1977, he filed for bankruptcy again. In 1979, his uninsured Florida home—including his baseball awards—burnt to the ground. In 1981, McLain suffered a heart attack. Sharon declared bankruptcy in 1983. Their daughter Kristin was killed by a drunk driver in 1992.

McLain hit bottom in 1985 when he was jailed on charges of racketeering, conspiracy, extortion, and possession with intent to distribute cocaine, among other things. Despite a 23-year sentence, due to a procedural error, he wound up being released in 1988. But he returned to prison in 1997 on new charges of embezzlement, money laundering, mail fraud, and conspiracy. During the six years Denny spent in prison this time, Sharon divorced him, but they were remarried on October 18, 2003. Denny had undergone intensive therapy while in prison, and claimed a new self-awareness.

McLain's weight had ballooned to over 350 pounds before he had bariatric surgery in 2014, helping him lose 156 of them. He said he did it to help

---

29. *The Sporting News*, June 23, 1973.
30. Associated Press. "Denny McLain Takes Another Step ... Back." July 11, 1973.
31. McLain, Denny, with Eli Zaret. *I Told You I Wasn't Perfect*. Chicago: Triumph Books, 2007, p. 118

in the care of Sharon, who has Parkinson's disease. "I am down 24 pants sizes," Denny said. "I'm seeing things now I forgot I had!"[32] Now in his 70s, McLain lives in Brighton, Michigan, and focuses on his family, including five grandchildren.

McLain, having pitched in 10 seasons, technically is eligible for the Hall of Fame. But he got a total of just six votes over three BBWAA elections before being dropped from the ballot. He remains the last 30-game winner in major league history.

"I am the poster child of why they take better care of pitchers today," McLain says. "They could abuse us back then. We had no control over our destiny. If you didn't go out there and pitch ... you were going to Toledo or worse, and you would lose your job."[33]

I met Denny McLain in Cooperstown while I was working on this book. He had to lift his right arm with his left in order to shake my hand.

Year	Team (League)	G	IP	W	L	PCT	SO	BB	H	ERA
1963	Detroit (AL)	3	21.0	2	1	.667	22	16	20	4.29
1964		19	100.0	4	5	.444	70	37	84	4.05
1965		33	220.1	16	6	.727	192	62	174	2.61
1966		38	264.1	20	14	.588	192	104	205	3.92
1967		37	235.0	17	16	.515	161	73	209	3.79
1968		41	*336.0	*31	6	*.838	280	63	241	1.96
1969		42	*325.0	*24	9	.727	181	67	*288	2.80
1970		14	91.1	3	5	.375	52	28	100	4.63
1971	Washington (AL)	33	216.2	10	*22	.313	103	72	233	4.28
1972	Oakland (AL)–Atlanta (NL)	20	76.1	4	7	.364	29	26	92	6.37
Totals		280	1886.0	131	91	.590	1282	548	1646	3.39

32. "Ex-Detroit Tigers Pitcher Denny McLain: I've Lost over 150 Pounds." *Detroit Free Press*, March 4, 2014.
33. Dow, Bill. "Denny McLain Recalls His 31-Victory Season in 1968." *Baseball Digest*, September/October 2013, p. 41.

Don Newcombe

Don Newcombe's major league career was delayed up to four years by the color of his skin. It was interrupted by two full years of military service.

And it was shortened by alcoholism. Yet Newcombe's peak and career won-lost records of 27–7 and 149–90 compare with those of Hall of Famers Dizzy Dean (30–7, 150–83) and Sandy Koufax (27–9, 165–87).

Donald Newcombe was born June 14, 1926, in Madison, New Jersey, son of Sadie Sayers and chauffeur James Roland Newcombe. Don was named after his maternal uncle, Donald Sayers, and joined older brother Roland, Jr., in the family; brothers Harold and Norman would follow.[1] Don survived a life-threatening battle with pneumonia in his youth.[2] He attended Lafayette Junior High and Jefferson High School in Elizabeth, New Jersey.[3] At 16 Don lied about his age and joined the Army, but they found out and sent him home; he later served in the Navy before World War II was over.[4]

After starring for his school team and the semi-pro Roselle, N.J. Stars, Don turned professional in 1944 with the Newark Eagles of the Negro National League. The right-hander went 1–3 that year, but blossomed to 8–4 (for a 21–17 team) in '45, pitching against the likes of Hall of Famers Josh Gibson, Buck Leonard, Cool Papa Bell, and Roy Campanella. Note that those won-lost records account only for documented league games; many if not most Negro leagues' games were exhibitions and barnstorming affairs against all levels of competition, including white major leaguers. One source says Newcombe's overall records in those two years were 7–6 and 14–4, with each of the four 1945 losses by one run.[5]

Don met a gal named Freddie Green in 1945 and they were married a month later.[6] After a decade of trying to start a family, they would adopt two children, Gregory and Evit.[7]

In the fall of 1945, Brooklyn Dodgers president and general manager Branch Rickey began the bold process of integrating major league baseball. After intensive scouting, the first four African American players he chose to sign were Jackie Robinson, John Wright, Campanella, and Newcombe. Newk debuted for Nashua in the New England League on May 16, 1946, just four weeks after Robinson's historic debut with Montreal of the International League.[8]

Despite being a teenager in an uncomfortable environment,

---

1. Poston, Ted. "The Don Newcombe Story." *New York Post*, June 12, 1955, p. 2M.
2. Cohane, Tim. "Don Newcombe: Next 30-Game Winner?" *Look*, 1950, p. 100.
3. Poston, Ted. "The Don Newcombe Story." *New York Post*, June 12, 1955, p. 2M.
4. Cohane, Tim. "Don Newcombe: Next 30-Game Winner?" *Look*, 1950, p. 100.
5. Gould, Paul. "Negro Hurler Nashua Hero." Unidentified clipping in National Baseball Library files, January, 1947.
6. Poston, Ted. "The Don Newcombe Story." *New York Post*, June 12, 1955, p. 2M.
7. Newcombe, Don, as told to Milton Gross. "I'm No Quitter." *Saturday Evening Post*, March 9, 1957, p. 90.
8. Kleinknecht, Merl. "Integration of Baseball after World War II." *Baseball Research Journal*, 1983, pp. 100–01.

Newcombe excelled from the start. He went 14–4 with a 2.21 ERA in 1946, and 19–6, 2.91 in '47, leading the New England League in wins and strikeouts. Promoted to Montreal in 1948, Newk was just as good, notching a 17–6 record (including a no-hitter vs. Toronto followed by a one-hitter vs. Rochester[9]) and 3.14 ERA. After starting the next IL season 2–2, 2.65, he finally got the call to the majors in late May 1949. He had run up a 52–18 record in the minors, good for a .743 winning percentage.

Obviously, Newcombe had the talent to pitch in the bigs three or four years earlier, but he was held back—why? Researcher Guy Waterman wrote that, in contrast to the articulate and controlled Robinson and the affable Campanella, "Newcombe had neither of these winning qualities. To white ballplayers who had never had to face a black pitcher before, he was perceived as just a big [6'4", 220 pounds] black man who was up to no good out there on the mound. In fact, for a while, Newcombe's promotion to the Major League level was delayed due to fears that he would not prove as tractable as Robinson and Campanella. [Dodgers manager] Burt Shotton, when sending Newcombe back down ... commented, 'I think he can pitch in the majors, but he might undo everything those other fellows have accomplished.' Black reporters charged that 'his habit of popping off' was why Newcombe was being held back."[10]

According to Newcombe, the Dodgers wanted to make him the trailblazer instead of Robinson, but there was too much worry about Newk's temperament. "If I was white, I would already have been called up, but Mr. Rickey said, 'I'm doing this on a stair-step procedure, so keep your mouth shut,'" recalled Newcombe. He acknowledged that it was the right call: "I was too young. The pressure would have killed me.... (I)f I were to throw a ball and hit someone? Oh, man."[11]

Newcombe made his major league debut on May 20, 1949, but gave up hits to four of the five batters he faced. His first start three days later was much more successful: Newk shut out the Reds on five hits and no walks, requiring only 99 pitches. He also impressed with his nimble defense and potent bat, driving in two of the Dodgers' three runs. One reporter described his pitching repertoire: "Newcombe not only has control but he is a 'stuff' pitcher. His fast ball ... is alive and tough to gauge. He has a slider, too, that throws the hitters off balance and his change-up is better than average."[12]

---

9. "Newcombe Traces Sore Arm to Porter." *Brooklyn Eagle*, March 24, 1949, p. 27.
10. Waterman, Guy. "Racial Pioneering on the Mound: Don Newcombe's Social and Psychological Ordeal." *Nine: A Journal of Baseball History and Social Policy Perspectives*, Spring 1992, p. 189.
11. Plaschke, Bill. "The Dodgers' Brooklyn Bridge." *Los Angeles Times*, August 28, 2005.
12. Murray, Arch. "Newcombe's Hitting, Fielding Stand Out." Unidentified clipping in National Baseball Library file, May 23, 1949.

Newcombe went on to an outstanding rookie year. Less than two months after his debut, he was pitching in the All-Star Game. In August and September, Newk hurled three straight shutouts amid a streak of 32 consecutive scoreless innings. Although he pitched in just over four months of the season, he won 17 games, tying for the NL lead with five shutouts and finishing just two strikeouts shy of Warren Spahn's league high in that category. Newcombe also finished in the top five in complete games, innings pitched, wins, percentage, and opposing on-base percentage. In addition he was the top batter (22 hits) and fielder (57 errorless chances) among NL pitchers. Newcombe easily won Rookie of the Year honors, receiving 21 of 24 votes (he got 105 of 116 in an Associated Press poll[13]), and even finished eighth in MVP voting. He was being touted as a possible future 30-game winner.

The Dodgers won the NL pennant, and Newcombe was their pitcher for Game One of the World Series. Newk throttled the Yankees for eight innings, surrendering just four hits and no walks or runs, and fanning 11. But he gave up a home run in the bottom of the ninth to lose, 1–0. Newcombe also lost Game Four as the Yanks steamrolled the Dodgers in five.

Big Don got a raise from $8,000 to $13,000 in 1950, and won 19 games, though he and the Dodgers lost the pennant on the last day of the season. He was even better in 1951, winning 20 and tying for the league lead in strikeouts. But once again, his season ended in October heartbreak. Brooklyn blew a 13½-game lead and wound up in a tie for first place with the New York Giants, necessitating a best-of-three playoff. In the finale Newcombe held a 4–1 lead after eight innings, but ran out of gas in the ninth and gave way to Ralph Branca. We all know the rest.

Just as he was approaching his athletic prime, Newcombe's burgeoning career was suddenly put on hold. He was inducted into the U.S. Army on February 26, 1952, not to be discharged until February 9, 1954. Newcombe was one of the few established major leaguers to miss two entire seasons in military service during the Korean Conflict. He returned not in prime shape, either physically or mentally. "When I got out in 1954, I couldn't get back in the pitching groove all that season," Newcombe recalled.[14] His weight had ballooned to 250 pounds, and he wound up with a mediocre record. But he was poised for a big comeback.

One thing which would help Newcombe in that regard was a new big bat in the lineup—his own. The lefty swinger had been restrained in his hitting ever since an incident in his rookie year. On August 16, 1949,

---

13. Young, Dick. "Newcombe Voted Top Rookie; Card-Dodger Deal Stutters." *New York Daily News*, November 4, 1949, p. 88.

14. Newcombe, Don, as told to Milton Gross. "I'm No Quitter." *Saturday Evening Post*, March 9, 1957, p. 92.

Newk took a big swing and the bat slipped out of his sweaty hands. It flew into the stands, injuring a woman, who sued Newcombe and the Dodgers for $3,000. "So all the years since, he has been fearful of hurting somebody," according to a 1955 article, thus "he checked his tremendous swing." The lady finally settled out of court for $250 that year. With that behind him, Newcombe started using resin to improve his grip, and the results were eye-popping.[15] He had hit for decent average (.245) through 1954, but had only one home run in 343 at bats. But in '55, Newk belted seven homers—still an NL record for pitchers—and hit .359 with a .632 slugging percentage (adding a steal of home for good measure). Over a six-year period encompassing 526 at bats—about the norm for a full-time player in one season—Newcombe would collect 158 hits (including 14 long-balls) for a .300 average. It seems likely he could have made it in the majors as a position-player if his pitching arm wasn't so valuable, and he was often used as a pinch-hitter.

Newcombe had a rocky start to the 1955 season, and then on May 5 was suspended by manager Walt Alston for refusing to pitch batting practice. He returned with a vengeance. On May 10, Newk pitched a near-perfect game against the Cubs. He allowed only one baserunner, Gene Baker, who singled and was caught stealing in the fourth. Newcombe kept rolling along from there, and by the end of July had an 18–1 record; he ran into a stretch of hard luck in August and illness in September, but finished 20–5. He led the NL in win percentage, fewest walks per nine innings, and lowest opposing OBP, and was second in complete games, wins, and ERA. Newcombe earned his fourth All-Star selection, finished seventh in MVP voting, and helped the Dodgers to their first world championship. His salary was raised from $17,500 to $25,000.

On July 9, 1956, by a 14–12 vote, the BBWAA approved a new award to recognize the major leagues' best pitcher each year. Commissioner Ford Frick, troubled by pitchers' lack of support in MVP voting, had spearheaded the creation of the Cy Young Memorial Award.[16] There was speculation as to whom the first honoree might turn out to be, but Don Newcombe—11–5 with a modest 3.51 ERA at that point—wasn't even mentioned. Yet Newk went an amazing 16–2, 2.30 in the second half of the season to become the landslide choice. With a 27–7 log, he won six more games than any other big league pitcher. He was also again best in the NL in win percentage and opposing OBP. Ironically, in light of Frick's concern, Newcombe was also named the league's Most Valuable Player. Until Justin Verlander joined him

---

15. "Suit Settled, Newk Finally Cuts Loose." Unidentified clipping in National Baseball Library file, June 18, 1955.

16. Deane, Bill. *Award Voting*. Kansas City, MO: Society for American Baseball Research, 1988, p. 64.

in 2011, Newk was the only man to win the Rookie of the Year, Cy Young, and MVP Awards during his career. His salary was upped to $30,000 for 1957.

At age 32, Don Newcombe was at the top of his profession. He had a 112–48 career record, good for a .700 win percentage. It is not far-fetched to think he might have had another 100 big league victories by that point, if not for the years he lost to the color line and military service. But his career and life were about to go on a downward spiral.

Newk had suffered arm stiffness in the closing weeks of the '56 season, and strained the limb in his last regular-season outing on September 30. "I didn't tell (Alston) my arm was hurting, which could have been another big mistake," Newcombe revealed weeks later. "It had been sore ever since the last game of the season against Pittsburgh, when I hurt it throwing a curve ball to Lee Walls in the eighth inning [Walls hit a home run, and Newcombe was removed from the game]. But my mind was made up that I wasn't going into (the World Series) complaining."[17] As a result, he was pounded by the Yankees in the Fall Classic, dropping his career World Series record to 0–4, and cementing an unfair reputation as a choker in big games. President Eisenhower even wrote to Newcombe, sympathizing with his "hard luck."[18] After being knocked out of the box for the second time, he was grabbed by a parking lot attendant who questioned his guts. Newk struck the man, leading to an assault suit.[19]

Overcoming elbow trouble in spring training, and finger and back ailments during the season, Newcombe did not pitch badly in 1957. His 3.49 ERA was .39 runs better than the league average, despite pitching his home innings in Brooklyn's band-box, Ebbets Field. Newk led the league in fewest walks per nine innings, and had the NL's third-best opposing OBP. But, based on his 11–12 record, everyone thought he was a flop, and he took a pay-cut after the season.[20]

Newcombe had even more trouble off the field. While driving home on August 21, 1957, he struck and critically injured a four-year-old boy in Linden, New Jersey. Though Newcombe wasn't charged by police, he was sued by the family, eventually to settle out of court two years later. Then, in February 1958, Don and Freddie separated, en route to divorce. To top it off, the Dodgers were moving to Los Angeles for that season, meaning that air travel would become a regular part of the game. Don had had a fear of

---

17. Newcombe, Don, as told to Milton Gross. "I'm No Quitter." *Saturday Evening Post*, March 9, 1957, p. 90.
18. Associated Press. "Ike to Newk: Forget about Hard Luck." November 10, 1956.
19. "Assault Charge is Dismissed, Big Newk Faces $25,000 Suit." *The Sporting News*, November 28, 1956, p. 10.
20. "Newk's Pay Cut." United Press International, December 10, 1957.

flying since witnessing a plane crash in Elizabeth, New Jersey, in 1951. He underwent hypnotism to overcome the fear so he could continue his baseball career.[21] Newcombe said this was also when he started on hard liquor. He had been a big beer-drinker since childhood ("I never drank the night before I pitched, but I drank every other night"), but needed something else to get him through flights. "You can't carry a six-pack on a plane with you," he explained, so "I started to drink whiskey. I'd carry two fifths on the plane." He later admitted that "alcohol shortened my career by at least five or six years."[22] Later in 1958, there was an incident outside a Newark tavern owned by Newcombe and his two brothers; the three were charged with assaulting a police officer on November 25. They ultimately were acquitted in court.[23]

After a predictably poor start in the 1958 season, Newcombe was traded to the Cincinnati Redlegs on June 15, 1958. He made a nice comeback in 1959, leading the NL in fewest walks per nine innings, posting the second-lowest ERA of his career, and going 13–8 for a sub-.500 team (helped by his .364 batting average). In later years he confessed to using a spitball that season. But that was pretty much the end of the trail. Newcombe was sidelined with a thigh injury in spring training, 1960, and was ineffective thereafter, finishing the year with the Indians after a mid-season sale. He spent 1961 in the Pacific Coast League, going 9–8, and then went to Japan for one final season of baseball—but not as a pitcher. Playing first base for the Chunichi Dragons, Newcombe batted .262 with 12 homers in 81 games.

Newcombe had married Billie Roberts immediately after his 1960 divorce. The couple would have three children, Don, Jr., Kelly, and Tony.[24] But by the mid–1960s Don's drinking had gotten out of control and, not coincidentally, his family was in financial ruin. He filed for bankruptcy in 1967.[25] Yet he was more concerned with the potential loss of his wife and young children. "In 1966 (Billie) told me that if I didn't stop drinking, she'd leave," he recalled. "She said she could stand not having any money, but she couldn't stand my drinking, my betting on horses and my carousing. I vowed that day I would never take another drink. I quit cold turkey."[26]

---

21. Klein, Willie. "Newk to Try Hypnotism to Overcome Fear of Flying." *The Sporting News*, November 20, 1957.
22. Coughlin, Dan. "Second Chance Saves Newcombe." *Cleveland Plain Dealer*, January, 1976.
23. "3 Newcombes Freed." *New York Times*, February 3, 1959.
24. Coughlin, Dan. "Second Chance Saves Newcombe." *Cleveland Plain Dealer*, January, 1976.
25. "Newcombe Bankrupt." *The Sporting News*, October 14, 1967.
26. Coughlin, Dan. "Second Chance Saves Newcombe." *Cleveland Plain Dealer*, January, 1976.

Newcombe remained sober for the remaining half-century of his life, and was very public in encouraging other alcoholics to do the same.

After a series of odd jobs, Newcombe returned to baseball in May 1970 as the Dodgers' Director of Community Relations.[27] Soon after, Dodger President Peter O'Malley handed Don an envelope. In it was the 1955 World Series ring he had pawned during his financial crisis, which O'Malley had secretly bought and stashed in a vault. Newcombe broke down and cried.[28] (Years later, Newcombe sold the ring, along with his Rookie of the Year, MVP, and Cy Young trophies, to film-maker Spike Lee.)[29] In 2009, Newk was named special adviser to Dodgers chairman Frank McCourt.[30]

Newcombe received several honors over the years. In 1971, he received KABC Radio's "Distinguished American" award.[31] In 1979, Newcombe followed the likes of Ernie Banks and Roberto Clemente as winner of the Ernie Weld Award as the "figure who has contributed greatly to the overall image of baseball both on and off the field."[32] And in 2007, Newk received the Jackie Robinson Lifetime Achievement Award at the Negro Leagues Baseball Museum's seventh annual Legacy Awards.[33]

Having played 10 big league seasons, Newcombe is eligible for the Hall of Fame. He was on the BBWAA ballot from 1966 to 1980, peaking at 59 votes (15 percent)—more than future Hall of Famer Orlando Cepeda, among others—in his last try. Newk did a bit better in veterans' balloting, with a high of 17 votes (21 percent) in 2007.

What was Newcombe's greatest memory of his long life and colorful career? "It's the day I swore on my four-year-old son's head that I'd never take another drink," he said. "He was scared of me, of the things I was doing. I have him back now. Baseball is a wonderful game but not *that* wonderful."[34]

Don Newcombe died at age 92 on February 19, 2019.

Year	Team (League)	G	IP	W	L	PCT	SO	BB	H	ERA
1949	Brooklyn (NL)	38	244.1	17	8	.680	149	73	223	3.17
1950		40	267.1	19	11	.633	130	75	258	3.70
1951		40	272.0	20	9	.690	*164	91	235	3.28
1954		29	144.1	9	8	.529	82	49	158	4.55

---

27. Los Angeles Dodgers news release, May 17, 1970.
28. Coffey, Wayne. "Fireballers on Firewater." *New York Daily News*, February 6, 1990.
29. Plaschke, Bill. "The Dodgers' Brooklyn Bridge." *Los Angeles Times*, August 28, 2005.
30. Associated Press. "Newcombe Named Special Advisor to Dodgers." March 23, 2009.
31. *The Sporting News*, February 27, 1971.
32. Waterman, Guy. "Racial Pioneering on the Mound: Don Newcombe's Social and Psychological Ordeal." *Nine: A Journal of Baseball History and Social Policy Perspectives*, Spring 1992, p. 193.
33. "A Task That Was Too Important to Fail." *Kansas City Star*, January 25, 2007.
34. Unidentified clipping in National Baseball Library file.

Year	Team (League)	G	IP	W	L	PCT	SO	BB	H	ERA
1955	Brooklyn (NL)	34	233.2	20	5	*.800	143	38	222	3.20
1956		38	268.0	*27	7	*.794	139	46	219	3.06
1957		28	198.2	11	12	.478	90	33	199	3.49
1958	Los Angeles–Cincinnati (NL)	31	167.2	7	13	.350	69	36	212	4.67
1959	Cincinnati (NL)	30	222.0	13	8	.619	100	27	216	3.16
1960	Cincinnati (NL)–Cleveland (AL)	36	136.2	6	9	.400	63	22	160	4.48
Totals		344	2154.2	149	90	.623	1129	490	2102	3.56

Note: As this book was going to press, Major League Baseball announced it would hereafter include the Negro leagues as "official" major leagues. The logistics were still under discussion, and different sources—based on ongoing and incomplete research—often give very different statistics for players in those leagues.

Dave Orr

Dave Orr was one of only four nineteenth-century players to compile a career slugging percentage over .500, but his career was abruptly ended just days after his 31st birthday.

David L. Orr was born September 29, 1859, in New York City, the youngest of four sons of James and Rachel Orr.[1] Dave began his baseball career on local amateur teams, including the Quickstep and Alaska teams of New York.[2]

Orr finally turned pro at age 23 in 1883 with teams in Newark, New Jersey, and Hartford Connecticut, and quickly drew the attention of the major leagues. Before the year was out, he had appeared in one game for the New York Gothams of the National League, and 13 for the New York Metropolitans of the American Association. He clinched his spot with the Mets on September 27–28, when he collected a single, double, two triples, and two home runs in a pair of games against Columbus.[3]

---

1. Smith, James D., III. "Orr, David L." In *Biographical Dictionary of American Sports: Baseball.*
2. "David Orr." *New York Clipper,* June 14, 1884.
3. *Ibid.*

At a time when the average player weighed about 170 pounds, Orr was a behemoth at 5'11" and 250. A right-handed batter and thrower, Orr played mostly first base, though he took an occasional turn in the outfield and even in the pitcher's box.

Orr was the Mets' regular first sacker in 1884, leading the team to the A.A. pennant and the first World's Series. As a rookie, Orr led topped the league in hits, total bases, RBI, and batting (.354), also finishing third in doubles, home runs, and slugging, and missing the Triple Crown by just two homers.

Orr also made news off the field that year. After a huge train wreck near Poughkeepsie, New York, in December, Orr freed a trapped child and carried him to safety.[4] Orr was a popular, easy-going guy, but not afraid to use his brute strength when a situation called for it.

Orr continued his heavy hitting in 1885. On June 12, he went 6-for-6 with two singles, two doubles, a triple, and a home run. In those days most parks were either spacious or not enclosed, so high triples totals were usually an indicator of a top slugger. Orr had 21 of them to top the A.A., also leading in slugging percentage and finishing among the top five in hits, doubles, homers, total bases, RBI, and batting.

In 1886, Orr amassed the amazing total of 31 triples. No one else in the league had more than 17, and only one player in major league history—Owen Wilson with 36 in 1912—ever surpassed that mark; Wilson had the advantages of batting left-handed

Dave Orr (1887) was one of the biggest and best sluggers of the 19th century. Library of Congress.

---

4. Smith, James D., III. "David L. Orr." *Nineteenth Century Stars*. Kansas City, MO: Society for American Baseball Research, 1989, p. 100.

and playing 16 more games. Orr also led in slugging, hits, and total bases, becoming the first man to reach 300 in a season. And he finished second in homers, fourth in RBI, and third in batting.

The 1887 season was a rough one for Orr. On April 27 he had a violent collision with teammate Pete Sommers while chasing a foul ball, breaking two teeth, almost slicing his tongue in two, and suffering bruises to his left knee and chest[5]; Orr was out for 13 days. He missed another 10 days after a leg injury on June 3, the same day he began an eight-game stint as interim manager following Bob Ferguson's firing.[6] On August 19, already nursing a sore hand, Dave got into a scuffle with a law clerk trying to serve divorce papers to his landlady (Orr would be acquitted of assault in October). The two men tumbled down a flight of stairs, with Orr suffering a broken arm and thumb and a sprained ankle; except for two games, he would not play again until October, and evidently could not swing a bat properly when he returned. He was batting an even .400 (and that's not counting walks as hits, as they did that year) through August 14, but went just 5-for-40 the rest of the season to slip to .368, still third in the league.

Remaining in the American Association after the Mets folded, Orr moved to Brooklyn in 1888 and Columbus in '89. He finished in the league's top five in batting in both years (in fact, he did so in each of the seven full seasons he played). In '89 Orr also finished second in the league in hits and fifth in total bases.

Orr moved to the newly-formed Players' League for 1890. In June he suffered two broken ribs when hit by a pitched ball; he tried playing through the pain for a while, but finally took a 20-day break when threatened with erysipelas.[7] But he hit as well as ever upon his return, finishing second in the league in RBI and batting and fourth in slugging. On October 4, the season finale, he went 2-for-4, including a triple, to complete one of his best years. Despite missing 26 games, Orr set career highs for RBI, batting average (.371), and on-base percentage. This gave him a lifetime averages of .342 (batting) and .502 (slugging) at age 31, with 162-game averages of 110 runs, 230 hits, 41 doubles, 22 triples, and 128 RBI (admittedly in a lesser league). The most similar player to Orr at that point was legendary slugger Dan Brouthers, with four other Hall of Famers also in the top 10.

According to Brouthers, "The greatest hitter that ever played ball was old Dave Orr. He didn't care whether they were over the plate or not. If they were within reach of that big bat of his he would hit them out, and when he hit them there was no telling whether they would be found again or not. I

---

5. *The Sporting Life*, May 11, 1887.
6. *The Sporting Life*, June 8, 1887.
7. *The Sporting Life*, July 12, 1890

have always held that Dave Orr was the strongest and best hitter that ever played ball."[8]

Three days after his final big league game, Orr's team was in Renovo, Pennsylvania, to play an exhibition contest, when he "was stricken ... with paralysis of the left side."[9] Early reports were hopeful of a quick recovery, but Orr was bedridden for months following the debilitating stroke, and would never play again. Having played in just eight seasons, he is not eligible for the Hall of Fame.

Orr recovered enough to find other employment, and even had some baseball jobs late in his life. He was a caretaker when Brooklyn's Ebbets Field was being built prior to the 1913 season, and was put in charge of the press box for the Brooklyn Federal League team of 1914–15.

At age 55 on June 3, 1915, Dave Orr died at the home of his niece in Long Island, New York.[10] His wife, Emily, had died nine years earlier; the couple had no children.

Year	Team (League)	G	AB	R	H	2B	3B	HR	RBI	SB	AVG	OBP	SLG
1883	New York (NL)-New York (AA)	14	53	6	16	4	3	2	11		.302	.302	.604
1884	New York (AA)	110	458	82	*162	32	13	9	*112		*.354	.362	.539
1885		107	444	76	152	29	*21	6	77		.342	.358	*.543
1886		136	571	93	*193	25	*31	7	91	16	.338	.363	*.527
1887		84	345	63	127	25	10	2	66	17	.368	.408	.516
1888	Brooklyn (AA)	99	394	57	120	20	5	1	59	11	.305	.330	.388
1889	Columbus (AA)	134	560	70	183	31	12	4	87	12	.327	.340	.446
1890	Brooklyn (PL)	107	464	89	172	32	13	6	124	10	.371	.414	.534
Totals		791	3289	536	1125	198	108	37	627		.342	.366	.502

8. *The Sporting Life*, September 22, 1894, p. 6.
9. *The Sporting Life*, October 18, 1890, p. 4.
10. "Dave Orr, Famous Ball Player, Dies." Unidentified clipping in National Baseball Library file.

Mark Prior

In 2003, Mark Prior led National League pitchers in the Sabermetric measures of WAR (7.4), Pitcher Wins (5.1), and Fielding-Independent Pitching (2.47). Having just turned 23, his future seemed limitless.

Except for one other, ominous measure he led the league in: most pitches per start.

Mark William Prior was born September 7, 1980, in San Diego, California, the youngest of three children of Jerry and Millie Prior (the oldest two were named after the parents). Mark starred in baseball and basketball at University of San Diego High School, but decided to give up hoops in his senior year to concentrate on his sport of choice. He led his team to the state championship with a 0.93 ERA, earned All-America selection, and attracted attention from pro scouts. Prior was drafted by the New York Yankees as the 43rd pick of the 1998 draft, but opted for college instead.

Prior spent one year at Vanderbilt before transferring to the University of Southern California. He grew into a 6'5", 225-pound righty with a rare combination of blazing stuff and pinpoint control. Mark had a mid-to-high-90s fastball and a snapping curve, and added an effective changeup. He pitched for the USA National Team in 1999 and 2000. As a junior in 2001, Prior led USC to the College World Series with some phenomenal numbers: 138.2 innings, a 15–1 record, 202 strikeouts, just 18 walks, and a 1.69 ERA. Prior earned the USA Baseball Golden Spikes Award, the Dick Howser Award, the R.E. Smith College Player of the Year Award, and the *Baseball America* and *Sporting News* College Player of the Year Awards. In June, the Cubs made Mark the #2 selection in the amateur draft, behind only Twins catcher and future MVP Joe Mauer, and signed Prior to a four-year, $10.5 million contract (a record not broken until Stephen Strasburg came along in 2009). "He is the most complete, polished pitcher ever to come out of the draft," said long-time pitching coach Tom House, who had worked independently with Prior in high school. Asked when Prior would be ready for the majors, House said "Two months ago."[1]

Prior was a few classes short of graduating, but he would make them up and earn his degree in business administration from USC on May 14, 2004.[2] He began his pro career in 2002 in the minors, but that lasted only nine games. After he went 5–2 with a 2.29 ERA and 79 strikeouts in just 51 innings (not to mention three homers in 19 at bats), the Cubs called him up. In his big league debut on May 22, Prior beat the Pirates, striking out 10 in six innings. By the end of the season, though he didn't pitch in September (strained left hamstring while running the bases), he was 6–6 for a 67–95 team, with an average of 11.34 strikeouts per nine innings. Among rookies with at least 100 innings pitched, only two—Kerry Wood (12.58) and Dwight Gooden (11.39)—had ever had a higher ratio. Prior's combined

---

1. Kurkjian, Tim. "Prior Destined for Greatness." ESPN.com, March 29, 2003.
2. Klein, Gary. "Prior Gets New Cap, and Gown to Match." *Los Angeles Times*, May 15, 2004.

major and minor league stats included 226 K's and 56 walks in 168 innings. Said ESPN's Tim Kurkjian, "there's little doubt that he's a future Cy Young Award winner."[3]

Prior should have won it in 2003. Despite missing 24 days (bruised right shoulder suffered in a July 11 basepath collision with Atlanta's Marcus Giles), he put together a brilliant campaign, leading the Cubs to a surprising divisional title. Prior rolled up an 18–6 record (the rest of the team was 70–68) with 245 strikeouts and just 50 walks in 211 innings. Despite pitching his home games in the friendly confines of Wrigley Field, he posted a 2.43 ERA, third in the league (he led the NL in road ERA at 2.08). Prior was chosen to the NL All-Star team, and voted the National League's Pitcher of the Month for both August and September. Besides the Sabermetric accomplishments mentioned earlier, he finished second in the NL in wins, percentage, and strikeouts. But voters gave the Cy Young to Eric Gagne, a juiced reliever who pitched just 82 innings. Prior finished third there, and ninth in MVP voting.

Prior continued his success into the post-season, with a two-hit, complete game victory over Greg Maddux and the Braves in the NLDS, and a Game Two win over the Marlins in the NLCS. But it all unraveled in Game Six, the "Bartman Game." Prior and the Cubs held a 3–0 lead in the eighth inning and were five outs away from the World Series. But fan Steve Bartman deflected a foul ball that Cubs left fielder Moises Alou seemed poised to catch, and the Cubs went into meltdown mode. Florida erupted for eight runs to win the game, and took the Series the next day.

The better Prior pitched, the more manager Dusty Baker let him pitch. On September 1, the 22-year-old Prior threw 131 pitches. Five days later, he tossed another 129. In Prior's last three regular-season starts, the counts were 124, 131, and 133, giving him a season average of 113.4 pitches per start, the most in the major leagues in 2003. Then he followed with 133, 116 (despite an early 8–0 lead), and 119 in his three post-season starts. Removing Prior for a pinch-hitter wasn't much of a factor; Mark was good with the stick, batting .250 with five extra-base hits among his 18 safeties, and was used as a pinch-hitter himself on a couple of occasions.

Prior developed a right Achilles tendon injury in the spring of 2004, and didn't pitch until June 4. While on the sidelines, he was stunned when former pitcher and Yahoo! Sports analyst Jack McDowell insinuated that Prior was a steroids-user. McDowell later issued a half-hearted apology. Another embarrassment occurred on June 3, when Prior walked out on a scheduled autograph session, leading to a successful breach-of-contract

---

3. Kurkjian, Tim. "Prior Destined for Greatness." ESPN.com, March 29, 2003.

suit against him.[4] Prior admits he was standoffish in those days, part of his disciplined regimen and focus on his job.

Once Prior returned to the Cubs (following a three-game rehab stint in Iowa), he battled a balky elbow, and his performance was less-than-spectacular, though he finished the season with three strong outings, including 16 K's in his last on September 30. After he started the 2005 season on the DL with an inflamed pitching elbow, Prior seemed to be returning to form. Then he missed a month after a 117 mph Brad Hawpe line drive rocketed off the same elbow, causing a hairline fracture.[5] Prior wound up with just 167 innings pitched, but led the NL in strikeouts per nine innings.

Prior's health problems continued in the spring of 2006, when he was sidelined with a sore shoulder. It was only at this time that people started writing about his (and teammate Kerry Wood's) high pitch counts and his coming back too soon from injuries. Prior didn't pitch in a big league game that year until June 18, and was shut down after his ninth start, most of them horrific, on August 10. Little did anyone know that Mark Prior's big league career was over at age 25.

Prior signed a 2007 contract with the Cubs, but didn't pitch a pro game that year. On April 24, he had exploratory arthroscopic surgery with Dr. James Andrews, turning up various problems. Prior had seven screws put in to shore up a torn labrum, rotator cuff, and anterior capsule. After the season, he became a free agent, signing with his hometown San Diego Padres in December.[6]

But once again Prior turned up lame in spring training, and didn't pitch a pro game all season. On June 4, 2008, he underwent his second shoulder operation. He signed a minor league contract with the Padres for 2009, but was released in August, having never pitched an inning in two years with the team.

Prior kept trying to rehab his arm and get back in the game. He joined the independent Golden Baseball League in August 2010, then returned to the minors. Between then and 2013, Prior pitched in relief in the minor league systems of the Rangers, Yankees, Red Sox, and Reds, but amassed fewer than 60 total innings in the four seasons. He finally announced his retirement in December 2013. His final major league numbers included a .592 win percentage and 10.37 strikeouts per nine innings.

Prior thinks the Giles and Hawpe incidents may have contributed to

---

4. Rozek, Dan. "Autograph Session Gone Bad Costs Prior $31,000." *Chicago Sun-Times*, May 5, 2006.
5. van Dyck, Dave. "Prior Breaks Elbow; Out 2 Months." *Chicago Tribune*, May 28, 2005.
6. Center, Bill. "Prior to Pitch for the Padres." *San Diego Union-Tribune*, December 27, 2007.

his breakdown, but doesn't fault his manager. "I don't blame Dusty for what happened to me," he says. "No matter how many pitches I threw, I never asked to come out of a game—doing so would have been unthinkable."[7]

Prior joined the Padres' baseball operations department in 2014, and became minor league pitching coordinator the next year. In 2018, he joined the Dodgers as bullpen coach. Mark and his wife, high school sweetheart Heather, live in San Diego with their three children, Amanda, Matthew, and Caitlyn.[8]

A 2016 article indicated that Prior had put things in perspective: "Would I love to still be pitching now, at 35? Without a doubt. But would I change where I'm at in life, the personal as well as the professional? Absolutely not."[9]

In 2014, Mark Prior was selected for induction into the Hall of Fame—the University of Southern California's Athletic Hall of Fame, that is.[10]

Year	Team (League)	G	IP	W	L	PCT	SO	BB	H	ERA
2002	Chicago (NL)	19	116.2	6	6	.500	147	38	98	3.32
2003		30	211.1	18	6	.750	245	50	183	2.43
2004		21	118.2	6	4	.600	139	48	112	4.02
2005		27	166.2	11	7	.611	188	59	143	3.67
2006		9	43.2	1	6	.143	38	28	46	7.21
Totals		106	657.0	42	29	.592	757	223	582	3.51

7. Prior, Mark. "I Have No Regrets, No One to Blame." SI.com, August 4, 2016.
8. Miller, Doug. "Mark Prior in the Present Tense." MLB.com, February 8, 2013.
9. Prior, Mark. "I Have No Regrets, No One to Blame." SI.com, August 4, 2016.
10. Gonzales, Mark. "Former Cubs Standout Prior Selected to USC's Hall of Fame." *Chicago Tribune*, July 7, 2014.

Pete Reiser

Up to 1947, most major league outfield fences were made of concrete, with nothing to warn fielders how close they were to the walls. That fall, the Dodgers installed foam-rubber padding to the walls at Ebbets Field.[1] A warning track followed soon after, and other teams gradually added similar accouterments. These safety improvements were inspired by the

1. Rosenthal, Harold. "Dodgers Send Pete..." *New York Times*, December 15, 1948, p. 34.

travails of Dodgers outfielder Pete Reiser—but they were too late to save his career.

Harold Patrick Reiser was born March 17 (thus the middle name), 1919 in St. Louis, Missouri. He was the seventh of 12 children (seven girls, five boys) of Stella Boody and George Reiser, a semi-pro pitcher.[2] As a youngster, Harold continually imitated a western movie serial character called Pistol Pete, and people soon bestowed the same nickname on him.[3] Pete attended Holy Ghost Catholic School and William Beaumont High School in the St. Louis area, and was a member of Sportsman's Park's "Knothole Gang," watching Cardinals and Browns games for free whenever he could.[4]

Pete became a baseball star at a young age, often playing with boys several years older than he. At age 17 in 1936, he attended a tryout camp held by his hometown Cardinals. Scout Charley Barrett recognized his talent immediately and the Cards signed him for the 1937 season. Showing lightning speed (9.8 in the 100-yard dash) and a rocket arm to go along with a strong bat, Pete quit school and played 77 games as a shortstop with Class-D teams in Newport, Arkansas, and New Iberia, Louisiana, hitting .283 and slugging .451 overall.

Reiser would trace a tiny cross into the dirt each time he came to the plate.[5] After that heavenly gesture, he would become a hell-bent-for-leather player, stopping for no man or barrier in his quest for extra bases or batted balls. As teammate Lonny Frey would later describe, "He's just a compact bundle of nervous energy inside a boy that's built for baseball."[6]

At that time, the Cardinals had a vast farm system, in four cases having more than one team in the same league. On March 23, 1938, Commissioner Kenesaw Landis intervened, saying that the players were being restricted, and declaring the 74 players on those teams to be free agents. Pete Reiser, one of the freed slaves, signed with the Brooklyn Dodgers for a mere $100.[7]

At Superior, Wisconsin, that year, Pete batted .302 with a hearty .563 slugging percentage, despite a left knee injury which required surgery to remove torn cartilage.[8] He impressed Dodgers manager Leo Durocher in spring training, 1939, then moved up to Elmira in the Class-A Eastern League. But Reiser soon suffered a right elbow injury which necessitated an operation to remove bone chips. When he returned to action, the

---

2. Meany, Tom. "Pistol Pete." Unidentified article in National Baseball Library file, 1942, p. 22.
3. Bernard, Tom. "Ace of Diamonds." *American Magazine*, 1947, p. 127.
4. Meany, Tom. "Pistol Pete." Unidentified article in National Baseball Library file, 1942, p. 22.
5. *Ibid.*, p. 20.
6. Bernard, Tom. "Ace of Diamonds." *American Magazine*, 1947, p. 126.
7. Meany, Tom. "Pistol Pete." Unidentified article in National Baseball Library file, p. 24.
8. *Ibid.*, p. 22.

ambidextrous Reiser actually played as a left-handed thrower for a while. He wound up playing only 38 games in '39 but batted .301 and slugged .512.

Reiser started the '40 season with Elmira, but soon moved up to Montreal of the International League, one step from the majors. After batting .370 and slugging .600 in 70 games for the two teams, Reiser was called up to the parent club in mid-season.

Reiser debuted with the Dodgers on July 23, and spent the rest of the season shuttling between third base, outfield, and shortstop. The 5'10½", 185-pounder didn't get his first hit until August 4, and was batting just .191 on August 20. But Pete hit .320 the rest of the way to finish at .293 for 58 games.

Earning the starting center fielder position for the 1941 season, Reiser burst into stardom, after overcoming some early-season injuries. First, he strained a muscle in his left side during a pre-season game, causing him to miss the first two regular-season games. Next, he survived a frightful beaning by Ike Pearson on April 23, sidelining him for a week. Then, on May 8, Reiser slammed into a wall after catching an Enos Slaughter fly ball, with an iron projection slicing a gash into Pete's lower back; this time, he was out 10 days. In August, he was hospitalized with a "troublesome sciatic nerve." But, when healthy, Pistol Pete was arguably the best player in the National League. "Pete has everything—power, speed, defensive ability and a throwing arm," said one anonymous report. "Name any ball player on my club and he's yours for Reiser," offered Cubs manager Jimmie Wilson,[9] whose team included established stars like Phil Cavarretta and Stan Hack.

In the heat of the pennant race, Reiser hit safely in 29 of the last 30 games in which he batted. By the end of the season, despite missing 20 games, he had led or tied for the NL lead in runs, doubles, triples, extra-base hits, total bases, batting average (.343), slugging percentage (.558), and even hit-by-pitch. Defensively, Reiser topped league center fielders in range factor and assists. Pete also was #1 in the Sabermetric measures of Win Shares, WAR, Runs Created, Win Probability Added, and OPS.

Reiser's brilliance helped Brooklyn win its first pennant in 21 years. The Dodgers lost the World Series to the Yankees in five games, but Reiser topped Brooklyn with a .500 slugging percentage in the Fall Classic, including the team's only home run. Pete finished second in MVP voting, behind his more-established teammate, slugger Dolf Camilli. But Reiser won the J. Louis Comiskey Award as the top rookie (defined then as someone with fewer than 100 previous games or 125 innings pitched) in the major leagues,

---

9. Patterson, Arthur E. "Reiser, Signed for $100, Hailed as $150,000 Dodger Property." *New York Herald Tribune*, June 1, 1941.

easily beating out Yankees future Hall of Famer Phil Rizzuto, 250–154.[10] After the season, Reiser signed a 1942 contract more than doubling his salary, from $4,500 to $10,000.[11]

More than half-way into the new campaign, Reiser had proven he was no flash-in-the-pan. On June 2, he slammed a single, three doubles, and a homer in one game. Reiser earned his second All-Star selection. Entering a doubleheader against the Cardinals at Sportsman's Park on July 19, 1942, the Dodgers were in first place by 8½ games over the Cards, and Brooklyn's young phenom was hitting .356, tops in the league again. But that date became a sad turning point for both the pennant race and Reiser's career.

With game two tied at six in the bottom of the eleventh inning, the Cards' Enos Slaughter (again!) hit a long fly ball to center field. According to *The Sporting News*, "it looked as though Reiser had caught the ball at the 405-foot marker when he crashed head-on against the concrete wall. He crumpled to the ground, but arose a few seconds later, chased the ball and started a belated, but futile, relay to the plate." Slaughter circled the bases for a game-winning, inside-the-park home run.

"A delegation of Dodgers went out and found Reiser weaving and groggy," continued *TSN*. "They escorted him to the clubhouse and he was still badly shaken. They called an ambulance and he was taken to St. John's Hospital, where he stayed as the team moved on to Pittsburgh. X-rays showed no skull fracture, but there was a concussion."[12]

Reiser was back in the lineup six days later, but by early August was relegated to the sidelines for another week with recurring headaches. Having trouble against lefties, he tried switch-hitting (he normally batted lefty in the majors, but switch-hit occasionally throughout his pro career). Later in the month, Reiser was hospitalized with a torn ligament in his left thigh, missing another week. After July, Pete hit just .221, and the Dodgers wound up losing the pennant to the Cardinals by two games. Reiser still batted .310 for the season, leading the NL in stolen bases, finishing in the top five in runs, doubles, and batting, and ranking sixth in MVP voting. Through age 23, the 10 most similar players to Reiser include Hall of Famers Fred Clarke, Goose Goslin, Duke Snider, and Al Simmons, along with current star Mookie Betts.

Pete married Patricia T. Hurst at Titusville, Florida, on March 29, 1942. They separated on January 6 of the following year, shortly before the birth of Sally Ann, whom they later learned was mentally challenged. Patricia

---

10. Burns, Ed. "Pete Gets Big Pat from 'Chi' Writers." *The Sporting News*, December 25, 1941, p. 5.
11. Parrott, Harold. "Reiser Agrees to 1942 Terms; Goes from $4,500 to $10,000." *Brooklyn Eagle*, December 1, 1941.
12. *The Sporting News*, July 23, 1942, p. 1.

was granted a divorce on February 14, 1944,[13] but the couple reconciled, having a second daughter, Shirley, in 1949, and remaining together until Pete's death in 1981. Pete and Pat became active in the St. Louis Association for Retarded Children.[14]

Pete was classified as 1A for military service in 1942, but got a deferment at the appeal of his parents, whom he was supporting financially.[15] A year later, despite a double-hernia, Reiser was sworn in as a private in the U.S. Army on January 13, 1943.[16] Though he was recommended four times for medical discharge, Reiser spent the next three years in military service.[17] Sometime during this period, he suffered a clavicle separation while playing ball.[18]

After threatening to jump to the outlaw Mexican League, Reiser returned to the Dodgers with a $15,000 pact in 1946.[19] He promptly reinjured his shoulder in spring training, had difficulty throwing all season, and was moved to left field. This was the start of a horrific season of physical woes. On May 28 and again on August 1, Reiser crashed into Ebbets Field's cement wall, being knocked unconscious the second time, but missing a total of just 11 days. On July 21, he endured a concussion after a beaning, but stayed in the lineup. On August 31, Pete suffered a charley horse in his right leg, hampering him the rest of the season. Somewhere along the line, he was burnt in a gas stove explosion. Finally, on September 26, Reiser broke his right fibula while sliding back into first base on a pickoff attempt.[20] Without his services in the final week, the Dodgers wound up losing the pennant in a playoff against St. Louis.

Somehow, Reiser managed to have a productive season between all the setbacks. He wound up leading the NL with 34 stolen bases in 40 attempts,[21] including a record-setting seven steals of home. Reiser batted .323 in the first half of the season, but just .218 in the second half as the ailments piled up. He still finished ninth in MVP voting.

Reiser made a prescient suggestion during spring training, 1947. "They ought to lay out a cinder running track on the fringe of the outfield

---

13. "Pete Reiser Divorced." *The Sporting News*, February 17, 1944.
14. Biederman, Lester J. "Dodger Coach Reiser Big Man in Fields Other Than Baseball." Unidentified clipping in National Baseball Library file, 1960.
15. Rose, Lester. "Reiser in 1A; Appeal Filed by Parents." Unidentified clipping in National Baseball Library file, April 14, 1942.
16. *The Sporting News*, January 21, 1943.
17. Bernard, Tom. "Ace of Diamonds." *American Magazine*, 1947, p. 127.
18. "Broken Leg Caps Long Run of Tough Luck for Reiser." Unidentified clipping in National Baseball Library file, September 27, 1946.
19. Young, Dick. "Bruised, Battered Reiser to Quit." *New York Daily News*, c. 1948.
20. "Broken Leg Caps Long Run of Tough Luck for Reiser." Unidentified clipping in National Baseball Library file, September 27, 1946.
21. John Tattersall research files, excerpted by L. Robert Davids.

here, so that an outfielder will know when he is coming close to the wall," he said.[22]

Reiser signed a $20,000 contract and went into the season still suffering from the effects of his leg injury and off-season shoulder surgery. Still, he was able to play regularly for the first two months, until his latest—and worst—encounter with an outfield wall.

On June 4, after making a spectacular catch on Cully Rikard's long drive, Reiser crashed headlong into Ebbets Field's concrete center field barrier. Rikard circled the bases as Reiser lay crumpled and bleeding, with no one realizing that the ball was still safely stuck in the webbing of his glove. Reiser was hospitalized with a severe concussion and didn't return to the field until July 12. The one positive for the Dodgers was that the injury opened a spot for a 20-year-old rookie, a fellow named Edwin Snider.[23]

Reiser quietly battled dizziness the rest of the season, but still batted .309, helping the Dodgers to another World Series against the Yankees. On October 2, in the first inning of Game Three, Reiser suffered a broken right ankle on a steal attempt, though the break wasn't diagnosed until after the Fall Classic. Reiser pinch-hit twice more in the Series, walking and being pinch-run for each time. The Dodgers lost in seven games.

According to author Roger Kahn, Reiser's career as a star effectively ended during the game before that injury. In Game Two, the outfielder—still battling vertigo, along with the Yankee Stadium sun—played three fly balls into triples, then made a two-base error, as the Dodgers lost, 10–3. When Reiser caught a routine fly, some in the crowd cheered sarcastically. "Reiser would play parts of five more seasons, but that sunny October day at the Stadium was really the end," wrote Kahn. "The best prospect Leo Durocher ever saw was washed up at the age of twenty-eight."[24]

Between 1948 and '52, Reiser played for the Dodgers, Boston Braves, Pittsburgh Pirates, and Cleveland Indians, doing whatever he could to stay in the majors, but collecting only 150 hits with a .246 average over the five seasons (dropping his career average from .310 to .295). Pete even tried out as a catcher in spring training, 1951. Veteran NL umpire Dusty Boggess watched the experiment and commented, "He was one of the greatest I've seen. Maybe if he had been a catcher all along he wouldn't have hit those fences. But he probably would have fallen into dugouts chasing fouls."[25]

After his playing career ended, Reiser returned to baseball as a minor

---

22. Goren, Herbert. "Reiser's Latest Crack-up Brings Gloom to Dodgers." *New York Times*, June 5, 1947.
23. *Ibid.*
24. Kahn, Roger. *The Era.* New York: Ticknor & Fields, 1993, p. 110.
25. Talbot, Gayle. "Hardluck Pete Reiser Has Hopes of Finishing Career as Catcher." *Elmira Advertiser*, March 16, 1951.

league manager (1955–59, 1965–66) and major league coach with the Dodgers (1960–64), Cubs (1966–69, 1972–74), and Angels (1970–71), with a brief stint coaching for the Toei Flyers in Japan in '66.[26] Even in those roles he couldn't escape the sickbed. Pete suffered a pinched nerve in 1957, three broken ribs (in an on-field collision) in 1958, heart attacks in 1964 and '65, and a fractured collarbone (in a brawl) in 1973.

As a skipper, Reiser won the Midwest League pennant in 1957, won *The Sporting News*'s 1959 Manager of the Year Award, and managed the likes of Frank Howard and Tommy Davis. According to a 1959 article, "the expectation is that some day he will manage the Dodgers."[27] Walter Alston had other ideas: he stayed on the job through the 1976 season, by which time Reiser was retired himself.

Reiser did play in parts of 10 seasons, so is eligible for the Hall of Fame. He got six votes in 1958 and eight in '60—not bad for a player with just 2662 career at bats. Pete won the New York writers' Casey Stengel "You Could Look It Up" Award in 1976.[28]

According to Kahn, Reiser's post-playing life "was dominated by bitterness and drink."[29] At just 62, he died at Palm Springs, California, on October 25, 1981—fittingly, as another Dodgers-Yankees World Series was in progress. Late in his life, Reiser was asked how long he might have lasted in the majors, and what accomplishments he might have authored, had he not played so recklessly.

"If I hadn't played that way," Pete said, "I may never have got there to begin with. It was my style of playing. I didn't know any other way to play ball.… You slow up a half step, and it's the beginning of your last ball game. It might take a few years, but you're on your way out. That's how I look at it. You can't turn it on and off anytime you want to. Not if you take pride in yourself."[30]

Year	Team (League)	G	AB	R	H	2B	3B	HR	RBI	SB	AVG	OBP	SLG
1940	Brooklyn (NL)	58	225	34	66	11	4	3	20	2	.293	.338	.418
1941		137	536	*117	184	*39	*17	14	76	4	*.343	.406	*.558
1942		125	480	89	149	33	5	10	64	*20	.310	.375	.463
1946		122	423	75	117	21	5	11	73	*34	.277	.361	.428
1947		110	388	68	120	23	2	5	46	14	.309	.415	.418

26. Graczyk, Wayne. *Americans in Japan*. Self-published, 1986.
27. Kamm, Herbert. "Fence-Crashing Pete Reiser Bears Big Personal Burden." United Feature Syndicate, 1959.
28. Pepe, Phil. "The Wall of Fame." *New York Daily News*, February 2, 1976, p. C24.
29. Kahn, Roger. *The Era*. New York: Ticknor & Fields, 1993, p. 110.
30. Reiser, Pete. "Pete Reiser: Why He Ran into Walls." *New York Times*, August 10, 1975.

Year	Team (League)	G	AB	R	H	2B	3B	HR	RBI	SB	AVG	OBP	SLG
1948	Brooklyn (NL)	64	127	17	30	8	2	1	19	4	.236	.382	.354
1949	Boston (NL)	84	221	32	60	8	3	8	40	3	.271	.369	.443
1950		53	78	12	16	2	0	1	10	1	.205	.367	.269
1951	Pittsburgh (NL)	74	140	22	38	9	3	2	13	4	.271	.389	.421
1952	Cleveland (AL)	34	44	7	6	1	0	3	7	1	.136	.208	.364
Totals		861	2662	473	786	155	41	58	368	87	.295	.380	.450

J.R. Richard

By mid-June 1980, the Astros' J.R. Richard had emerged as the best pitcher in baseball. Over his team's last 120 games dating back to July 25, 1979—three-fourths of a season—Richard was 20-5 with 257 strikeouts, seven shutouts, and a microscopic 1.33 ERA.

He would pitch just 13 more big league innings.

James Rodney Richard was born March 7, 1950, in Vienna, Louisiana, one of six children of Lizzie Frost and Clayton Richard, a sawmill owner. Known mostly by his middle name during his youth, Rodney became a physical giant (eventually reaching 6'8" and 240 pounds, with the ability to hold eight baseballs in one hand) and an athletic prodigy, starring in football, basketball, and baseball. Stories of his sports exploits at Lincoln High School in Ruston, Louisiana, frankly defy belief. Supposedly he posted a 28-0 pitching record there, including four perfect games. The year he graduated, Richard was chosen by the Houston Astros as the second pick overall in the 1969 draft. He eschewed scholarship offers in the other sports to start a pro baseball career, signing for $100,000.[1]

Richard pitched for Covington in the Appalachian League that year, showing two qualities which would characterize the majority of his pitching career: blazing speed, and godawful control. In 56 innings, he struck out 71, but walked 52. His huge hands made it difficult to control the ball's flight.

---

1. "Astros' Richard Dominates before Stroke of Bad Luck." *The Baseball Draft*, p. 69.

Under the mentorship of Hub Kittle, Richard showed progress with Cocoa of the Florida State League in 1970, belying his 4–11 won-lost record. He fanned 138 in 109 innings, posted a 2.39 ERA, and tossed a no-hitter vs. Daytona Beach on August 28. Moving up to Oklahoma City of the AAA American Association the next year, Richard went 12–7, topping the league in shutouts, strikeouts, and ERA (2.45)—but also in walks and wild pitches. Still, this was good enough to earn his first taste of major league action.

Before Richard even made his Astros debut, columnist Bob Hertzel described the hype accompanying his arrival in the bigs: "Build a new wing on the Hall of Fame up there in Cooperstown, N.Y. You're gonna need it. The Hall isn't big enough any more. It's going to have to expand just to keep tabs on James Rodney Richard."[2]

Three days later, on September 15, 1971, Richard made Hertzel look like a prophet. J.R. threw a complete game to beat the division-leading Giants, 5–3, tying Karl Spooner's record of 15 strikeouts (including three of Willie Mays) in a big league debut. But Richard's other three starts in September were not as memorable: he walked 13 batters in 12 innings, and failed to retire a batter in his last outing. He returned to Oklahoma City for '72.

The next three seasons were more of the same: lots of strikeouts and walks in the minors, brief trials in the majors each year. Richard's 1969–74 minor league numbers included a 42–42 record, 3.46 ERA, and 10.57 strikeouts and 5.68 walks per nine innings.

Meanwhile, Richard went 11–6 with a 4.34 ERA in his four stints with the Astros. He looked like he had made the majors to stay in 1973. Called up on May 30, he was 5–1 with a 2.97 ERA as a spot-starter through August. But after being roughed up his next two outings, Richard suffered a separated right shoulder in a motorcycle accident on September 13. He was done for the season and back in the minors the next spring, still not fully-recovered from the injury.

Despite his limited big league experience, Richard was attracting the admiration—and fear—of some of the league's biggest names. "I've batted against Nolan Ryan and Tom Seaver, and they're tough," said Cardinals future Hall of Famer Ted Simmons. "But when I go to the plate against Richard, I say, 'Hey, that's too damn fast.'"[3] Astros pitching coach Roger Craig opined, "Richard has the best arm in the league. It's just a matter of time before he is the best righthanded pitcher in the league."[4] Pirates slugger Willie Stargell said, "I'll tell you, when that Richard gets his stuff

---

2. Hertzel, Bob. "The New 'Phenom' in Baseball." *Cincinnati Enquirer*, September 2, 1971.
3. *The Sporting News*, April 27, 1974.
4. Shattuck, Harry. "With Astro Experiments." *The Sporting News*, October 4, 1975.

together, I hope I'm a designated hitter somewhere in the other league. He throws so hard he could start a forest fire."[5]

Nineteen-seventy-five was considered a make-or-break year for Richard, and he came through. After spending the winter in the Dominican League, J.R. finally made the Astros for good. He filled the rotation spot left by the death of Don Wilson, and went a respectable 12–10 for a 64–97 team, though he led the NL in walks and wild pitches for the first of three times each. Richard also contributed with the bat, driving in 13 runs (he would collect 10 home runs during his career, batting .168). His defense was unpredictable: he would lead the NL with 10 errors in 1976 and five in '79, but make only five errors total in his other eight seasons, once leading the league in putouts.

In the four years after his breakthrough season, J.R. Richard became one of the best pitchers in the game. Besides his blazing fastball, he had developed a slider which analysts Bill James and Rob Neyer rate as one of the 10 best in baseball history.[6]

- In 1976, Richard won 20 games—including three wins in the last nine days of the season—for an 80–82 team, earning "Most Valuable Astro" honors.[7] Overcoming late-season muscle soreness, he was second in the league in games started, innings pitched, and strikeouts, and allowed the fewest hits per nine innings. One game in particular illustrates the Jekyll-Hyde nature of Richard's performance at that time. On July 6, Richard walked 10 batters, and surrendered eight hits and two wild pitches—yet shut out the Mets, 1–0, in 10 innings. The game set a record for most runners (15) stranded in a shutout. His estimated number of pitches, based on Tom Tango's formula, was 184.
- In 1977, despite tendinitis in August, Richard went 18–12 for an 81–81 team, finishing second in strikeouts and fewest hits allowed per nine innings. He underwent an emergency appendectomy on October 26.[8]
- In 1978, Richard went 18–11 for a 74–88 team. He led the league in fewest hits allowed per nine innings (6.28), and in strikeouts (303), breaking Tom Seaver's league record for right-handed pitchers. Richard was named NL Pitcher of the Month for July, and finished fourth in Cy Young Award voting. He particularly impressed two all-time greats in one early-season outing against the Reds. "He was

---

5. Unidentified clipping in National Baseball Library file, July 6, 1975.
6. James, Bill, and Rob Neyer. *The Neyer/James Guide to Pitchers*. New York: Fireside, 2004, p. 38.
7. *The Sporting News*, December 11, 1976.
8. *The Sporting News*, November 12, 1977.

awesome and you spell that with a capital 'A,'" said Pete Rose. "[H]e was the best I ever faced," added Joe Morgan.[9] More and more, opposing hitters came down with mysterious maladies on the days Richard was scheduled to pitch. The Dodgers' Bill Russell once began shaking uncontrollably while batting against J. R., and had to give way to a pinch-hitter.[10]

- In 1979, Richard led the NL in ERA, won 18 for the third straight year, and again had the fewest hits allowed per nine innings (6.77) and the most strikeouts (313), breaking his own league record for right-handed pitchers. More significantly, he seemed finally to have mastered his control problems, averaging an NL-best 3.2 strikeouts per walk, with just three walks per nine innings. In the last two-plus months of the season, Richard went 11–2 with a 1.26 ERA—including 25 straight scoreless innings to end the season—earning NL Pitcher of the Month honors for September. On August 3 and again on September 21, he matched his career high of 15 strikeouts in a game. Richard finished a strong third in Cy Young voting.

As good as Richard's records were, his performance was even better. According to Bill James's stat, "component ERA," Richard's expected ERAs for 1976–80—based on his hits and walks allowed, etc.—were 2.93, 2.74, 2.53, 2.23, and 1.41, respectively. He was very good to begin with, and getting better every year.

Richard's contract ended after the 1979 season, and he could have become the most sought-after free agent on the market. But on October 11 Houston signed him to a four-year contract reported at 2.4 million dollars, making him one of the highest-paid players in the game.[11] Yet that number would soon be dwarfed by a teammate. On November 19, the Astros signed Angels free agent Nolan Ryan, making him the first million-dollar-per-year player in baseball history. With Ryan and Richard, Houston now had the two most overpowering pitchers in baseball.

But Richard was still the ace of the staff, picking up in the 1980 season right where he left off in '79. On April 19, he allowed only an infield single in tossing a one-hit shutout over the Dodgers, his 13th straight win against Houston's arch rivals. Six days later, Richard earned his 100th career victory. He was named NL Pitcher of the Month for April. On May 31, he hurled a three-hit shutout over the Giants. On June 6, J.R. again tossed a three-hit whitewash against San Francisco, striking out 13 and walking

---

9. *The Sporting News*, May 6, 1978.
10. Sakamoto, Bob. "J.R. Richard Still Going Strong." *Washington Post*, April 19, 1989.
11. Shattuck, Harry. "$2.4 Million Keeps Richard in Houston." *The Sporting News*, October 27, 1979.

none. On June 11, he notched his third straight shutout, beating the Cubs. He was in the midst of 33 consecutive scoreless innings. "And J.R. gets better when the weather gets hot," noted teammate Enos Cabell. "If he's this good now, what's he gonna do when it gets hot?"[12]

By June 17, 1980, Richard was 9–3 with a 1.51 ERA. He was on pace to go 25–8 with 291 strikeouts for the season, and he finally earned an All-Star selection. But something wasn't right.

On that date, Richard departed after just five effective innings against the Cubs, saying his arm "went dead."[13] It was the tenth time in his 14 starts he had failed to go the distance, an oddity for someone who had hurled 19 complete games the year before. He had been complaining of back and shoulder stiffness, and that his pitching hand was cold and numb.

J.R. didn't start again until June 28, and didn't make it through the fourth inning against the Reds, this time complaining of a "tired arm." People joked, "At least it's improved from dead to tired."[14]

On July 3, Richard lasted just six frames vs. the Braves, giving up his first home runs in 135+ innings, but earning the win. Next came the All-Star Game at Dodger Stadium on July 8. Richard was the starting pitcher, tossing two shutout innings (including strikeouts of future Hall of Famers Reggie Jackson and Carlton Fisk) to launch the NL to a 4–2 victory. At least one of his pitches was clocked at 100 mph, making him only the second pitcher ever officially timed at three digits (Ryan, at 100.9, was the first).

Richard's next start was on July 14 against the Braves. He cruised through three innings, giving up just one hit and no runs. As his teammates went on the field for the fourth, J.R. remained in the dugout, and manager Bill Virdon had to urge him out to the mound. Richard walked Dale Murphy, who was then retired on a Chris Chambliss force-out. That was it for J.R. He walked off the field, looking glassy-eyed and feeling nauseated. He said he had been having trouble seeing the catcher's signs. The Astros put him on the 21-day disabled list two days later. Diagnostic tests on July 23–25 "found no neurological, arthritic or muscle disorders, but ... an occlusion or blockage of the distal subclavian and axillary arteries on the right arm." Despite the blood clot, "no surgical intervention was indicated."[15] Richard was cleared to work his way back to the field. The Astros needed him on the mound.

By now, the media and even teammates were questioning Richard's

---

12. Shattuck, Harry. "Astro All-Stars: Cruz, Richard." *The Sporting News*, July 5, 1980.
13. Associated Press. "Richard Tames Cubs but Arm Goes 'Dead.'" June 18, 1980.
14. Shattuck, Harry. "Astros Find Batting Eyes as Hurling Sags." *The Sporting News*, July 19, 1980.
15. Madden, Michael. Unidentified clipping in National Baseball Library file, August 4, 1980.

"guts," some wondering if he was on drugs—"Who Shot up J. R.?" was one throwaway line, a play on that year's *Dallas* TV show mystery. How could something be wrong with Richard if he was still firing 100 mph fastballs? People wondered if he was malingering in jealousy of Ryan's contract. Richard did little to quiet the whispers and rumors, with his erratic behavior and conflicting statements.

On July 30, Richard was doing some light throwing at the Astrodome, when he collapsed. A photo depicts the crumpled giant surrounded by team personnel, whose faces and postures show more annoyance than concern, as if to ask, "What drama is J.R. creating now?" But this was no act. J.R. Richard, 30, had suffered a massive stroke.

Richard underwent emergency surgery to remove the clot which had lodged in his neck and cut off circulation to his brain for several hours. For a long time he could not even feed himself or button his shirt. Though he made significant progress, J.R. remained hospitalized until September 12, having suffered permanent damage. Many reporters apologized for the way they had questioned his heart and conditioning, but the damage had been done. On September 27, Richard made a pre-game appearance at the Astrodome, walking deliberately and somberly out to home plate to a standing ovation. He did not wave or smile; he gave a few words of restrained gratitude, and left the field.

J.R. had a second operation on October 14, this one taking 18 hours and clearing obstructions in his pitching shoulder. Doctors have theorized that the strain of pitching led to the circulatory problems, much like those which impaired Sandy Koufax and Whitey Ford in the 1960s, and would later sideline David Cone in 1996 and kill Darryl Kile in 2002.

Richard—whom one writer likens to "Randy Johnson with a chest"—finished the 1980 season with a 107–71 (.601) career record and 3.15 ERA, compared to Johnson's 81–62, 3.70 at the same age. Through ages 29 and 30, the most similar pitcher to Richard was his idol, Hall of Famer Bob Gibson. "He was on his way to the Hall of Fame," said teammate Enos Cabell,[16] reflecting the opinion of many. "He was the best pitcher in baseball, no question about it," said Astros manager Bill Virdon. "He probably created more headaches and stomach-aches for right-handed batters than anybody who ever played."[17]

Against the odds, Richard prepared for a comeback in 1981. He pitched some batting practice for the Astros, throwing about 85 mph from behind a protective screen. The team was more concerned with his impaired reflexes, and ability to react to hard-hit balls up the middle, than with his throwing

---

16. Sakamoto, Bob. "J. R. Richard Still Going Strong." *Washington Post*, April 19, 1989.
17. Crowe, Jerry. "A Bitter J. R. Richard is Busy at Nothing." *Los Angeles Times*, June 29, 1987.

speed. The baseball strike from June to August pretty much scuttled Richard's hopes to return in '81, but the Astros reactivated him on September 1, to avoid losing him to another team. There was talk of his pitching that month, but it never happened.[18]

Richard became depressed, and was overweight and out of condition by the time 1982 rolled around. He was also preoccupied with a medical malpractice suit he filed on March 26.[19] He would eventually settle out of court for an amount estimated between one and two million dollars.

J.R. finally made it back to competitive baseball on June 28, 1982. Hurling for the Daytona Beach Astros of the Class-A Florida State League, he went 3-1 with a 2.79 ERA over six games. His comeback inspired even the U.S. President. "If we can focus as clearly on our goal as J.R. Richard has on his," said Ronald Reagan, "then I believe we, too, can find the strength to make our dreams come true."[20]

But any illusion that Richard was ready to return to the majors was shattered by a move up to Triple-A. In six appearances with the Tucson Toros, J.R. was torched for a 0–2 record and 13.68 ERA. He was again put on the Astros' roster in September, but again remained on the sidelines.

Richard was set back further by surgery to replace a graft in his left leg in March 1983. When he returned, it was with the Gulf Coast Astros, the team's lowest-level pro team. J.R. went 2–3 with a 3.18 ERA. His Astros contract expired on October 31, and he opted for free agency. No one signed him, but the Astros gave him one last shot, inviting him to spring training in 1984 as a non-roster player. It didn't work out; they released him on March 27 and his pro baseball career was over. "This was an extremely difficult decision for us," said Astros Chairman of the Board John McMullen. "J.R. has been an example to everyone, whether they be a baseball fan or not."[21]

Over the next 11 years, Richard's life cascaded. Some articles depicted him as at peace, comforted by his faith; others as bitter and unmotivated. He went through a series of short-lived jobs and disastrous business ventures. In 1984, Richard and his wife of 15 years, Carolyn, were divorced; the split cost him $669,000 and estranged him from their five children, Paula, J.R. Jr., Patrick, Eric, and Crystal.[22] In 1985, it was revealed that J.R. had had a "chemical abuse problem" throughout his career, including cocaine use in 1980. In 1988 he married Zemphery Volcy, with whom he already had a daughter, but this union also ended in divorce. In 1989, J.R. signed with the

---

18. Shattuck, Harry. "Astronotes." *The Sporting News*, September 19, 1981.
19. "Richard Charges Malpractice." *The Sporting News*, April 10, 1982.
20. "Reagan: J. R. an Inspiration." *New York Daily News*, July 14, 1982.
21. Associated Press. "Astros Cut Richard to End Comeback Try." March 28, 1984.
22. Wade, Ed, et al. *Astros '81 Media Guide*, p. 39.

Orlando Juice of the newly-formed Senior Professional Baseball Association, but he was released before the season started for being out of shape at over 300 pounds.[23] Richard filed for bankruptcy on January 9, 1990.[24] He soon became homeless, shuttling between friends until he was discovered living under a Houston bridge with $20 to his name in 1995.[25]

Richard's baseball pension kicked in when he turned 45 in '95, and he began piecing his life back together. He pitched in the Legends Game before that year's All-Star Game in Arlington, Texas.[26] He became an ordained minister, and still serves as an associate pastor for the Mary Olive Baptist Church in Houston. His third wife, Grethan, gave him a son, J.R. III. An inspirational film, *Resurrection: The J.R. Richard Story*, was released in 2005.[27]

On June 1, 2012, J.R. Richard was inducted into the Astros' Walk of Fame, and on August 3, 2019, into their Hall of Fame. On June 9, 2018, he became part of the Negro Leagues Baseball Museum's fifth "Hall of Game" class. And on May 5, 2019, he was elected into the "Shrine of the Eternals." Richard did pitch in parts of 10 major league seasons, so is eligible for Cooperstown's Hall of Fame. But he received just seven votes in the 1986 election, and was dropped from the ballot.

Year	Team (League)	G	IP	W	L	PCT	SO	BB	H	ERA
1971	Houston (NL)	4	21.0	2	1	.667	29	16	17	3.43
1972		4	6.0	1	0	1.000	8	8	10	13.50
1973		16	72.0	6	2	.750	75	38	54	4.00
1974		15	64.2	2	3	.400	42	36	58	4.18
1975		33	203.0	12	10	.545	176	*138	178	4.39
1976		39	291.0	20	15	.571	214	*151	221	2.75
1977		36	267.0	18	12	.600	214	104	212	2.97
1978		36	275.1	18	11	.621	*303	*141	192	3.11
1979		38	292.1	18	13	.581	*313	98	220	*2.71
1980		17	113.2	10	4	.714	119	40	65	1.90
Totals		238	1606.0	107	71	.601	1493	770	1227	3.15

---

23. "J. R. Richard is Too Plump for the Juice." *USA Today*, October 31, 1989.
24. "J. R. Files Bankruptcy." *Albany Times-Union*, January 28, 1990.
25. Aron, Jaime. "J. R. Richard is Trying Not to be Bitter." *Philadelphia Inquirer*, July 22, 1995.
26. "Richard Comes Back after Stroke Following '80 Game." *USA Today*, July 11, 1995.
27. Beaton, Rod. "Richard's Rise, Fall on Screen." *USA Today*, February 24, 2005.

Al Rosen

Delayed by military service and bad timing, Al Rosen didn't play his first full major league season until he was 26. Hampered by two serious injuries, he was through at 32. But in between, for peak value, Rosen was among the very best third basemen in baseball history.

Albert Leonard Rosen was a leap-day baby, the son of Louis and Rose Levine Rosen, born February 29, 1924, in his mother's hometown of Spartanburg, South Carolina. Like many players from that era, Rosen fudged his birth year to appear younger, but in so doing had to change his birthday, too: *Sporting News Registers* from the 1950s list his birthdate as March 1, 1925. Al's parents were divorced soon after the birth of his younger brother, Jerry. His mother moved the kids to Miami, Florida, where they joined her mother and sister. There, the Jewish family dealt with harsh anti-Semitism.

Despite severe asthma which afflicted him until his mid-teens, Al grew into an excellent athlete. This was particularly true in softball, where he earned the nickname "The Flipper," shortened to "Flip," supposedly due to his pitching style (though he said he got it while playing basketball[1]). Rosen transferred from Miami Senior High School to Florida Military Academy, St. Petersburg, on a full athletic scholarship. There he competed at football, basketball, and baseball, in addition to boxing, in which he won a state championship.[2]

Rosen was offered a puny pro baseball contract in 1941, but declined, and enrolled in the University of Florida that fall. Switching to the University of Miami, and majoring in business administration, he would continue his studies around pro ball and military service, eventually graduating in 1948.[3]

Rosen looked to begin his pro baseball career at age 18 in 1942. After being rejected by the Red Sox, he went to Thomasville, North Carolina, where he had received his previous pro offer. Rosen walked into a café, asking for the manager of the local team. Someone asked him what position he played, and he said third base. "They fell all over themselves rushing out to round up [Thomasville manager] Jimmy Gruzdis before I could get away," Rosen recalled. "It seems that their third baseman had just broken his leg. Gruzdis signed me right up and had me in the line-up that night."[4] After a

---

1. Albert Rosen player questionnaire, National Baseball Library files.
2. Paxton, Harry T. "The Clouting Kid from Cleveland." *Saturday Evening Post*, August 11, 1951, p. 87.
3. *Ibid.*, p. 88.
4. *Ibid.*

slow start, Rosen wound up batting .307 in 86 games in the class-D North Carolina State League.

Rosen's fledgling career then was put on the back burner. He joined the U.S. Navy V-12 training program at the University of Miami in the fall of 1942. In 1944, he spent six weeks at Camp Shelton, Virginia, moved into small-boat training, and then into full-fledged World War II action. Rosen navigated the USS Procycon, an assault boat which was in Okinawa on D-Day. He was discharged in 1946 as a lieutenant.

After a couple of false starts, Rosen—now 22—resumed his baseball career with Pittsfield, Massachusetts, of the class-C Canadian-American League. Splitting his defensive time between the three bases, the right-handed hitter wound up batting .323 and slugging .600 over 107 games, leading the league in triples (19), home runs (15), and RBI (86), and earning the league's "Star of the Year" honors.

Moving all the way up to the Indians' AA team in Oklahoma City in 1947, Rosen didn't miss a beat. He led the league in hits (186), doubles (47), total bases, RBI (141), and batting (.349), falling three homers shy of the Triple Crown, while slugging .619 over 146 games. Rosen was selected as Texas League MVP.[5] In September, he got his first cup of coffee with the Indians.

With Kansas City of the AAA American Association in 1948, Rosen had 25 homers, 110 RBI, and a .327 average. On July 27–28, he belted five consecutive home runs and knocked in 13 runs in two games.[6] After the season Rosen won a $100 savings bond as the league's "Outstanding Freshman," an annual award that went to a player with no previous AAA experience.[7] He again finished the season with Cleveland, even getting an at bat against Warren Spahn in the World Series.

Surely Rosen would have made the majors much sooner in another place and time. Besides the 3½ years of military service, he was delayed by sheer numbers. By 1949, there were some 448 minor league teams siphoning their talent into just 16 big league clubs, so Rosen was but one of thousands of minor leaguers waiting for an opening—and the hot corner in Cleveland was not one of them. The Indians already had a popular and talented third baseman, Ken Keltner. Keltner had joined the team in 1937, earned seven All-Star selections, and set career highs in homers and RBI in the pennant year of 1948.

---

5. Cronley, John. "Player Prizes Won by Rosen and Beers." *The Sporting News*, September 10, 1947, p. 29.
6. Mehl, Ernest. "Five Homers in Five Trips Move Rosen Closer to Tribe." *The Sporting News*, August 18, 1948, p. 19.
7. American Association press release, August 24, 1948.

Rosen wed Evelyn Silverstein in Kansas City in October 1948,[8] but that marriage ended in divorce just a few months later.[9] On October 12, 1952, he married Terese Ann Blumberg,[10] a union producing sons Rob, Andy, and Jim. On March 1, 1971, Terry left a note indicating despondency, and plunged to her death from the 19th floor of a Philadelphia hotel.[11] The third time was the charm for Al. Wife #3, Rita Lowenstein, was with him the last 43 years of his life, and added two stepchildren, Gail and David, to his family.

The Indians gave Rosen a shot as a pinch-hitter and backup to Keltner in the first half of the 1949 season, but Flip failed to hit his weight in limited action and was sent back to AAA. With the San Diego Padres of the Pacific Coast League, Rosen batted .319 in 83 games. He finished his 549-game minor league career with 86 homers, a .328 batting average, and a .563 slugging percentage.

Meanwhile, Keltner seemed to get old overnight, slumping badly over the last two-thirds of the '49 season. He batted just .178 with one home run after June 18, failing to drive in a single run in July or August. The Indians released Keltner on April 18, 1950. At 26, Al Rosen would finally get his chance—and he would make it count. By the end of the season, he had played every game, topped the AL with 37 home runs and 10 times hit by pitch, and finished in the league's top five in walks, slugging, OPS, Win Shares, and WAR.

Although record-keepers long listed Rosen as the holder of the AL rookie home run record (finally topped by Mark McGwire in 1987), Al was not considered a first-year player in 1950, nor would he be under modern rules. While he had accumulated just 58 at bats in 1947–49, he had spent all of May and June 1949 on the Indians' squad. Current Rookie of the Year voting rules say that, if someone has spent more than 45 days on a roster before September 1 of any previous season, he is no longer eligible. There was no formal definition of "rookie" until 1957, but Rosen failed to get a vote in 1950 ROY voting, the consensus being that his previous experience was "tantamount to veteran status."[12]

Rookie or not, Rosen's performance, in context, was exceptional. In that era, third base was not generally a position reserved for power-hitters: in 1950, the seven starting AL third sackers other than Rosen averaged five home runs and 50 RBI apiece. Rosen hit more homers than all of them

---

8. "Rosen Aims for Majors." *Detroit News*, October 30, 1948.
9. Paxton, Harry T. "The Clouting Kid from Cleveland." *Saturday Evening Post*, August 11, 1951, p. 88.
10. Albert Rosen player questionnaire, National Baseball Library files.
11. Associated Press. "Plunges to Death." March 6, 1971.
12. Deane, Bill. *Award Voting*. Kansas City, MO: Society for American Baseball Research, 1988, p. 58.

combined, 37 to 35. In so doing, he set a major league single-season record for home runs by a third sacker.

Rosen was not big for a power-hitter: 5'10½" and 180 pounds. But the blue-eyed, prematurely-graying, nattily-dressed youngster—nicknamed "Captain America" by his teammates, and "the Hebrew Hammer" by sportswriters—was strong, well-conditioned, and dedicated to his craft. Rosen trained and practiced year-round, did not drink during the season, and did not smoke at all (though he received $500 for endorsing Chesterfield cigarettes[13]). He sought hitting advice from the likes of current and future Hall of Famers Tris Speaker, Max Carey, Hank Greenberg, Ted Williams, and Ralph Kiner.[14]

Some sources have claimed that Rosen's defense was substandard, but the numbers don't bear that out. In the minors, he made a lot of errors, but also covered a lot of ground: in 1947, his first full season at the hot corner, he topped the Texas League in putouts and chances accepted. In the majors, both his range factor and fielding percentage were above league average over his career. After working with Indians coach Oscar Melillo, Flip led the AL third basemen in assists in 1950 and '53, also leading in double plays and range factor in the latter year. He also saw some action at each of the other infield positions.

Over the first 50 games of the 1951 season, Rosen was nearly duplicating his '50 performance. He had played every game and was on pace for 117 RBI and a .283 average. But on June 10, a bullet shot off the bat of Boston's Walt Dropo took a bad hop right into Rosen's nose, fracturing it. Al claimed it was the 11th broken nose he had suffered in athletic competition: two in boxing, six in football, and three in baseball.[15] He missed the second game of the doubleheader, and—with his eyes almost swollen shut by internal bleeding—no one expected him to play again for at least a week. But Rosen was right back in the lineup in the next game, going 3-for-4 with a double, homer, and four RBI to lead the Indians to an 8–6 win. He did not miss a game the rest of the season, and wound up fifth in the league with 102 RBI, including a record-tying four grand slams. "He was a fierce competitor," recalled Hall of Famer Hank Greenberg, the Indians' GM at the time. "[H]e was back in there with two black eyes. There was no doubt he was the leader of our club."[16]

---

13. Shaw, Bud. "Ex-Tribe Great Rosen Has Finally Seen it All." *Cleveland Plain Dealer*, July 13, 2003, p. C3.
14. Gibbons, Frank. "Rosen—Indians' Mr. America." *Baseball Digest*, August 1952, pp. 51–55.
15. Paxton, Harry T. "The Clouting Kid from Cleveland." *Saturday Evening Post*, August 11, 1951, p. 86.
16. Bush, David. "Taking Stock of Al Rosen." Unidentified clipping in National Baseball Library file, 1985, p. 62.

Nevertheless, Greenberg and the Indians cut his pay for the '52 season, pointing out that his numbers were below his '50 standards. "I've got a chance to get it back if I have a good year, so I figure it's money in the bank," Rosen said. "I'm going to have a good year."[17]

And he did. Despite being benched briefly due to a slump in August, Rosen wound up leading the AL in total bases and RBI. He was also third in runs, extra-base hits, slugging, and OPS, fifth in hits, doubles, and WAR, sixth in homers (including three on April 29) and on-base percentage, seventh in batting and walks, and even tenth in stolen bases. Rosen earned his first All-Star selection, and finished tenth in MVP voting.

As good a year as 1952 was, it was only a prelude to arguably the greatest season ever by a third baseman. In 1953, Al Rosen played in all 155 games, and led the AL in runs (115), home runs (43), RBI (145), extra-base hits, total bases (367), slugging (.613), OPS, Runs Created, WAR (10.1), and Win Shares (42). In most of those categories, he didn't just lead the league, he blew away the field. Rosen had 52 more total bases, 30 more RBI, and 13 more Win Shares than anyone else in the league, and was clear of the #2 man in slugging by 54 points and in OPS by 113. He also finished second in batting and OBP, third in hits, fifth in walks, and eighth in steals, and had his best defensive season. Rosen's RBI total would remain the most ever by a third baseman until Alex Rodriguez recorded 156 in 2007.

Rosen narrowly missed the Triple Crown. Washington's Mickey Vernon led the batting race, but Al hit safely in the last 20 games and, entering his last at bat of the season, a hit would have enabled him to squeak past Vernon, .33723 to .33717. Rosen almost beat out an infield grounder but was out because he missed the bag, losing out to Vernon, .337-.336.

According to Craig Wright, Rosen totaled more Win Shares in 1953 than any other third basemen in history, topping the best totals for Hall of Famers Mike Schmidt (39 in 1974), Eddie Mathews (39 in 1953), Frank Baker (39 in 1912), George Brett (37 in 1985), and Wade Boggs (37 in 1986). Bill James calls Rosen's '53 season the best ever by a third baseman, adding that Al's career average of 111 RBI per 162 games played is the most of any third sacker.[18]

Though the Indians had finished in second place for the third straight year, there was no doubt about the league's Most Valuable Player. Rosen won the award unanimously, the first man to do so since the electorate was expanded to three writers from each league city in 1938. He had more than twice as many points as his nearest competitor, 336 to 167 for the Yankees'

---

17. Gibbons, Frank. "Rosen—Indians' Mr. America." *Baseball Digest*, August 1952, p. 55.
18. James, Bill. *The New Bill James Historical Baseball Abstract*. New York: Free Press, 2003, p. 554.

Yogi Berra. Rosen wept openly when he received the news, and later sent "thank you" notes to each of the 24 MVP voters.[19]

Rosen looked like he was going to have an even better season in '54. Through May 28, he had played in all 37 games and was batting .372 and slugging .693. He had 13 homers and 48 RBI, a pace of 54 and 200. There was talk of his breaking Hal Trosky's team RBI record of 162, and even Lou Gehrig's league mark of 184. But a position change led to Al's undoing.

On April 25, Rosen had moved to first base at management's request, replacing the light-hitting Bill Glynn, and making room for hot prospect Rudy Regalado (who would wind up playing just 91 big league games with two homers and a .249 average). But calamity struck on May 31, when Rosen was attempting to field a sharp grounder hit by Jim Rivera of the White Sox.[20] The ball struck Rosen's throwing hand, resulting in a badly-broken right index finger, though it wasn't diagnosed until sometime later. "What's the use of X-raying it," team physician Don Kelly asked rhetorically. "Rosen will play regardless of what the film shows."[21] Indeed, Rosen attempted to play through the injury, but couldn't grip the bat properly, managing only an occasional single over the next few games.[22] He finally sat out from June 4–15, but that wasn't enough. "I waited too long, and then I came back too soon," recalled Rosen. "It never did heal properly."[23] He hit a pedestrian .270 with just 11 homers in 329 at bats after his hot start.

The season was far from a total "bust" for Rosen, though. On July 13, playing in his third of four straight All-Star Games, he was the star of the AL's 11–9 victory with a single, two homers and five RBI (through 2020, only Hall of Famers Arky Vaughan, Ted Williams, Willie McCovey, and Gary Carter have matched the feat of two homers in a Midsummer Classic). Rosen finished with his third consecutive .300 season and his fifth straight 100-RBI campaign (it would be 23 years before another AL player, Thurman Munson, strung together three 100-RBI, .300-average seasons). Rosen led the AL in sacrifice flies and finished in the league's top five in homers, OBP, and slugging. Most importantly, he helped the Indians to an AL record 111–43 log, enabling them to end the Yankees' five-year grip on the AL pennant (though Cleveland was upset by the Giants in the World Series).

---

19. Ingraham, Jim. "Rosen Worth Remembering." *Morning Journal* (Lorain, OH), August 25, 2013.

20. Rosen, Al, as told to Milton Richman. "They Pay Off on Runs-Batted-In." *SPORT*, October 1954, p. 94.

21. *The Sporting News*, June 9, 1954, p. 4.

22. Warsinskey, Tim. "One Last At-Bat, One Last Chance for a Crown." *Cleveland Plain Dealer*, September 27, 2013.

23. Storm, Stephanie. "Competitive Streak Still Burning in Al Rosen." *Beacon (OH) Journal*, February 29, 2004.

Rosen's reward for all this? Another pay-cut, from $42,500 to $37,500.[24]

Rosen had averaged 31 homers, 114 RBI, and a .298 average over his first five full seasons, but his days as a dominant player were over. Still bothered by the finger injury, and adding a badly-pulled left leg muscle (which had benched him during the 1954 World Series[25]), Rosen suffered through an off-year in 1955. Nevertheless, Ralph Kiner, who joined Cleveland for his final season that year, was impressed. "He was the leader of the team and the best all-around player I ever played with," recalled Kiner.[26]

In January 1956, Rosen was further injured in an auto accident. A driver in front of Rosen stopped short, and he did the same, but the driver behind him didn't, sandwiching Al's car between the two vehicles. Rosen suffered neck and leg injuries,[27] and his production declined even more. He repeatedly reinjured the neck on swings of the bat, and the fans started booing him. "I don't want you to think this is an excuse," Rosen said following the season, "but after I got hurt I could hardly turn my head. I had to take injections so that I could get full use of my neck and shoulders while playing."[28]

Despite the setbacks, Rosen was just 32 years old and three years removed from an MVP season. So it came as a surprise when he announced his retirement on January 31, 1957, "because I can't do the job anymore."[29] Rejecting the Indians' efforts to woo him back over the next year, Rosen remained retired.

Unlike most players of that era, Rosen was well-equipped to leave his baseball career behind. Putting his business degree to work, he had joined a Cleveland stock brokerage business in 1953, and now could put full-time effort into it. Rosen spent over two decades as a successful stockbroker.

But Rosen was not done with baseball altogether. He served as an Indians spring training batting instructor, and on January 18, 1968, was elected to the team's Board of Directors.[30] In December 1971, he led a group of investors, including Cleveland magnate George Steinbrenner, in making an

---

24. Warsinskey, Tim. "One Last At-Bat, One Last Chance for a Crown." *Cleveland Plain Dealer*, September 27, 2013.
25. Olderman, Murray. "Al Rosen Held Prime Seat for Baseball Record." *The Desert Sun*, September 27, 2014.
26. Goldstein, Richard. "Al Rosen, Who Missed Triple Crown by a Step, Dies at 91." *New York Times*, March 15, 2015.
27. Lebovitz, Hal. "Neck Injury Puts Rosen in 'Collar.'" Unidentified clipping in National Baseball Library file, January, 1956.
28. Associated Press. "'Boos Didn't End Career'—Rosen." February 12, 1957.
29. United Press International. "Rosen of Indians Quits Baseball; Infielder 'Can't Do Job Anymore.'" January 31, 1957.
30. "Ex-Slugger Rosen on Indian Board." *The Sporting News*, February 3, 1968.

offer to buy the Indians, but it was rejected.[31] A year later, he joined a group led by Steinbrenner in buying the New York Yankees. Rosen was named the team's executive vice-president, soon elevated to president, after the 1977 season.[32]

Rosen had gotten some lessons in team management decades before. "I was very fortunate in that my locker with the Indians many years ago was next to [future manager] Birdie Tebbetts," Rosen said. "One thing he always said in building a team was to determine what your need is and fill it."[33]

Rosen's rookie season in the front office was a smashing success. He helped the club to its second straight world championship in 1978, and later engineered a trade which brought future pitching star Dave Righetti to the team. Rosen even helped save Bob Fishel's life when the AL official had a medical emergency during a league meeting.[34] Rosen was named Miami University's Alumnus of the Year.[35]

But things turned sour after Steinbrenner fired manager Bob Lemon, Rosen's friend and former teammate, and rehired Billy Martin to replace him in June 1979. Rosen and Martin had a personality conflict which dated back to 1951, when they were rival AL players. Rosen resigned on July 19, and promptly accepted an executive vice president position for Bally's Casinos.[36] He resigned from that post amid some financial controversy on October 6, 1980.[37]

Following rumors that he was going to join the front office of the A's or White Sox, Rosen was named president and general manager of the Astros on October 27, 1980.[38] He was replacing the popular Tal Smith right after Houston's most successful season, so Rosen found himself in a hostile situation. To add to that stress, Rosen underwent open-heart surgery on January 5, 1981.[39] The Astros made it to the post-season in 1981, but then sunk into mediocrity. Rosen did land future All-Stars Dickie Thon and Mike Scott in trades, but the effects did not show in the standings over the next four years (though the team won more games than it lost during his regime). Rosen was fired on September 13, 1985.[40]

Five days later, Rosen signed as president and general manager of the

---

31. Schneider, Russell. "Stouffer Snubs Local Bid for Injuns." *The Sporting News*, December 25, 1971, p. 33.
32. Pepe, Phil. "Yankees Lose Blomberg, Take on Rosen." *The Sporting News*, December 3, 1977.
33. Spander, Art. "G. M. Story: Best of Two Worlds." *The Sporting News*, October 23, 1989.
34. Young, Dick. "Young Ideas." *The Sporting News*, September 2, 1978.
35. "Yankee Doodles." *The Sporting News*, December 16, 1978.
36. Associated Press. "Rosen Accepts Casino Position." July 31, 1979.
37. Associated Press. "Rosen Resigns from Casino Job." October 6, 1980.
38. "New Pact for Rosen." *The Sporting News*, October 24, 1981.
39. "Astronotes." *The Sporting News*, February 28, 1981.
40. Associated Press. "Astros Dismiss Rosen." September 14, 1985.

San Francisco Giants, a team completing a 100-loss season and its second straight last-place finish. Rosen cleaned house, and showed quick results. The Giants improved by 21 games and three spots in the standings in '86, then—with the help of new acquisition Kevin Mitchell—won the NL West title the following year. Rosen was named Executive of the Year by *The Sporting News* and UPI, becoming the first former MVP ever to win that honor. He remained with San Francisco for seven years, including the 1989 NL pennant, retiring after the 1992 season. One bad feature of his Giants stint was the loss of most of his baseball memorabilia, to fire and water damage during the 1989 San Francisco earthquake.[41]

Rosen enjoyed a lot of honors and recognition in his golden years. On June 5, 1988, he was inducted into the Jewish Sports Hall of Fame in Irvine, California.[42] On July 13, 2003, marking the 50th anniversary of his MVP season, the Indians honored him with Al Rosen Day at Jacobs Field.[43] On July 29, 2006, he was inducted into the Cleveland Indians' Hall of Fame (joining six others, including Ray Chapman and Herb Score, subjects of other chapters in this book).[44] And in 2013, he was the subject of a documentary DVD, *Beating the Odds, the Al Rosen Story*.[45]

Al Rosen died at 91 on March 13, 2015, at Rancho Mirage, California.

Year	Team (League)	G	AB	R	H	2B	3B	HR	RBI	SB	AVG	OBP	SLG
1947	Cleveland (AL)	7	9	1	1	0	0	0	0	0	.111	.111	.111
1948		5	5	0	1	0	0	0	0	0	.200	.200	.200
1949		23	44	3	7	2	0	0	5	0	.159	.275	.205
1950		155	554	100	159	23	4	*37	116	5	.287	.405	.543
1951		*154	573	82	152	30	1	24	102	7	.265	.362	.447
1952		148	567	101	171	32	5	28	*105	8	.302	.387	.524
1953		155	599	*115	201	27	5	*43	*145	8	.336	.422	*.613
1954		137	466	76	140	20	2	24	102	6	.300	.404	.506
1955		139	492	61	120	13	1	21	81	4	.244	.362	.402
1956		121	416	64	111	18	2	15	61	1	.267	.351	.428
Totals		1044	3725	603	1063	165	20	192	717	39	.285	.384	.495

---

41. "Rosen Loses Memorabilia." *New York Times*, October 23, 1989.

42. "Honors for Rosen." Unidentified clipping in National Baseball Library file, June 13, 1988.

43. Lubinger, Bill. "Indians Great Rosen Endured, Prevailed in the Face of Bigotry." *Cleveland Plain Dealer*, October 12, 2010.

44. Milicia, Joe. "Hall of Fame a Long Time Coming for Indians." *The Morning Journal* (Lorain, OH), July 12, 2006, p. C4.

45. Ingraham, Jim. "Rosen Worth Remembering." *Morning Journal* (Lorain, OH), August 25, 2013.

Herb Score

The May 11, 1957, issue of the *Saturday Evening Post* had a four-page feature article on Herb Score. "This is not just the story of another promising young pitcher," it said, echoing the thoughts of most baseball followers. "This Cleveland left-hander is the kind who can finish up in the Baseball Hall of Fame.... He could be one of the very greatest."[1]

But by the time the magazine hit the newsstands, Score's career path had taken a tragic turn.

Herbert Jude Score was born June 7, 1933, at Rosedale, Long Island, New York, the son of Herbert A. (a New York City traffic cop) and Ann Score. The child's middle name came from the patron saint of desperate causes. Sisters Helen and Anna Mae followed over the next nine years before Herbert and Ann split up. Bound by Catholic taboos, they never divorced, but the separation was permanent, and the marriage wouldn't officially end until Herbert's death on November 8, 1957.[2] Ann would die on April 12, 1963.[3]

Young Herb, called "Buddy" by his family, had his first of many health crises at age three. He toddled out into the street and was struck by a bakery truck, crushing both legs just below the pelvis. Herb spent 10 weeks in traction, and there was doubt if he would ever walk again. Surgery to install a steel plate was scheduled, but cancelled at the last minute, when a pre-op X-ray showed the bones had surprisingly worked themselves back into place.

At age 10, Herb came down with rheumatic fever, spending eight months in bed and missing a year of school (ultimately delaying his high school graduation by a year). There were also bouts with pneumonia, appendicitis, and a broken ankle. He had high blood pressure, which caused him to be rejected for military service. Somehow, Herb always recovered with no significant after-effects.[4]

In sixth grade at Holy Name of Mary parochial school in Valley Stream, New York, Herb became a pitcher under the tutelage of his coach, Father Thomas Kelly. He kept improving over the next three years, until his parents' separation forced him to new surroundings. Seeking a warmer climate for her kids' health, Ann Score took them and moved to Lake Worth, Florida.

---

1. Lebovitz, Hal. "Cleveland's Left-Handed Lightning." *Saturday Evening Post*, May 11, 1957, p. 42, 124.
2. "Herb Score's Father Dies." *New York Times*, November 10, 1957.
3. United Press International. "Score's Mother Dies." April 12, 1963.
4. Score, Herb. "Dear Mom..." *Guideposts*, May 1958, p. 3.

Herb continued his pitching dominance at Lake Worth High School, pitching a no-hitter in his first game for the Trojans (also becoming a basketball star for the school). He soon drew the attention of Indians scout Cy Slapnicka, the man who had signed Bob Feller. Score pitched five more no-hitters for the Trojans over the next four years, going 8–0 in his final season, 1952.[5] Declining higher bids, Score eventually signed with the Indians for $60,000, payable in five annual installments.[6]

Score went right from high school to AAA, joining the Indianapolis Indians of the American Association. He displayed amazing speed but awful control, striking out 61 but walking 62 in 62 innings, resulting in a 2–5, 5.23 record. Sent all the way down to Reading in the Eastern League (A) in 1953, though he missed much of the season due to a dislocated left collarbone, Score showed enough progress (7–3, 4.68) to return to Indianapolis for the next campaign.

Score had a breakout year in 1954. By the time it was over (ended by a second bout with pneumonia), he had gone 22–5, leading the A.A. in wins, percentage (.815), strikeouts (330), and ERA (2.62). Score gave up just 140 hits in 251 innings, barely five per nine frames. He shattered the league strikeout record (264 by Heine Berger in 1906),[7] and was named Minor League Player of the Year by *The Sporting News*.[8] At 21, Herb Score would be going to the big leagues.

Score was a solidly-built athlete, standing 6'2" and weighing 185 to 200 pounds. He had an all-out pitching style. His sweeping follow-through drove his head downward and caused his left elbow to crack against his right knee, so he had to wear a sponge-rubber pad to cushion the impact.[9] As a consequence, Score was not good at fielding his position or reacting to shots hit back to the box—but then, not many batters were hitting the ball hard against him.

Though he was making the minimum salary of $6,000,[10] Score was hardly flying under the radar. Associated Press sports editor Joe Reichler wrote that "the Cleveland left-hander may well develop into one of the greats of baseball. Reputed by some to be as fast as Lefty Grove, Score also

---

5. George, Dave. "Herb Score: Lake Worth's Lost Legend." *Palm Beach (Florida) Post*, May 7, 2015.
6. Lebovitz, Hal. "Cleveland's Left-Handed Lightning." *Saturday Evening Post*, May 11, 1957, p. 124.
7. Johnson, Lloyd and Miles Wolff, Editors. *The Encyclopedia of Minor League Baseball*. Durham, NC: Baseball America, Inc., 1993, p. 280.
8. Obojski, Robert. "Score Completes 32nd Year as Indians Broadcaster." *Sports Collectors Digest*, November 24, 1995, p. 130.
9. Lebovitz, Hal. "Cleveland's Left-Handed Lightning." *Saturday Evening Post*, May 11, 1957, p. 122–23.
10. *Ibid.*, p. 124.

owns a wicked curve that many batters find harder to hit than his blazing fast ball."[11]

In those days, strikeouts were far less plentiful than they are today. There was a stigma about whiffing, and many batters shortened up on the bat or their swing, just trying to put the ball in play. Prior to 1955, no pitcher had ever averaged a strikeout per inning pitched over a season of 150+ innings. That was about to change.

Score made his major league debut against the hard-hitting Tigers on April 15, 1955. He pitched a complete-game, 7–3 victory, striking out nine and walking nine. In his fourth game on May 1, Score fanned 16 Red Sox, just two strikeouts shy of the modern major league record at the time. He made the cover of *Sports Illustrated* (May 30) and the AL All-Star team. Score was a bit erratic, though, and through the Indians' 100th game was a modest 9–9 with a 3.21 ERA.

But Herb went 7–1, 2.43 the rest of the way to complete a remarkable rookie season. His 2.85 ERA was fourth-best in the league, and he ranked third in pitching WAR. Among his 16 wins were two four-hitters, three three-hitters, a two-hitter, and a one-hitter; he finished second in the AL for fewest hits allowed per nine innings. Score's 9.73 strikeouts per nine innings set a record, and his 245 K's easily led the league and broke Hall of Famer Grover Alexander's rookie mark (227 in 1911). Score overwhelmingly was named AL Rookie of the Year by both the BBWAA and *The Sporting News*.

Raised to $12,000, Score destroyed the sophomore jinx in 1956. He set lofty goals of 20 wins and 260 strikeouts, and reached both.[12] Despite missing two weeks in June due to a spastic colon, he won 20 games, made his second All-Star team, and led the AL in strikeouts (263–71 more than the #2-man), shutouts (5), and most strikeouts and fewest hits per nine innings. He finished second in ERA and in pitching WAR, and was tops in three other modern metrics to evaluate pitchers, Adjusted ERA, Fielding Independent Pitching, and Win Probability Added. Score was named Sophomore of the Year.[13] Triple Crown winner Mickey Mantle named Score as his toughest pitcher to hit.[14]

At 23, Score was more than an up-and-coming prospect—he was already close to the best pitcher in the American League. Among major league hurlers in 1955–56, his 2.68 ERA was bettered only by Whitey Ford's

---

11. Obojski, Robert. "Score Completes 32nd Year as Indians Broadcaster." *Sports Collectors Digest*, November 24, 1995, p. 130.
12. Bang, Ed. "Will Herb Score be Greatest Lefthander?" *The Sporting News*, April 10, 1957.
13. Lebovitz, Hal. "Cleveland's Left-Handed Lightning." *Saturday Evening Post*, May 11, 1957, p. 122.
14. "Score Toughest, Says Mantle." *New York World Telegram-Star*, February 5, 1957.

2.55. Score's 508 strikeouts were far ahead of second-place Sam Jones's 374. In the AL, only future Hall of Famers Bob Lemon (38), Early Wynn (37), and Ford (37) topped Score's 36 wins. Seeking to reach the top of his profession, Score regularly picked the brains of teammates Lemon and Wynn, along with pitching coach Mel Harder.[15]

Score was raised to $20,000 for 1957,[16] an unheard-of sum for a 23-year-old pitcher at that time. Earning nicknames like "Hurricane Herb" and "The Howitzer," Score was already being talked about as a potential all-time great. In a 1956 BBWAA poll, he was rated as one of the top 10 fastball pitchers in history, joining the likes of Walter Johnson, Bob Feller, and Dizzy Dean.[17] In the spring of 1957, Red Sox' general manager Joe Cronin offered the Indians one million dollars for Score, at a time when an entire team could be bought for two or three million.[18] "This kid is going to be one of the great ones," said Hall of Famer Tris Speaker.[19] Indians general manager Hank Greenberg was always quick to add, "provided nothing happens to him."[20]

According to Cleveland scribe Hal Lebovitz, Score sometimes threw as many as 180 pitches in a game.[21] Given his high totals of strikeouts, walks, and complete games, it is not far-fetched. On opening day, 1957, for instance, Score pitched 11 innings and faced 50 batters, with 10 strikeouts and 11 walks, losing to the White Sox, 3–2. Based on Tom Tango's pitch estimating formula, that would be 208 pitches—in his first outing of the season! Score followed that with a four-hit shutout of the ChiSox and a three-hit, 2–1 win over the Tigers. After a no-decision in the Tribe's 13th game on May 1, in which he fanned 12 in six-and-a-third innings, Score had a 2–1 record with 39 K's and a 2.04 ERA. He was on track for his greatest season yet.

On Tuesday night, May 7, 1957, Score faced the world champion Yankees in Cleveland. New York's Hank Bauer grounded out to lead off the game. This brought up Gil McDougald, a hard-hitting infielder and former Rookie of the Year who would earn five All-Star selections in his 10-year career. McDougald worked the count to 2–2. The time was 8:05 p.m.

---

15. Lebovitz, Hal. "Cleveland's Left-Handed Lightning." *Saturday Evening Post*, May 11, 1957, p. 123.
16. *Ibid.*, p. 124.
17. Obojski, Robert. "Score Completes 32nd Year as Indians Broadcaster." *Sports Collectors Digest*, November 24, 1995, p. 130.
18. Bang, Ed. "Will Herb Score be Greatest Lefthander?" *The Sporting News*, April 10, 1957.
19. Kamm, Herb. "Faith in St. Jude Buoys Herb Score in Adversity." *New York World Telegram-Star*, March 31, 1959.
20. Lebovitz, Hal. "Cleveland's Left-Handed Lightning." *Saturday Evening Post*, May 11, 1957, p. 123.
21. *Ibid.*

Score let loose with his twelfth pitch of the game, a fastball. "After I released the ball," recalled Score three months later, "I didn't see it again until it was three feet away from me. I heard the crack of the bat while my head was down in my follow-through. All I ever saw as my head came up was this white blur bulleting at me. I snapped up my glove, but the white blur blasted through the finger tips and smashed into my right eye."[22] The ball ricocheted to third baseman Al Smith, who threw out McDougald, giving Score a hard-earned assist. "If he loses his sight, I'll quit baseball," said the distraught McDougald.[23]

Score left the field on a stretcher and was transported to Lakeside Hospital, where he would remain until May 28. He had suffered severe hemorrhaging and a swollen retina, along with a broken nose. It was four days before Score could see even light from his right eye, and his vision remained blurry for months afterward. He talked about returning to baseball that season, but it soon became apparent that wouldn't happen. Drugs and medications slowed his ability to return to fitness, and Score was unable to focus his eyes properly, reaching for things that weren't there.[24]

Herb took the opportunity to move up his wedding date. He had met Nancy McNamara at Lake Worth High School, but they didn't start dating until afterward, and became engaged in January 1957.[25] They were married in Boynton Beach, Florida, on July 10, with the Rev. Thomas Kelly—Herb's old baseball coach—officiating.[26] Herb and Nancy would remain married for more than a half-century, raising four children, Judy, Mary, David, and Susan (Susan, who had Down Syndrome, would die in 1994).

People wondered if Score would be gun-shy when he returned in 1958. "I'd be foolish to say I won't be more conscious of a liner coming back at me," he said. "I'll be trying to get my head up faster after my follow-through."[27] There is evidence that Score changed his delivery to leave himself in better fielding position: before the injury, he averaged just 0.81 chances accepted per nine innings; afterward, it was up 38 percent to 1.12. But the Indians weren't worried that it would affect his pitching, signing him to another $20,000 contract.[28]

Score seemed to be back on track in the early weeks of the new

---

22. Score, Herb. "The Things I Saw in the Darkness." *Look*, August 20, 1957, p. 24.
23. George, Dave. "Herb Score: Lake Worth's Lost Legend." *Palm Beach (Florida) Post*, May 7, 2015.
24. Kamm, Herb. "Faith in St. Jude Buoys Herb Score in Adversity." *New York World Telegram-Star*, March 31, 1959.
25. Lebovitz, Hal. "Cleveland's Left-Handed Lightning." *Saturday Evening Post*, May 11, 1957, p. 124.
26. Murphy, Jimmy. "Score's Discoverer Officiated at his Marriage." *New York World Telegram-Star*, July 12, 1957.
27. Score, Herb. "The Things I Saw in the Darkness." *Look*, August 20, 1957, p. 25.
28. United Press International. "Herb Score Signs Indians' Contract." January 8, 1958.

season. In the month of April, he was 2–2 with a 3.00 ERA and 32 K's in 30 innings. On April 23, he struck out 13 in a three-hit shutout over the White Sox. But in his next start, April 30 vs. Washington, something went wrong. He began feeling a "muscle knot" in his forearm in the eighth inning, and by the ninth was unable to get the ball to home plate.[29] The injury eventually was diagnosed as a torn tendon; he would pitch only 11 more innings all season. Teammate Rocky Colavito said that, after this setback, Score "slung the ball instead of popping it." Manager Joe Gordon opined that he had "a mental block which prevents him from cutting loose." Score denied it.[30]

Score attempted another comeback in 1959. "Herb got off to a good start, but then a ball was hit back through the box and it brought back memories" recalled Bob Lemon, by then an Indians scout. "He became mechanical. He wasn't bringing it like he used to, not holding anything back."[31] At the All-Star break Score was 9–5 with 111 K's, but he went 0–6 with a 6.31 ERA thereafter. He finished with the league's second-worst ERA out of 33 qualifiers and had a losing record for a team that finished just five games out of first place. Still, Score actually led the AL in most strikeouts and fewest hits allowed per nine innings.

On April 18, 1960, Score was traded to the White Sox for Barry Latman. Three years after being offered a million dollars for Score, the Indians instead got a journeyman on his way to a 59–68 career record. Indians general manager Frank "Trader" Lane defended the deal, saying Score was a complainer whose problems stemmed from the 1957 beaning, and were "more psychological than physical.... On the mound, when he's delivering the ball, he sneaks a peek at the batter. Before the injury he never looked at the batter—just at the catcher and the strike zone."[32]

Score's career continued downhill. He went 6–12 with a 4.25 ERA in parts of the next three seasons with the White Sox. He spent most of 1961 (San Diego, Pacific Coast League) and '62 (Indianapolis, American Association) in the minors, going 7–6 and 10–7, but with ERAs of 5.10 and 4.82. After a 0–6, 7.66 log with Indianapolis in 1963, it was obvious Score's pitching career was over.

But Herb was not done with the game. At the end of the 1963 season, the Indians invited him to try his hand at broadcasting. He teamed with Bob Neal to call Cleveland's last two televised games of the season on WJW,

---

29. Daley, Arthur. "Learning the Score." *New York Times*, May 7, 1958.
30. United Press International. "Score Denied 'Mental Problem' Hinders Pitching." September 18, 1958.
31. Goldstein, Richard. "Herb Score, Derailed by a Line Drive, Dies at 75." *New York Times*, November 12, 2008.
32. Associated Press. "Lane Defends His Latest Deals." April 19, 1960.

as an audition for an opening the following year. Score got high marks as a color commentator and won the job.[33]

Score became a beloved Indians broadcaster over the next 34 years, noted for his folksy delivery and malapropisms. He switched to radio play-by-play with WERE in 1969, later moving along with the team to WWWE and, in 1992, to WKNR.[34] His knowledge of the game and his innate goodness shone through his broadcasts. "He has no ego," said broadcasting partner Tom Hamilton. "He wears a suit and tie to games on the road and he goes to Mass every Sunday."[35] Indians player Buddy Bell said, "Herb is such a nice guy, he probably makes his bed in the hotel room in the morning."[36]

Score also served the Indians as a ticket salesman and batting practice pitcher. "I'm a great BP pitcher," he joked. "Now I realize I was throwing BP the last few years of my career."[37]

Score announced his retirement effective at the end of the 1997 season. He wanted to bow out while still healthy and spend more time with his family, which now included eight grandchildren. The Indians honored him with a 20-minute pregame ceremony on "Herb Score Night" on September 7. He was given a key to the city and three long standing ovations.[38]

Score didn't get to enjoy his retirement for long. On October 8, 1998, the day after being inducted into the Broadcasting Hall of Fame in Akron, Ohio, he was nearly killed in an auto accident. Score ran a stop sign and swerved into the path of a tractor-trailer, sustaining brain, lung, face, and rib injuries, and was put on a ventilator in critical condition. He was hospitalized until December 11.[39] Score's health was problematic the rest of his life. He underwent hip replacement surgery in 2000, and had the first of a series of debilitating strokes in 2002. Herb Score died at 75 on November 11, 2008. The Indians wore a uniform patch in his memory the following season.

Score received several more honors in his final years. He was inducted into the Press Club of Cleveland Journalism Hall of Fame in November

---

33. Lebovitz, Hal. "Score Fires Strikes with Old Zip in Tryout at Wigwam Video Mike." *The Sporting News*, October 5, 1963.
34. Obojski, Robert. "Score Completes 32nd Year as Indians Broadcaster." *Sports Collectors Digest*, November 24, 1995, p. 131.
35. Cabot, Mary Kay. "Soon Score-less." *Cleveland Plain Dealer*, September 21, 1997.
36. George, Dave. "Herb Score: Lake Worth's Lost Legend." *Palm Beach (Florida) Post*, May 7, 2015.
37. Dolgan, Bob. "Former Cleveland Indians Broadcaster and Pitcher Herb Score Dies at Age 75." *Cleveland Plain Dealer*, November 12, 2008.
38. Cabot, Mary Kay. "Pregame Salute Honors Score." *Cleveland Plain Dealer*, September 8, 1997.
39. "Score Goes Home." *New York Post*, December 12, 1998.

1998. Score threw out the first pitch in the Indians' home opener in 1999.[40] And on July 29, 2006, he was inducted into the Cleveland Indians' Hall of Fame.[41]

It's clear that arm trouble led to Score's demise as a pitcher. Was it the result of the McDougald incident, making him gun-shy and upsetting his mechanics? Was it the old story of overuse of a young arm? Or a combination of the two? Regardless, Score went from a pitcher who seemed bound for Cooperstown, to one who couldn't retire even minor leaguers.

He refused to dwell on the negative, though. "I'm a lucky fellow," he said. "I'm glad God gave me the ability to throw a baseball well for a few years. That drive could have killed me."[42]

Year	Team (League)	G	IP	W	L	PCT	SO	BB	H	ERA
1955	Cleveland (AL)	33	227.1	16	10	.615	*245	154	158	2.85
1956		35	249.1	20	9	.690	*263	129	162	2.53
1957		5	36.0	2	1	.667	39	26	18	2.00
1958		12	41.0	2	3	.400	48	34	29	3.95
1959		30	160.2	9	11	.450	147	115	123	4.71
1960	Chicago (AL)	23	113.2	5	10	.333	78	87	91	3.72
1961		8	24.1	1	2	.333	14	24	22	6.66
1962		4	6.0	0	0	.----	3	4	6	4.50
Totals		150	858.1	55	46	.545	837	573	609	3.36

40. Dolgan, Bob. "Former Cleveland Indians Broadcaster and Pitcher Herb Score Dies at Age 75." *Cleveland Plain Dealer*, November 12, 2008.
41. Milicia, Joe. "Hall of Fame a Long Time Coming for Indians." *The Morning Journal* (Lorain, OH), July 12, 2006, p. C4.
42. George, Dave. "Herb Score: Lake Worth's Lost Legend." *Palm Beach (Florida) Post*, May 7, 2015.

Louis Sockalexis

Can you imagine the White Sox changing their name to "Cubans" in honor of Cuban-born slugger Jose Abreu? Can you imagine it having happened in spring training of 2014, before Abreu had ever played a major league game?

That's what happened with Lou Sockalexis 117 years earlier.

Louis Francis (or Lewis M., according to his death certificate) Sockalexis was born October 24, 1871, the son of Native Americans Francis P.

and Frances P. Sockabeson Sockalexis. Louis grew up at Indian Island, the Penobscot tribe reservation in Old Town, Maine.[1] Francis's father was Governor of the Penobscots, and the family was active in tribal affairs.

Louis soon developed into a solidly-built athlete; at 5'11" and 185 pounds, he was bigger and stronger than most men of that era. Separating fact from fiction in the stories of Sockalexis is a challenging task. He supposedly could run the 100-yard dash in 10 seconds flat (the winning time for the 100-meter dash in the 1896 Olympics was 12 seconds), throw a baseball over 400 feet, and hit one even farther. As H.G. Salsinger wrote, "The legends about him are often vague and contradictory. At times he appears to have been a mythical, rather than a legendary, figure."[2] But it is clear that Lou had exceptional talent and was what today we would call a five-tool player.

The left-handed hitter and right-handed thrower began playing amateur and semi-pro ball in Maine, quickly standing out wherever he went. Among the nicknames Sockalexis gathered in his travels were Sock or Sox, Aleck, Deerfoot, and—like most Native Americans who followed Lou to the diamond—Chief. It is said that Corinth, Maine, author Gilbert Patten was inspired by Sockalexis in creating his famous fictional baseball player, Frank Merriwell, while writing under the pseudonym Burt Standish. Patten supposedly managed a team in the Maine summer leagues which Sockalexis dominated.[3]

In 1894, the Poland Spring resort hotel fielded a baseball team, playing a couple of games per week between July 7 and September 6. Among its players were two future major leaguers: catcher Mike "Doc" Powers, and Sockalexis. The resort's official newspaper, *The Hill-Top*, reported on the games, with box scores of 10 of them. In those 10, Sockalexis batted .326 with a .698 slugging percentage—and that's not including the September 1 game (no box score), when he hit two home runs in the first inning! Besides detailing his hitting exploits, *The Hill-Top* claimed that "Sockalexis is the best thrower in New England" and was the team's "star fielder." As the season concluded, the paper reported that Lou would be moving on to Ricker Classical Institute in Houlton, Maine.[4]

Recommended and lured by Doc Powers, Sockalexis instead joined the College of the Holy Cross in Worcester, Massachusetts, in the fall of 1894.[5] He soon became the most celebrated collegiate baseball player of

---

1. Gagnon, Cappy. "SOCKALEXIS, Lewis M." In *Biographical Dictionary of American Sports: Baseball*, edited by David L. Porter.
2. Salsinger, H. G. "The Facts about Sockalexis." *Baseball Digest*, June, 1954, p. 54.
3. Rice, Ed. *Baseball's First Indian*. Tidemark Press, 2003, p. xiii.
4. *The Hill-Top*, July 15–September 9, 1894.
5. "The Sockalexis Story." *Kaleidoscope*, July 27, 1964.

his time. According to Holy Cross records, Sockalexis batted .436 in 1895 and .444 in 1896, with a season of football in between. Sixty years later, the school would create an Athletic Hall of Fame, inducting Sockalexis as a charter member.[6]

Cleveland Spiders star Jesse Burkett, a future Hall of Famer and part-time Holy Cross coach, recommended that the Spiders sign Sockalexis. Arrangements were made for Lou to join the team after his 1897 college season. During the winter of 1896–97, Powers transferred to Notre Dame and Sockalexis did too. But in March, Lou left or was expelled from Notre Dame, expediting his path to the majors. He joined the Spiders in spring training to a hero's welcome.

Sockalexis would be the first full-fledged Native American to play in the major leagues, blazing the trail for the likes of Chief Bender and Chief Meyers. Fans would flock to the ballparks to see this much-hyped novelty. Sockalexis would good-naturedly endure racial taunting and war whoops from the fans and stereotyping by the press, often turning the taunts into cheers with his play on the diamond.

When the Spiders arrived in camp, *The Sporting Life* printed the following:

> THEY'RE INDIANS NOW
>
> There is no feature in the signing of Sockalexis more gratifying than the fact that his presence on the team will result in relegating to obscurity the title of "Spiders," by which the team has been handicapped for several season (sic), to give place to the more significant name "Indians."[7]

Granted, team nicknames then did not have the "official" status they do today, and "Spiders" remained in common usage for the three remaining years of the team's existence. Nonetheless, it was a unique distinction for a team to be renamed in honor of a man who was still a month from his major league debut.

That debut, following an impressive spring training season, came on April 22. It did not take Sockalexis long to live up to the hype. On April 30, the day after making a game-saving catch in right field, he connected for his first home run, off Bill Hutchison (featured in another chapter of this book). An unidentified clipping described it as "one of the longest hits ever made on the (St. Louis) grounds." The following day, Lou collected four hits, including a triple, and two stolen bases. On May 5, he hit his second homer (this in a season in which no one would hit more than 11 round-trippers). On May 7, Sockalexis again had a four-hit game with a triple and two steals,

---

6. Rice, Ed. "Baseball Hall Needs to Acknowledge Sockalexis." *Bangor Daily News*, April 5, 2004, p. C5.

7. "Cleveland Chatter." *The Sporting Life*, March 27, 1897, p. 3.

adding a great running catch. On May 10 and again on May 13 (the latter game against future Hall of Famer Kid Nichols), he swatted a double and triple. According to *The Sporting Life*, Cleveland manager Patsy "Tebeau predicts that after one full season in the National League, (Sockalexis) will be one of the greatest players ever joining the organization."[8]

By May 22, 24 games into the season, Sockalexis was batting .385 with a .583 slugging percentage and 13 stolen bases. Newspapers didn't keep track of league leaders in those days, but I checked 13 others who wound up as the top players of 1897: Hall of Famers Jesse Burkett, Fred Clarke, George Davis, Ed Delahanty, Hugh Duffy, Billy Hamilton, Willie Keeler, Joe Kelley, Nap Lajoie, and Bobby Wallace, plus Harry Davis and Jake Stenzel. Here's how Sockalexis compared in batting and slugging:

Major League Leaders Through May 22, 1897

Batting Average		Slugging Percentage	
.437	Willie Keeler, BAL	.643	Nap Lajoie, PHI
.398	Joe Kelley, BAL	.613	Willie Keeler, BAL
.388	Fred Clarke, LOU	**.583**	**Louis Sockalexis, CLE**
.385	**Louis Sockalexis, CLE**	.581	Ed Delahanty, PHI
.381	Ed Delahanty, PHI	.573	Fred Clarke, LOU

Sockalexis also was in the top five in hits, doubles, triples, homers, RBI, and total bases; he was sixth in steals, but just four behind the leader. His salary, already high for a first-year player at $1,500, soon was raised to the maximum $2,400.[9] The *Boston Traveler* reported that "each season the league generally produces something in the way of a sensation. This year the sensation is Sockalexis, and the chances are that he will grow greater as he becomes more seasoned."

After that, Lou's highlights started coming farther apart. He stopped stealing bases, and stopped hitting for power. After a long home run against the immortal Amos Rusie on June 16, Sockalexis would collect only three more extra-base hits in 1897. But he was still collecting one-base hits. On July 1 he went 5-for-5 in the midst of a 14-game hitting streak.

At some point in 1897, Sockalexis was introduced to liquor, and it soon took over his life. There are fanciful accounts of it happening after he hit a game-winning grand slam and went out to celebrate, but Sockalexis never had such a hit. A more-credible story indicates he had taken up the bottle before he even reached the majors, and it was a drunken escapade that caused his expulsion from Notre Dame.[10]

---

8. *The Sporting Life*, May 15, 1897.
9. Rice, Ed. *Baseball's First Indian*. Tidemark Press, 2003, p. 23.
10. Salsinger, H. G. "The Facts about Sockalexis." *Baseball Digest*, June 1954, p. 55.

Though he was still hitting for average, his fielding had become intolerably erratic. In his first 53 games, Sockalexis had made seven errors in 118 chances for a .941 percentage, six points better than the league average for outfielders that year. But in his last 13 games, he made nine errors in just 25 chances, a woeful .640 mark. In mid-season, Sockalexis injured his foot and/or ankle; author David Fleitz pinpoints it to the wee hours of July 4, when the inebriated Sockalexis fell or was thrown from the second-story window of a brothel. In any case, he played just three games in the final 10 weeks of the season. On July 20, the *Boston Globe* reported that "Sockalexis has been laid off by Cleveland for indifferent playing." *The Sporting Life* remarked that "much of the stuff written regarding the dalliance with grape juice and his tryst with paleface women is pure speculation."[11] Two weeks later, they reported that "Sockalexis has been fined by the Cleveland club various sums aggregating $175 for dissipation and has suspended him without pay until such time as he shall come to his senses."[12] Louis wound up appearing in exactly half of the team's 132 games with a .338 batting average.

At the close of the season, *The Sporting News* lamented the corruption of two spectacular phenoms:

> Two young stars, who entered the National League within the last twelve months with the most brilliant prospects, have almost thrown away their fortunes by the excessive use of liquor. One is [Napoleon] Lajoie of the Philadelphia club. The other is Sockalexis, the much talked of player on the Indian team. Both were recognized as players who had abilities to stay among the major stars from the outset. Neither could stand flattery and success. Probably they had the love of strong drink before they reached the goal of their ambition in the baseball profession, and their success among the top notchers set that love on a riot run....
>
> (Sockalexis) entered the big league under the most flattering conditions. His ballplaying, particularly his batting, surprised the veterans of the profession. Then the fact that he was a full-blood Indian, though highly educated and possessed of all the refinements of a white man, made him doubly a hero in every city where the Cleveland team played. Suddenly his heavy batting declined, his fielding became ragged, and his playing in general ranged from poor to bad. Finally he dropped out of the nine entirely. The real cause was for a while suppressed. A bad ankle was the excuse given the public but the facts cannot be strangled and the truth went abroad. Sockalexis had succumbed to the curse which had been the bane of his nationality ever since civilization in America put whiskey in the reach of the aborigines. Sockalexis admitted it himself and seemed to be determined to redeem his great error. What is the queerest part about his case is his claim that until he became a ballplayer he did not know the taste of whiskey. But when he rose to be a hero and a public pet his admirers surrounded him. They must do him homage. Mere flattery is not sufficient. More seemed to be required to show their admiration for the young Indian ballplayer.
>
> Indians instinctively like whiskey. Sockalexis was importuned to join us. His first

---

11. *The Sporting Life*, July 24, 1897.
12. *The Sporting Life*, August 7, 1897.

refusals were soon broken down. A step was taken. All the national love of firewater lying dormant in his soul flamed out and the famous new star of the base ball field went out like a meteor.[13]

Lajoie would recover to fashion a Hall of Fame career. Sockalexis would play only 28 more big league games.

Sockalexis arrived the next spring vowing to be on his best behavior. "I am in good condition again and will play as well as ever," he said. "As to my falling by the wayside again there is no chance for it. I made a big fool of myself and know it. (The team management) stuck to me longer than I deserved and I mean to repay them. When I get to Cleveland I intend to get a place near the ball grounds to live at and then I will not go down town all the season. My mind is made up and it is no joke. I have a good future as a ball player and only have to take care of myself to keep in this game."[14]

But Sockalexis's resolution apparently didn't last long, or else management didn't have faith in him. Playing only sporadically, he was batting .320 through May 11, but it was all downhill from there. Sockalexis appeared in just seven games after June 7, going 2-for-20.

Sockalexis played in his final seven major league games in May 1899. He had one last hurrah, going 5-for-5 on May 11, but had just one hit in the other six games before being released at age 27. Two years after taking the league by storm, Sockalexis was not even good enough for the worst team in baseball history, the 1899 Cleveland team which finished 20–134 and vanished from the big leagues.

Sockalexis drifted around the Eastern, Connecticut, and Maine State Leagues over the next three years, before his playing career ended. He then returned to the Penobscot reservation in Old Town, Maine.

By 1912, Sockalexis was an old 40, described as "fat and lazy," and at least once arrested for vagrancy. He was captain and deckhand of a ferry which crossed the Penobscot River near Old Town. He occasionally served as an umpire in local games, and followed major league baseball through the newspapers.[15]

Louis's second cousin, Andrew Sockalexis, was getting his name in the sports pages around this time. He finished second in the Boston Marathon in both 1912 and '13, and fourth in the Olympic marathon in 1912.[16]

The Louis Sockalexis legend was already starting to grow by this time. "When the great Book of Baseball is written," said one sportswriter (no doubt anticipating the book you are reading now), "there will be a short but

---

13. *The Sporting News*, October 2, 1897.
14. Unidentified clipping in National Baseball Library file, April 9, 1898.
15. Unidentified clipping in National Baseball Library file, July 31, 1912.
16. Rice, Ed. "Negro League Team Played in Bangor." *Bangor Daily News*, August 5, 2006.

graphic chapter on 'Sockalexis, the Man Who Might Have Been.'"[17] Future Hall of Famers John McGraw and Hugh Jennings—rival NL players on the Baltimore Orioles—were among those who recalled Sockalexis as an all-time great, presumably based on peak value. (Ed Barrow was another, but since he was Atlantic League President at the time Sockalexis was in the majors, it must have been based on hearsay.)

On Christmas Eve, 1913, Sockalexis was working as a logger in Burlington, Maine. He was chatting with coworkers when he suddenly turned pale, stared blankly into space, and literally dropped dead.[18] A lifelong bachelor, Louis Sockalexis was just 42.

By this time, Cleveland had a team in the fledgling American League. For nearly a decade they were known as the "Naps," in honor of player-manager Napoleon Lajoie. Lajoie left the team after the 1914 season, and the team needed a new nickname. A contest was held for that purpose, and the winning name, announced on January 17, 1915, was Indians. The nickname is still in use over a century later. There has been debate about who or what inspired the moniker, but an editorial in the next day's *Cleveland Plain Dealer* leaves little doubt:

> Many years ago there was an Indian named Sockalexis who was the star player of the Cleveland base ball club. As batter, fielder and base runner he was a marvel. Sockalexis so far outshone his teammates that he naturally came to be regarded as the whole team. The 'fans' throughout the country began to call the Clevelanders the 'Indians.' It was an honorable name, and while it stuck the team made an excellent record.
>
> It has now been decided to revive this name. The Clevelands of 1915 will be the 'Indians.' There will be no real Indians on the roster, but the name will recall fine traditions. It is looking backward to a time when Cleveland had one of the most popular teams in the United States. It also serves to revive the memory of a single great player who has been gathered to his fathers in the happy hunting grounds of the Abenakis.[19]

In 1934, during the depths of the Great Depression, a reporter from the *Old Town Enterprise* raised money to erect a bronze tablet at Sockalexis's barely-marked grave. It reads, "In memory of Louis Sockalexis whose athletic achievements while at Holy Cross and later with the Cleveland major league baseball team won for him national fame."[20]

Over a century after his 94-game career, Louis Sockalexis still inspires wistful memories. In 2003, not one, but two biographies—one by Ed Rice, the other by David Fleitz—were published. In 2009, the Maine House of Representatives and Senate issued a joint resolution "to honor Maine

---

17. "Sockalexis, Fat and Lazy, Takes Ease in His Tribe." *Philadelphia North American*, August 4, 1912.
18. "Sockalexis Dies of Heart Disease." Unidentified clipping in National Baseball Library file, December, 1913.
19. *Cleveland Plain Dealer*, January 18, 1915.
20. "Sockalexis Memorial in Maine." *The Sporting News*, June 7, 1934.

baseball great Louis Sockalexis." And currently, a Maine group calling itself "Friends of Sockalexis" is raising money for a commemorative bronze statue.

Year	Team (League)	G	AB	R	H	2B	3B	HR	RBI	SB	AVG	OBP	SLG
1897	Cleveland (NL)	66	278	43	94	9	8	3	42	16	.338	.385	.460
1898		21	67	11	15	2	0	0	10	0	.224	.246	.254
1899		7	22	0	6	1	0	0	3	0	.273	.304	.318
Totals		94	367	54	115	12	8	3	55	16	.313	.355	.414

Karl Spooner

Brooklyn Dodgers fans were always saying "Wait 'til next year!" The team's track record of near-misses was historic. By 1954, they had yet to win a world championship, despite seven trips to the World Series. In the past nine seasons, they had lost four Fall Classics, and finished in second place in the NL four other times, twice losing out in a pennant playoff after tying for first.

The fans were sure that Next Year was finally going to come in 1955, thanks to a spectacular rookie pitcher named Karl Spooner. And the Dodgers did indeed finally win the world title that year—but Spooner had precious little to do with it, and would never throw a big league pitch after 1955.

Karl Benjamin Spooner was born June 23, 1931, at Oriskany Falls, New York. His father died when he was 11 and his mother when he was 17, and Karl and brother Maurice were left with various relatives. Karl worked on a local farm while attending Oriskany Falls High School. He played basketball and football there, and was a left-handed catcher on the baseball team. "Our pitcher graduated when I was a senior," Karl recalled, "and since I was the hardest thrower on the team—we only had a squad of 11—I was nominated to pitch."[1]

Spooner was an instant success on the mound, and continued pitching after high school. While playing for a Clinton, New York, town team in

---

1. "Spooner's Story—One of Sadness." *Los Angeles Times*, April 9, 1965.

1950, he was discovered by Dodger scout Greg Mulleavy. Karl signed for a $600 bonus.

Spooner began his pro career in 1951 not far from home. Pitching for Hornell of the Class-D Pennsylvania-Ontario-New York (PONY) League, Spooner had a mediocre record (10–12, 4.18), but showed great stuff. He topped the league with 200 strikeouts in 170 innings, and hurled a no-hitter vs. Bradford.

Karl also met his future wife, Carol Pratt, in Hornell. They would marry in February 1954, and have four daughters and one son, all with "K" first names: Karen, Kim, Kelley, Karrie, and Kevin. All would become competitive athletes, the girls in softball and Kevin in baseball.[2]

Spooner's 1952 season was split between three teams and leagues: Greenwood (Cotton States), Newport News (Piedmont), and Miami (Florida International). He had trouble as he moved up the ranks from Class D to B, going 4–12 all told. But he showed enough (including a 19-strikeout game with Greenwood[3]) to be promoted to Class A the next year.

Spooner started 1953 with Elmira of the Eastern League where, despite a respectable 3.42 ERA, he went 1–6, and was thinking about quitting the game. From there he was sent to Pueblo of the Western League, where he made a breakthrough. Spooner went 11–6 for Pueblo, including a no-hitter vs. Denver, with a 2.53 ERA. Though he didn't join the league until June 14, he led it in strikeouts with 198 in just 153 innings. Included among those K's were 18 vs. Wichita on June 22, and 16 vs. Des Moines on July 7.[4]

Spooner moved up to AA with Ft. Worth for 1954. After a decent start, he suffered a freak right knee injury while playing pepper in June, costing him the better part of a month of action. But when he returned, he was better than ever. Shortening his stride in favor of the knee, he found that he could throw just as hard but with better control. By the end of the season, he led the Texas League in wins and strikeouts, going 21–9 for an 81–80 team with 262 K's in 238 innings. That was the league's highest strikeout total since Dizzy Dean in 1931. Among his wins were a one-hitter, three two-hitters, a three-hitter, a four-hitter, and three five-hitters.[5] Spooner added two victories in the league playoffs before losing his last outing, 3–2 in 17 innings.

Spooner was not an especially imposing physical specimen, standing a shade under six feet tall and weighing 180 pounds, but he could bring the

---

2. Sins, Ken. "Karl Spooner—A Career Marked by Destiny, Disappointment." *Oriskany Falls* (NY) *Sentinel*, July, 1975.
3. Smith, Red. "Strikeout Spooner." *New York Herald Tribune*, December 7, 1954.
4. Johnson, Lloyd, and Miles Wolff, editors. *The Encyclopedia of Minor League Baseball.* Durham, NC: Baseball America, Inc., 1993, p. 274.
5. Shosid, Joe. "Spooner Dishes up Best Whiff Mark Since Dean." *The Sporting News*, September 8, 1954.

ball. "Karl's windup is a thing of complicated grace," described one article, "unhurried even after his left arm starts through its forward movement. At the last split second, his tight grip on the seams, a limber wrist and elbow coordinate like a flashing whiplash."[6]

The Brooklyn Dodgers purchased Spooner from Ft. Worth on September 20, and he reported that day—which happened to be the day the New York Giants beat the Dodgers to clinch the NL pennant. There were only six days left in the season. Spooner joined another Dodgers southpaw recently called up from the minors, Tommy Lasorda.

Two days later, according to Lasorda, "Billy Loes was scheduled to start the game for us against the Giants. But when the Giants clinched, Loes packed his things and went home. So [manager Walt] Alston needed a pitcher. It was between Spooner and me and Alston at the last minute made up his mind on Spooner."[7]

After a shaky first inning, Spooner dominated the Giants, on their way to a world championship. He not only hurled a three-hit shutout, but struck out 15 batters, a big league record for a major league debut (later matched by J.R. Richard). Included were six straight K's in the seventh and eighth innings. Strikeouts were not as common in 1954 as today; no other NL pitcher had fanned more than 13 in a game that year. "He's the greatest young pitcher I've ever seen," said Dodgers Hall of Fame catcher Roy Campanella about Spooner. "I didn't let him rely on his fast ball. I called for the curve and the change-up, and he fanned them on them, too."[8]

Spooner was given one more start in the season finale, September 26. This time he four-hit the Pirates, 1–0, with 12 strikeouts. He became only the seventh pitcher (including Boo Ferriss) ever to toss shutouts in each of his first two major league starts; only one man has done it since. Spooner's 27 K's were reported as the most by an NL pitcher over *any* two consecutive games, let alone their first two.

Spooner's big league statistical line for 1954 still jumps off the page: two games, 18 innings, a 2–0 record, 27 strikeouts, just seven hits allowed, and a 0.00 ERA. Dodgers fans spent the next half-year lamenting what they might have accomplished had the lefty been on the team all season ("We shoulda had Spooner sooner!"), and dreaming about what numbers he would rack up in 1955. There were predictions of 25 or even 30 wins for the electrifying youngster.

---

6. Holmes, Tommy. "Spooner's Speed Ball 'Fascinates' the Pros." *New York Herald Tribune*, July 3, 1955.

7. Gurnick, Ken. "Karl Spooner: Memories of 1954." *Los Angeles Herald Examiner*, May 30, 1984.

8. McGowen, Roscoe. "Rookie Lifts Bums' 'Next Year' Hopes." *The Sporting News*, September 29, 1954.

Spooner was more realistic. "This probably is the worst thing that could have happened to me," he said. "[N]ext year when I start pitching, everybody will expect me to pitch a shutout and strike out a lot of guys every time out, and I certainly can't, and don't expect to, do that."[9] Spooner spent some of the off-season on the banquet circuit, then had surgery to remove cartilage from his knee in December.

There are several versions of how Spooner hurt his arm before the 1955 season. It could simply have been the effects of his pitching nearly 300 innings on a bum knee at age 23 in 1954. His brother said Karl injured it throwing snowballs at the Old Forge Winter Carnival. Vin Scully said it happened on the first day of spring training, when Spooner fired a throw for a photographer without warming up. Karl himself said it happened when he was rushed into an early spring training game and tried to throw too hard, too soon. On a curveball to the White Sox' Jim Rivera, "I felt a sharp twinge in my shoulder … but thought nothing of it. The next morning I couldn't comb my hair."[10] Contemporary newspapers said that Spooner complained of a stiff shoulder as early as March 13, had a negative X-ray on March 28, and tried rest and various treatments over a two-month period, but the soreness persisted.

Spooner didn't make his regular-season debut until May 15, and was blasted out of the box in the third inning. He didn't return to the mound until June 12, and after a couple of weeks of effective work out of the bullpen, went through a two-month period of rather wretched pitching.

Spooner finally began showing signs of hope late in the season. On August 28, he tossed his first complete game of the year, defeating the Cardinals, 6–1, and fanning nine. On September 2, he threw a four-hit shutout to beat the Pirates, 2–0. And on September 8, he entered a game with one out in the fourth inning, and pitched hitless, scoreless ball the rest of the way, striking out nine Braves to earn a 10–2 victory. This gave the Dodgers the NL title, the earliest pennant-clinching in a full season in NL history.

Spooner pitched sparingly and poorly the rest of the regular season, finishing the year a rather mediocre 8–6 with a 3.65 ERA. But considering the league ERA was 4.04, that wasn't terrible. His 7.11 strikeouts per nine innings would have ranked second in the league, as would his 7.21 hits allowed per nine, had he pitched enough innings to qualify.

Spooner got into two games in the World Series against the Yankees. In Game Two, he hurled three scoreless innings in relief, fanning five. This earned him a start in Game Six, but he was shelled in the first inning, facing six batters and giving up five runs. Bill "Moose" Skowron finished the

---

9. McGowen, Roscoe. "Misery in Arm Gone, Declares Spooner, Who'll Start Early." *The Sporting News*, January 9, 1957.

10. "Spooner's Story—One of Sadness." *Los Angeles Times*, April 9, 1965.

carnage with a three-run homer, on what turned out to be Spooner's last major league pitch. The Dodgers recovered to win Game Seven the next day.

Still hurting, Spooner started the 1956 season with the Dodgers, but didn't get into a game before he was optioned to St. Paul of the American Association on May 16. Between stints on the DL, he appeared in just four games with St. Paul in 1956, 13 with Macon in '57, and 11 with Dothan and Houston in '58, going a combined 3–6. He had shoulder surgery on November 2, 1957,[11] was drafted by the Cardinals before the 1958 season, and was cut in spring training, 1959. Karl Spooner's pro baseball career was over at age 27. "After pitching didn't work out, I was heartbroken," he recalled. "My arm went dead on me overnight. I just had no strength in the damn thing. I'll never understand it."[12]

Spooner eventually took a job at Jerry Haffield Citrus Corporation in Vero Beach, Florida. He became packing house manager, and remained there the rest of his working life.[13] He avoided going to baseball games. "I stay away purposely," he explained. "When I go it eats my innards up.... I can't help thinking about what might have been."[14]

On April 10, 1984, Spooner died at Vero Beach after a long battle with Hepatitis-C which begat liver cancer; he was just 52. Eighteen years later, on July 2, 2002, a baseball field in his hometown of Oriskany Falls (which, incidentally, is only about 30 miles from Cooperstown) was rechristened Karl Spooner Memorial Field.

Spooner endured pain the last three decades of his life. As one article put it two decades after his final professional pitch, "every time it rains, even a little, a pain runs through an arm that struck out 105 in 116 innings, reminding him of what might have been."[15]

Year	Team (League)	G	IP	W	L	PCT	SO	BB	H	ERA
1954	Brooklyn (NL)	2	18.0	2	0	1.000	27	6	7	0.00
1955		29	98.2	8	6	.571	78	41	79	3.65
Totals		31	116.2	10	6	.625	105	47	86	3.09

---

11. McGowen, Roscoe. "Spooner Pins Comeback Hopes on Arm Operation." *The Sporting News*, November 13, 1957.
12. "Karl Spooner." *Inside Sports*, April 1981, p. 62.
13. Hankins, Dona. "Karl Spooner Lifts Orange Crates, Dreads Rain." *The Daily Press* (Utica, NY), January 10, 1978, p. 11.
14. "Spooner's Story—One of Sadness." *Los Angeles Times*, April 9, 1965.
15. Hankins, Dona. "Karl Spooner Lifts Orange Crates, Dreads Rain." *The Daily Press* (Utica, NY), January 10, 1978, p. 11.

Monty Stratton

One could say that Monty Stratton's story is like something out of Hollywood.

Monty Franklin Pierce Stratton was born May 21, 1912, on the family farm in Wagner, Texas. One of nine children—four boys and three girls lived to adulthood—Monty was named after an uncle and the 14th U.S. President. Two of his younger brothers, Roland and Leslie, would also become pro baseball prospects.

Monty's father died when he was a teenager, forcing the youngster to curtail his Wagner High School attendance in order to help on the farm. He still found time for baseball, becoming an instant success as a pitcher. In a time where the average man stood about 5'8", Monty grew to six-feet-five, naturally earning him the nickname "Shorty" (later on, he was called "The Texas Gander"). Between farm chores, Stratton continued playing after high school, gaining fame as a semi-pro hurler.

While pitching in the Red River Valley League, Stratton was discovered by a husband-wife scouting team, Mr. & Mrs. Roy Largent, in the employ of the Chicago White Sox. They signed him for $1,200 in 1934. The gangly right-hander began his pro career with the Galveston Buccaneers of the Class-A Texas League, appeared in one game for the White Sox, and finished the year with the Omaha Packers of the Class-A Western League, going 9–14 overall.

Stratton followed with a fine year with the St. Paul Saints of the American Association, the highest level of minor league ball. Filling out from 175 to 205 pounds, Monty went 17–9 for a team that was only 75–78. "He is the most promising young pitcher I've seen in this league in ten years," said Hall of Fame umpire and executive Billy Evans.[1] Stratton finished the 1935 season with the White Sox, not to return to the minors for over a decade.

Stratton's pitching style was compared to that of Hall of Famers Grover Alexander and Dazzy Vance. "[H]is best pitch ... is his low, sidearm sinker," wrote John P. Carmichael. "Hitters don't like to face a Stratton type, because he is a triple threat. He winds up and first he throws his foot at them. Then he throws his glove out and finally the ball. It is most deceiving."[2]

"Stratton had a lot of stuff," wrote another reporter. "He had a natural sinker, a good curve, and he often used a change of pace pitch. To right-handed batters he threw mostly side-arm; to the left-handed batters

---

1. "Monty Franklin P. Stratton." *The Sporting News*, August 22, 1935.
2. Carmichael, John P. "The Barber Shop." Unidentified newspaper, May 18, 1937.

he usually employed an overhand motion. Every once in a while he would vary his style and throw under-handed or in three-quarter fashion. It was hard for batters to get into the rhythm of his pitching."[3]

Stratton was a pretty good hitter and fielder, too. He would bat .224 with 14 extra-base hits in 192 big league at bats, and make only three errors (with above-average range factors) in his career.

Set back by operations for appendicitis and tonsillitis, Stratton struggled to a 5–7 record for the Sox in 1936. Then came a breakout year. He was picked for the 1937 AL All-Star team, and through August 5 was 14–4—including four three-hitters—with a microscopic 2.02 ERA. But, on that date, he tore an arm muscle while throwing a submarine fastball to the Yankees' Red Rolfe.[4] Stratton pitched only four-and-a-third innings the rest of the season, giving up eight runs to swell his final ERA to 2.40. Still, that was 2.22 runs better than the American League's 4.62 mark. How impressive was that? In the first 80 years after ERA became an official statistic, only three other qualifiers—all Hall of Famers—had bigger differentials in a season. But one of them was Lefty Gomez in the same year, so Stratton's performance got lost in the shuffle:

Pitchers with Biggest Difference, ERA vs. League ERA, Season, 1913–93

Year	Pitcher, CLUB (LEA.)	ERA	LG	DIFF
1930	Dazzy Vance, BKN (NL)	2.61	4.97	2.36
1931	Lefty Grove, PHI (AL)	2.06	4.38	2.32
1937	Lefty Gomez, NY (AL)	2.33	4.62	2.29
1936	Lefty Grove, BOS (AL)	2.81	5.04	2.23
1937	**Monty Stratton, CHI (AL)**	**2.40**	**4.62**	**2.22**
1953	Warren Spahn, MIL (NL)	2.10	4.29	2.19
1934	Lefty Gomez, NY (AL)	2.33	4.50	2.17
1930	Lefty Grove, PHI (AL)	2.54	4.65	2.11
1939	Lefty Grove, BOS (AL)	2.54	4.62	2.08
1937	Johnny Allen, CLE (AL)	2.55	4.62	2.07

Despite missing most of the last two months of the season, Stratton wound up second in the AL in winning percentage, ERA, shutouts, and fewest hits allowed per nine innings, and first in fewest baserunners allowed per nine innings—WHIP.

Stratton reinjured his arm in a spring exhibition game the following

---

3. The Old Scout. "Stratton Felt Proud of Being a Country Boy." Unidentified newspaper, November 30, 1938.
4. *Ibid.*

year, and didn't make his 1938 regular-season debut until May 13. But once he started pitching, he was again the ace of a staff which included Hall of Famer Ted Lyons. Stratton finished 15–9; the rest of the ChiSox team was 50–74. Monty finished among the league's top five in win percentage, wins above team, and fewest hits and baserunners allowed per nine innings. His 4.01 ERA does not look too impressive until you consider that the league average was 4.79. Stratton received 15 points in MVP voting.

Some have claimed Stratton was one of the best pitchers in the AL at this point in time. "[W]ith Bob Feller," said one 1938 article, Stratton "was rated as one of the outstanding two pitching phenoms in the league, from a future standpoint."[5]

Others have said that this is an exaggeration. But among those pitching 300+ innings in 1937–38, only Hall of Famers Lefty Gomez (2.80), Lefty Grove (3.04), and Red Ruffing (3.14) had a better ERA than Stratton's 3.26; and among those with 30+ wins, only Ruffing (.745) and Grove (.705) topped Stratton's .682 win percentage.

By this time, Monty was a family man. He and the former Ethel Milberger would have two sons, Monty, Jr., and Dennis Lee. Tragically, Dennis would commit suicide at age 23 in 1964—using a gun. Ethel would outlive her husband by 34 years.

On November 27, 1938—his namesake's first birthday—Monty, carrying a holstered .22 caliber revolver, set out to hunt rabbits on his mother's Greenville, Texas, farm. While grabbing at the gun, it accidentally discharged through the holster into his right thigh, severing the popliteal artery. Gushing blood, Stratton had to crawl a quarter-mile before he was discovered (some accounts say by his wife, others by a brother). Stratton was rushed to a hospital in Greenville, where doctors were unable to find the bullet or diagnose the damage. From there, he was taken by ambulance some 50 miles to Dallas, where the bullet was removed, the artery was tied off, and multiple blood transfusions were administered.

By the next day, Stratton's condition was critical as gangrene set in. In order to save his life, doctors were forced to make a dire decision. As the Associated Press reported, "The brilliant baseball career of Monty Stratton, 26-year-old pitching star of the Chicago White Sox, was at an end today, cut short by the amputation of his right leg at the knee."[6]

White Sox' president J. Louis Comiskey offered Stratton a lifetime job with the organization, presumably an office position. "Monty has a job with us as long as he wants it," said Comiskey. "He was a fine pitcher and a

---

5. *Ibid.*
6. Associated Press. "Comiskey Mourns End of Stratton's Career." *Brooklyn Eagle*, November 29, 1938.

finer man. Baseball can't afford to lose him."[7] A benefit exhibition game was scheduled between the White Sox and the cross-town Cubs. Played on May 1, 1939, it raised some $30,000 for the Stratton family.

But Monty was not content to sit at a desk. Fitted with an artificial leg, he became a White Sox' base coach, and still had dreams of pitching again. On June 1, 1939, Stratton began pitching in practice.[8] Thereafter, he pitched batting practice to the Sox, in addition to his coaching duties. He practiced pitching year-round, and repeatedly expressed interest in returning to the Comiskey Park mound, but it never happened. Stratton did pitch in a charity game on July 27, 1941.[9]

After three years of coaching, Stratton landed a job as manager of the Lubbock team in the West Texas-New Mexico League. On May 12, 1942, he put himself into a game as a relief pitcher. Though he took a pounding, he had played in a professional game for the first time in nearly four years. Stratton resigned as manager three days later.[10] World War II practically stopped minor league baseball for the next three years, though Stratton appeared in at least one independent league game in 1944.

Pro baseball returned with a vengeance in 1946, with the minors expanding from 12 leagues to 41. With so many new jobs open, the 34-year-old Stratton was able to find a roster spot with the Sherman Twins of the Class-C East Texas League. Fans and players marveled at his ability not only to pitch with speed and control, but to field his position and hit the ball. The only concession to his disability was a special league rule, permitting a courtesy runner any time he reached base.[11]

By the end of the season, Stratton had rolled up an amazing 18–8 record for a team that was 70–70. The performance inspired an MGM major motion picture: *The Stratton Story*, released in 1949 and starring Jimmy Stewart as the pitcher.

Stratton moved up to the Class-B Big State League in 1947, going 7–7 for Waco, but that was essentially the end of his pitching career. He spent 1948 as an advisor in the film production, and appeared in six scattered minor league games between 1949 and 1953, going 3–3.

Stratton returned to Greenville, Texas, running a small cattle ranch for most of the rest of his life. He was inducted into the Texas Sports Hall of Fame in 1961 and the Texas Baseball Hall of Fame in 1980.[12] Stratton helped

---

7. Associated Press. "White Sox Offer Stratton Lifetime Job." *Brooklyn Eagle*, December 11, 1938.
8. "Monty Stratton Hurls Again." *Chicago Daily News*, June 2, 1939, p. 41.
9. *The Sporting News*, July 31, 1941.
10. *The Sporting News*, May 21, 1942.
11. "Stratton in New Comeback." *The Sporting News*, April 11, 1946.
12. Associated Press. "Ex-White Sox Pitcher Stratton Dead at 70." September 1982.

start the Greenville Little League, and a local baseball field was named in his honor.[13] He appeared in major league old-timers' games as late as the 1970s.[14]

The Stratton Story ended on September 28, 1982, when he died after a long bout with cancer.

Year	Team (League)	G	IP	W	L	PCT	SO	BB	H	ERA
1934	Chicago (AL)	1	3.1	0	0	.----	0	1	4	5.40
1935		5	38.0	1	2	.333	8	9	40	4.03
1936		16	95.0	5	7	.417	37	46	117	5.21
1937		22	164.2	15	5	.750	69	37	142	2.40
1938		26	186.1	15	9	.625	82	56	186	4.01
Totals		70	487.1	36	23	.610	196	149	489	3.71

13. Claybourn, David. "Ethel Stratton Dead at 90." *Herald-Banner*, 2006.
14. Barnard, William. "Stratton Roots for Texas Teams." Associated Press, July 14, 1974.

Dickie Thon

Dickie Thon's 15-year major league career ended after the 1993 season. But his career as a "future Hall of Famer" ended almost a decade before that.

Richard William Thon was born June 20, 1958, son of Evangeline and Fred Thon, Jr. Fred, the grandson of a German immigrant who had settled in Puerto Rico, had just graduated from Notre Dame University, thus Dickie was born in South Bend, Indiana.[1] The family—including older son Freddie—moved to the Rio Piedras part of San Juan, Puerto Rico shortly after; two other boys, Kenneth and Francis (Frankie), followed.[2] Fred had had some success as a pitcher before physical problems intervened. His father had played one season of pro ball as an outfielder-pitcher in 1940, batting .262 and going 6–0, 2.28 on the mound. Fred Sr., also played in the Puerto Rican winter leagues and was close friends with Negro league stars who played there, including Monte Irvin and Willard Brown. In later years, those legends would visit Puerto Rico to spend time with Fred, Sr. As one writer put it, "When [Dickie] Thon's career began to take off, he stepped into his greatness with the

1. Hecht, Henry. "Thon: The Best Kept Secret in Baseball." *New York Post*, May 4, 1983.
2. Telephone interview with Dickie Thon, November 20, 2017.

understated air of expectation of someone who had grown up in the presence of Hall of Famers."[3]

Dickie attended San Antonio High School, playing basketball and volleyball in addition to baseball.[4] Fred, Jr., coached his sons throughout their youth, hoping one or more of them would complete the professional baseball dreams that he was unable to realize for himself. Dickie and Frankie soon became highly-regarded pro prospects.

Dickie Thon got a $20,000 bonus in signing with the California Angels as an undrafted free agent on December 23, 1975,[5] and began his pro career in '76 with the Quad City Angels of the Class-A Midwest League. The right-handed batter and thrower hit a respectable .276 with 19 stolen bases in 69 games. After 56 games for Salinas in the California League in 1977, Thon moved all the way up to AAA with the Salt Lake City Gulls of the Pacific Coast League. His combined stats in the two leagues included 95 runs, 12 homers, 87 RBI, 24 steals, and a .301 average—pretty impressive for a slightly-built (5'11", 160 pounds), teen-aged middle infielder. "The name to remember is Dickie Thon," reported *The Sporting News*. "Scouts from both leagues rate the 19-year-old shortstop as one of baseball's prime prospects."[6]

Thon married Maria Soledad "Sol" Rauchle on December 23, 1977. Their first child, daughter, Soleil Maria, arrived on September 24, 1978.[7] Vanessa, Mariana, Richard "Dickie Joe," and Cecilia would follow, the five children producing four grandchildren.[8]

Thon did have one setback in 1977. While playing for Salt Lake City, he was struck behind the ear by a pitched ball, resulting in a concussion which hospitalized him for a few days. It was one of three beanballs Thon suffered in the minors.[9] He was a hitter who crowded the plate and stood his ground. "They pitched inside more in those days," recalls Thon, "but I was pretty good at getting out of the way."[10] Indeed he was, for the most part: Thon would be hit by just nine pitches in his 15-year big league career.

By this time, younger brother Frankie had turned pro, signing with the Giants, but not before suffering a horrific injury. Between innings of a November 1977 game in Puerto Rico, Thon at second base was not paying

---

3. Hanlon, Greg. "Lost Greatness, Scar Tissue, and Survival: The Life of Baseball's Brief Superstar, Dickie Thon." *Vice Sports*, May 7, 2015.
4. *Milwaukee Brewers 1993 Media Guide*, p. 86.
5. *Ibid.*
6. *The Sporting News*, February 25, 1978.
7. E-mail from Dickie Thon, November 25, 2017.
8. Telephone interview with Dickie Thon, November 20, 2017.
9. Spencer, Lyle. "For Dickie Thon, Seeing is Believing." *New York Post*, April 22, 1985, p. 38.
10. Telephone interview with Dickie Thon, November 20, 2017.

attention when the catcher fired the ball toward him after the pitcher's warm-ups. The ball smashed into Frankie's face, fracturing his left cheekbone. Despite three operations, he would suffer from blurred vision thereafter, and would never advance beyond A-ball, batting .246 with no power over three seasons. He has remained in baseball as a scout, currently with the Orioles.[11]

Dickie was invited to the Angels' spring camp in 1978, then spent the rest of that year and the start of the next back at Salt Lake City. The Angels called Dickie up to the majors early in the 1979 season, and he made his debut on May 22. Thon served mostly as a defensive replacement, but showed he could play some offense, too, with a .339 average in limited action, helping California to the AL West title.

When Thon started the 1980 season with a PCL-leading .394 average in his first 40 games, the Angels brought him up to the big leagues to stay. He made an instant impression, going 5-for-5 in his first game of the season on May 28, but finished at .255 as a multi-position backup player. Afterward, Thon hit .331 for Bayamon to win the Puerto Rican Winter League batting title, setting a league record with 82 hits in the 60-game schedule.[12]

The Angels weren't sure if Thon's future was as a second baseman or a shortstop, but their focus was on winning then instead of building a team for the future. They already had a standout at second in Bobby Grich, and when they acquired three-time All-Star shortstop Rick Burleson from the Red Sox on December 10, 1980, it was obvious that Thon's days in Anaheim were numbered. On April 1, 1981, the Angels traded Dickie to the Houston Astros for veteran pitcher Ken Forsch. "No one wants to give up a Thon," said Angels GM Buzzie Bavasi, "but we want to win now and Forsch can help us."[13]

One thing which would work against Thon's development was his new team's home park, the Astrodome. It was the worst hitters' park in baseball, due in large part to its poor visibility. In 1979, for example, the entire Astros team—good enough to go 52–29 at home—hit just 15 home runs in its 81 Astrodome games. "It was tough to see there," Thon recalls. "[Opposing p]layers would reach second base and tell me how hard it was to pick up the ball."[14]

Another factor was his position. In this era, before the likes of Cal Ripken, Alex Rodriguez, and Derek Jeter came along, shortstops were not

---

11. *Ibid.*
12. Miller, Dick. "The Future is Now for Thon." *The Sporting News*, February 14, 1981, p. 40.
13. Shattuck, Harry. "Quick-Acting Astros Patch Infield Leaks." *The Sporting News*, April 18, 1981.
14. Telephone interview with Dickie Thon, November 20, 2017.

expected to hit much, and most didn't. The average NL starting shortstop in 1980 had hit only two homers (none had more than five), with 37 RBI and a .253 average. The Astros had Craig Reynolds, a popular two-time All-Star, at short.

Backing up Reynolds and playing sparingly, Thon had a poor start in 1981. He was hitting just .157 when a strike stopped the season for two months, and was still below .200 as late as August 28. But a 13-for-29 finish enabled him to wind up at a respectable .274. Thon then won his second straight Puerto Rican Winter League batting title, with a .333 mark.[15]

When Reynolds was sidelined with vertigo problems in 1982, Thon got his chance to play regularly. But he was pressing, and hitting just .204 on June 13. The Astros liked his speed on the bases and range in the field, however, and stuck with him. Thon finally started hitting, bringing his average up to .276, including a 21-game hitting streak, a league-leading 10 triples, and his first three major league home runs. But his overall value was largely hidden, except to analysts. According to WAR, Thon was the sixth-best position-player in the National League in 1982. Bill James raved about Thon's baserunning (37 steals, just eight times caught) and ability to turn a double play, also calling him "The second-best lead-off man (and the) best-hitting shortstop in the National League.... I believe he will be the best shortstop in the National League in the 1980s."[16]

In 1983, he was.

Thon's fielding was extraordinary in '83. He led the NL with 533 assists and, though he finished a distant second to Ozzie Smith in Gold Glove Award voting, James said that Thon should have won. "I have been writing for years that Ozzie was the best defensive player in the major leagues at any position," wrote James. "But recognition usually lags a couple of years behind the fact, and Thon passed him by last year: he is now the best defensive shortstop in baseball. His arm is better than Ozzie's; he turns the double play better."[17]

As good as his defense was, Thon's offense was even better. His average was over .300 for most of the year, and he started hitting for power, earning a move up to #3 in the batting order. Thon had six homers in a 12-day span in June, and became the first Astro since 1977 to hit 20 homers in a season. Sixteen of those 20 came in road games, suggesting he could have been a 30+-homer man in a better home park; only four NL players hit more road homers that year. Thon finished fourth in the NL in total bases, topped the

---

15. *The Sporting News*, March 6, 1982.
16. James, Bill. *The Bill James Baseball Abstract 1983*. New York: Ballantine Books, 1983, p. 172
17. James, Bill. *The Bill James Baseball Abstract 1984*. New York: Ballantine Books, 1984, p. 209.

league with 18 game-winning RBI, made the All-Star team, won the Silver Slugger Award, and ranked fourth in Win Shares and seventh in MVP voting. Moreover, according WAR, he was the best position-player in the National League. Thon is proud to say that, among Puerto Rican players, only he and Roberto Clemente ever led their leagues in WAR.[18]

And Thon was still just 25, the youngest regular on the Astros, a bona fide franchise player. Teammate Phil Garner predicted he would win a batting title someday. "When I see Dickie Thon," said club GM Al Rosen, "I see a future Hall of Famer."[19]

The Astros played their fifth game of the 1984 season at the Astrodome on April 8. Thon, off to a .353 start, dug in against Mets veteran pitcher Mike Torrez in the third inning. A 92 mph fastball sailed up and in, and Thon had a split-second of difficulty in picking it up. "I didn't move," recalled Thon. "I just stood there. When I saw it, it was too late."[20] The ball slammed into Thon's head, catching a bit of his helmet, but mostly his left eye. As it turned out, his season was over, and his career would never be the same.

Thon didn't blame the pitcher. "Torrez called me in the hospital the day after it happened," he said. "He told me he was sorry, that the ball got away from him, that he wasn't throwing at me. I don't think he was."[21] The two wouldn't see each other in person again until 2011, during an old-timers' event. Torrez would apologize again, but Thon would tell him what he told him in 1984: That he had no hard feelings, and that it was part of the game.[22]

On April 11, Thon had surgery to repair a tripod fracture of the inferior orbital rim. But that did nothing to improve the scar tissue behind his retina, causing blurred vision, measured at 20–300. As time went on, the vision got better, with reports of it improving all the way to 20–30. Thon now admits that wasn't the truth. "[I]n reality Thon was gaming the tests," reported a 2015 article, saying that Dickie was just trying to stay in the game so he could support his family. "He underwent so many tests that he took progressively more educated guesses based on the blurriest fragments of visual information." More than three decades later, Thon says the vision in his left eye is still like "looking through a sheet of wax paper."[23]

Astros fans were reminded of previous tragedies involving Houston players: Jim Umbricht (age 33 in 1964), Walt Bond (29, 1967), and Don

---

18. Telephone interview with Dickie Thon, November 20, 2017.
19. Etkin, Jack. "Never Say Die." *The Sporting News 1990 Baseball Yearbook*, pp. 34–35.
20. Edes, Gordon. "Dickie Thon: His Future Appears Blurry." *Cincinnati Enquirer*, March 24, 1985, p. C4.
21. Anderson, Dave. "Will Thon See the Ball?" *New York Times*, March 5, 1985.
22. Hanlon, Greg. "Lost Greatness, Scar Tissue, and Survival: The Life of Baseball's Brief Superstar, Dickie Thon." *Vice Sports*, May 7, 2015.
23. *Ibid.*

Wilson (29, 1975) all died prematurely, and J.R. Richard's career was ended by a stroke at age 30 in 1980.

Thon was working out within two months of the beaning. Late in the summer, he began hitting against live pitching in practice. There was talk of Thon's returning to the diamond in September, but it didn't happen. He suffered from severe headaches and his depth perception wasn't there. After the season, Thon played in five games in the Arizona Instructional League, and three games in the Puerto Rican Winter League, before shutting it down for the year. "I wasn't ready to play," he said. "I was frustrated not seeing the ball."[24]

With his $675,000 contract renewed, Thon rejoined the team for spring training, 1985. Downplaying his difficulties, he batted .366 in 23 ST games.[25] People thought Thon's problems were behind him and he was ready to resume his role as a star. He got a long standing ovation on Opening Day, April 9, and scored the Astros' first run of the regular season. But still not seeing the ball well, he slumped, and soon relinquished his starting job back to Craig Reynolds. In May and June, Thon spent three weeks on the disabled list at his request. By July 5, he was hitting a weak .183 with just three RBI over the team's first 79 games. Dickie rebounded to bat .299 with decent production the rest of the season, again creating the illusion that he was almost back to his old self. The Astros re-signed him as a re-entry free agent on January 3, 1986.

After starting 7-for-13 in the first five games of 1986, Thon slumped again. He was down to .205 when he was put on the disabled list on June 6. Thon returned to complete another season of frustration and underperformance.

Things only got worse in 1987. Thon, complaining of vision problems during spring training, walked out on the team on March 14, sought psychiatric help, and was fined. In April, he was sent on a rehab assignment to the Pacific Coast League. After batting .271 in 14 games for Tucson, Thon was reinstated, returning to the Astros on May 10. But he continued to struggle and left the team again on July 3, going onto the disqualified list. The Astros had had enough of Thon's lack of production and what they seemed to consider malingering and insubordination. It looked like his career was over. "It's difficult to walk away from a game that I would do anything to play again," said Thon, "but I can't keep playing this year. I can't see the ball well enough."[26]

But Thon continued working out, and the rest from the daily grind seemed to help his vision problems. After he settled his grievances with the

---

24. Anderson, Dave. "Will Thon See the Ball?" *New York Times*, March 5, 1985.
25. Muniz, C. L. Smith. "A Goal in Sight." *New York Daily News*, May 2, 1985.
26. Hohlfield, Neil. "Thon Leaves Astros." *The Sporting News*, July 20, 1987.

Astros, he signed with the Padres as a free agent on February 8, 1988, and he performed adequately as a backup that year. On January 27, 1989, the Padres sold Thon's contract to the Phillies, with whom he would get a shot at playing regularly for the first time in six years.

Though Thon was far from the star he had been before the injury, he was a solid and durable player over the next three seasons with the Phils, averaging 144 games each year. In 1989, he led NL shortstops with 15 home runs, and his salary was raised to $1.1 million. The following year Thon topped the league in double plays. In 1991, he won the Tony Conigliaro Award, presented to a major league player who has overcome adversity.[27]

Thon became a free agent again, playing one season each with the Texas Rangers and Milwaukee Brewers before hanging up his spikes for good. Having played 15 years in the majors, Thon theoretically became eligible for the Hall of Fame in 1999—but the screening committee eliminated him from even reaching the ballot.

Thon represented his 18-year-old son, Dickie Joe, helping him receive a $1.5 million bonus to sign with the Blue Jays in the fifth round of the 2010 draft. But Dickie Joe did not advance above AA ball, batting just .241 with 30 homers in eight seasons as a minor and independent league middle infielder.

Dickie also had a nephew who played pro ball. Freddie Thon—born the day after Dickie's 1984 beaning—was a minor league first baseman between 2004 and 2011, batting .284. He was named the Mariners' director of international amateur scouting in 2018.

Dickie Thon stays busy teaching the game to children and working with the Puerto Rican Winter League. A devout Catholic and family man, he tries not to think too much about what might have been, though it's hard not to wonder: What if the visibility was better in the Astrodome? What if the 1984 batting helmets were more advanced? What if pitchers didn't throw inside as much? "It's a tough game, but it's getting softer," Thon says. "If I could have continued playing at (my 1982–83) level, I think I could have had a Hall of Fame career."[28]

Thon prefers to focus on the positive. "Sometimes I say, 'What if I didn't have that accident?'" he says. "But I try not to dwell on it. It's part of the game. It happens to pitchers, with their arms. That's why the game is hard.... I've had a lot of good things happen to me. I try to think about it that way."[29]

---

27. Associated Press. "Thon is Honored." *New York Times*, December 10, 1991.
28. Telephone interview with Dickie Thon, November 20, 2017.
29. Hanlon, Greg. "Lost Greatness, Scar Tissue, and Survival: The Life of Baseball's Brief Superstar, Dickie Thon." *Vice Sports*, May 7, 2015.

Year	Team (League)	G	AB	R	H	2B	3B	HR	RBI	SB	AVG	OBP	SLG
1979	California (AL)	35	56	6	19	3	0	0	8	0	.339	.393	.393
1980		80	267	32	68	12	2	0	15	7	.255	.282	.315
1981	Houston (NL)	49	95	13	26	6	0	0	3	6	.274	.337	.337
1982		136	496	73	137	31	*10	3	36	37	.276	.327	.397
1983		154	619	81	177	28	9	20	79	34	.286	.341	.457
1984		5	17	3	6	0	1	0	1	0	.353	.389	.471
1985		84	251	26	63	6	1	6	29	8	.251	.299	.355
1986		106	278	24	69	13	1	3	21	6	.248	.318	.335
1987		32	66	6	14	1	0	1	3	3	.212	.366	.273
1988	San Diego (NL)	95	258	36	68	12	2	1	18	19	.264	.347	.337
1989	Phila. (NL)	136	435	45	118	18	4	15	60	6	.271	.321	.434
1990		149	552	54	141	20	4	8	48	12	.255	.305	.350
1991		146	539	44	136	18	4	9	44	11	.252	.283	.351
1992	Texas (AL)	95	275	30	68	15	3	4	37	12	.247	.293	.367
1993	Milwaukee (AL)	85	245	23	66	10	1	1	33	6	.269	.324	.331
Totals		1387	4449	496	1176	193	42	71	435	167	.264	.317	.374

Cecil Travis

Over his first eight full seasons, 1934–41, Cecil Travis batted .327. No other AL player with as many hits had a higher batting average during that period.

Over his remaining big league career, from 1945 to 1947, Travis batted .241. Only four AL players had as many at bats with a *lower* average.

Cecil Howell Travis was born August 8, 1913, on a 200-acre family farm just a few miles from Atlanta in Riverdale, Georgia. He was the youngest of 10 children—six boys and four girls—of James and Ada Travis. Cecil graduated from Fayette County High School in 1930.[1]

---

1. Boylan, Michael. "From Senator to Farmer." *The Citizen*, February 10, 1999.

Travis also played semi-pro baseball in Fayetteville in the summers of 1929 and '30, gaining a local reputation.[2] He was recommended to Norman "Kid" Elberfeld, a 14-year major league shortstop who ran a winter baseball school in Atlanta. Elberfeld gave him a trial near the end of the 1930–31 session, and liked what he saw: a strong-armed infielder who could put his bat on any pitch. He got Travis placed on Elberfeld's hometown minor league team, the Chattanooga Lookouts of the Southern Association, a Washington Senators farm club. They signed Cecil, but first sent him to Newport, Tennessee, to play more semi-pro ball, rather than ride the Lookouts' bench at age 17.

Travis joined Chattanooga at the end of the season, was stationed at third base, and batted .429 in 13 games. With Chattanooga all year in 1932, he hit .356 and led the league with 17 triples, helping the team win the Dixie Series. Still just 19, Travis returned to the Lookouts for another season in '33. Many though Cecil was ready for the bigs, but the Senators were set at third base: Ossie Bluege, a popular player, fine fielder, and adequate hitter, had held down the job since 1923.

When Bluege was sidelined with an injury early in the 1933 season, the Senators summoned Travis. Cecil, nursing a hand injury, took an overnight train to Washington, arriving on May 16, a half-hour before the Nats' scheduled game with the Indians—the first major league game he would ever see. Put right into the lineup, Travis hardly looked like a starry-eyed teenager: he rapped base-hits in the second, third, fourth, and sixth innings. He reached on an error in the eighth, and then collected his fifth single in the tenth; the Senators wound up winning, 11–10, in 12. The five hits tied Hall of Famer Fred Clarke's 1894 record for most in a big league debut, and has not been matched since.

Travis played nine games in nine days before Bluege returned, and Cecil went back to Chattanooga. He wound up batting .352 for the Lookouts, then rejoined the Senators for the final few weeks of the season, never to return to the bushes; he finished his minor league career with a .356 average. Travis wound up hitting .302 in 18 games for the Senators, who won the 1933 AL pennant. Though he wasn't eligible for the World Series, the team voted him a partial share of post-season money. That would be the closest he ever got to a Fall Classic.

Travis stood six feet, 1½ inches tall, and weighed between 180 and 195 pounds. He batted left-handed and threw right. At the plate, Travis would wait until the last possible moment before committing to a pitch, then typically slash it to left field. He rarely struck out, fanning a total of just 215

---

2. Farrington, Dick. "Cecil Travis of Washington Got Start in Tennis Shoes as Invited Guest of Elberfeld's Spring Training School." *The Sporting News*, c. 1935.

times in his first eight full seasons—less than some modern players do in a single year! Travis was clean-cut, soft-spoken, and well-liked, a manager's and umpire's dream.

At 20, Travis was ready to take Bluege's job. After a torrid first half, Travis finished his rookie season at .319, including a 20-game hitting streak. "He is one of the most natural hitters I ever saw come into the big leagues," said Senators Hall of Fame player-manager Joe Cronin. "As a rookie he has more poise and polish at the plate than many veterans of ten years major league experience. No pitcher of reputation will disturb his calm, no delivery of a ball will disconcert him. He is a perfect picture at the plate.... He is keenly interested in his career and quite willing to accept advice."[3]

Travis did have one setback in his freshman campaign, when he was slammed behind the ear by a Thornton Lee fastball on May 5. Cecil played only one game in the next 12 days, but then picked up right where he left off (though the oft-told tale, of his returning after four weeks in the hospital to hit a triple off Lee his next time up, is a fable). Travis was prone to pitched balls, and would lead the league with nine times hit by pitch in 1935. "Cecil becomes paralyzed when a ball comes right at him," reported *The Sporting News*.[4]

Travis defeated the sophomore jinx in 1935, batting .318. Though he was considered just adequate defensively, his range factor and fielding percentage were well above the AL average, and he led the league in double plays.

With the arrival of rookie sensation Buddy Lewis in 1936, the Senators had to find a new position for Travis. He played 52 games in right field and four at second base that year, but found his new home at shortstop. Travis kept up his batting average (.317), while increasing his run-production (92 RBI).

Travis kept hitting over the next five years, earning three All-Star selections, and finishing among the AL's top 10 in batting four times and in WAR three times. His only sub-.300 year was 1939, when he battled influenza and dropped to 157 pounds, settling for a mere .292. The Tigers reportedly offered the Senators $150,000 for Travis in 1940.[5]

Between his slap-hitting style and the Senators' cavernous park, Travis had hit only 18 home runs—five of them inside-the-park—during his first eight seasons. In 1941, manager Bucky Harris asked him to try to pull the ball more and hit for more power. Travis moved back in the batters' box,

---

3. Bloodgood, Clifford. "Cecil Travis, Coming into Favor." *Baseball Magazine*, August 1934, p. 402.
4. *The Sporting News*, April 16, 1936.
5. Povich, Shirley. "This Morning." *Washington Post*, June 26, 1947, p. 17.

switched to a huge 36-inch, 36-ounce bat, and didn't choke up as much.[6] The results were astounding. Travis still got more than his share of singles—153 of them, leading the league—but also was fourth in the league in doubles (39) and second in triples (19), and set career highs in homers (7) and RBI (101—ninth in the AL). His .520 slugging percentage was one of the best ever by a shortstop to that point:

Highest Slugging PCT., Season, Shortstop
(Min. 100 G at SS, 1876–1941)

SLG	Player	Year	G @ SS	HR	RBI	AVG
.607	Arky Vaughan	1935	137	19	99	.385
.553	Bill Dahlen	1896	125	9	74	.352
.543	Glenn Wright	1930	134	22	126	.321
.542	Honus Wagner	1908	151	10	109	.354
.536	Joe Cronin	1938	142	17	94	.325
.529	Travis Jackson	1930	115	13	82	.339
.520	Honus Wagner	1904	121	4	75	.349
.520	**Cecil Travis**	**1941**	**136**	**7**	**101**	**.359**

In this year that Ted Williams batted .406 and Joe DiMaggio hit in 56 straight games, Travis also led the AL in hits (218) and finished second in batting (.359). He ranked sixth in MVP voting.

At this point, Travis had a .327 career batting average. Among long-term players who performed mainly at shortstop, only the immortal Honus Wagner had a higher mark—and by less than one point. Historically, the most similar players to Travis at this age are Billy Herman, Joe Sewell, and Eddie Collins, with three other Hall of Famers (plus current star Jose Altuve) in the top 10. Still just 28, Travis was in the prime of his career—but everything was about to change.

The U.S. entered World War II and Travis was sworn into the Army exactly one month later, January 8, 1942. He was stationed close to home at first, close enough that he could start a family. Cecil married Helen Hubbard on September 12, 1942.[7] The couple would have three sons, Cecil Anthony, Mike, and Rickey, in a marriage lasting over six decades until Helen's death in 2004.

With the war still raging, Sgt. Travis's 76th Infantry Division was sent to the European Theatre in the summer of 1944. It arrived in Belgium that winter, just after the Battle of the Bulge. The Division served as a cleanup

---

6. *The Sporting News*, 1941.
7. Kavanagh, Jack. "Cecil Travis." Unidentified article in National Baseball Library file, 1997.

unit and didn't see actual combat, but was imperiled by booby traps and bitter weather. Travis suffered severely-frostbitten toes, spending three weeks in a French hospital before returning to duty. He spent several months in Europe, and 3½ years in military service overall, receiving the Bronze Star for his efforts. "You never think about what you lost," he said. "We had a job to do, an obligation, and we did it. I was hardly the only one."[8]

Travis finally returned to the diamond on September 8, 1945, but he just didn't have it any more, at bat or in the field. "Immediately, it was evident something was missing, and that something was the spring in his legs," reported *The Sporting News*.[9] Some blamed his frozen feet, but Travis said the reason was more subtle. "[M]y timing was completely gone. I'd see the ball coming and nothing," he said.[10] "You didn't have to be off but just a hair and you couldn't play."[11]

Travis batted a soft .252 in 1946, then slipped to .216 and lost his starting job the next year. The Senators gave him a "Day" on August 15, 1947, showering him with gifts including a DeSoto automobile for his driveway and a Hereford bull for his farm.[12] After the season, Travis quietly asked to be put on the "voluntarily retired" list, and his playing days were over.

"The war definitely put a period to the Senator infielder's career," wrote *The Sporting News*. "Travis was one of the outstanding shortstops in the majors when he entered the military service in 1942. He never came close to being the same ball player after his discharge."[13]

Though his career average dropped to .314 after his post-war seasons, Travis still stands third all-time among shortstops, behind only Hall of Famers Wagner (.328) and Arky Vaughan (.318). "Cecil Travis is one of the five best left-handed hitters I ever saw," said Ted Williams,[14] who was a pretty good one himself.

Travis returned to the family farm, also serving as a Senators scout from 1948 to 1955.[15] Helped by his baseball earnings, the farm had more than doubled in size. He still worked on it well into his eighties, though

---

8. Appel, Marty. *Yesterday's Heroes*. New York: William Morrow, 1988.
9. The Old Scout. "Travis Closes out Career as Player." *The Sporting News*, January, 1948.
10. Heller, Dick. "Kuhn Goes to Bat for Travis as Cooperstown Candidate." *Washington Times*, April 22, 2002.
11. Kindred, Dave. "Memories Frozen in Time." *The Sporting News*, January 2, 1995, p. 6.
12. Povich, Shirley. "Even Umpires Share in Tribute to Travis." *The Sporting News*, August, 1947.
13. The Old Scout. "Travis Closes out Career as Player." *The Sporting News*, January, 1948.
14. Povich, Shirley. "Baseball's Out in Left on Nats' Sweet-Swinging Travis." *Washington Post*, c. 1994.
15. Carter, Craig, Editor. *Daguerreotypes*. St. Louis: *The Sporting News* Publishing Co., 1990, p. 287.

he had sold of much of it by then.[16] Travis died at age 93 on December 16, 2006.

Travis received several honors in his golden years. On February 8, 1975, he was inducted into the Georgia Sports Hall of Fame, along with Hank Aaron.[17] On November 28, 1993, Travis was inducted into the Hall of Stars at Washington's RFK Stadium (to show how low-profile he was, the committee wrote to his family, saying they were planning to induct him posthumously).[18] And on February 6, 1999, he was named to the Fayette County Sports Hall of Fame.[19]

But Travis never got a Baseball Hall of Fame vote in any BBWAA election. Part of the reason he never got the recognition he deserved was his team: Washington averaged only 70 wins and 377,658 fans a year from 1934 to 1941, his hey-day. "If he were playing with any other club than the hopeless Senators, he'd be hailed as one of the game's great stars," opined one writer.[20] "[H]e put the right numbers in the book but had the wrong letter on his cap," wrote another.[21]

Theoretically, Travis is still a viable Hall of Fame candidate via the veterans' committee (he received 12 of a possible 82 votes in his most recent time on the ballot, 2007). Former Commissioner Bowie Kuhn, who had been a teenaged Griffith Stadium scoreboard operator from 1939 to 1943, campaigned mightily for Travis.[22] But Cecil never campaigned for himself. "If I had played a few more years then yes I should have made it," said Travis. "They need to hold higher standards. There's too many people in there as it is."[23]

Year	Team (League)	G	AB	R	H	2B	3B	HR	RBI	SB	AVG	OBP	SLG
1933	Washington (AL)	18	43	7	13	1	0	0	2	0	.302	.348	.326
1934		109	392	48	125	22	4	1	53	1	.319	.361	.403
1935		138	534	85	170	27	8	0	61	4	.318	.377	.399
1936		138	517	77	164	34	10	2	92	4	.317	.366	.433

---

16. Kavanagh, Jack. "Cecil Travis." Unidentified article in National Baseball Library file, 1997.
17. "Aaron, Travis Picked." *The Sporting News*, January 10, 1975.
18. Siegel, Morris. "Contrary to Reports, Ex-Senator Alive, Well." *Washington Times*, September 18, 1993.
19. Boylan, Michael. "From Senator to Farmer." *The Citizen*, February 10, 1999.
20. McAuley. "Senators' Travis Turns on Power by Request." Unidentified newspaper article, August 19, 1941.
21. Holway, John B. "A Nat Stopped Short." *Washington Post*, April 5, 1992.
22. Heller, Dick. "Kuhn Goes to Bat for Travis as Cooperstown Candidate." *Washington Times*, April 22, 2002.
23. Boylan, Michael. "From Senator to Farmer." *The Citizen*, February 10, 1999.

Year	Team (League)	G	AB	R	H	2B	3B	HR	RBI	SB	AVG	OBP	SLG
1937	Washington (AL)	135	526	72	181	27	7	3	66	3	.344	.395	.439
1938		146	567	96	190	30	5	5	67	6	.335	.401	.432
1939		130	476	55	139	20	9	5	63	0	.292	.342	.403
1940		136	528	60	170	37	11	2	76	0	.322	.381	.445
1941		152	608	106	*218	39	19	7	101	2	.359	.410	.520
1945		15	54	4	13	2	1	0	10	0	.241	.293	.315
1946		137	465	45	117	22	3	1	56	2	.252	.323	.318
1947		74	204	10	44	4	1	1	10	1	.216	.273	.260
Totals		1328	4914	665	1544	265	78	27	657	23	.314	.370	.416

Hal Trosky

At the end of the 1940 season, Hal Trosky was 27 years old, and his career statistics included 205 home runs, 860 RBI, a .314 batting average, and a .559 slugging percentage. He already ranked 17th on the all-time home run list. The 10 most similar players at the same age are Orlando Cepeda, Eddie Murray, Miguel Cabrera, Jim Rice, Hank Aaron, Duke Snider, Frank Robinson, Lou Gehrig, Joe DiMaggio, and Joe Medwick—all Hall of Famers, except for Cabrera, only because he is not yet eligible.

Yet Trosky not only didn't make the Hall of Fame, he never received a single vote.

Harold Arthur Trojovsky was born November 11, 1912, in Norway, Iowa, one of four children of John and Mary Siepman Trojovsky. Hal would drop the middle three letters of his surname when he started pro ball, legally changing his name to Trosky on July 14, 1939.[1]

Hal played baseball for fun, and had no dreams of playing pro ball. He got some local recognition as a pitcher on his high school and town teams, and one day came home to find an Indians scout, Cy Slapnicka, waiting for him. A distant relative of Hal's knew Slapnicka and recommended the youngster to him. "You can believe it or not, but I didn't know what a scout was," said Trosky. "I liked Slap, and after we had talked baseball for a while he suggested that I sign with him. He asked my father if it was all right and Dad said, 'He might as well. I can't get him to do any work around the farm.

---

1. "Harold Arthur (Hal) Trosky." *The Sporting News*, October 19, 1939.

All he wants to do is play ball.'" So Trosky "simply signed with the first fellow who stuck an actual contract under my nose."[2]

Trosky began his pro career at age 18 in 1931, playing near home for Cedar Rapids and Dubuque in the Class-D Mississippi Valley League. After five games on the mound (2–2 record), he developed a sore arm. But management liked his bat, switched him from a cross-handed righty to a lefty swinger, and put him in the outfield; he batted .302, and his pitching days were over. In 1932, Trosky played for Quincy of the Class-B Three-I League and Burlington on the Mississippi Valley, hitting .324 and slugging .572 overall. In 1933, he was at the top rung of the minors, playing first base, and batting .323 with 33 homers for Toledo of the American Association. Trosky joined the Indians at the end of the season and, at age 20, was in the majors to stay.

Trosky married Lorraine Evelyn Glenn on November 15, 1933. She was the sister of two of his high school baseball teammates. The Troskys would have four children: Hal, Jr., James, Lynn, and Mary Kay, the only girl.

Before he even started his first full season, Hal Trosky was being touted by some (including Hall of Fame executives Will Harridge and Connie Mack) as heir-apparent to Babe Ruth as the American League's premier slugger. Like Ruth, Trosky was a big (6'2½", 207 pounds), left-handed pull-hitter who had shown the ability to hit for both power and average. He was also a hard-working, good-natured young man.

Hal had a slow start in 1934, but switched from a 40-ounce bat to a 34-ounce one at the advice of a teammate. The change worked wonders, and Trosky soon became one of the top sluggers in the league. In the second game of a Memorial Day doubleheader, he cracked three straight home runs. By the end of the season, Trosky had completed one of the best rookie seasons ever, finishing second in the AL in RBI (142) and total bases (374), behind only Triple Crown-winner Lou Gehrig. While not regarded as a graceful fielder, Trosky wound up leading the league in putouts, assists, and double plays. He finished seventh in MVP voting, and was named the majors' top rookie by *Baseball Magazine*.

The following year didn't go as well, and Trosky was called a flop, a victim of the sophomore jinx. He suffered from a mysterious stomach ailment, losing some 20 pounds. Trosky slumped, tinkered with his stance, tried switch-hitting (on September 15, he had a homer and two RBI-singles while batting right-handed[3]), and was the subject of trade rumors. Yet when all was said and done with the 1935 season, he had topped the AL in

---

2. Cobbledick, Gordon. "Trosky Never Heard of Foxx or Simmons Until He Accidentally Tuned in '30 Series." Unidentified newspaper, March 9, 1935.
3. Johnson, William H. *Hal Trosky, a Baseball Biography*. Jefferson, NC: McFarland & Company, Inc. Publishers, 2017, p. 142–44.

games played and finished in the league's top five in homers and RBI. His salary was raised to $7,500.[4]

Trosky came back with a monster year in 1936. In the highest-scoring season in American League history, among such immortal sluggers as Gehrig, Jimmie Foxx, and Joe DiMaggio, Trosky emerged as the biggest run-producer of them all. He put together a 28-game hitting streak from July 4–August 2, and in mid–September had nine consecutive hits, including two doubles and four home runs, good for 15 RBI. Trosky set or matched his ultimate career bests in runs (124), hits (216), doubles (45), triples (9), homers (42), RBI (162), batting (.343), and slugging (.644). Hal led the majors in RBI, extra-base-hits, and total bases (405), and finished second in homers and slugging. Curiously, he finished only tenth in MVP voting. The Indians' fifth-place finish had much to do with it, but it also exemplified Trosky's being overshadowed throughout his career. He had the poor timing to play in the same era, at the same position, and in the same league as three of the greatest sluggers of all time in Gehrig, Foxx, and Hank Greenberg. Trosky never played in an All-Star Game nor on a pennant-winner.

Trosky had another productive season (32–128-.298) in 1937, including a three-homer game on July 5, and an inside-the-park grand slam on September 21. But management encouraged him to change his hitting style the following year. Hal was a dead-pull hitter, and teams stacked the right side of the field against him. Trosky was offered a bonus of $10 for every hit he made to the left side of second base. He collected a reported $700[5] and boosted his batting average to .334, but his home run output fell to 19.

After playing 762 of a possible 776 games in the previous five seasons, Trosky began missing chunks of time in 1939: 32 games in all, including nine straight in May–June, and 11 straight in September. He still had a productive year, finishing fourth in batting, fifth in slugging, and sixth in homers. He was voted "Most Popular Indian" in a newspaper poll.[6] Trosky was having another good season in 1940, until he missed 10 straight games in September and went just 8-for-57 the rest of the year, while the Indians missed the AL pennant by a single game. The cause of his 1939–40 absences would not become publicly known until 1941.

The 1940 season was punctuated by the Indians' "Crybaby Revolt," where 12 players petitioned ownership to fire manager Ossie Vitt. The petition was dismissed, and the players were excoriated by the press and fans. Trosky, as team captain, was given a disproportionate share of blame for the

---

4. *Ibid.*, p. 58.
5. Ruhl, Oscar. "From the Ruhl Book." *The Sporting News*, January 11, 1945, p. 19.
6. Johnson, William H. *Hal Trosky: A Baseball Biography.* Jefferson, NC: McFarland & Company, Inc. Publishers, 2017, p. 92.

incident, which he believed was due to his name being reminiscent of former communist leader Leon Trotsky's.

Trosky had a strong start to the 1941 season, but then started slumping and missing games again. On July 12, he finally revealed that a "thumping headache" had bothered him at least half of the time during the previous three seasons, to the point that it impaired his vision, making the ball look like a bunch of white feathers. "If I can't find some relief, I'll simply have to give up and spend the rest of my days on my farm in Iowa," Trosky said.[7] He played sporadically until August 17, when a collision resulted in a season-ending fractured thumb. On February 18, 1942, Trosky—still suffering from migraines—asked the Indians to put him on the "voluntarily retired" list; they did so on March 5. "[P]oor health deprived the blond Iowan of his chance to become one of the truly great hitters of all time," lamented one noted writer.[8]

Away from the diamond all of 1942 and '43, Trosky saw improvement in his pain, and talked about coming back. The Yankees expressed interest, but Trosky said he would consider returning only to Chicago or St. Louis, so he could be relatively close to home. After securing reinstatement through the Commissioner's office, Trosky was sold to the White Sox on November 6, 1943. Ironically, the migraines would allow him to return to baseball, as they gave him a 4-F military draft rating.

But despite some relief attributed to vitamin shots, the headaches persisted, and Trosky was far from the player he had been. Though he led the White Sox in doubles, homers and RBI, he slugged just .374. Trosky quit again on March 9, 1945.

Trosky attempted one last comeback in 1946, but it was a bust and he retired to his farm for good with lifetime averages of .302 (batting) and .522 (slugging)—still one of the top 60 of all time. He remained on the White Sox' payroll as a scout for the next few years. In 1951, Trosky became one of the original 10 members of the Cleveland Indians' Hall of Fame, along with the likes of Cy Young, Nap Lajoie, and Tris Speaker.

Hal Trosky's name returned to the limelight in the late 1950s, when his eldest son became a prized pitching prospect. After going 9–5, 14–10, and 13–9 in the minors, Hal, Jr., got a brief trial with the White Sox in 1958, winning his only decision.

Hal Trosky, Sr., died of a massive heart attack at Cedar Rapids, Iowa, on June 18, 1979.

---

7. Associated Press. "Chronic Headache May End Hal Trosky's Baseball Career." July 12, 1941.
8. McAuley, Ed. "Trosky Gone—and it May Be Forever." Unidentified newspaper article, August, 1941.

Year	Team (League)	G	AB	R	H	2B	3B	HR	RBI	SB	AVG	OBP	SLG
1933	Cleveland (AL)	11	44	6	13	1	2	1	8	0	.295	.340	.477
1934		*154	625	117	206	45	9	35	142	2	.330	.388	.598
1935		*154	632	84	171	33	7	26	113	1	.271	.321	.468
1936		151	629	124	216	45	9	42	*162	6	.343	.382	.644
1937		153	601	104	179	36	9	32	128	3	.298	.367	.547
1938		150	554	106	185	40	9	19	110	5	.334	.407	.542
1939		122	448	89	150	31	4	25	104	2	.335	.405	.589
1940		140	522	85	154	39	4	25	93	1	.295	.392	.529
1941		89	310	43	91	17	0	11	51	1	.294	.383	.455
1944	Chicago (AL)	135	497	55	120	32	2	10	70	3	.241	.327	.374
1946		88	299	22	76	12	3	2	31	4	.254	.330	.334
Totals		1347	5161	835	1561	331	58	228	1012	28	.302	.371	.522

Brandon Webb

What pitcher finished in the top two in Cy Young Award voting for three straight years, then never won another game in the majors? If you ask a baseball expert that question, chances are he will guess Hall of Famer Sandy Koufax.

The correct answer is Brandon Webb.

Brandon Tyler Webb was born May 9, 1979, at Ashland, Kentucky, the son of Mr. & Mrs. Philip Webb. Ashland, despite being a small town, has a significant baseball history connection: just three months after Brandon's birth, it hosted the first Negro League Baseball Reunion, leading to the Negro League Baseball Hall of Fame, now housed in Kansas City, Missouri.

Webb went to Ashland High School and then the University of Kentucky in Lexington. Despite his size (6'3" and 190–230 pounds), the right-hander relied on curves more than power: his fastball was clocked at an unimposing 88–92 mph.[1] The 2000 major league draft

---

1. Bloom, Barry M. "Webb Reflects on 'Devastating' End to Career." MLB.com, June 2, 2014.

went into the eighth round before Webb was selected by the Arizona Diamondbacks.

Webb pitched in relief for South Bend Indiana and the Arizona League Diamondbacks in 2000, winding up with no wins or losses, two saves, and a 3.57 ERA over 13 appearances, before spending the final month of the season on the disabled list with right arm soreness.[2] But he developed his signature pitch, a heavy sinking fastball. Coach Royal Clayton saw Webb toying with it on the sidelines and encouraged him to work on it and throw it more often. It eventually developed into "a two-seam fastball that approaches the batter at thigh level, then suddenly plummets to his ankles, as if sucked into a vacuum."[3] The result was a lot of ground-ball outs and batters muttering the word "filthy" on their ways back to the dugout.

The next year, Webb was with Lancaster of the California League. He had trouble harnessing his new pitch, as evidenced by his 27 hit batsmen and 6–10 record; but he had 158 strikeouts against just 44 walks, impressive enough to move up to AA and then AAA in 2002. With El Paso and Tucson that year, Webb combined for a 10–7 record and 3.17 ERA. He then pitched for Scottsdale in the Arizona Fall League, going 2–0 with a 0.55 ERA over eight appearances.[4]

Back with Tucson in 2003, Webb got the call to the parent team after just three games, when future Hall of Famer Randy Johnson went on the disabled list with a sore knee. Webb made his debut on April 22, pitching a hitless inning in relief vs. the Expos. Five days later, he got his first start, hurling seven shutout innings, fanning 10, and giving up just three hits in a 6–1 win over the Mets. Webb wouldn't pitch in the minors again for eight years.

The D'backs' pitching rotation was led by the twin towers of Johnson and Curt Schilling, who had combined for the unfathomable records of 43–12 in 2001 and 47–12 in '02. But when injury and misfortune saw them plummet to 14–17 in 2003, Webb was one of those pleasant surprises who stepped up to fill the void and keep the team competitive. Despite missing the first few weeks of the season, and another 15 days on the DL with right elbow tendinitis, Webb wound up with a 10–9 record. More impressively, he ranked among the NL's top six in ERA, strikeouts per nine innings, fewest hits allowed per nine innings, pitching WAR, WHIP, and Fielder-Independent Pitching (FIP). Webb finished third in Rookie of the Year voting, was named the majors' top rookie by *Baseball America*, and earned a three-year, $3.3 million contract starting in '04.

2. *2009 Arizona Diamondbacks Media Guide*, p. 177.
3. Taylor, Phil. "One-Pitch Wonder." *Sports Illustrated*, June 12, 2006, p. 47, 50.
4. *2009 Arizona Diamondbacks Media Guide*, p. 177.

Webb married his high school sweetheart, Alicia Berginnis, on January 19, 2004.[5] They soon had a daughter, Reagan.[6]

Webb suffered through a rough season in 2004. Though he led the NL in games started and ground ball-to-fly ball ratio (G:F), and had a respectable 3.59 ERA (compared to the league's 4.30), he also led in losses. Some of that was his own doing: he was tops in walks and wild pitches. But most of it was due to Arizona's poor team (51–111), especially its shaky infield, deadly for a ground-ball pitcher; the team made 36 errors[7] in his 35 starts, leading to 28 unearned runs. It should be noted that Webb made five of those errors himself, leading the league. Overall, Webb was a good fielder, usually among the league leaders in assists and range factor.

Webb made a nice comeback in 2005, cutting his walks in half, topping the majors in G:F, and finishing sixth in the NL in innings and eighth in pitcher WAR. This got him a four-year contract extension worth $19.5 million,[8] and set the stage for a three-year run of dominance.

In 2006, Webb roared out to an 8–0, 2.01 record through May, including a string of 30 consecutive scoreless innings. He faltered in June, came on strong again in the summer (earning All-Star selection; he retired Derek Jeter, David Ortiz, and Alex Rodriguez in his one inning, not permitting a ball to leave the infield), then dropped his last two decisions. All in all, Webb tied for the NL lead in wins and shutouts, and topped the league in pitcher WAR, FIP, G:F, and adjusted ERA. He was also second in innings, complete games, wins above team, and WHIP, and among the leaders in several other categories. It all earned him the NL Cy Young Award.

Webb was arguably better in 2007. He earned another All-Star selection, and put together a streak of 42 consecutive scoreless innings in July and August, the 12th-longest ever, and the most since Orel Hershiser set the all-time mark of 59 in 1988.[9] Included were three straight shutouts, making Webb the first pitcher to do that since Roger Clemens in 1998.[10] By the end of the season, Webb had led the NL in innings, complete games, shutouts, and adjusted ERA, and finished second in games started, wins, ERA, and pitcher WAR, third in FIP, and even fourth in strikeouts. In post-season play, Webb pitched a gem (7 innings, 4 hits, 9 K's, 0 walks) to beat the Cubs in the NLDS, but took a loss against the Rockies in the NLCS.

As impressed as people were with Webb's pitching, they were even

---

5. Bordow, Scott. "Webb Holds Up Under Spotlight." *East Valley Tribune*, February 24, 2004.
6. Taylor, Phil. "One-Pitch Wonder." *Sports Illustrated*, June 12, 2006, p. 49.
7. *Ibid.*, p. 51.
8. *Ibid.*, p. 49.
9. *2009 Arizona Diamondbacks Media Guide*, p. 175.
10. Boivin, Paola. "Streak Ends for Webb, but That's a Good Thing." *Arizona Republic*, August 23, 2007.

more impressed with his work ethic. "There's something to be said for a guy who works hard, labors to improve every year and goes about his business with very little ego," wrote one observer.[11] He was also big in community activity, starting the Brandon Webb K Foundation to benefit critically and chronically ill Arizona children, and serving as team spokesman for the Domestic Violence Prevention program.[12] Webb finished second in Cy Young Award voting, behind San Diego's Jake Peavy.

And 2008 was more of the same. Webb started the season 9–0, becoming just the fifth pitcher since 1919 to win his first nine starts, and joining Clemens as the only starters to start 8–0 or better more than once. Webb was NL Pitcher of the Month in April (he was the first since Randy Johnson in 2002 to finish April 6–0, giving him an 18–2 career record before May), earned a third straight All-Star selection, and had another eight-game winning streak during the summer.[13] Webb had top-five finishes in games started, complete games, innings, wins, percentage, adjusted ERA, FIP, G:F, and pitcher WAR. With a 22–7 record, Webb was the NL's first 20-game winner since 2005, and again wound up second in Cy Young voting, behind San Francisco's Tim Lincecum.

For 2005–08, Webb led all major league pitchers in wins (70) and innings (927).[14] If he wasn't the best pitcher in baseball, he was certainly in the discussion. At age 29, the most similar pitcher to Webb was Hall of Famer Jim Bunning, with Bob Gibson and Gaylord Perry near the top 10.

Nobody could have guessed that Brandon Webb would never win another pro game.

Webb had been struck by a line drive late in the 2008 season, and may have altered his motion thereafter to compensate. Yet, he won his last three decisions, and was again the D'backs' opening day pitcher in 2009. It was a sunny day at Chase Field against the Rockies on April 6. Webb had a 2–0 lead with one out in the third inning. Then everything fell apart.

Before the inning ended, a single, a double, an RBI-groundout, and two walks were followed by a bases-clearing two-bagger. The Rockies started the fourth with back-to-back homers. By the end of the frame, Webb had already thrown 77 pitches, and was complaining of a sore shoulder. His day—and, as it turned out, his big league career—was suddenly over.

Over the next three months, Webb saw five specialists and had three MRIs. The consensus was some sort of "internal impingement," not

---

11. Ibid.
12. *2009 Arizona Diamondbacks Media Guide*, p. 177.
13. Ibid., p. 175.
14. Ibid., p. 174.

requiring surgery.[15] But, after rest and rehab failed to improve the arm, Webb underwent shoulder debridement surgery on August 3, 2009. His season was officially over and his career in question, but the Diamondbacks exercised their 2010 contract option for $8.5 million, citing his promising progress and significant past contributions to the team.[16]

There was talk of Webb's rejoining the D'backs as a relief pitcher in the second half of the 2010 season, but he wound up spending the whole year in rehab. He became a free agent on November 1.

On January 3, 2011, Webb signed a contract with the Texas Rangers for $3 million plus considerable incentive bonuses.[17] He debuted with Frisco of the AA Texas League on May 30. But after going 0–2, 9.75 over four games, Webb shut it down again. "I was taking Toradol shots to get through my starts," Webb recalled, referring to a pain-killing drug. "On the last one, that didn't help, so I figured something was up again. It wasn't going to work, so let's move on. Let's spend some time with the family."[18]

On August 1, 2011, Webb underwent rotator cuff surgery. He became a free agent again on October 3. Finally, after 18 more months of unsuccessful rehab, Webb formally announced his retirement on February 4, 2013. "The thing I remember about Webby," said D'backs coach Kirk Gibson, "is that he gave everything he had, all of his heart, all of his soul."[19] Webb returned to his Ashland, Kentucky, home, and later became an analyst for the Diamondbacks in a limited amount of televised games.

A 2013 article by Nick Piecoro put a good perspective on Webb's story: "In the spring before (Webb) was hurt, teammate Dan Haren told him he was on a path to the Hall of Fame. Webb was taken aback and reminded Haren of how hard it was to maintain his level of production.

"Haren was right. Webb was that good. Unfortunately, Webb was right, too."[20]

Year	Team (League)	G	IP	W	L	PCT	SO	BB	H	ERA
2003	Arizona (NL)	29	180.2	10	9	.526	172	68	140	2.84
2004		35	208.0	7	*16	.304	164	*119	194	3.59
2005		33	229.0	14	12	.538	172	59	229	3.54

15. Gintonio, Jim. "Webb Determined to Pitch This Season." *Arizona Republic*, July 6, 2009.
16. Associated Press. "Webb Has Option Picked up by Arizona." ESPN.com, November 6, 2009.
17. Durrett, Richard. "Rangers Officially Welcome Pitchers." ESPN.com, January 3, 2011.
18. Bloom, Barry M. "Webb Reflects on 'Devastating' End to Career." MLB.com, June 2, 2014.
19. *Ibid.*
20. Piecoro, Nick. "Injury Kept Brandon Webb from Full Promise." Azcentralsports.com, February 5, 2013.

Year	Team (League)	G	IP	W	L	PCT	SO	BB	H	ERA
2006	Arizona (NL)	33	235.0	*16	8	.667	178	50	216	3.10
2007		34	*236.1	18	10	.643	194	72	209	3.01
2008		34	226.2	*22	7	.759	183	65	206	3.30
2009		1	4.0	0	0	.---	2	2	6	13.50
Totals		199	1319.2	87	62	.584	1065	435	1200	3.27

Joe Wood

After Joe Wood's meteoric pitching career ended, he became a solid position-player in the majors. Which gave him more satisfaction? "Hitting is very nice," he recalled, "but it's much nicer to be like I was—practically among the best of them, pitching."[1]

Howard Ellsworth Wood was born October 25, 1889, at Kansas City, Missouri, the son of Rebecca Stephens and John F. Wood, an eccentric lawyer. When small boys, Howard and his older brother, Harley, attended a circus and were inspired by two clowns called Pete and Joe. The Wood brothers were known as Pete and Joe ever after.

The family moved to Ouray, Colorado, in 1900. Joe went to Ouray High School, and played with some distinction for the local town baseball team at age 15. Next, the Woods moved to Ness City, Kansas, in 1906. Playing shortstop and pitcher in local leagues (and supposedly for the University of Kansas), Joe earned the nickname "The Kansas Cyclone," and his first taste of professional ball—on a girls' team! From the 1890s through the 1930s, there were teams called the "Bloomer Girls" in hundreds of cities and towns across the country. They were ostensibly all-female teams who challenged local men's teams, but according to Wood, four of the players on his Bloomer Girls squad were men in disguise. The 16-year-old Wood, playing as "Lucy Totton," earned $20 to join the team for the final three weeks of the season.[2]

Still just 17, Wood began his organized baseball career in 1907. He signed a $90-per-month contract with Cedar Rapids of the Three-I League,

---

1. Amore, Dom. "'Smoky' Joe Wood Provides a Voice from the Past." *Hartford Courant*, June 17, 2013.
2. Wood, Gerald C. *Joe Wood: The Biography of a Baseball Legend*. Lincoln, NE: University of Nebraska Press, 2013, p. 37.

but before the season started he was transferred to Hutchinson, Kansas, in the Class-C Western Association. Wood was signed as a shortstop, but due to injuries to the pitching staff was given a chance on the mound. "Once they saw me pitch, they wouldn't let me do anything else," he recalled.[3] Wood had 19 strikeouts in an April game, and held Webb City to two scratch hits in September[4] (he reportedly had a no-hitter that season, too). He finished the season 18-11 with 224 strikeouts in 196 innings.

Sold for $300 to Kansas City of the American Association, Wood (sometimes referred to as "Woods") jumped all the way to the top rung of the minors. He went just 7-12 for the seventh-place team, but had a 2.26 ERA. On May 21, he no-hit the Milwaukee Brewers, 1-0, retiring the first 25 batters before the 26th reached on an infield error.[5] The Red Sox bought his contract for a reported $3,200 on August 12, and he was a big leaguer at age 18. Wood made his major league debut on August 24, and appeared in six games all told, including a one-hit shutout vs. the Athletics on October 3, stopped by darkness after six innings.

A right-handed thrower and batter, Wood stood a shade under six feet tall and eventually filled out to about 185 pounds. He had a blazing fastball—earning him the nickname "Smoky Joe"—and an effective "drop ball." Wood also took his fielding duties seriously, including covering and

Smoky Joe Wood, here at the height of his powers (1912), had a 1.99 ERA in eight seasons with the Red Sox. Library of Congress.

---

3. Green, Paul. "Joe Wood—Still Waiting for Cooperstown." *Sports Collectors Digest*, November 26, 1982, p. 34.
4. Unidentified clippings in National Baseball Library file, 1907.
5. Unidentified clipping in National Baseball Library file, 1908.

backing up bases, not common practice in those days. According to one article, "He fields his position better than almost any other man playing the game, especially when it comes to covering the first bag."[6] Another said, "When 'Woody' was on the pitcher's mound there was an extra infielder in the game. Not only was he a great bunt 'hawk' but he invariably knocked down any hard hit ball that came close to the pitcher's box."[7] Writers also marveled at the fact that Wood, unlike most players from that era, actually kept in condition during the off-season.

It didn't help in 1909, as Wood didn't take the mound until summer. He apparently had a knee injury,[8] and the team didn't want to rush him into action until he was "in the proper shape."[9] Once Smoky Joe joined the Boston staff, he became a key member. He debuted on June 21 with a two-hitter to beat the Athletics. On July 17, Wood struck out 10 batters in an amazing four-inning relief stint vs. Cleveland. Three days later, he shut out the same team, 4–0. On August 7, he pitched a three-hit shutout to top the White Sox; on August 18, he duplicated the feat against New York, giving him three straight three-hitters. On September 11, Wood whitewashed the A's, 1–0. He finished with an 11–7 record and a 2.18 ERA; only five teenagers since 1900 (including Hall of Famers Chief Bender and Bob Feller) won more games in one year. Smoky Joe finished fifth in the league for fewest hits allowed per nine innings. After the season, the Sox played the New York Giants in an exhibition series; Wood pitched the first game against Christy Mathewson and lost, 4–2.

Smoky Joe started the 1910 season well. A three-hit shutout on June 4, and seven-and-two-thirds innings of relief to win an extra-inning game on June 7, gave him a 7–3 record. But Boston put Wood right back in the box for another four innings of relief the next day, starting him on a five-game losing streak. Wood finished the season 12–13, despite a 1.69 ERA, the second-highest strikeouts-per-nine-innings rate in the AL, a league-leading six wins in relief, and even a .261 batting average. The reward for all this? A pay-cut offer from Red Sox' president John I. Taylor! "I don't consider that Joe delivered the goods this year, and it was purely a business proposition," said Taylor.[10] Wood refused and Taylor wished him well on his future endeavors.

Obviously the two eventually came to terms, and Wood again had a strong start in 1911. In back-to-back starts against the Yankees on May 4 and

---

6. Unidentified clipping in National Baseball Library file, September, 1912.
7. McHale, Marty. "A Closeup of Smoky Joe Wood." Unidentified article, 1918.
8. Neft, David, Richard M. Cohen, and Michael L. Neft. *The Sports Encyclopedia: Baseball*. New York: St. Martin's Griffin, 2000, p. 44.
9. *The Sporting Life*, April 24, 1909, p. 7.
10. Whipple, Sid. "Wood, Denied Raise, Quits the Red Sox." Unidentified article, 1910.

8, he hurled a two-hitter followed by a one-hitter, both shutouts. On June 5, he struck out three pinch-hitters in the ninth inning to finish off a relief win, one of a league-leading six he earned that year. On July 7, Smoky Joe fanned 15 St. Louis Browns, allowing only one hit—a two-out, ninth-inning single by Burt Shotton. On July 29, against the same team, Wood finally got his no-hitter, striking out 12 in the 5–0 win; he remains the youngest Boston hurler to pitch a no-no. In between, he was picked as the starting pitcher for an all-star team formed for a July 24 game to benefit the family of Hall of Famer Addie Joss, who had died at 30 earlier that year. Wood had 19 wins by August 2, then sputtered a bit, dropping six of his next nine. But he finished the season strongly, two-hitting the Yankees with 13 K's in a 7–0 win on October 3. He wound up 23–17 for a team that was otherwise below .500; among his victories were ones over former and future 30-game winners Cy Young, Ed Walsh, Jack Coombs, and Walter Johnson. Wood was third in the league in games, opponents' OBP, and ERA (2.02), second in strikeouts and in fewest hits per nine innings, and first in strikeouts-per-nine. Factoring in his hitting (.261) and defense, under Pete Palmer's system, Wood was the best all-around pitcher in the AL in 1911—and he hadn't even reached his peak! Smoky Joe Wood was about to embark on a historic pitching season.

Wood's 1912 campaign started modestly. He was 3–2 through May 1, then ran off five consecutive wins, a loss, and eight straight wins, before a Fourth of July defeat left him at 16–4. Then came the longest streak of all: Smoky Joe would not lose another game for 2½ months.

By this time, Wood was being compared with the top pitchers in baseball. The Senators' Walter Johnson, in the early stages of a Hall of Fame career which would produce 417 wins and 110 shutouts, was universally regarded as the fastest and best in the game. But the Big Train was quick to deflect such praise. "Listen, my friend," Johnson supposedly said. "There's no man alive can throw harder than Smoky Joe Wood."

Future Hall of Famer Napoleon Lajoie agreed. "Wood looks like the swiftest pitcher I've ever faced," Lajoie was quoted in 1912 newspaper articles. "He seems to have more speed than Amos Rusie, Rube Waddell, Rube Marquard, Walter Johnson and others I could name.... It is not exaggerating it a bit when I say that at times I have been unable to see Wood's fastball as it sped over the plate.... He perfected his curve ball so that it's about the quickest breaking ball I've ever tried to hit.... Wood has all the American League batsmen tabbed. He never overlooks a fault."

That year, Johnson set an American League record by winning 16 consecutive decisions between July 3 and August 23. But Joe Wood was already threatening the mark, having run up 10 straight wins over the same period. By the time the Senators came to Boston in early September, Wood had 13 straight.

Senators manager Clark Griffith came up with an idea: How about a match-up between the two aces? "They challenged our manager, Jake Stahl, to pitch me against Walter, so Walter could stop my streak himself," recalled Wood. "Jake agreed, and to match us against each other he moved me up in the rotation from Saturday to Friday. The newspapers publicized us like prizefighters: giving statistics comparing our height, weight, biceps, triceps, arm span, and whatnot. The champion, Walter Johnson, versus the Challenger, Joe Wood."[11] So the showdown was set for September 6, 1912. Johnson entered the contest with a 28–10 record, while Wood was 29–4. The game lived up to the hype. Johnson gave up just five hits, one walk, and one fifth-inning run. But that was all Wood needed as he scattered six hits and fanned nine to prevail, 1–0, en route to a 32-inning scoreless streak.

Wood matched Johnson with his 16th straight win on September 15, before finally taking a loss on the 20th. Over a century later, Johnson's and Wood's AL mark of 16 straight wins in a season has been matched three times—by Lefty Grove (1931), Schoolboy Rowe (1934), and Roger Clemens (2001)—but never surpassed.

Wood finished the 1912 season with a spectacular 34–5 record, good for an .872 winning percentage, highest in history to that point. Besides topping the AL in wins and percentage, Smoky Joe was first in complete games (35) and shutouts (10), and second (behind Johnson) in ERA, strikeouts (258, which would stand as a Red Sox' record until Clemens topped it 1988), and fewest hits allowed per nine innings. Part of Wood's success was due to his own bat and glove. He hit .290, and among his 36 safeties were 13 doubles, a record for a pitcher. On May 15, he set a record (since broken) with five putouts in one game, en route to a league-leading 41 for the year. But Wood's season wasn't done yet: the Red Sox had won the AL pennant and were on their way to face the New York Giants in the World Series.

Wood won Game One on October 8, 4–3, going the distance and striking out 11, a Series record at the time. After a tie game (called after 11 innings due to darkness) and a Giants victory, Wood came back on two days' rest to win Game Four, 3–1. He again pitched the complete game, whiffing eight and walking none. The teams split the next two games, and there was a rumor that Wood came to blows with teammate Buck O'Brien after Buck lost Game Six, Joe getting the worst of the fracas.[12] Whatever the reason, the next day Wood had easily his worst performance of the year. The Giants knocked him out of the box with seven hits and six runs in the first inning, evening the Series at 3–3–1 with an 11–4 triumph. It was all down to Game Eight the next day, October 16.

---

11. Schechter, Gabriel. *Unhittable!* Los Gatos, CA: Charles April Publications, 2002, p. 62–63.
12. "That Red Sox Row." *The Sporting Life*, December 21, 1912.

The game was tied at one after seven innings, but the Sox had pinch-hit for pitcher Hugh Bedient, so a reliever was needed. In came Wood. Smoky Joe dispatched the Giants easily in the eighth and ninth, but the immortal Christy Mathewson did the same to the Red Sox, sending the game into extra innings. The Giants touched Wood for a run in the top of the tenth, but Wood quashed a potential rally with a great stop on a come-backer. New York's defense then abandoned them in the bottom of the frame, allowing the BoSox to tally twice and win the world championship. Wood's record-tying three World Series victories gave him a 37–6 overall record for the year. In the victory parade after the Fall Classic, Wood sat in an open car next to Mayor John "Honey Fitz" Fitzgerald, grandfather of JFK; the mayor gave Joe an inscribed gold pocket watch.

It's interesting to note that Wood not only did not win that year's Chalmers Award (emblematic of the league's most valuable player), but ranked just fifth, behind a teammate (Tris Speaker) and two other pitchers (Ed Walsh and Walter Johnson). But some writers named just one player from each AL team, choosing either Speaker or Wood from the Red Sox, whereas Walsh was the only Chicago player named on any ballot. Speaker had batted .383, leading the league in doubles, homers, and OBP, while playing his usual brilliant center field.

Through age 22, the 10 most similar pitchers to Wood include five Hall of Famers, among them Mathewson and Johnson. But despite Wood's ascension to the top of the baseball heap, there were some ominous predictions being voiced in 1912. "He has tremendous speed," said Johnson. "But he acquired that speed in such a way that he can't stand it long.... I am afraid he will soon cease to be as effective as he is now, if he does not have to retire altogether."[13] An anonymous reporter, comparing the two aces, wrote, "The chances are that (Johnson's) strength will carry him into a more enduring pitching life than will fall to the lot of Wood. The motion of the Boston pitcher is against him. Sooner or later that snap of the wrist will destroy the efficiency of a baseball pitcher."[14]

It happened sooner.

In countless articles, most written more than a half-century after the fact, Wood said that his downfall began when he slipped on wet grass during a 1913 spring training or early-season game, breaking his pitching thumb. He came back too soon, injured his arm, and was never the same. But the details don't quite add up.

Wood was Boston's opening day starter in 1913, and pitched well in the first half of the season, though he missed three weeks early in the

---

13. "Wood's Strong Wrist Great Aid in Pitching." *The Sporting Life*, November 30, 1912.
14. Unidentified clipping in National Baseball Library file, November, 1912.

campaign. Through the Sox' 83rd game of the season, he was on a pace to go 20–9 for a team which was otherwise barely over .500, with 220 K's and a 2.31 ERA over 263 innings. But something happened to Smoky Joe on July 18; *The Sporting Life*, citing an X-ray, called it a "sprained thumb." Wood pitched just one more inning the rest of the season, a one-two-three frame with two K's on September 17 (he had hurled three innings of one-hit ball in an exhibition game in Manchester, New Hampshire, on September 8[15]).

Trying to pinpoint what happened to Joe before his two long absences in 1913, only adds more mystery. At Philadelphia on April 21, Wood was relieved after just two innings "because he became wild in the second," according to one source, and didn't pitch again until May 12. Following are some newspaper accounts from during this period:

- The April 22, 1913, *Reading* (Penn.) *Times* reported, "Boston started with Joe Wood, who injured his hand sliding to base and was compelled to retire, [Hugh] Bedient taking his place." Wood's biographer, Gerald C. Wood, says the injury happened in a slide to second base, and resulted in erratic control upon his return.[16]
- The *New Castle* (Penn.) *News*, April 29, 1913, said "Smoky Joe Wood, the Red Sox twirler, cannot pitch for a week or so because he is suffering from an injury to the metatarsophalangeal joint, the same being in his thumb."
- The *Altoona Tribune*, April 30, 1913, reported "'Smoky Joe' Wood, the Boston champion's star twirler, won't be able to pitch for a week or more until his heaving arm gets into the right condition. The injury is the result of being hit by a batted ball."
- The May 5, 1913, *Albuquerque Journal* said, in a list of "maimed and crippled" major leaguers, that Wood is suffering from "general indisposition, induced by his beaning Bobby Byrne in the Hot Springs series." Pittsburgh's Byrne had been struck in the head by a Wood pitch during spring training, and accounts throughout the season indicate that Smoky Joe was emotionally scarred by the incident.
- The May 7, 1913, *Delaware County* (Penn.) *Daily Times* wrote that Wood received five X-rays "to determine, if possible, whether the long-standing trouble on Wood's [right] hand was due to fracture of any kind." A specialist determined there was nothing indicative of

---

15. "Wood Returns to Diamond." Unidentified clipping in National Baseball Library file, September 8, 1913.
16. Wood, Gerald C. *Joe Wood: The Biography of a Baseball Legend*. Lincoln, NE: University of Nebraska Press, 2013.

a fracture, and Wood left for the west with Boston, "but it is hardly expected that he will be able to pitch for a couple of weeks at least."

- The May 8, 1913, *Fort Wayne Daily News* wrote, "of late [Wood's] absence from the fray has been attributed to a bothersome injured finger, although Trainer Quirk has all along been inclined to make light of it."
- The May 15, 1913, *St. Louis Post-Dispatch* offered a bit of everything, saying "Wood was suffering from nervousness resulting from having hit [Byrne] in the head with a pitched ball at Hot Springs. Wood also is reported to have a bad hand. But there is some reason to believe that the strain of the tremendous season of 1912 helped kill the wonderful arm of Wood. Wood outdid Walter Johnson, many believe, by throwing out all there was in his arm. These believe his arm 'dead' today, as a result." It added that, "Wood today said he had been nursing a sprained thumb on his right hand, which has prevented him from throwing a curve ball without pain. He injured the thumb sliding into the plate in Philadelphia."

After his return, Wood was looking more and more like his old self until July 18, when he left a game at Detroit with two out in the fourth frame. The next day's *Pittsburgh Post-Gazette* said, "In fielding [Bobby] Veach's grounder in the fourth inning, Joe Wood injured the thumb joint of his right hand and it was announced he probably will be unable to pitch again for at least two weeks." A United Press story three days later reported that Wood "is out of the game for an indeterminate period. Examination of his injured right thumb under an X-ray shows a crack in the end of the big bone with indications that a piece of the bone has been chipped off."

Whatever happened that year, there is little evidence that Wood had reduced effectiveness or speed when he pitched. His 7.60 strikeouts per nine frames was the highest rate of his career, higher than any other AL pitcher that year; Walter Johnson wound up leading with 6.32. Despite starting only 18 games, Smoky Joe finished tenth in the league in strikeouts, going 11–5, 2.29. He also batted .268, including two doubles in one inning on July 4.

At least one good thing happened to Wood in 1913. On December 20 he married Laura T. O'Shea, a gal he had met back when he pitched in Kansas City. This began a union lasting almost 66 years, and producing four children: Joe, Jr. (born May 20, 1916), twins Robert K. and Virginia, and Stephen L. By Joe, Sr.'s death, he would have 14 grandchildren and 10 great-grandchildren.

Wood had his appendix removed on February 22, 1914,[17] and didn't

---

17. *Ibid.*, p. 165.

make his first start of the year until May 27. They didn't believe in easing pitchers back in those days. Wood pitched a complete game victory, then missed the next 19 games. On July 3, he pitched a ten-inning win, then sat out the next 31 games. Wood was effective when he pitched (10–3), but was able to hurl only 113 innings, and his strikeout rate per nine innings was down to 5.32, indicating a loss of velocity. To make up for it, he developed an "emery ball."[18]

By 1915, Wood was in constant pain ("rheumatism," according to one clipping) and pitching on guile alone. His strikeout rate sunk all the way to 3.60, less than half of his peak rate. Wood again had a late entry to the season, not making his first start until May 16, and he hurled only three games after August 16. Yet, when Smoky Joe pitched, he was the most effective in the league, winding up tops in the AL in both win percentage and ERA (1.49). He won nine straight decisions between June 1 and July 7, and barely missed a no-hitter on August 7. Cleveland's only hit was by Bill Wambsganss, who beat out an eighth-inning infield single when backup shortstop Hal Janvrin was slow in fielding the ball. Wood wound up with his fifth one-hitter, to go along with his no-no, four two-hitters, eight three-hitters, and 16 four-hitters.

By the end of the season, Wood's arm was totally shot, and he was unable to play in the World Series. In fact, he would never pitch another game for Boston. His final career stats with the Red Sox included a .676 win percentage (117–56) and 1.99 ERA, with just ten home runs allowed. He is still the Sox' all-time leader in ERA, but Pedro Martinez finally topped him in percentage.

Wood didn't play in the pros at all in 1916. In later years, he said he was ill, refused a pay-cut, retired to the family farm in Pennsylvania, and contemplated his situation, but the contemporary reports paint a slightly different picture. In March, Wood was put on waivers, and all 15 of the other major league teams passed on him.[19] In July, he sent Boston President Joe Lannin a letter, saying he had been working out at home and was almost ready to return to the Sox; he never did.[20] On September 3, Wood pitched a no-hitter in an amateur game in Pennsylvania.[21] After the season, he sought chiropractic care in New York.[22]

---

18. "Truth about the Emery Ball." Unidentified clipping in National Baseball Library file, February, 1915.
19. Broun, Heywood. "Fifteen Clubs Refuse to Give Joe Wood a Trial." Unidentified clipping in National Baseball Library file, March, 1916.
20. "Joe Wood Will Rejoin Red Sox." *Boston Sunday Post*, July 23, 1916.
21. Lobb, Graham Roger. "Remembering 'Smoky Joe' Wood." *Wayne Independent* (Honesdale, PA), August 8, 1985, p. 7B.
22. Horgan, Tim. "Let's Clear the Air on Smoky Joe." *Boston Herald American*, April 25, 1982, p. 69.

Wood appealed to his former roommate, Tris Speaker, for a job. Speaker was now player-manager of the Indians, and convinced team owner Jim Dunn to take a chance on his friend. The Indians purchased Wood's contract for $15,000 on February 24, 1917.[23] Smoky Joe made his Indians debut against the Yankees on May 26, went eight innings, strained his arm, and lost, 4–3; he would face only 34 more batters the rest of the year. Except for mop-up appearances in 1919 and '20, his pitching career was over (an unfortunate consequence of his Cleveland hurling efforts was raising his career ERA above two).

Wood decided that, if he could not contribute on the mound, maybe he could serve elsewhere on the field; after all, he was a ballplayer, not just a pitcher. The Indians had 14 players who would miss time in 1918 due to World War I service, so the openings were there. And the idea of Wood becoming a position-player was hardly new. As early as 1911, an article said, "He points to his [1910] batting record of .261 with pride and sees in it comfort in his old age—an outfield job, perhaps."[24] The following year, another article said "if ever he goes back as a pitcher and wants to remain in the game, there are many clubs which would like to secure him as an infielder."[25] But no one could have foreseen Smoky Joe's instant success.

Wood wound up playing 119 of the team's 129 games in the war-shortened season, including 84 in left field, 19 at second base, 10 in right field, four at first base, and one in center field. He "arrived" as a regular player on May 24, hitting a game-tying home run in the seventh inning and a game-winning blast in the 19th—this in a season when the entire *league* hit only 96 homers. Wood had a 12-game hitting streak in June, and a 4-for-4 game in July. By the end of the year, he ranked tied for fifth in the AL in homers and tied for third in RBI, leading the second-place Indians in both categories. He batted .296, 42 points above the league average.

With players returning from the military, Wood saw decreased playing time the next three seasons, but performed well when called upon. He helped the Indians to the 1920 world championship, and in 1921 batted .366 with 60 RBI in just 194 at bats. Wood was Cleveland's regular right fielder in 1922, hitting .297 (including a 17-game hitting streak) with 92 ribbies. It turned out to be his final season. He wound up batting .298 in his five seasons as a position-player, finishing up one of the most remarkable pitcher-batter careers in history.

After the '22 season, Wood was offered a coaching position at Yale

---

23. "Joe Wood is Sold to Indians for $15,000." Unidentified clipping in National Baseball Library file, February 24, 1917.
24. "Wood to Show Them." *The Sporting News*, March 9, 1911.
25. "Joe Wood, Who Will Face New York in World Series, Idol of Boston." *The Sunday Star*, September 7, 1912.

University. Following a year in charge of the freshmen, he served as varsity coach for nearly two decades, running up a 283–228 record.[26] His most memorable game during that period was on April 21, 1941, when Yale defeated Colgate in a home game featuring all three of Joe's sons. The opposing pitchers were Joe, Jr., for Yale and Steve for Colgate, while Bob played first base for the visitors. Joe, Jr., would go on to a pro career, hurling a no-hitter in the Eastern League on August 7, 1941, appearing in three games for the Red Sox in 1944, and pitching through 1947. Steve's and Bob's pro prospects were derailed by World War II. Steve pitched in the minors in 1945–46, going 16–10, but at 28 was no longer considered a prospect.

Joe, Sr.'s Yale career ended unceremoniously. On March 19, 1942, he and two other long-time coaches were dismissed effective June 30 in a "war-time economy move."[27]

Wood maintained a home in New Haven, Connecticut, but spent most of the rest of his life at the family farm in Shohola ("Woodtown"), Pennsylvania. Joe now had more time for his many hobbies. He was an avid hunter and fisherman, and an accomplished pool player and golfer. For a time, Wood managed a Los Angeles-area driving range owned by his brother. Later, Joe coached a Delaware Valley League baseball team in 1956–57.

The 1970s were tough on Wood. In 1972, he underwent a hernia operation, and in 1978 he was seriously injured in a fall from a ladder. His son Stephen died at 56 in January 1975, and Joe's wife Laura followed on August 2, 1979.

Wood received many honors in the second half of his life. He was elected to the State of Kansas Hall of Fame in 1943, and was similarly honored by Connecticut on January 30, 1967, and by Pennsylvania on October 18, 1996. On April 20, 1962, Joe was recognized at Fenway Park upon the 50th anniversary of the stadium and the 1912 championship team; on April 12, 1982, he threw out the first ball—left-handed—at the Red Sox' home opener. In 1966, Wood was featured in Larry Ritter's historic *The Glory of Their Times*, which told the stories of 22 former stars (including seven Hall of Famers) of the game in their own words. From 1977 until his death, the Pike County, Pennsylvania Commissioners designated October 25 as "Smoky Joe Wood Day." And on January 3, 1985, he received an honorary doctorate degree from Yale, presented to him in a ceremony at his home by Yale President Bart Giamatti, and reducing Wood to tears. Composer Cole Porter was the only previous recipient of an honorary Yale degree.

But the ultimate baseball honor eluded Wood. He received votes in

---

26. Clark, Ellery H., Jr. "Joe 'Smoky Joe' Wood." In *Biographical Dictionary of American Sports: Baseball* (David L. Porter, editor).

27. Associated Press. "Yale to Drop Three Coaches on June 30." *New York World Telegram*, March 19, 1942.

nine BBWAA Hall of Fame elections, peaking at 29 nominations in 1947. Since then, many—most notably Alex Preuss, Bob Wood (Joe's son), and Doug Roberts—have campaigned vigorously for his election through the various veterans' committees. Among those who supported the campaigns were Presidents Gerald Ford and George H.W. Bush. But there is no evidence Smoky Joe ever got serious consideration. The 1953–2001 Veterans' Committees did not publicize results, but in 1995, for example, their ballot listed 27 former players, and Wood was not among them. Under the restructured committees since then, Wood got just two of 80 votes in 2005, and didn't make the ballot in any other year. His next opportunity to be considered is in 2021. Throughout his long life, Wood professed disinterest in being elected, but nobody really believed him.

Smoky Joe Wood died at age 95 on July 27, 1985, at West Haven, Connecticut. It was the day before that year's Hall of Fame induction ceremony.

Year	Team (League)	G	IP	W	L	PCT	SO	BB	H	ERA
1908	Boston (AL)	6	22.2	1	1	.500	11	16	14	2.38
1909		24	160.2	11	7	.611	88	43	121	2.18
1910		35	196.2	12	13	.480	145	56	155	1.69
1911		44	275.2	23	17	.575	231	76	226	2.02
1912		43	344.0	*34	5	*.872	258	82	267	1.91
1913		23	145.2	11	5	.688	123	61	120	2.29
1914		18	113.1	10	3	.769	67	34	94	2.62
1915		25	157.1	15	5	*.750	63	44	120	*1.49
1917	Cleveland (AL)	5	15.2	0	1	.000	2	7	17	3.45
1919		1	0.2	0	0	.---	0	0	0	0.00
1920		1	2.0	0	0	.---	1	2	4	22.50
Totals		225	1434.1	117	57	.672	989	421	1138	2.03

Appendix A
Honorable Mentions

Included here are players who didn't quite make the featured 40. Some had long, distinguished careers, despite a disability or derailing event; some were players whose best years were behind them when their careers were ended; and others are subjects of miscellaneous tales of woe. I could easily have added more, but had to stop someplace.

Jim Abbott—Despite having been born with no right hand, Abbott was able to pitch 10 years in the major leagues. He developed a deft routine wherein he would release the ball with his left hand and put on his glove, which had been wedged under his stump, in the same motion. Abbott proved nay-sayers wrong every step of the way, capturing the Sullivan Award as the nation's top amateur athlete in 1988, finishing fifth in AL Rookie of the Year voting the next year, winning 18 games in 1991, and hurling a no-hitter in 1993.

Abbott had some bad years and bad luck, too, and finished with an 87–108 record in the bigs. He received 13 votes in the 2005 Hall of Fame election.

Harry Agganis—"The Golden Greek" was an all-American boy, and became an All-American football player at Boston University, earning the Cleveland Browns' #1 draft pick. He opted for baseball, though college and U.S. Marine Corps service delayed his pro career until he was 24.

Agganis had a respectable rookie year for the Red Sox in 1954, batting .251 with 11 homers in 132 games, and showing good defense at first base. He was hitting .313 in his first 25 games in '55 when he was sidelined with pneumonia and leg pain. Agganis was hospitalized on May 6 and again on June 5. On June 21, the Associated Press reported that he was "very much improved," but Dr. Eugene E. O'Neil warned that he wasn't out of the woods. "Harry was a lot sicker than realized when he entered the hospital," said O'Neil. "His case is very complicated and very serious. He could be idle all season. It's too early to say just yet."[1]

Six days later, a massive blood clot travelled from the ballplayer's leg to his lungs. Harry Agganis, 26, was dead of a pulmonary embolism.

Moises Alou—The most recent and most accomplished member of a distinguished baseball family, Moises Alou was a very good player when he was healthy. He hit as many as 39 homers and batted as high as .355, earning six All-Star selections and two third-place MVP finishes. Unfortunately, he often wasn't healthy. Alou missed the entire 1991 and '99 campaigns with injuries, and spent time on the disabled list in 11 other seasons, including all but 15 games of his final year (2008). His 814 total days on the DL rank second all-time among position-players, according to Gary Gillette and Pete Palmer; Nick Johnson (987) is the leader.

After debuting in the majors in 1990, Alou missed the '91 season due to surgery to correct a recurring shoulder problem. Although he didn't miss much time because of it, his most gruesome injury came on September 16, 1993, when his spikes caught on artificial turf and he suffered a fractured left fibula and dislocated left ankle.

In February 1999, Alou was working out on a treadmill when he fell off, tearing the ACL in his left knee. He was set to come back for the final month of the season when he fell off a bicycle, re-aggravating the injury. Alou had also spent time on the DL in 1992, '95, and '96, and would do so in 2000, '01, and '02.

The injuries really started to pile on after 2004. Alou spent 31 days on the DL in 2005, 49 in '06, and 75 in '07, with injuries including a badly-sprained ankle, a hamstring strain, and a back problem. He missed the first month of 2008 after hernia surgery, then strained his left calf. Finally, a torn left hamstring on July 9 ended Alou's season and career.

Despite all the missed time, Alou finished with 1941 games, 332 homers (more than Felipe, Matty, and Jesus Alou combined), a .303 batting average, and a .516 slugging percentage. He received six votes in 2014 Hall of Fame balloting.

Lady Baldwin—Charles "Lady" Baldwin had only a 12–10 career record at age 27, but then had a remarkable season in 1886. Pitching 487 innings for the Detroit Wolverines, the southpaw posted a 42–13 record, topping the National League in wins, shutouts (7), strikeouts (323), and opposing

---

1. Associated Press. "Agganis 'Improved' but Not Enough." *New York World Telegram-Star*, June 21, 1955.

batting and on-base averages. Plagued by arm trouble thereafter, he won just 16 more games before retiring to his Michigan farm. Baldwin finished with a 73–41 career record, with the 1886 season accounting for 58 percent of his career victories.

Gene Bearden—Bearden was a 27-year-old overnight sensation in 1948. The rookie southpaw went 20–7 with a league-leading 2.43 ERA. Six of those wins came in the last 16 games of the season, including the clincher, as the Indians took the AL pennant in a one-game playoff over the Red Sox. Bearden then tossed a five-hit shutout to win Game Three of the World Series over the Braves, and got the last five outs to save the sixth and final game, giving Cleveland the world championship. Bearden finished eighth in MVP voting, and surely would have won the AL Rookie of the Year had each league had its own award. The Braves' Alvin Dark was the major leagues' honoree, but Bearden was the top vote-getter among AL players, and also was named the league's top freshman in an Associated Press poll.

Bearden started the 1949 season 3–0 with a 2.33 ERA, but reinjured his left leg while trying to field a fourth-inning bunt against the Senators on May 8 (he had originally hurt the leg, what he called a "pulled sciatic nerve," in a spring training game against the Giants). He went 5–8 with a 5.94 ERA the rest of the season, and won only 17 more big league games in four seasons with five teams after that.

Charles "Lady" Baldwin (c. 1887) batted .231, but was best known for his pitching. Library of Congress.

Besides the injury, one theory offered for Bearden's sudden decline was that batters learned to take his sinking knuckler for a ball rather than flail helplessly at it. It seems likely that overwork was a factor, too. After hurling 205 minor league innings in 1947, Bearden spent the whole winter pitching in Mexico, tossed another 240+ innings of regular- and post-season ball for Cleveland in '48, then pitched in a post-season exhibition tour.

What took Bearden so long to reach the majors? World War II, mostly. Bearden began his pro career in 1939 as a pitcher-first baseman. The following year, he topped the Class-D Florida East Coast League in shutouts and ERA (1.63), going 18–10. Bearden was 17–7, 2.41 with the same team in '41, then jumped up to Class B in '42, before joining the U.S. Navy. On July 6, 1943, Bearden was aboard the U.S.S. Helena near the Solomon Islands when it was torpedoed by the Japanese, killing 168. He suffered severe head and leg wounds, and spent two days on a rubber life raft before being rescued. Bearden underwent numerous surgeries over the next year-and-a-half, including the placement of metal plates in his skull and knee. He received the Purple Heart.

Against the odds, Bearden was able to resume his pro baseball career in 1945. He went 15–5, 2.41 in the Eastern League that year, and 15–4, 3.13 and 16–7, 2.86 in the Pacific Coast League the next two years. He pitched in one game for the Indians in 1947 before making the team the next year, though he didn't make his season debut until May 8.

Bearden returned to the minors after his big league career ended, posting an 18–12 record in the PCL in 1955. He also did some work in Hollywood, including a role in *The Stratton Story*.

Johnny Beazley—Beazley was the toast of the baseball world in 1942. Although he didn't join the Cardinals' starting rotation until July, the rookie rolled up a 21–6 record and 2.13 earned run average, finishing second in the National League in wins, percentage, and ERA. Beazley then earned two complete-game World Series victories, including the clincher, over the mighty Yankees. He was named the majors' "Most Valuable Rookie."

But with World War II heating up, Beazley promptly enlisted in the U.S. Air Force. When he returned 3½ years later, he was suffering from arm and stomach ailments, and what today we would call PTSD. Johnny Beazley won only nine big league games after his spectacular rookie season.

Beazley paid $15 for a baseball school conducted by the Cincinnati Reds in his hometown of Nashville, Tennessee. Upon its conclusion, Beazley signed a minor league contract for the 1937 season.[2] He pitched for nine different teams over the next four seasons, suffering elbow and back

---

2. "John Beazley." Unidentified clipping in National Baseball Library file.

injuries, and losing more games than he won. He had a good fastball (he was nicknamed The Weasel, because it popped), but little else. Beazley made a breakthrough in the Southern Association in 1941. With manager Ray Blades teaching him a new pitch, Beazley went 16–12 for a team that was otherwise below .500. "Blades taught me much about pitching," Beazley said. "He told me how to throw a let-up pitch without telegraphing it, and he told me when to throw it. And he showed me how to pace myself so that I could be as strong in the closing innings as in the early part of a ball game."[3] The Cardinals called him up to The Show, where he made his debut on the final day of the season, September 28. Beazley hurled a complete-game, 3–1 victory over the Cubs.

Making the big league team in 1942, Beazley was tutored further by coach Mike Gonzalez, catcher Gus Mancuso, and veteran pitcher Lon Warneke, who helped Johnny master the curveball.[4] Beazley pitched mostly in relief for the Cards in the first half of the season. In 20 appearances out of the bullpen, he went 6–3 with three saves. Manager Billy Southworth decided Beazley could help the team more in the regular rotation, and he unloaded the popular Warneke to make room for Johnny. Beazley rewarded his skipper's faith, winning more games the rest of the season than Warneke would the rest of his career. In 23 starts, Beazley chalked up 13 complete games and a 15–3 record, leading the team to a 63–19 second half, enough to overcome a large deficit against the defending champion Brooklyn Dodgers.

By the end of the season, Beazley ranked second in the NL in wins and ERA behind only teammate Mort Cooper, who took the league's MVP Award with a 22–7, 1.78 campaign. The Cardinals won the pennant by two games over the Dodgers, but few gave St. Louis much of a chance in the World Series. They would be facing off against the dynastic New York Yankees, featuring Joe DiMaggio, Bill Dickey, and four other future Hall of Famers. Over the past 15 seasons, the Yanks had captured all eight World Series in which they appeared, in the process winning 32 games while losing just *four*. New York kept on rolling in the '42 opener, building up a 7–0 lead and knocking Cooper out of the box, before settling for a 7–4 victory.

Southworth gave Beazley the ball for Game Two—a somewhat bold decision, considering no rookie had won a World Series game since Paul Dean in 1934. Beazley shut down the Bronx Bombers for seven innings, before allowing them to tie the game with three runs in the eighth. But Southworth stuck with his young star, the Cards scored in the bottom of the frame, and Johnny held on for the 4–3 victory. As the Series moved to

---

3. The Old Scout. "Beazley Hopes to Win Rookie Honors." Unidentified clipping in National Baseball Library file, 1942.
4. *Ibid.*

Yankee Stadium, St. Louis followed with 2–0 and 9–6 triumphs, and was one win away from a big upset. Beazley got the call to pitch Game Five on three days' rest.

All he did was hurl another complete-game victory, subduing the Yanks, 4–2. The Cardinals were world champions! After the game, the immortal Babe Ruth entered the Cardinals' clubhouse, wanting to meet "that guy that whooped my Yankees."[5] Beazley returned to Nashville to a hero's welcome on October 7.

On November 24 Beazley was named winner of the Chicago BBWAA chapter's J. Louis Comiskey Award as the major league's "most valuable rookie," forerunner of the modern Rookie of the Year Award. In earning the honor, he polled 192 points, beating out up-and-coming stars Johnny Pesky (136), Vern Stephens (112), and Stan Musial (72).[6]

Though he was sole supporter of his mother, giving him a potential draft exemption, Beazley was determined to join the World War II effort. After flirting with the Marines and Navy, he enlisted in the U.S. Army Air Force on November 3, 1942.[7] "Baseball's a thing of the past for me," Beazley said. "I'm going to make a career out of the Army."[8] He was commissioned a second lieutenant on March 3, 1943, and served until his honorable discharge as Captain in 1946.

According to his son, Terry Morton Beazley (named after Johnny's teammates, Terry Moore and Mort Cooper), "when he got out of OCS, he was assigned to a special branch which was a morale type unit. Really what he did was to travel around to all the bases in Hawaii and ... California. They had baseball games and everywhere he went he was asked to play.... [H]e agreed to play and pitch two or three innings before getting on a bus and traveling 40 miles to the next base. He didn't cool down his arm and without proper training all the pitching eventually hurt his arm."[9]

Contemporary articles from his National Baseball Library file indicate Beazley wasn't always pitching just two or three innings, either. It is likely that his pitch count often exceeded 150. On April 24, 1943, he lost a 12-inning game, 5–4, despite notching 18 strikeouts. On August 12, 1943, he gave up 10 hits and struck out 10 in a 6–5 win. On June 11, 1944, he gave up 12 hits, but fanned 14 in a 9–3 win. On September 11, 1945, he hurled a 4–0 no-hitter.

When Beazley returned to spring training in 1946, his pitching was

---

5. Traugher, Bill. "Johnny Comes Marching Home after '42 World Series." Nashville *Sports Weekly*, August 10, 1999, p. 25.
6. "Beazley Rookie of the Year." *The Sporting News*, November 26, 1942.
7. "Beazley Mechanic in Army Air Corps." New York *World Telegram*, November 4, 1942.
8. "Beazley to Quit Game." New York *Times*, November 10, 1942.
9. *Ibid.*, p. 25.

labored and he was further bothered by a chronic upset stomach (which may or may not have been related to an appendectomy he wound up having in January 1948). One article described his arm ailment as a "calcified bursa."[10] According to another contemporary source, "His arm bothered him considerably. He was the victim of ptomaine poisoning and was extremely nervous."[11] Expanding on that, noted writer Dan Daniel indicated that Beazley was experiencing what today we would call post-traumatic stress disorder. "The Cardinal right-hander is suffering from war fatigue," wrote Daniel. "He had some harrowing experiences in the South Pacific and doesn't appear to be able to get down to regarding baseball as serious business."[12]

Beazley stumbled in with a tepid 7–5 record and 4.46 ERA for 1946. The Cardinals wound up winning the pennant and then beating the Red Sox for the world championship, but Beazley's only contribution was a scoreless inning in a Game Five loss.

Beazley reported in March 1947 "that he had developed a new kink in his arm and was finished," asking for his unconditional release.[13] He was sold to the Boston Braves for a reported $25,000 on April 18. Southworth was now managing the Braves, and was hopeful Beazley could regain his magic. It was not to be. Beazley pitched fewer than 30 innings before going on the disabled list on June 1, 1947. The following spring, Braves president Lou Perini said, "I am resigned to the loss of money we paid to the Cardinals for pitcher Johnny Beazley a year ago."[14] Beazley was reinstated on September 3, 1948, but pitched just 16 innings that year and two in 1949 before leaving the majors for good. His career record of 31–12 (.721 percentage) and 3.01 ERA only hinted at what he might have accomplished with good health.

Albert Belle—Few players have encountered as much controversy as Albert Jojuan Belle. After playing parts of two seasons as .220-hitting Joey Belle, the youngster went through alcoholism treatment, returning in 1991 as Albert Belle, and becoming one of the most feared sluggers in baseball. Over the next decade, Belle averaged 37 homers, 120 RBI, and a .298 average each year.

But every year was marred by controversy linked to his erratic behavior and temper. In 1991, Belle was suspended for throwing a ball at a fan's chest. He was suspended in each of the next three seasons as well, for

---

10. "Moore, Beazley Turn Up Ailing." New York *World Telegram*, March 2, 1946.
11. "John Beazley." Unidentified clipping in National Baseball Library file.
12. Daniel, Dan. "Daniel's Dope." New York *World Telegram*, May 15, 1946.
13. Daniel, Dan. "Cuban Diamond Bonanza a Fizzle." New York *World Telegram*, March 19, 1947.
14. Daniel, Dan. "Beazley's Arm a Dead Loss." New York *World Telegram*, March 31, 1948.

infractions including a corked bat, charging the mound, destroying a bathroom, and hitting a fan with a Ping-Pong paddle. In 1995, he was fined for a World Series clubhouse tirade against reporter Hannah Storm, and sued for knocking down a kid who had egged his house on Halloween. In 1996 he fired a ball at a *Sports Illustrated* reporter's hand, and earned a suspension for stiff-arming 170-pound second baseman Fernando Viña on a force play. In 1997, he was fined for an obscene gesture toward fans, and named in a gambling scandal. In 1998, he was charged with battery in a domestic dispute. He staged a clubhouse tirade in spring training, 1999. Along the way, Belle beat out Barry Bonds in a sportswriters' poll to name "Baseball's Biggest Jerk." Even after his career, Belle made negative headlines, with a DUI in 2002 and a stalking charge in 2006.

But, oh, how Belle could hit a baseball. In 1993, he led the AL with 129 RBI. In the strike-shortened 1994 campaign, he batted .357 with 36 homers and 101 RBI (projecting to 52–145 over a full season). In 1995, also abbreviated by strike, Belle led the league in runs (121), doubles (52), homers (50), RBI (126), and slugging (.690), becoming the first man ever to hit 50 doubles and 50 homers in the same season; pro-rated for 162 games, he might have amassed 59 doubles and 56 homers. In 1996, he won his third RBI title, collecting 48 homers and knocking in 148 runs. After joining the White Sox as a free agent, and becoming the highest-paid player in the game, Belle came through with 49 homers, 152 RBI, and a league-leading .655 slugging average in 1998.

Late in 2000, Belle was en route to his ninth straight 100-RBI season, but suffering from the pain of an arthritic, degenerative hip. Few could have guessed that his career was coming to a close at age 33. Belle's home run off Denny Neagle on October 1, 2000, helping the Orioles to a 7–3 win, proved to be the final swing of his career. He retired the next spring, naturally amidst controversy: he fought to have insurance pay his salary for the remaining years of his contract.

Belle finished with 381 lifetime homers and a .564 slugging average over 1539 games. If not for the premature end to his career, he would have amassed surefire Hall of Fame numbers—but would he have made it to Cooperstown with all his baggage? Even with career totals comparable to Hall of Famers Orlando Cepeda and Jim Rice, Belle received just 8 percent of the votes on his first try at the Hall of Fame in 2006, then sunk to 3 percent the next year and was dropped from the ballot. He went on the Veterans' ballot in 2016 and '18, but his vote total was reported only as fewer than five of a possible 16 each time.

Paul Blair—Blair is remembered for his defense—eight Gold Gloves in center field—but he was also emerging as a fine hitter until a horrific beaning. In his first full season in 1967, he led the AL with 12 triples and finished fifth in batting at .293. Two years later, he helped the Orioles to the first of three straight AL titles with 26 homers and a .285 average.

On May 31, 1970, Blair was hit in the face by a Ken Tatum pitch. He missed three weeks, and was never quite the same hitter. Blair remained in the majors for another decade, but batted just .243 with an average of six homers per year after 1970. He received eight votes in the 1986 Hall of Fame election.

Steve Blass—The phenomena of an established player who seemingly forgets how to throw a baseball is often called "Steve Blass Disease," after one of the first and most drastic examples.

After three nondescript seasons with the Pirates, Blass had a breakout year in 1968, leading the NL in win percentage on an 18–6 record with a 2.12 ERA. He followed with 16–10 and 10–12 logs, then was a key figure in his team's 1971 world championship drive. Blass was 15–8 with a league-leading five shutouts and a 2.85 ERA. He capped the year off with two masterful complete-game victories over the Orioles in the World Series, allowing just seven hits and two runs in 18 innings. Blass followed with arguably his best season in '72, setting career highs in innings and wins as he went 19–8, 2.49 and finished second in Cy Young Award voting. At age 30, his career record was 100–67 with a 3.24 ERA and an average of fewer than two walks per nine innings.

But in 1973, Blass suddenly could not throw strikes. His season started poorly, and got worse, until he was removed from the rotation in mid-season. "You can't imagine the feeling that you suddenly have no idea what you're doing out there," Blass said. There was no physical explanation for Steve's sudden collapse, and he tried everything from psychotherapy to hypnosis to Transcendental Meditation, with no improvement.[15]

By the end of the campaign, Blass had pitched 89 innings and been battered for 109 hits, 84 walks, 12 hit batsmen, and a 9.85 ERA. After giving up seven walks and eight runs in five innings in his first game of the '74 season, he was sent down to AAA. He fared no better there, posting a 9.74 ERA for Charleston, and surrendering 103 walks in 61 innings. After Blass showed similar results in his only spring training game the following year, his pro career was over at age 32. He later spent decades as a broadcaster for the Pirates.

Blass got two Hall of Fame votes in 1980.

---

15. Pietrusza, David, Matthew Silverman, and Michael Gershman, editors. *Baseball: The Biographical Encyclopedia*. Kingston, NY: Total Sports Illustrated, 2000, p. 95.

Vida Blue—Blue made his debut with the Oakland A's before his 20th birthday in 1969, but really arrived the following September. The 21-year-old southpaw hurled a one-hit shutout to beat the Royals on the 11th, then no-hit the hard-hitting Twins 10 days later. With barely 80 major league innings under his belt, and a salary of just $14,750, Blue became Oakland's opening day pitcher the next year.

Vida Blue was sensational in 1971. After being knocked out of the box in his season debut, he reeled off 10 consecutive victories, five by shutout. Following a 4–3 loss on May 28, he won six more in a row. Blue had the best outing of his young career on July 9: 11 innings, 17 strikeouts, zero walks, and zero runs allowed in a no-decision (this was the game that pushed Tony Conigliaro into retirement). Blue entered the All-Star break with a 17–3 record, 188 strikeouts, and a 1.42 ERA. He was the starter and winner of the Midsummer Classic (the only game the AL won between 1962 and 1983), and had a 22–4 record by August 15, before two straight 1–0 losses. He finished the season 24–8 with 301 K's, leading the league in shutouts (8) and ERA (1.82), and handily won the AL MVP and Cy Young Awards.

Throughout the season, people—even President Richard Nixon—remarked that Blue was the most underpaid player in the game. Blue came to believe them, and sought a raise to $115,000 in '72—at a time when only the *crème de la crème* of established players received six figures. A bitter holdout and feud with A's owner Charlie Finley followed, with Blue announcing his "retirement" on March 16, and Commissioner Bowie Kuhn even intervening, before the pitcher signed for $63,000 in May. Blue said that Finley had soured his stomach on baseball, and that he had learned that baseball is a business, not a game. Vida didn't pitch his first game of the season until May 24, or earn his first win until June 18, and finished just 6–10.

Blue went on to pitch another 13 years in the majors, including five All-Star selections and two 20-win seasons, but he never again had the magical touch he displayed in 1971. His strikeout high after his MVP season was 189, just one more than he had at the All-Star break in '71. He went to prison on cocaine charges, missing the '84 season, and his career ended three years later due to a failed urine test. Blue finished 209–161 with a 3.27 ERA, and received 60 Hall of Fame votes in his two years on the ballot (he was mistakenly left on an extra year, after failing to make the 5 percent cut in 1992). He went on the Veterans' ballot in 2011, but did not receive enough votes for them to be publicized.

Tiny Bonham—Ernest "Tiny" Bonham was just shy of his 27th birthday when he debuted with the Yankees, going 9–3 with a 1.90 ERA in the last two months of the 1940 season. Two years later, he went 21–5, 2.27, leading the AL in complete games, shutouts, and win percentage. He was 15–9, 2.27 in 1943, but he lost more than he won after that season.

By 1949, Bonham's chronic back trouble (which kept him from military service) had reduced him to a spot-starter, and he planned to retire after the season at age 36. But on September 15, just 18 days after his last appearance, Bonham suffered complications from an appendectomy and died. He finished with a 103–72 career record and 3.06 ERA.

Britt Burns—Burns went 18–11 in his final season, 1985, before his career was ended at age 26 by a painful and deteriorating hip condition. The southpaw had had his first cup of coffee at age 19, and followed with an excellent rookie season in 1980, going 15–13 with a 2.84 ERA for the 70–90 White Sox. He had a 10–6, 2.64 mark in the strike-shortened '81 season, earning All-Star selection, and went 13–5 in '82. Two losing seasons followed before his '85 campaign, which earned him a lucrative free agent contract with the Yankees, although his physical problems had already begun. After he underwent hip replacement surgery in May 1986, and spent the entire season on the DL, Burns announced his retirement on April 1, 1987. He finished with a 70–60 record and 3.66 ERA. Burns tried a comeback with the Yankees in Spring Training, 1990, but it failed.

Chris Carpenter—When healthy, Chris Carpenter could be the best pitcher in the league. But Carpenter spent 1059 days on the disabled list, second only to Steve Ontiveros (1068) on the all-time list, ruining a fine career.

Carpenter won the NL Cy Young Award in 2005, when he posted a 21–5 record with a 2.83 ERA for the Cardinals. He was even better four years later, when he went 17–4, 2.24, topping the league in ERA and finishing second in Cy Young balloting. He also won the Tony Conigliaro Award that year.

But injuries cost him almost the entire seasons of 2003, 2007–08, and 2012–13. He finished with a 144–94 record and 3.76 ERA. He went onto the Hall of Fame ballot in 2018, but received just two votes and was dropped.

Rico Carty—Few players have had as many physical problems as Rico Carty. He was one of the best hitters of his generation, but missed two entire seasons and chunks of many others due to health woes.

After a terrific rookie season in which he batted .330 and slugged .554 in 1964, Carty suffered from back and thumb injuries, playing just 83 games (with a .310 average) the following year. He came back to play 151 games and hit .326 in 1966, giving him the highest lifetime batting average (.323) among all active players.

Carty was involved in a serious auto accident on January 18, 1967, injuring his face and back. He recovered and started the season well, batting .313 through May 16, but began slumping. In early June he dislocated his right shoulder, the beginning of a chronic problem. By the end of the season his average had fallen to .255. After showing weight loss the following spring training, Carty was diagnosed with tuberculosis on March 29. He missed the entire 1968 campaign.

Carty came back in 1969, but suffered at least three shoulder separations (seven, according to Carty), along with leg cramps. In between, he batted .342 and slugged .549 in 104 games. Despite a thigh injury in 1970, he had his best year, posting the highest batting average (.366) since Ted Williams, and slugging .584 (but finishing just tenth in MVP voting). Carty still led active players with a .322 lifetime average.

On December 11, 1970, Carty collided with fellow-outfielder Matty Alou in a winter league game. Carty suffered a crushed left kneecap and cartilage and ligament damage. He had surgery, with a pin put in his leg for 11 months. During his recovery period, he contracted pleurisy and phlebitis. Just as it looked like he might be ready to return to the field, Carty was clubbed by a police officer on August 24, 1971, suffering right eye damage. He did not play a single game in '71, and was never the same afterward.

In 1972, Carty suffered continuing issues with his left leg, tendinitis of his right elbow, and a torn right hamstring, putting him on the DL from July 18–August 20. He played just 86 games and batted a pedestrian .277. Then, in a winter league game that December, Carty suffered a broken jaw when hit by a pitch.

The designated hitter rule gave Carty new hope in 1973, but he wound up batting just .229 for three teams. He broke a bone in his right foot and was on the DL from July 23–August 13. By the next year he was in the minors.

Carty made another amazing comeback in 1974, batting .354 in the Mexican League, then returning to the majors to hit .363 in 33 games. Between hamstring injuries, he became one of the top designated hitters in the AL over the next four years, topping .300 in 1975 and '76, and hitting a career-high 31 homers in 1978. Plagued by an ankle injury in 1979, Carty slipped to .255 and retired, with his career average having dropped to .299. Somehow, he had managed to play 1651 big league games despite all the setbacks. He went on the Hall of Fame ballot in 1985, got just one vote, and was dropped from further consideration.

Bob Caruthers—Although he notched his last pitching victory at age 28, Caruthers finished with a 218–99 career record, good for an outstanding .688 win percentage. But the shortening of his career appears to have been mostly of his own doing. Unidentified clippings in his National Baseball Library file mention his "carousing," his "bad habits," and his frequent threats to quit baseball.

Caruthers had most of his success in the American Association, a lower-level rival to the NL. From 1885–89 he averaged 408 innings and a 34–12 won-lost record each year. Through age 25, he had amassed a 175–64 record and become "the highest priced player in the Association."[16] Joining the National League in 1890, he had more-modest marks of 23–11 and 18–14, then fell off the earth with a 2–10 record in 1892, the last year he took the mound.

As SABR's *Nineteenth Century Stars* relates, "His pitching arm was nearly gone, but his hitting made him a regular outfielder for St. Louis."[17] Caruthers played right field for the Cardinals,

Bob Caruthers (1887) had a .688 win percentage and a .282 batting average for his career. Library of Congress.

Cubs, and Reds over the next two seasons before becoming a minor league umpire. He finished his playing career with a .282 career batting average. SABR chose him as an "Overlooked 19th Century Baseball Legend" in 2017, and placed a marker at his Chicago gravesite in 2018.

Dean Chance—At times, Chance was the best pitcher in baseball, and at others he appeared to be just phoning it in. After an impressive 14–10 rookie season with the expansion Angels in 1962, he slipped to 13–18 the following year, and was just 5–5 at midseason in '64, having spent nearly a month demoted to the bullpen.

---

16. *The Sporting Life*, November 9, 1887.
17. Tiemann, Robert L., and L. Robert Davids. "Robert Lee Caruthers." *Nineteenth Century Stars*. Kansas City, MO: Society for American Baseball Research, 1989, p. 26.

Chance was lights-out the rest of that year, and finished 20–9 with a microscopic 1.65 ERA. He led the AL in complete games, innings, wins, shutouts (11), and ERA, and earned the major leagues' Cy Young Award. But after going 27–27 over the next two years, and gaining a reputation as a carouser, he was traded to the Twins.

Chance rebounded with his second 20-win season, helping keep Minnesota in the pennant race until the final day of the season. He led the AL in games started, complete games, and innings, and pitched two no-hitters in August, including a five-inning perfect game ended by rain. In '68, Chance posted a 2.53 ERA and set career highs in innings and strikeouts (234), though he finished 16–16 for the sub-.500 club. But he would win just 18 more games the rest of his career.

After a holdout in '69, Chance came back without sufficient training. He suffered shoulder and back trouble, spending nearly two months on the DL, and then finished the season with a bad case of the flu. His fastball gone, Chance pitched for four teams over his final three seasons, losing more games than he won, before his career ended at age 30 in 1971. He finished 128–115 with a 2.92 ERA.

Spud Chandler—Due to his attending the University of Georgia, his less-than-impressive minor league records, and the strength of the Yankees' staff, Chandler was nearly 30 when he finally debuted in 1937. Arm trouble in 1937 and '38 and a broken fibula in '39 limited him to just 273 innings in his first three seasons. Spud finally made a breakthrough in the second half of the 1941 season, going 10–1 with a 1.99 ERA after June. He followed with records of 16–5 and 20–4, winning the 1943 AL MVP after leading the league in complete games, wins, shutouts, and ERA (1.64). But Chandler spent most of the next two years in military service. He returned to make the All-Star team in 1946 (20–8) and '47 before his arm gave out on him for good. Despite his late start and career interruptions, Chandler finished with a 109–43 record for a remarkable .717 winning percentage. He received 12 Hall of Fame votes over five elections.

Joe Charboneau—Surely no non-pitcher got as much notoriety out of a 201-game big league career as Joe Charboneau. Charboneau won the 1980 AL Rookie of the Year Award, earned the nickname "Super Joe," and even had a song written about him, before he flamed out.

After Charboneau played 55 games in the Phillies' system in 1976–77, he briefly quit the game, then went to the Twins and finally the Indians. After batting .350 in A ball in 1978 and .352 in AA the next year, Charboneau made the majors in '80. He brought with him a reputation as a hard-drinking, street-fighting character.

An injury to Andre Thornton opened up a lineup spot for Charboneau. He proceeded to post a 23–87–.289 season and was an easy choice for the league's top rookie. He earned a raise to $90,000. But, as a wild 25-year-old freshman who failed to get a single point in MVP voting, it was hard to take Charboneau seriously as a future star; historically, the most similar players to him at that age are the likes of Larry Sheets and Sam Bowens.

Super Joe slumped in the first two months of 1981. Though he denied being hurt, he suffered injuries to his back (during a spring training slide), right hand, and both ankles, along with ulcers. After the players went on strike, he was sent to AAA, and he got just 13 at bats for the Indians after the big league season resumed. He finished his sophomore campaign batting .210 in the majors and .217 in the minors. He had his first back operation after that season.

Nineteen-eighty-two was much the same story. Hitting .214 through June 1, Charboneau was demoted back to the minors, where he fared little better (.226). At 27, he was no longer a prospect; he would never play in the big leagues again. A second back operation and a compound leg fracture followed. Joe's pro career ended after the 1984 season (the year he appeared as one of Roy Hobbs's teammates in *The Natural*), except for a one-game stunt with the independent Frontier League in 2000.

Ed Cicotte—Of the eight men banned in the Black Sox Scandal, only Shoeless Joe Jackson and Ed Cicotte played the 10+ years necessary for Hall of Fame eligibility. Both were ignored in Hall voting for decades, before they were formally made ineligible by the "Pete Rose Rule" in 1991.

Rose was put on baseball's "Ineligible List" by Commissioner Bart Giamatti on August 24, 1989. While it left him unemployed, Rose's banning did not immediately affect his Hall of Fame eligibility. Having last played in 1986, he was due to go onto the ballot in the fall of 1991, with the results announced in January 1992. There was a lot of speculation as to how Rose would fare. Rose, whom Bill James and others had previously predicted might be the Hall's first unanimous selection, now was expected to receive less than the 75 percent required for election, at least in his first try. The writers would have to weigh Rose's integrity and character (at the time, two little-known and rarely-considered criteria for election) with his playing record and contributions to his teams.

Some people, particularly Hall of Famer Bob Feller, started mouthing off on the issue. Rapid Robert said that if Rose were elected to the Hall, Feller would never return to the annual induction ceremonies (Feller didn't mention that he started coming regularly to the ceremonies only when the Hall's sponsors began paying him $500 per hour to participate in their autograph sessions). This concerned Hall of Fame officials, particularly

Public Relations Director Bill Guilfoile. Guilfoile drafted a new voting rule: "Any player on Baseball's Ineligible List shall not be an eligible candidate." He packaged it with another rule designed to appease the writers (making it harder for BBWAA rejects to get voted in by the Veterans' Committee), but nobody would be fooled.

In January 1991, Guilfoile called me over to bounce the proposed voting changes off me, the Hall's Senior Research Associate at the time. If this rule were adopted, Rose could not be elected to the Hall of Fame unless his name was removed from the Ineligible List by the commissioner—the guy that put Rose's name on the list on the first place (true, 1991 Commissioner Fay Vincent technically did not put Rose's name on the list but, as Giamatti's Deputy-Commissioner in '89, he was instrumental in the process; and, Vincent was not about to reverse the decision made by his best friend and mentor). After mulling it over, I sent Guilfoile a memo saying "While I realize that it may not count for much, I want to go on record as strongly opposed to this proposition. I don't feel that anyone's Hall of Fame eligibility should be left at the mercy of one man."

Guilfoile proposed rule number 3(E), anyway and, in February, it was approved by the Hall of Fame's Board of Directors—a group that included Fay Vincent! Thus, the "Pete Rose Rule" was pasted into the books just months before he would have become eligible.

This rule change forced the Commissioner's Office to draft up an "Ineligible List," since it apparently existed only in theory before 1991 (at least, they could not locate one in their archives; they asked me who should be on it). Ironically, in the first draft the Commissioner's Office released, they forgot to include Rose! They did name the members of the "Black Sox" charged with throwing the 1919 World Series, and banned after the 1920 season. So, this officially made Joe Jackson and Eddie Cicotte ineligible for Cooperstown for the first time, too.[18]

Cicotte was 36 when his career ended, but seemed to be near the top of his game. He had had his three winningest seasons over the past four years: 28–12 in 1917, 29–7 in '19, and 21–10 in '20. He finished 209–148 with a 2.38 ERA.

King Cole—Cole burst into the majors by pitching a shutout on the last day of the 1909 season, then led the Cubs into the 1910 World Series with a brilliant 20–4 rookie campaign, including a seven-inning no-hitter. Cole had the league's highest winning percentage (.833), lowest opposing batting average, and second-lowest ERA (1.80). He followed with a strong sophomore season (18–7), but 1912 was a nightmare. He pitched poorly, was

---

18. Deane, Bill. *Baseball Myths*. Lanham, MD: Scarecrow Press, Inc., 2012, p. 175–76.

suspended for training violations, and was traded to the Pirates, finishing the year 3–4 with a 7.68 ERA. Cole seemingly resurrected his career in the minors in 1913, going 23–11 including a no-hitter, and he was acquired by the Yankees. He pitched creditably, going 10–9 for a 70–84 team, but he was stricken with cancer the next year. Cole died on January 6, 1916, aged 29.

Leonard "King" Cole (1912) had gone 20–4 with a 1.80 ERA as a rookie in 1910. Library of Congress.

Hub Collins—Hubert Collins was a solid player over seven big league seasons, topping the American Association in doubles in 1888 and the National League in runs (148) in '90. He scored 653 runs in 680 big league games, the last of which was on May 14, 1892. One week later Collins died of typhoid at age 28. *The Sporting Life* reported, "He was a fine, hard hitter, a fine fielder and a very daring base-runner, and his fine all-around work went far towards helping the Brooklyns win the championship in 1889, of the American Association, and, in 1890, of the National League."[19]

Jim Creighton—Major League Baseball's Official Historian, John Thorn, calls Jim Creighton "The first great pitcher" and the sport's first professional player. Creighton first worked from the box at age 18 in 1859, an era when the fledgling game of "base ball" was barely-organized and ostensibly amateur. He soon was the most dominant hurler in the game—and its best hitter as well.

On October 14, 1862, Creighton—who had hit four doubles in four at bats already—cranked a home run. As he crossed the plate he said, "I must

---

19. *The Sporting Life*, May 28, 1892.

have snapped my belt." In fact, he had suffered a fatal injury, probably a ruptured inguinal hernia. After four days of suffering, Creighton died at age 21.[20]

In 2019, SABR picked Creighton as an Overlooked 19th Century Baseball Legend.

Hugh Daily—After losing his left hand in a childhood rifle mishap, Hugh "One Arm" Daily used his right to strike out 483 batters in one season. Granted, it was in the weak Union Association with different rules than today, but nobody else in the league was within 100 K's of him, and only two major leaguers ever had more whiffs in a season.

The Irish-born Daily debuted in the majors at the advanced age of 34 in 1882. After winning seasons in the NL with Buffalo and Cleveland, including a no-hitter, the surly hurler moved to the UA where he logged a 28–28 record in its lone season. Returning to the established major leagues, Daily went 7–26 with just 76 strikeouts over three seasons, and his career ended with a 73–87 record. From there he seemingly vanished, and no one knows when or where he died.

Steve Dalkowski—The career minor leaguer was the quintessential example of a pitcher with incredible speed but no control. Many called him the fastest pitcher of all time, and even the immortal Ted Williams expressed fear in facing him. The 5'10", 170-pound southpaw pitched in the minors for nine seasons (1957–65), getting as high as AAA, but the lack of control was too much to overcome. Alcoholism and an arm injury didn't help, either. Dalkowski struck out 1396 batters in 995 pro innings—but walked 1354, and finished with a 46–80 record and 5.59 ERA.[21]

Eric Davis—Davis had immense talent, but could not stay in the lineup. In various seasons, he hit as many as 37 home runs, stole as many as 80 bases, and batted as high as .327—yet he never played in more than 135 games.

Most of Davis's health problems stemmed from his slight frame (6'3" and 165 pounds, when he started out) and aggressive play, but he also missed most of the 1997 season due to colon cancer (winning the Tony Conigliaro Award after his return). Davis spent a total of 463 days on the DL, and that doesn't count the entire 1995 season, when he retired due to injuries. He came back to play six more years.

Davis finished with 282 homers, 349 steals (with only 66 times

---

20. Thorn, John. "The First Great Pitcher." Thorn, John, Phil Birnbaum, and Bill Deane, editors. *Total Baseball*. Wilmington, DE: SPORT Media Publishing, Inc., 2004, p. 51–53.

21. Society for American Baseball Research. *Minor League Baseball Stars*. Manhattan, KS: Ag Press, Inc., 1984, p. 104.

caught), a .269 average, and three Gold Glove Awards. He received three votes in 2007 Hall of Fame balloting.

Willie Davis—Bill James devoted nearly four pages (740–43) of his 2001 *Historical Baseball Abstract* to show that Davis "was a terrific player" whose stats were severely deflated by the era and the park (Dodger Stadium) in which he played his prime years. Adjusting for a more normal context, James projects Davis to have amassed 2860 hits and a .302 average (as compared to the 2561 and .279 he actually wound up with). Davis's 322 career Win Shares put him in the top 150 all time, yet he was not even put on the BBWAA's Hall of Fame ballot.

"Skill-wise, talent-wise, athletic-wise, he was the best athlete on the team," said long-time teammate Wes Parker. "He was the fastest man who ever put on a baseball uniform."[22]

Paul Dean—Paul "Daffy" Dean is remembered mostly as Jay "Dizzy" Dean's younger, lesser brother. But for a time, it looked as if Paul might turn out to be everything Dizzy was—and possibly more. "A goodly number of observers," said one article the year Dizzy won 30, "declared they thought Paul had more speed than Dizzy and that as soon as the younger Dean learned to throw slow stuff and catch batters off balance he would surpass Dizzy in victories."[23] A 1935 article added: "Dizzy gets more than twice as much money, but any number of baseball experts will tell you that Paul is just as good a pitcher, and that in time may become a greater pitcher than Dizz."[24]

The statistics indicate this wasn't just hype. In early June 1936, Paul was two months shy of his 24th birthday. Here's how his career numbers at that point compared to Dizzy's at the same age:

Pitcher	IP	W	L	PCT	ERA	ERA+
Dizzy Dean	588	39	33	.542	3.14	116
Paul Dean	580	43	26	.623	3.34	121

But, while Dizzy burst into greatness at age 24 and went on to the Hall of Fame, Paul won just seven more big league games.

Paul started pitching semi-pro ball in 1930, winning 11 of 13 games, and turned pro with the St. Louis Cardinals' farm system at age 18 the following year. After brief stops in the Texas League and American Association, Paul finished the 1931 season with Springfield, Missouri, of the Class-C

---

22. Telephone interview with Wes Parker, May 17, 2020.
23. Unidentified clipping in National Baseball Library file.
24. Braucher, Bill. "Dizzy Great, but his Work is in Vain if Paul Falls Down." *Brooklyn Times Union*, January 22, 1935.

Western Association. He posted an 11–3 record there with 139 strikeouts in 136 innings.

The next year Dean moved up to Columbus in Double-A, the highest level of the minors in that era. He raised eyebrows by one-hitting the defending champion St. Paul team on April 21, defeating the New York Giants in an exhibition game in May, and pitching a no-hitter vs. Kansas City on August 30.[25] In between he suffered through a wretched 7–16 season, though he did lead the American Association with 169 strikeouts.

Back with Columbus in 1933, Dean blossomed. He went 22–7, topping the league in wins, strikeouts (222), and ERA (3.15), and leading his team to the A.A. pennant. He then hurled three victories in the league's Little World Series as Columbus beat second-place Minneapolis, four games to two. Turning down substantial offers from the Yankees and Red Sox, among others, the Cardinals purchased Dean's contract in September.[26] He would be joining brother Dizzy on the Cards' pitching staff for the 1934 season, at a salary of $3,000. Dizzy had become the team's ace, going 18–15 and 20–18 in his first two full campaigns, and establishing himself as one of the most colorful players in the game.

Paul's main pitch was a sinking fastball, thrown at about three-quarters from the right side. "Crimminy," said Cards player-manager Frank Frisch, "he didn't need a curve, not when he threw the damndest, heaviest sinker you ever saw."[27]

Before the 1934 season even started, Dizzy predicted that the Dean brothers would win 45–50 games between them—pretty bold, considering they had only 39 combined big league wins in their *careers* to that point. Writers tried to hang the nickname "Daffy" on Paul, but it didn't match the younger brother's quietly confident personality, and never really stuck.

Once the season got going, Dizzy was the one making the headlines. He wound up going an amazing 30–7, leading the league in wins (seven more than anyone else), percentage, strikeouts, and shutouts, en route to the MVP Award. Dizzy still stands as the last National Leaguer to win 30 games in a season, and the only one since 1917.

But his younger brother put together a pretty remarkable season himself, especially for a 21-year-old rookie. Paul won 19 games, had the highest strikeout-per-nine-inning rate in the league, and did something Dizzy never did (nor did many other pitchers in the hard-hitting 1930s): toss a no-hitter. It was one of his five shutouts, second in the league behind Dizzy.

---

25. Johnson, Lloyd, and Miles Wolff, editors. *The Encyclopedia of Minor League Baseball.* Durham, NC: Baseball America, Inc., 1993, p. 181.

26. "Cards Snub $50,000 and Keep Paul Dean." *The Sporting News*, September 7, 1933.

27. Broeg, Bob. "The 'Other Dean' Makes Pitch for Handicapped Kids." *St. Louis Post-Dispatch*, September 22, 1968, p. 2C.

Paul finished ninth in NL MVP voting. The Associated Press opined that Paul "has led critics to believe that he is even a better pitcher in his first year than Dizzy was when he came up."[28]

It was not all smooth sailing. On August 13, the brothers were fined and suspended for refusing to accompany the team to an exhibition game the day after both had pitched. They were both reinstated within a week.[29]

In the second game of a doubleheader on September 21, Paul no-hit the Dodgers (.281 team batting average), 3–0, retiring the last 25 batters in order. The elder Dean had allowed just three hits in winning the first game, 13–0. "If'n Paul had told me he was gonna pitch a no-hitter," Dizzy supposedly said, "I'da throwed one, too." Paul's was the only no-no in the NL between 1929 and 1938.

Fulfilling Dizzy's pre-season prediction, the Dean brothers were credited with 49 of the Cardinals' 95 wins as the team won the NL pennant by two games. Then, the Deans captured all four of the team's victories in a seven-game World Series defeat of the Tigers. Dizzy won Games One and Seven (with a loss in between), while Paul took Three and Six, both complete-game efforts, posting a 1.00 ERA.

The brothers Dean picked up in 1935 where they had left off in '34, with Dizzy earning 28 wins and Paul another 19 (plus five saves). Paul again finished third in the league in strikeouts, increasing his workload while reducing his ERA.

But late in the campaign, the younger Dean hinted that he was ready to quit baseball. Wanting his salary doubled to $15,000, he held out before the next season, said "there's no use of conditioning if I can't play,"[30] and reported out of shape. "It was just plain ignorance that brought me to spring training in 1936, a holdout at 225 pounds when I pitched ordinarily at 185," Dean recalled decades later.[31] It is possible he was mixing memories with what happened in another season; the press mentioned his being 40 pounds overweight in 1938,[32] but I've seen no contemporary mention of his weight gain in '36.

In any case, Paul appeared to be on his way to another good year in 1936. Through June 2nd, 42 games into the season, he was 5–3 with a 2.93 ERA (as compared to the league's 4.02 mark). He was approaching his 24th birthday, the age at which Dizzy made his big breakthrough.

But Paul pitched just 15⅓ more innings the rest of the year, being

---

28. Associated Press. "Dean Boys Big Stars in American Comedy." *Brooklyn Eagle*, c. 1935.
29. Charlton, James, editor. *The Baseball Chronology*. New York: Macmillan Publishing Co., 1991, p. 280.
30. Associated Press. "Notice Served by Paul Dean upon St. Louis." March 20, 1936.
31. Broeg, Bob. "The 'Other Dean' Makes Pitch for Handicapped Kids." *St. Louis Post-Dispatch*, September 22, 1968, p. 2C.
32. "About Paul Dean." *The Sporting News*, March 1, 1938.

blasted for 31 hits and a 12.91 ERA. What happened? Contemporary reports indicated he hurt his shoulder in a clubhouse wrestling match with teammate Pepper Martin on June 17.[33] But Dean recalled that he entered a game on one day's rest and "felt something snap" in his pitching arm.[34] He added, "The next day, I couldn't even raise my arm."[35] That jibes with the game of June 4. Pitching on one day's rest (after toiling into the ninth inning on June 2), Dean entered in the eighth frame of a game against Brooklyn, trying to protect a 3–2 lead. He gave up two runs on three hits to take the loss, didn't pitch again for 10 days, and didn't win another big league game for 27 months.

Team surgeon Robert F. Hyland examined Dean that summer and declared he had bursitis.[36] Paul was placed on the "voluntarily retired" list in August, and reinstated in January 1937. After a rough spring training, Dean returned to the mound on April 24, facing three batters; all three reached base and scored. Nine days later, he underwent surgery by Hyland to remove torn cartilage from his shoulder. "My arm felt fine after the operation," Dean recalled, "but the old zip wasn't there."[37] His recovery was slow, and once again he was placed on the "voluntarily retired" list, not to be reinstated until March 1938.

His fastball gone, Dean kicked around pro ball until 1946, with only intermittent success and a few brief stints in the majors.

Bill Delancey—Delancey was the regular catcher for the Cardinals' Gas House Gang in 1934–35, posting a .316 batting average and .565 slugging percentage in 93 games as a 22-year-old rookie. But he contracted tuberculosis in '35, had only four more big league hits after that, and eventually died on his 35th birthday in 1946.

Jim Devlin—Jim Devlin won 30 and 35 games in his two major league seasons before his career ended in disgrace at age 28.

Devlin began his professional career as an infielder-outfielder in the National Association in 1873, and batted .287 overall in the pros. He found his home on the mound two years later, and became the most prolific hurler in the first two years of the National League. Devlin pitched 129 of the Louisville Grays' 130 games in 1876–77, completing all but two. He led the NL in games, complete games, and innings each year, while posting a 1.89 ERA. Ironically, he gained praise for his integrity in '76, when he provided

---

33. *The Sporting News*, June 25, 1936.
34. Broeg, Bob. "Paul Dean Had Talent but Not Luck." *St. Louis Post-Dispatch*, March 18, 1981, p. 2C.
35. *The Sporting News*, April 4, 1981.
36. *The Sporting News*, August 6, 1936.
37. Burnes, Robert L. "'Me and Paul,' the Best of the Gas House Gang." *St. Louis Globe-Democrat*, March 18, 1981, p. 4F.

evidence against teammate George Bechtel in getting Bechtel banned from the game for attempted game-throwing.

Devlin and Louisville were on the top of the baseball world late in the 1877 season. Through August 13, the Grays had lost only 13 games and were five ahead of their nearest rival, the Boston Red Stockings. But Louisville won only one of its next 10 games, including four losses against Boston, and wound up losing the pennant. Rumors of game-fixing arose, and after the season Devlin confessed to his role in the scandal which led to the permanent expulsion of four Grays.

Until his death at age 34 in 1883, Devlin expressed great remorse for what he had done and literally begged for reinstatement, to no avail.

Turkey Mike Donlin (1909) was known more for his bat than his glove, hitting .333 in the Deadball Era. Library of Congress.

Dominic DiMaggio—Joe D's younger brother has gotten support as a Hall of Fame candidate, despite missing three prime years due to military service. Dom was one of the best defensive outfielders of all time, statistically superior to his more-celebrated brother, and was also a fine leadoff man, posting a .383 OBP and twice topping the AL in runs scored. But even if we pencil in normal seasons for 1943–45 (based on his averages in the surrounding seasons), his career totals are simply not Hall of Fame caliber: 1338 runs, 2183 hits, 117 home runs, and a .297 average. DiMaggio was on the BBWAA ballot between 1960 and 1973, with a high of 43 votes (11 percent) in his last try.

Mike Donlin—Turkey Mike Donlin was a star hitter when he played, but he often felt he had better things to do.

Donlin was a hard-drinking playboy and a mediocre fielder, but was also among the best batsmen in the game. Debuting in 1899, he hit .300+ with power almost every year. His best season was 1905, when he batted .356 for the Giants, led the NL in runs, and finished among the league's top four in hits, doubles, triples, homers, total bases, batting, and slugging. He was off to another good start (.339) the next season, but suffered a broken ankle on a slide on May 15, 1906. He did not return until August, and went 1-for-12 the rest of the year.

Donlin missed three entire seasons due to contract disagreements. When he and the Giants couldn't come to terms in either 1907 or 1909–10, he spent the seasons on the vaudeville circuit with his wife, noted actress Mabel Hite. Donlin played his last full season at age 30 in 1908, though his career didn't end until 1914.

Despite playing during the "Deadball Era," Donlin finished with a .333 average over 1049 games.

Dave Dravecky—On August 10, 1989, Giants southpaw Dave Dravecky made an inspirational comeback from cancer, pitching eight innings to earn a 4–3 win over the Reds. Five days later, he hurled five shutout innings against the Expos, before giving up a home run and a hit batsman to start the sixth. On his final pitch of the game, Dravecky's left arm—the bones weakened by cancer treatments—snapped. The Giants held on to give him a 3–2 victory, but Dravecky would never pitch again, and eventually would lose his arm.

Dravecky had undergone arthroscopic surgery on the arm in 1988, at which time a cancerous tumor was discovered. The tumor, along with half of his deltoid muscle, was removed on October 7.[38] His return to a big league mound 10 months later inspired millions, but the joy was short-lived. Dravecky, 33, finished his career with a 64–57 record and 3.13 ERA.

Fred Dunlap—On April 20, 1891, "Sure Shot" Dunlap, a former .400-hitter, saw his 12-year career end on the basepaths. Dunlap, just 32, "broke the small bone of his left leg while stealing third base," according to *The Sporting Life*.

Dunlap was a "meh" player for most of his career, but he had one great season, thanks to low-level competition in a league that lasted just one year, yet somehow is historically considered major. He led the 1884 Union Association in runs (160 in 101 games), hits, homers, batting (.412), OBP, and slugging. The rest of his career, he batted .276 with little power, and was

---

38. Pietrusza, David, Matthew Silverman, and Michael Gershman, editors. *Baseball: The Biographical Encyclopedia*. Kingston, NY: Total Sports Illustrated, 2000, p. 306.

chiefly known for his defense at second base. Dunlap received two votes in the first Hall of Fame veterans' election in 1936.

Fred Dunlap (1888) had batted a flukish .412 in 1884. Library of Congress.

Luke Easter—Easter hit 385 professional home runs—not bad for a guy who didn't hit his first until he was nearly 32. "Had Luke come up to the big leagues as a young man," said teammate Al Rosen, "there's no telling what numbers he would have had."[39]

Easter started his organized baseball career with the 1947–48 Homestead Grays of the Negro National League. In 434 at bats in league games, the 6'4½", 240-pound Easter batted .336 with 23 homers—including one into the center field bleachers at New York's Polo Grounds—and a slugging percentage well above .600. He then played winter ball in Venezuela, leading the league in homers. Indians owner Bill Veeck bought his contract for $5,000 and sent him to the Pacific Coast League for "seasoning."

In a pattern which would repeat itself everywhere he went, Easter quickly became a prodigious slugger and fan favorite. Though he played just 80 games for San Diego before being sidelined by a broken kneecap, Easter batted .363 with 25 homers and 92 RBI. He joined the Indians that August, claiming to have just turned 28 years old; in reality, he was at least 34. The official records now say he was born August 4, 1915, though he once admitted it was actually 1911.[40]

Easter played in the Puerto Rican Winter League in 1948–49, batting .402 and leading the league in runs, doubles, triples, and homers toward a .751 slugging percentage.

---

39. Cattau, Daniel. "So, Maybe There Really is Such a Thing as 'The Natural.'" *Smithsonian*, July 1991, p. 119.

40. Associated Press. "Luke Easter Confesses ... to 52." *New York World Telegram-Star*, August 17, 1963.

It took Easter a while to make his mark in the majors; he didn't hit his first big league homer until May 6, 1950. But on June 23, he hit what has been called the longest home run in Cleveland history, a 477-foot bomb into the upper deck. By the end the season, the 35-year-old rookie ranked sixth in the AL in homers, and eighth in RBI.

Easter suffered torn cartilage in his left knee at the start of the 1951 season, and missed 27 games; he still wound up fourth in homers and RBI and ninth in slugging. In 1952, Easter was named *The Sporting News*'s American League Player of the Year, after finishing second in homers, sixth in RBI, and fourth in slugging—despite missing 28 games, mostly due to a curious mid-season demotion to the minors.

Despite the setbacks, Easter slugged 86 homers and knocked in 307 runs for the Indians in 1950–52. Only two AL players had more homers and just three had more RBI during that period.

Easter suffered a fractured left foot when hit by a pitch in the fourth game of the 1953 season; he played only 70 more big league games before being sent down to the minors for good in early 1954.

But Easter's pro career was far from finished; he continued in AAA ball over the next decade. In both 1956 (35, 106) and '57 (40, 128), past his 40th birthday, Easter led the International League in home runs and RBI; he was still playing as late as 1964, the year he turned 49, or 53. He finished with 269 minor league homers, all at the highest level of the minors.

Obviously, the color line delayed Easter's arrival in Major League Baseball, but it's something of a mystery why it took him so long to join the Negro leagues. He played semi-pro ball in St. Louis but, according to his younger brother, performed poorly in exhibitions against pro teams, thus blowing his auditions for the big time.[41] Then, in June 1941, Easter broke both legs below the ankles in an auto accident, shelving him for 2½ months; he would be bedeviled by leg problems thereafter. After that, Easter spent 13 months in the U.S. Army, before finishing out World War II in the Portland, Oregon, shipyards. Finally, north of his 30th birthday, Luke Easter was ready to start his colorful pro baseball career.

Jim Eisenreich—The Twins were excited by the arrival of rookie Jim Eisenreich in 1982. The 23-year-old Minnesota native had batted .309 with some power and speed in his two minor league seasons, and seemed just the tonic for a team which just finished a .376 season. But in the majors, Jim's odd behaviors and twitching repeatedly forced him out of the lineup. All kinds of theories were advanced and remedies tried, but the problems

---

41. Cattau, Daniel. "So, Maybe There Really is Such a Thing as 'The Natural.'" *Smithsonian*, July 1991, p. 122.

persisted. Though he batted .282 over the next three seasons, he got into just 48 games.

Eisenreich was finally diagnosed with Tourette's syndrome, a little-known ailment at the time, and was out of baseball entirely in 1985 and '86. But with the help of medication and monitoring, he was able to return to the field as a veritable 28-year-old rookie in '87. After putting up a .382/.469/.705 slash line in 70 games of AA ball, Eisenreich returned to the majors with the Royals. Following six decent seasons in KC, he joined the Phillies as a free agent. He batted .324 over four years as a platoon player for the Phils, before winding up his career with the Marlins and Dodgers.

Eisenreich finished his 15-year career with 1160 hits, 52 homers, and a .290 average. He was the first winner of the Tony Conigliaro Award in 1990, and received three Hall of Fame votes in 2004.

Nick Esasky—Esasky put up a 30–108–.277 season in 1989, earning a lucrative free agent deal. But he would never hit another big league homer.

Esasky had been a platoon player for the Reds for six seasons, showing some power, but with too many strikeouts and too little spirit for manager Pete Rose's taste. Traded to the Red Sox, and given a chance to play regularly in a great hitters' park, Esasky flourished, finishing in the AL's top five in homers and slugging. But after signing with the Braves for 1990, he suffered from dizzy spells which made it practically impossible for him to perform. After managing just six singles in 35 at bats, along with five errors in the field, he was put on the DL, and eventually diagnosed with vertigo.

After two years of inactivity, Esasky tried a comeback in 1992, playing 30 games in the Braves' AAA system, before hanging up his spikes for good at age 32. He finished his career with 122 homers and a .250 average over 810 big league games.

In his final season (1920), Happy Felsch finished in the AL's top five in homers and slugging. Library of Congress.

Happy Felsch—Oscar "Happy" Felsch had a banner season in

1920, hitting 14 homers (fourth in the AL), knocking in 115 runs, batting .338, and slugging .540 (fifth). It turned out to be his final season in the majors, as he was banned for his alleged role in the Black Sox Scandal. Felsch, a fine center fielder, finished his career at age 29 with a .293 lifetime average over six seasons, all but the last one in the Deadball era.

Jocko Flynn—When a hurler goes 23-6 as a 22-year-old rookie, then never pitches in the majors again, it sounds like the making for a chapter in this book. Alas, Jocko Flynn doesn't quite measure up as a great "what if."

Flynn posted his fancy record for the 1886 Chicago White Stockings. Included was a run of 14 straight victories from July 17 through September 22. He was a good pitcher, but his record was not as impressive as it seems.

Teams in those days did not have pitching rotations, per se. Playing four or five games a week, they typically used their best pitcher as often as they could, and their second-best hurler in the other games. Some teams had the luxury of a third-string pitcher. Such was Flynn's role on the great White Stockings, who finished 90-34. Only when John Clarkson (467 innings, 36-17 record) or Jim McCormick (348 IP, 31-11) were both unavailable or unnecessary did Flynn get his chances. Five times, he went 10 days or more between starts. He was used disproportionately against the league's patsies, going a combined 13-0 against Washington (28-92 on the season) and Kansas City (30-91). Among Flynn's victories were ones by scores of 17-8, 10-8, 14-8, and 13-11. When not pitching, Flynn often played in the outfield. By October, his arm was shot. With the pennant on the line, he did not pitch in the last four days of the season, nor did he appear in the six-game World's Series that followed.

Flynn started one game in the outfield in 1887, suffered a split finger on the first ball hit to him, and never played in the majors again. According to SABR BioProject author Justin Murphy, "It seems clear that Flynn was suffering from the twin curses of booze and a bad arm." He kicked around in minor league and independent baseball for a few years, then worked mostly clerical jobs until his death of pneumonia at age 43.

Ray Fosse—Everyone knows the play. Pete Rose is roaring around third base in the bottom of the twelfth inning of the 1970 All-Star Game. Young catcher Ray Fosse—three inches taller, 20 pounds heavier, and covered by protective gear—blocks the plate as he awaits the throw from center fielder Amos Otis. Rose starts to go into his trademarked head-first slide, realizes he can never reach the plate that way, and crashes into Fosse to score the winning run. Fosse suffers an undiagnosed shoulder injury and is never the same player.

But was Fosse really on track for a great career, or was his first-half performance of 1970 just a fluke? And was the All-Star Game mishap truly the turning point of his career, or just one of a series of incidents on the ledger of an injury-prone player?

Fosse was a highly-touted catcher, drafted in the first round of the 1965 amateur draft. But his offensive performance in the minors over the next five years did little to predict major league stardom. He batted .283, but with a total of just 17 home runs and a weak .377 slugging percentage. In three trials with the Indians over that span, the oft-injured Fosse hit just .159 with two homers in 132 at bats, enough to lose his rookie status for 1970.

But the 23-year-old Fosse had a terrific first half in 1970, putting together a 23-game hitting streak, and batting .312 with 16 homers and a .527 slugging percentage. This earned him a spot on the AL All-Star team, and his date with destiny.

Fosse didn't miss any games immediately following the collision, and continued to hit for average (he finished the year at .307, fifth-best in the league, though four plate appearances shy of qualifying for the title), but not power. He hit only two more homers before his season was ended by a broken finger on September 3. Years later, Fosse claimed he suffered a separated shoulder in the All-Star encounter, and couldn't lift his left arm above his shoulder.[42] Even after his fine season, the most similar players to Fosse through age 23 were journeymen Ed Herrmann and Russ Nixon.

Fosse had a decent year in 1971, with 12 homers and a .276 average, despite injuries caused by hitters' back-swings, and another suffered in a brawl. He earned a second All-Star selection and a second Gold Glove Award. After a mediocre '72 season, he was dealt to the Oakland A's.

Fosse helped Oakland to the 1973 world championship. Then came the injury which really derailed his career. On June 5, 1974, he was attempting to break up a locker-room fight between teammates Reggie Jackson and Bill North. Fosse suffered a neck injury, requiring cervical disc fusion.[43] He missed the next 2½ months, finished the year hitting .196, and was never a full-time player after that.

Fosse played for four teams over the next five years, getting only 736 more at bats. He had surgery on his right knee in 1976 and his left in '78, retiring after the '79 season, his twelfth.

Nomar Garciaparra—In August 1999, *Baseball America* published Bill James's career projections for three great young shortstops, based on their ages and career numbers through the '99 All-Star break. Derek Jeter was

---

42. Nightingale, Dave. "Flashback: The Rose-Fosse Crash." *The Sporting News*, July 15, 1985.
43. Spander, Art. "In Harm's Way." *The Sporting News*, September 16, 1985.

projected to collect 3489 hits, 252 homers, and a .306 average; 15 years later, he finished with 3465 hits, 260 homers, and a .310 mark. Alex Rodriguez was forecast to hit 689 homers with a .305 average; his actual final numbers 17 years later were 696 and .295.

And Nomar Garciaparra was predicted to amass 3517 hits and 552 homers. He didn't reach half of those totals.

Nomar (his father's name, spelled backwards) joined the Red Sox at age 23 and quickly garnered respect for his hard play and strenuous training regimen. He earned unanimous Rookie of the Year selection in 1997, after batting .306 with 30 homers, and leading the AL in hits and doubles. He also authored a 30-game hitting streak, set a record (since broken) with 98 RBI from the leadoff spot, topped shortstops in putouts and double plays, and finished eighth in MVP voting.

Garciaparra was even better the next year, having a 35–122–.323 season, good for runner-up in MVP balloting. He won the AL batting title in both 1999 and 2000, with marks of .357 and .372, and became only the fourth player to finish in the top 10 in MVP voting in each of his first four full seasons. He followed Joe Jackson, Joe DiMaggio, and Mike Piazza; Albert Pujols and Mike Trout have joined them since then. Nomar finished the 2000 season on a 20-game hitting streak.

Garciaparra's first major injury came in 2001. On April 2, he had surgery to repair a frayed tendon in his right wrist (originally injured by a pitch in September 1999), and he wound up playing only 21 games that year. After Nomar returned for All-Star seasons in 2002–03, the injuries started piling up (about the same time as PED-testing started). In 2004, he battled problems with his Achilles tendon, left wrist, and right groin, spending 66 days on the disabled list; he was traded to the Cubs on July 31, missing Boston's world championship (though he was voted a full share of post-season money). On April 20, 2005, Garciaparra suffered a torn left groin, requiring surgery; he was out until August 5. In 2006, he had rib cage and left quadriceps issues. He averaged just 84 games per year from 2004 to 2009, and finally retired on March 10, 2010.

Garciaparra finished with 1747 hits, 229 homers, a .313 average, and 564 days on the DL. He got 30 votes in the 2015 Hall of Fame election, then slipped to eight votes in '16, and was dropped from the ballot.

Wayne Garland—After going 7–11 as a mop-up man over the previous three seasons, Garland had what appeared to be a breakout year at age 25 in 1976. He went 20–7 with a 2.67 ERA for the Orioles, then signed a lucrative free-agent deal with the Indians. Without the O's vaunted defense behind him, Garland slipped to 13–19 in '77, then underwent rotator cuff surgery on May 5, 1978. He quit three years later with a 55–66 career record.

Dwight Gooden—At age 21, people were saying that Dwight Gooden might win 400 games. But he wound up with less than half of that total.

Gooden joined the Mets at age 19 in 1984. After a decent start, Gooden finished the season in a blaze, earning the Rookie of the Year Award with a 17-9 log, a rookie-record 276 K's, and a 2.60 ERA. In his last nine starts, he went 8-1 with a 1.07 ERA and 105 strikeouts against just 13 walks in 76 innings. But Doctor K was just getting warmed up.

Gooden authored a pitching season for the ages in 1985. He wound up going 24-4 with a microscopic 1.53 ERA—second-lowest by any qualifier since 1919—while leading the NL in innings, complete games, wins, strikeouts (268), and ERA. He naturally earned unanimous selection for the Cy Young Award.

Gooden started the 1986 season 5-0. At that point, in a span of 50 starts, he had gone 37-5 (.881) with a 1.38 ERA, 412 strikeouts, 25 complete games, and 12 shutouts. Though he wasn't quite as dominant the rest of the year, he finished 17-6, giving him a three-year record of 58-19 at age 21.

Unfortunately, the rest of Doc's career was continually interrupted by injuries and drug-related absences. Though he continued to be a winning pitcher for the rest of the 20th century, Gooden never again won 20 games, led the league in anything important, nor finished higher than fourth in Cy Young voting. He ended his career in 2000 with a 194–112 record (.634) and a 3.51 ERA. Doc got 17 votes in the 2006 Hall of Fame election and was dropped from the ballot.

Vean Gregg—After gathering 32 wins and 376 strikeouts in the Pacific Coast League in 1910, Gregg joined the Indians and became the American League's rookie pitching sensation of 1911. He went 23-7, posting a league-best 1.80 ERA and allowing the fewest hits and baserunners per nine innings. Gregg followed up with 20-win seasons in both

Vean Gregg (1912) won 20-plus games in each of his first three major league seasons. Library of Congress.

1912 and '13 as well, and started the 1914 season 9–3 before a blockbuster trade to the Red Sox on July 28. His seeming disinterest in baseball and his clashes with management had made him expendable. But an arm malady described as "neuritis" or "rheumatism" hampered him, and Gregg struggled to a 9–11 record for the Sox over the next two years before returning to the minors on July 15, 1916.

Gregg came back to go 21–9 with 249 strikeouts and a 1.72 ERA in the International League in 1917, and was acquired by the woeful Philadelphia A's for the 1918 campaign. But Gregg went 9–14 for the last-place team and, at 33, was no longer a promising young prospect. He pitched for most of the next decade in the minors (including a 25–11 record in the PCL in '24) and independent ball, with only one brief return to the majors.

Pedro Guerrero—Guerrero was one of the NL's best sluggers in the 1980s, but was bedeviled by injuries, mostly to his legs. The worst was on April 3, 1986, when, sliding during an exhibition game, he ruptured the tendon that held his left knee-cap in place. According to *The Sporting News*, "as he started his slide into third base he had a change of mind, his spikes caught in the dirt and he tumbled over the bag." Guerrero wouldn't return until August or get his first hit of the season until September. It was noted that Pedro had suffered several previous sliding injuries. He fractured a leg at the ankle in the Pacific Coast League, missing the last four months of the 1977 season. He damaged ligaments in his left knee sliding into second in 1980. He tried sliding head-first for a while, and injured his shoulder. "I guess the best thing to do is not to slide," reflected Guerrero.

Guerrero earned his first of five All-Star selections in 1981, and finished third and fourth in MVP voting the following two years. He had his best season in 1985, leading the NL in OBP (.422) and slugging (.577), and finishing third in MVP voting, despite back spasms and a sprained wrist.

After missing most of the next season with the knee injury, Guerrero came back to set career highs with a .338 batting average in '87 and 117 RBI in '89. In between, he was traded from the Dodgers to the Cardinals and spent 54 days on the DL with a pinched nerve in his neck.

From 1990–92, Guerrero's production declined steeply and he spent 178 days on the DL (broken leg, shoulder separation) before his career ended at age 36. He finished with 215 homers and a .300 average, and got six votes in his only try on the Hall of Fame ballot.

Noodles Hahn—In the early part of the 20th century, Noodles Hahn ranked among the winningest left-handers of all time. Yet he won his last game at age 27.

Frank Hahn supposedly got the nickname "Noodles" as a child, due to his fondness for his mother's noodle soup.[44] He began pitching professionally at age 16, joining the Chattanooga team of the Southern League in 1895. With Mobile in the same league the following year, he was released in July "because he objected to being overworked." Nevertheless, he was offered a contract by the Cincinnati Reds in 1897—but he deemed their offer insufficient, and wound up pitching for Detroit of the Western League in 1897–98.[45]

Cincinnati came calling again in 1899, and this time Hahn accepted the terms. *The Sporting News* reported that he had "terrific speed, good curves, and the best control ever displayed by a green southpaw."[46] The diminutive pitcher went on to have a brilliant rookie season, going 23–8 and leading the NL in strikeouts.

Hahn did not train with the Reds in the spring of 1900, and had a slow start.[47] He wound up with a 16–20 record for a 62–77 team. But he led the NL in strikeouts again and tied for the league lead with four shutouts. One of them was a no-hitter to beat the Phillies, 4–0, on July 12. It was the major leagues' only no-no that year.

Hahn came back with a remarkable season in 1901. On a last-place team that was 30–68 in games he did not get a decision, he managed to go 22–19, thus accounting for 42 percent of his team's victories. This stood as a post-1900 record until Steve Carlton broke it with 46 percent in 1972. Hahn led the NL with 41 complete games (in 42 starts), 375 innings, and 239 strikeouts. On May 22, he struck out 16 batters in one game, which at the time was a record from the 60'6" pitching distance. "I am wise enough to know that I cannot last forever," Hahn later remarked, "and that I am greatly shortening my career by pitching as I did last season."[48]

At one point, Boston reportedly offered Hahn a $4,500 contract to jump to the fledgling American League. Hahn did not want to leave Cincinnati and the girl he had fallen in love with there, but he was able to use the offer to negotiate a nice raise from the Reds.[49]

Hahn had another strong season in 1902, going 23–12 with the second-best ERA (1.77) in the league. In '03, he went 22–12, including his 100th career victory, making him only the eighth lefty ever to reach that milestone—and the youngest with either arm to win 100 at the 60'6"

---

44. "Frank. G. (Noodles) Hahn." *The Sporting News*, February 17, 1960.
45. Unidentified clipping in National Baseball Library file, August, 1899.
46. Simon, Tom, editor. *Deadball Stars of the National League*. Washington, DC: Brassey's, Inc., 2004, p. 233.
47. Unidentified clipping in National Baseball Library file, c. May, 1900.
48. Simon, Tom, editor. *Deadball Stars of the National League*. Washington, DC: Brassey's, Inc., 2004, p. 233.
49. "How Noodles Hahn Got a Big Salary." Unidentified clipping in National Baseball Library file, July, 1916.

pitching distance (a record later broken by Bob Feller).⁵⁰ In both seasons, the Reds were under .500 in games Hahn did not pitch. Despite posting a 2.06 ERA and leading the NL in fewest walks per nine innings, Hahn slipped to 16–18 in 1904. Nevertheless, in comparison with his statistics through age 26, the seven most similar pitchers to Hahn include five Hall of Famers.

Over a four-year period, Hahn had completed 143 of 146 starts for Cincinnati, averaging over 320 innings per season. He paid the price with reduced pitch speed and a sore arm in 1905. He was released by the Reds in August after pitching just 77 innings with a 5–3 record. "Hahn has failed to reach his old standard," reported the *Cincinnati Commercial-Gazette*. "Without his speed, he was robbed of much of his effectiveness."⁵¹

Picked up by the New York Highlanders the following year, Hahn pitched just six games, going 3–2, and asked for and got his release. His major league baseball career was over at age 27. Hahn finished with a 130–94 (.580) lifetime record and 2.55 ERA.

In later years, even into his 60s, Hahn would often visit the Reds and work out with them at Crosley Field.⁵² In 1963, he was inducted into the Cincinnati Reds Hall of Fame.

George Hall—The British-born Hall batted .311 over five National Association seasons, then starred in the first National League campaign, batting .366 with a league-leading five homers in 1876. But after hitting .323 at age 28 in '77, Hall was banned for his confessed role in the Louisville Scandal (along with Jim Devlin). Hall retreated into obscurity, making one reinstatement attempt by mail, and serving out his remaining 46 years in Brooklyn as an engraver and clerk.

Josh Hamilton—Hamilton may well deserve a spot among the featured 40. Assuming his major league career is over, he is the only man to win an MVP Award, but not last the requisite 10 seasons to qualify for Hall of Fame consideration.

At 18, Hamilton was the #1 pick in the 1999 amateur draft, receiving a $3.96 million signing bonus from the Tampa Bay Devil Rays. He was a five-tool player; the only question was whether he would make the big leagues as a position player or pitcher: he had a 96 mph fastball and 110 mph bat speed. Nobody would have guessed it would be eight years before he made it to the majors in any capacity.

---

50. Simon, Tom, editor. *Deadball Stars of the National League*. Washington, DC: Brassey's, Inc., 2004, p. 233.
51. *Ibid.*, p. 234.
52. *The Sporting News*, September 17, 1942, April 30, 1944.

From 1999 through 2002, Hamilton moved up the minor league ladder, batting .295 with power. But a 2001 back injury suffered in an auto accident cost him most of that season, and gave him the free time and self-pity to discover alcohol and drugs. He soon burned through his bonus money and got himself banished from baseball, ultimately missing four years from July 2002 until July 2006. Doctors later told him that the drug abuse compromised his immune system, making him prone to illness and injury.

After hitting rock bottom on October 6, 2005, Hamilton quit the booze and drugs and began an improbable comeback. He played just 15 lackluster games in the minors in 2006, and was left unprotected. The Cubs claimed him for a mere $50,000 in the Rule 5 Draft, and promptly sold to the Reds.

Nearing his 26th birthday, Hamilton batted .403 in spring training, 2007, and made the Reds' opening day roster. His was the "feel-good" story of the year. Though his season was interrupted by two stints on the DL, he showed he still had the skills the scouts had drooled over eight years before. Hamilton batted .292 and slugged .554, with 19 homers in 90 games. After the season, the Reds traded him to the Rangers for two promising pitchers, including Edinson Volquez.

Hamilton proceeded to have five straight All-Star seasons with the Rangers. In 2008, he starred in the Home Run Derby at Yankee Stadium, hitting a total of 35 balls out of the park, including 13 in a row. Hamilton wound up with a 32–130-.304 season, leading the AL in RBI and total bases. He earned the Players' Choice most outstanding player award and his first of three Silver Slugger Awards, finishing seventh in MVP voting.

After a brief fall off the wagon in early 2009, Hamilton was injured while crashing into an outfield wall on May 17, requiring abdominal surgery. He played only 89 games that year, but returned with a vengeance in 2010. Despite missing most of September with broken ribs, he went 32–100-.359, leading the league in batting, slugging (.633), OPS, and WAR. He was named AL MVP, *Sporting News* Player of the Year, and Player's Choice most outstanding player, and also earned the ALCS MVP after he led the Rangers to their first of two straight World Series appearances.

A bout with pneumonia set back Hamilton's 2011 training, and then he broke his right humerus bone in a slide on April 12, costing him six weeks of action. Before the 2012 campaign, Hamilton had another alcohol relapse. He put it all behind him with a spectacular start to the season. Hamilton was named AL Player of the Month in both April and May, and entered June with 21 homers, 57 RBI, and a .368 average. On May 8, he became the 16th major leaguer to hit four homers in one game, adding a long double for an AL-record 18 total bases; his bat was sent to the Hall of Fame. Hamilton received 11.1 million All-Star votes, shattering the record by nearly 50 percent. Though he had a long mid-season slump, he finished 43–128-.285 and fifth in MVP voting. A feature film about Hamilton's life, directed by Casey Affleck, was planned. After the season, Hamilton signed a five-year, $125 million contract, joining the Angels as a free agent.

It has been downhill ever since.

Hamilton had an off-year in '13, then suffered a torn thumb ligament on April 8, 2014, costing him nearly two months. He underwent right shoulder surgery on February 4, 2015, and had another substance abuse relapse. The disgusted Angels returned Hamilton to the Rangers in April, eating most of his contract in the process. He played only 50 games in 2015, and has not appeared in the majors since. His nine-year career totals show 1027 games, 200 homers, a .290 batting average, and a .516 slugging percentage.

Four left knee surgeries have followed, the most recent on February 27, 2017. The Rangers released him less than two months later. In October 2019, Hamilton was charged by police after allegedly assaulting his 14-year-old daughter.

There has been no talk of a movie lately.

Zaza Harvey—Ervin ("Zaza" or "Zeke") Harvey quit the Indians at age 23 in May 1902, complaining of debilitating stomach pain. He had batted .332 in 76 games (also going 3–7 on the mound) in parts of three big league seasons as an outfielder-pitcher. Harvey became a writer and lived another 52 years before dying of bronchopneumonia.

Willard Hershberger—Hershberger was backup catcher behind Hall of Famer Ernie Lombardi for the 1938–40 Reds, and batted .316 over 160 major league games. But his career ended tragically on August 3, 1940, when he took his own life at age 30, slitting his throat at Boston's Copley Plaza Hotel.

Hershberger had been pressed into regular duty due to an ankle injury suffered by Lombardi. The Reds were on their way to a second straight NL pennant, and Hershberger had done exceptionally well (.378 through July 23) in his limited role. But some tough losses and poor play during an eastern heat wave sunk him into despondency. Through August 2, Hershberger was in a 4-for-33 slump and the Reds had lost five of the last six games he had played. That day, they fell to the Boston Bees, 4–3 in 12 innings, and Willard went 0-for-5. "My father took his own life, and so will I," he told manager Bill McKechnie.[53] The next day, he did.

In the wake of this tragedy, Hershberger became the first NL player ever to have his number retired. The Reds announced that Hershberger's uniform #5 would be taken out of commission indefinitely, presumably

---

53. Barbour, James. "The Death of Willard Hershberger." *The National Pastime*, Winter, 1987, p. 64.

following the example of the Yankees, who had started the tradition of retiring numbers with Lou Gehrig's seven months earlier. However, by 1942, Reds #5 had reappeared on the roster. It would later be used by Johnny Bench, and retired for good following Bench's retirement in 1983.

Bug Holliday—James W. "Bug" Holliday was a solid slugger in the late nineteenth century, but his career was essentially ended by a ruptured appendix.

After becoming a prominent amateur player in his native St. Louis, Holliday actually made his pro debut in the World Series. The National League's Chicago White Stockings squared off against the American Association's St. Louis Browns in for the "world's championship" in October 1885. The White Stockings found themselves short a player for Game Four and picked up the 18-year-old local player to fill in.

Holliday starred with St. Joseph, Topeka, and Des Moines in the Western League in 1886–88, setting off a major league bidding war for his services. Cincinnati of the American Association won, and he began his big league career with them in 1889. The *New York Clipper* rated him a brilliant center fielder and "one of the most promising young players of the day."[54] As a rookie, Holliday batted .321 and tied Harry Stovey for the home run lead with 19.

Moving with the Reds to the National League in 1890, Holliday won a second homer title in 1892 and batted .376 in '94.

According to historian David Nemec, Holliday nearly died when his appendix burst in 1895. He played in only 120 more games after that year, and finished his 10-year career with a .312 average. Holliday died at age 43 in 1910 of gangrene of the foot and leg, arteriosclerosis, and septicemia.[55]

Charlie Hollocher—Between physical and/or mental setbacks, Hollocher was considered among the top shortstops in the NL over a six-year period. As one writer put it, "It's open conjecture as to whether or not Hollocher was suffering from hypochondria, mental illness, or an undisclosed ailment."

Hollocher had a sensational rookie year in the war-shortened 1918 season, compiling a 20-game hitting streak, leading the league in hits and total bases, finishing in the league's top five in batting (.316), OBP, runs, and stolen bases, and helping the Cubs to the World Series. Hollocher was drafted by the Army after the season, but a bout with the flu prevented him from serving.

---

54. *New York Clipper*, September, 1889.
55. Certificate of Death, James W. Holliday.

Charlie Hollocher (1918) was one of the best offensive shortstops in the NL, when he felt up to playing. Library of Congress.

Hollocher suffered a series of freak injuries the next year, slipping to .270, and some illnesses and surgeries in 1920, costing him 74 games, though he batted .319. But he was healthy the next two years, leading NL shortstops in fielding in both and putting together his best offensive season in '22. He batted a robust .340, striking out just five times in 592 at bats, and collecting three triples in one game.

By 1923 Hollocher was team captain. But he missed the first four weeks of the season due to what was variously reported as the flu or a mysterious stomach ailment. "My health first broke when at Catalina Island in the spring of 1923," Hollocher recalled. "I returned to St. Louis for an examination by Dr. Robert F. Hyland, who examined me and then turned me over to a specialist. They advised me that I would ruin my health if I played ball that season. But Bill Killefer, then manager of the Cubs, came to St. Louis and urged me to join the team, telling me that I didn't have to play when I didn't feel well. I yielded to Bill, and, once in uniform, couldn't stay on the bench." However, physicians hired by the Cubs could find nothing wrong with Hollocher, asserting "it was a state of mind."[56]

Once Hollocher started playing, he picked up where he left off, batting .342 in 66 games. But he suddenly quit the team on August 3, leaving

---

56. *The Sporting News*, August 22, 1940.

a note for Killefer: "Feeling pretty rotten so made up my mind to go home and take a rest and forget baseball for the rest of the year. No hard feelings, just don't feel like playing anymore."[57]

Hollocher attempted a comeback in 1924, signing a two-year contract, but he quit for good after just 76 games, citing stomach trouble and nerves. He finished with a .304 career average.

Hollocher continued to complain about his health, and committed suicide by shotgun in 1940. He had quickly remarried after going through a nasty divorce in 1939, and his new wife "said the stomach ailment which forced him to retire from baseball had been particularly troublesome in the last three or four months." One theory is that Hollocher suffered from syphilis, but it is noteworthy that his brother had died of "acute gastritis" in 1937.

Dummy Hoy—The most successful deaf-mute player in history was William Hoy, and in the sensitivity of the late nineteenth century, he was nicknamed "Dummy." Hoy was a center fielder for 14 seasons, admired for his brainy play and fast feet. He was good at getting on base—accumulating over 2000 hits and 1000 walks toward a .386 OBP—and in moving his way around the bases, amassing 596 stolen bases and 1429 runs scored in 1797 games. In 2018, SABR named Hoy as an Overlooked 19th Century Baseball Legend.

One thing Hoy did *not* do is something he is often credited with: inspiring umpires' hand signals. Those came into the major leagues about 1906, four years after Hoy retired, and were designed for the benefit of fans.[58]

William "Dummy" Hoy (c. 1888) overcame deafness to become a solid big leaguer for 14 seasons. Library of Congress.

---

57. Ahrens, Arthur. "The Tragic Saga of Charlie Hollocher." *The Baseball Research Journal*, 1986, p. 8.
58. Deane, Bill. *Baseball Myths*. Lanham, MD: Scarecrow Press, Inc., 2012, p. 15–21.

LaMarr Hoyt—After going 18–6 mostly as a reliever for the 1979–81 White Sox, Hoyt was promoted to the starting rotation. He promptly led the AL in wins in both 1982 (19) and '83 (24), winning the Cy Young Award in the latter year. After slipping to 13–18, Hoyt went to the Padres, where he made the NL All-Star team and posted a 16–8 log in '85. But 1986 was a disaster, not as much for his 8–11 record as for his three drug-related arrests, the final one landing him in federal prison. As it turned out, Hoyt's big league career was over with a 98–68 record at age 31. His drug-related problems continued, however, and he was back in prison by 1988.

Tex Hughson—Along with those of Boo Ferriss and Mel Parnell, which are told elsewhere in this book, Hughson's was one of three sad stories in the pitching rotation of the post–World War II Red Sox.

Hughson was the rare Depression-era athlete who actually went to college, the University of Texas at Austin. By the time he climbed from Class C to the majors in 1941, he was 25 years old. He joined the Sox' regular rotation the following year.

Hughson was brilliant in 1942. He went 22–6 with a 2.59 ERA, leading the AL in complete games, innings, wins, and strikeouts, and finishing sixth in MVP voting. Hughson posted a 2.64 ERA in '43 and again led in complete games, though his record dipped to 12–15 for the seventh-place Sox. He earned his third straight All-Star selection in '44, and became the baseball season's first 18-game winner on August 9, but that turned out to be his last game before he was inducted into the U.S. Army. Tex finished the year 18–5 with a career-best 2.26 ERA, and topped the league in win percentage.

After 20 months out of baseball, Hughson returned in 1946 to go 20–11, 2.75, helping Boston to its first World Series since 1918. He held out the next year, then suffered from a sore right elbow; he was 4–7 with a 4.72 ERA in late June, before finishing at 12–11, 3.33, but didn't pitch after September 3. Hughson underwent two operations on his pitching arm after the season, the first in San Antonio to cut the scalene nerve, and the second at Johns Hopkins in Baltimore to repair a bone growth which had first bothered him in '44.

Tex never really recovered. Trying to come back too soon, he complained of a "gnawing feeling in his arm" the next spring, and was demoted to the minors for two months. Hughson pitched a total of just 97 innings for the Red Sox in 1948–49, with an ERA of 5.29. He was sold to the New York Giants on December 15, 1949, but never again pitched in the pros, and his career was over at 33.

Hughson finished with a 96–54 career record (granted, much of it against competition diluted by the war), good for a .640 win percentage, and a 2.94 ERA.

Bo Jackson—Jackson was a two-sport star whose career was cut short by hip replacement surgery.

After the Auburn running back won the 1985 Heisman Trophy, he shocked the pundits by eschewing the NFL for a pro baseball career. Jackson's athletic gifts overcame his technical flaws to get him to the major leagues in 1986, and make him an All-Star three years later.

Bo drew criticism in 1987 when he decided to also play pro football as a "hobby." Joining the Raiders after the baseball season was over for the next four years, he rushed for 2782 yards in 38 games, averaging 5.4 yards per carry. A 1990 hip injury would end his hobby and effectively do the same to his baseball career.

Jackson had his most productive MLB season in 1989, with 32 homers, 105 RBI, 26 steals, and the All-Star Game MVP Award; he finished tenth in AL MVP voting. He was arguably better in '90, setting career highs in batting, OBP, and slugging (.523), and hitting three consecutive homers on July 17 before going on the DL; he returned on August 26 to hit a record-tying fourth straight homer.

Jackson missed most of the 1991 season and all of '92 following his hip injury and surgery. But he was able to return to the bigs for two more years as a part-time slugger (winning the 1993 Tony Conigliaro Award) before he hung up his cleats at age 31. Bo finished with 141 homers and a .250 average in 694 games.

Joe Jackson—Of all those banned as the result of the Black Sox Scandal, Jackson's is the most tragic story. Despite playing most of his career in the Deadball Era, Shoeless Joe finished with a .356 lifetime

Shoeless Joe Jackson (right), shown with Ty Cobb in 1913. Only Cobb was considered a superior hitter to Jackson, but Joe outslugged Ty over their careers, .517 to .512. Library of Congress.

average, third-highest of all time—but he is not eligible for the Hall of Fame.

After three cups of coffee totaling 115 at bats, Jackson became a regular in 1911 at age 21, and proceeded to tear up the league. He batted .408, leading the AL in OBP, and finishing second behind only the immortal Ty Cobb in runs, hits, doubles, total bases, batting, and slugging. Jackson also finished as runner-up to Cobb in the AL batting races of 1912 (.395) and '13 (.373); but Joe topped the league in hits, triples, and total bases in 1912, and in hits, doubles, and slugging in '13. He led the White Sox to the world championship in 1917 and the AL title in 1919; despite the scandal, he led all World Series players in hits, homers, batting, and slugging in the '19 Fall Classic.

In 1920, Jackson batted .382 while leading the AL in triples and setting career highs in homers and RBI. It turned out to be his last season in the majors; he was banned the following year, though he was acquitted of conspiracy in court.

Though Jackson was 31 when his pro career ended, he still had a lot of baseball left in him. He played semi-pro ball under assumed names until well into his 40s, his amazing bat always giving away his identity. There is no reason to doubt that he would have excelled in the majors throughout the hard-hitting 1920s. Here's how Shoeless Joe stacked up between 1911 and 1920, as compared to three other great hitters on their ways to Cooperstown:

Player	DOB	AB	H	AVG
Ty Cobb	12/18/1886	4956	1927	.389
Eddie Collins	5/2/1887	5176	1718	.332
Joe Jackson	7/16/1889	4876	1737	.356
Tris Speaker	4/4/1888	5304	1852	.349

Here's how the other three did the rest of their careers:

Player	AB	H	AVG
Cobb	3705	1333	.360
Collins	3253	1110	.341
Speaker	3674	1282	.349

It seems reasonable to believe that Jackson, younger than the other three, would have maintained his .350+ career average while approaching if not surpassing 3000 hits, which only a handful of players had done to that point.

Jackson received two Hall of Fame votes in the very first (1936) election, and two more in 1946, then was ignored by the Veterans' Committee for four decades before he was formally stripped of Hall eligibility in 1991 (see the Ed Cicotte entry).

Jackie Jensen—Jensen was considered a talented underachiever until he moved to a hitters' park at age 27. For the Red Sox between 1954 and 1959, he amassed 667 RBI, leading the league three times, and winning the 1958 MVP Award.

A year later, Jensen abruptly retired, citing a fear of flying and wanting to spend more time with his family. He tried a comeback at age 34 in '61, but slugged just .392 and quit for good. Jensen received a total of 11 Hall of Fame votes between 1967 and 1972.

Bill Joyce—Joyce was a slugging third baseman in the 1890s, before his career ended at age 33 under "mysterious circumstances." Scrappy Bill, as he was called, made his pro debut at 24 in 1890, playing all his team's games and leading the Players' League in walks, while also finishing in the top 10 in triples and stolen bases. He moved to the American Association in 1891 and National League in '92, both seasons cut short by mid-season broken legs. After sitting out 1893 in a salary dispute, Joyce returned to become one of the top sluggers in the NL. From 1894–98, Joyce won one league home run title, and finished second three other times, batting as high as .355. On May 20, 1894, he had a home run and triple in the same inning. On August 20, 1894, Joyce became one of the earliest players to belt three homers in one game, adding a single. On May 18, 1897, he hit four triples in one game, a record which has not been matched since.

Joyce became player-manager of the Giants over his last three seasons, earning the loyalty and affection of his players, and leading the club to a .595 percentage. But his career ended abruptly after the 1898 season, and he returned to his hometown to open up an eatery—the Home Run Buffet—with a fellow St. Louis-born player, Patsy Tebeau. Joyce later claimed he quit the Giants on a matter of principle over management's treatment of his players.

Joyce's big league playing career lasted only 906 games, but his 162-game averages included 147 runs, 19 triples, and 129 walks. He batted .293 with a .435 on-base percentage.

Benny Kauff—The Federal League was formed in 1913, and a year later claimed major league status, raiding some players from the two established leagues, and giving many minor leaguers a shot at the big time. One of them was 24-year-old Benny Kauff, who proceeded to lead the circuit in runs, hits, doubles, batting (.370), and OBP, earning the sobriquet "The Ty Cobb of the Federal League." The following year, Kauff again led the league in batting (.342) and OBP, also topping it in slugging.

Benny Kauff (1915) was called the "Ty Cobb of the Federal League." Library of Congress.

The Federal League folded after the 1915 season, and Kauff joined the New York Giants. He did not become the Ty Cobb of the National League. Against true major league competition, Kauff batted .287 over the next five seasons—good, but not great—before his career ended in disgrace at age 30. Often mentioned in connection with gambling scandals, Kauff was sent down to the minors in mid-1920, despite homering in both games of a doubleheader on July 2 (the only other player with two homers on his last day in the majors was Hall of Famer Cap Anson, who hit both in the first game of a doubleheader on October 3, 1897). The following year, Kauff and his brother were arrested for auto theft, and despite his acquittal in court, Commissioner Landis banned Benny from baseball.

Dickey Kerr—Kerr got a total of 75 votes in Hall of Fame elections—not bad for someone who played in just four big league seasons. Dickey—that's how he spelled it—gained favor among voters for his performance in the 1919 World Series, where he excelled despite his teammates' conspiring to throw the Series.

Kerr, a crafty southpaw, succeeded in the minors for nearly a decade before getting his shot in the majors. Kerr went 142–76 between 1910 and 1918, including consecutive seasons of 19–8, 22–7, 21–10, and 24–12. He claimed that scouts who were impressed by his records were turned off by his size (5'7" and 145 pounds) when seeing him in the flesh. Finally, after a 17–7, 2.04 season with Milwaukee, the White Sox added him to their staff for the 1919 season.

Kerr became the team's #3 starter, helping them to the AL pennant with a 13–7 record. In the Fall Classic, after aces Eddie Cicotte and Lefty Williams had tanked the first two games of a best-of-nine series against Cincinnati, Kerr tossed a three-hit shutout to win Game Three, 3–0. After Cicotte and Williams lost the next two, Kerr came back in Game Six to stave off elimination with a gutsy 10-inning, 5–4 victory. When the Black Sox Scandal was revealed a year later, Kerr went down in history as a hero and a martyr.

Kerr proved he was no flash in the pan in 1920, going 21–9 and leading the AL in saves. In light of Chicago's 62–92 record in '21, after eight of their players were banned, Kerr's 19–17 record that year may have been even more impressive.

Kerr claimed that White Sox' owner Charles Comiskey refused to give him a $500 raise for 1922, so he quit the team to play in "outlaw" industrial leagues. Over the next couple of years, he even played against some of his banned former teammates, earning a suspension from organized baseball. By the time it was lifted on July 14, 1925, Kerr was an old 32 and didn't have it any more. He finished his brief big league career with a 53–34 (.609) record.

Kerr returned to organized ball as a minor league manager between 1937 and 1947, in which role he made perhaps his biggest contribution to baseball. In the Florida State League in 1940, one of Kerr's players was a promising pitcher who injured his shoulder and thought his career was over. He had a new bride and a baby on the way, and didn't know how he was going to support them. Kerr allowed the couple to move in with him to weather the financial hardship, and convinced the player that he could succeed as a hard-hitting outfielder. The player's name: Stan Musial. Stan named his newborn son Richard Kerr Musial, and in 1958 bought Kerr a new house as a birthday present.

Kerr served as a Cardinals scout in the 1940s and '50s, and got Hall of Fame votes as early as 1937. Even after the 10-year rule went into place, he continued to get votes, peaking at 25 in 1955 (more than 13 future Hall of Famers who received votes that year), his final year before being removed from the ballot. Ignorant of the rules, in 1958 Kerr said "To be voted into the Hall of Fame" was his only remaining goal in life.

Kerr would have to be satisfied with a couple of lesser honors. In 1961, he was voted the first recipient of the Houston BBWAA chapter's Tris Speaker Award; later that year, Commissioner Ford Frick presented Kerr with a silver tray. Dickey Kerr died in 1963.

Darryl Kile—On June 22, 2002, Cardinals 33-year-old pitcher Darryl Kile was found dead in his hotel room, a victim of a circulatory problem much like that which ended J.R. Richard's career.

Kile had a checkered career. As an example, he went 19–7 for the 1997 Astros and 20–9 for the 2000 Cards, but was 21–30 in the two years in between. He finished with a 133–119 record, including a no-hitter. Kile became one of the few beneficiaries of the "Roberto Clemente Rule," allowing him onto the Hall of Fame ballot just months after his death rather than after a five-year wait. He received seven votes.

Matt Kilroy—Who had the most strikeouts in one season? Most would answer Nolan Ryan, who notched 383 K's in 1973. But the answer is Matt Kilroy.

Kilroy struck out 513 batters as a rookie. Granted, it was in 583 innings, in an inferior league, and at a time it took seven balls for a walk. But no other big leaguer has ever topped it.

Kilroy debuted at age 19 with the 1886 Baltimore Orioles of the American Association. Along with the K's, he managed to go 29–34 and toss a no-hitter for the last-place team, which was 19–49 in games he did not get a decision. A year later, Kilroy was 46–19 while the rest of the club was 31–39, almost single-handedly lifting the team to third place.

Kilroy led the AA in games and complete games in each of those two seasons, pitching a staggering 1172 innings. Not surprisingly, his effectiveness dropped off after that, and he was essentially washed up by age 24, though he kicked around until 1898. Kilroy finished 141–133, and received one Hall of Fame vote in the very first (1936) old-timers' election.

Matt Kilroy in 1887, the year after he set the all-time record with 513 strikeouts in one season. Library of Congress.

Silver King—Born Charles Frederick Koenig, the big fastball pitcher was called Silver King due to his platinum-blonde hair and the translation of the German word "koenig." Starting his pro career at age 17, he had a brief big league trial the next year, and then followed with a spectacular rookie season at 19. For the St. Louis Browns of the American Association, King went 32–12 in 1887, followed by logs of 45–20 (leading the league in innings, wins, and ERA) and 35–16. Included were three one-hitters. He jumped to Chicago of the short-lived Players' League in 1890, posting his fourth straight 30-win season (30–22), turning in an eight-inning no-hitter on June 21, and again posting the best ERA in the league. That gave King 142 wins at age 22, but it was sharply downhill from there. Moving to the more-competitive NL (after being expelled from the AA), he pitched creditably but slipped to 14–29 and 22–24 the next two years. When the mound was moved back in 1893, King's ERA leaped to 6.08, and he quit baseball for the next two years. He resurfaced for a couple more mediocre seasons before retiring for good at age 29, with a 203–152 career record. Along the way, there was a paternity scandal and a suspension without pay for listless play.

Charles "Silver" King (c. 1888) began his career with four straight 30-win seasons. Library of Congress.

Dave Kingman—Until David Ortiz surpassed it in 2016, Kingman held the record for most home runs in a player's final season. Despite his 35 homers in 1986, giving him 100 in the past three seasons, Kingman was unable to find a job for '87, and his career ended abruptly. Club owners were later found guilty of collusion against free agents during this period. At least one writer has made the case that this cost Kingman Hall of Fame enshrinement: if not for the owners' illegal action, Kingman would surely have reached 500 homers (he finished with 442), which at that time was a virtual guarantee for Cooperstown honors.

But it's hard to imagine the voters could have overlooked all the negatives in giving Kong a Hall pass. Kingman was the quintessential one-dimensional player, batting .236 lifetime (.182, when he didn't hit the ball out of the park), fielding atrociously, and supplying a toxic clubhouse influence.

Kingman received three votes in the 1992 Hall of Fame election, and was dropped from the ballot.

Chuck Knoblauch—By the time he was 28, analysts were comparing Knoblauch with the best second basemen in history, in terms of peak value. But by the time he was 35, he was out of baseball.

Knoblauch was AL Rookie of the Year for the world champion 1991 Twins, and earned four All-Star selections over the next six years. He really blossomed in 1994, batting .312 with a league-leading 45 doubles in the strike-shortened season. Knoblauch followed with marks of .333 and .341, leading the AL with 14 triples in '96, and winning a Gold Glove in '97. Through age 27, the most similar player was Rod Carew, with Billy Herman and Ryne Sandberg also in the top 10. Knoblauch was traded to the Yankees before the '98 season for four prospects and cash.

In New York, he began suffering a form of "Steve Blass Disease." By 1999, Knoblauch couldn't seem to make even routine throws to first base. Two years after winning a Gold Glove, he led the AL in errors. In 2001, the Yankees moved Knoblauch to left field, and a year later they moved him to the Royals. By then, he seemed to have forgotten how to hit, too. After Knoblauch batted .210 with a .584 OPS in 2002, his career was over. He received one vote in the 2008 Hall of Fame election.

Harry Krause—Krause was the pitching sensation of the first half of the 1909 season. The 20-year-old A's southpaw won his first 10 games of the season, six by shutout, four of those 1–0 games, and allowed only five runs in that stretch. He finished his rookie

Harry Krause (1911) won 316 professional games. Library of Congress.

season 18–8 with a league-best 1.39 ERA. After starting the following year 3–0 with two shutouts, Krause suffered from shoulder trouble and illness; he finished that season 6–6, then went 11–8 in 1911 and 0–3 in '12. Krause returned to the minors where he developed a spitball (not yet banned) and became an effective pitcher again. He hurled until 1929, winning 281 games in the minors, mostly in the Pacific Coast League.

Terry Larkin—Frank "Terry" Larkin was a 32-year-old rookie for the Hartford NL Team in 1877 when he posted a 29–25 record. The team folded, and Larkin joined the Chicago team, going 29–26 and 31–23 the next two seasons. He never won another big league game. Larkin was evidently plagued by alcoholism and mental illness, with the rest of his life marked by violent crimes and suicide attempts. His final one was successful, as he slit his throat with a razor in 1894.

Frank Lary—During his first seven full seasons, 1955–61, Frank Lary—not Whitey Ford, Early Wynn, nor Jim Bunning—was the winningest pitcher in the American League, and the only AL pitcher to post 20-win seasons in both the 1950s and '60s. During that period, "The Yankee Killer"—he was 28–13 lifetime against the perennial champs—topped the league in complete games and innings pitched three times each. But after going 23–9 at age 31 in 1961, Lary turned up lame the following spring, suffering what the team physician called "an inflammatory condition in the ligaments attaching to the sub-scapularis muscle in his [pitching] shoulder."[59]

"I had a little trouble with it in 1961, but not much," said Lary. "This year I started having trouble in spring training. I think I probably started throwing a little hard too soon."[60]

Lary kicked around for another four seasons, winning only 11 more big league games.

Sal Maglie—It took Sal "The Barber" Maglie 12 years to become an overnight sensation.

At age 33 in 1950, the New York Giants' pitcher had an unimposing 5–3 record through July 20 (making him 10–7 for his career). Maglie then won 11 straight decisions, including a stretch of 45 consecutive scoreless innings, and finished the season 18–4 with a 2.71 ERA. To prove it was no fluke, he followed up with 23–6, 2.93 and 18–8, 2.92 records the next two years.

By 1956, Maglie appeared to be washed up. Dealt away to Cleveland and then Brooklyn within a year, he had just a 2–3 record and 4.11 ERA

---

59. Falls, Joe. "Frank Lary en route to ?" *SPORT*, June 1963, p. 76.
60. Land, Charles. "'Arm Feels Sound, Nothing Seriously Wrong,' Says Lary." *The Sporting News*, November 10, 1962.

through July 23. But he went 11–2 the rest of the way, including a no-hitter on September 25, sparking the Dodgers to the NL pennant. Maglie finished second in MVP voting, his third top-10 finish.

The Barber finished his 10-year career with a nifty 119–62 record and 3.15 ERA. Despite his abbreviated tenure, he got 13 Hall of Fame votes in 1964 and 11 in '68. But what took him so long to reach the top of his profession?

Mostly, it was because he just wasn't good enough in his younger years. Maglie began his pro career in 1938, but went a combined 6–19 with an ERA near five over his first three years. After decent seasons in 1941 and '42, he spent two years working in a defense plant (he was rejected for military duty due to a chronic sinus condition[61]). Maglie returned to pro ball in 1945 and, despite a 3–7 record in the minors (giving him a 38–47 lifetime log in the bushes), the pitching-starved Giants called him up for the last two months of the season. He went 5–4.

Maglie jumped to the outlaw Mexican League the next year, and as a result was banned from organized baseball. But he truly learned his craft there under the tutelage of former major league star Dolf Luque, and posted a couple of 20-win seasons before the league folded. By the time the ban was lifted in late 1949, Sal Maglie was finally ready to become a star big league pitcher.

Don Mattingly—Mattingly went on the Hall of Fame ballot in 2001, the same year as Kirby Puckett. Following are their career numbers:

Player	G	AB	R	H	2B	3B	HR	RBI	AVG	OBP	SLG
Mattingly	1785	7003	1007	2153	442	20	222	1099	.307	.358	.471
Puckett	1783	7244	1071	2304	414	57	207	1085	.318	.360	.477

Mattingly led his league in hits twice, doubles three times, total bases twice, and RBI, batting, and slugging once each. He won nine Gold Gloves and six All-Star selections, earned 2.22 MVP Award shares (winning it once), and was a very popular player.

Puckett led the same league in hits four times, total bases twice, and RBI and batting once each. He won six Gold Gloves and 10 All-Star selections, earned 2.55 MVP Award shares (never winning it), and was a very popular player.

Pretty similar careers, wouldn't you say? Yet Puckett won first-ballot selection to the Hall of Fame with 82 percent of the vote, while Mattingly received just 28 percent of the vote, and went downhill from there.

---

61. Overfield, Joe. "A Giant among Men." *Bison Tales*, April-May 1993, p. 27.

The difference was their career trajectories. Puckett was still going strong when his career was cut short by glaucoma. Mattingly, on the other hand, had labored through a half-dozen seasons of mediocrity after dominating early in his career.

Between 1984–87, Mattingly averaged 211 hits, 46 doubles, 30 homers, 121 RBI, and a .337 average each year. He won the 1985 AL MVP, and finished fifth, second, and seventh in the other three seasons. At age 26, he appeared to have a long, productive career ahead of him; seven of his 10 most similar players at that age are Hall of Famers, and another is Manny Ramirez.

After two more All-Star seasons, Mattingly suffered a back injury in 1990, and was never the same player. He averaged just 10 homers, 64 RBI, and a .286 average over his last six years, retiring at age 34 in 1995. Following his 28 percent first-year showing on the Hall of Fame ballot, his percentage dropped to 20, then 14, and all the way down to 8 before his time on the ballot expired.

Carl Mays (1922) had two 20-win seasons for the Red Sox, two for the Yankees, and one for the Reds. Library of Congress.

Carl Mays—See the chapter on Ray Chapman. Mays received six Hall of Fame votes in 1958, then did better in Veterans' Committee voting. After the committee was restructured and its results made public, Mays got 16 of 79 votes (20 percent) in 2003, before dropping to 12, 6, and fewer than 3 votes in his next three tries.

Von McDaniel—If you're reading this book in order, you've already read about Rick Ankiel: a young Cardinals pitcher who was the talk of the baseball world, then suddenly forgot how to pitch, and later made a semi-successful comeback as a position-player.

Now, read about the original Rick Ankiel.

Max Von McDaniel was one of three brothers, all of whom played pro ball. Lindy, the oldest, would pitch 21 seasons (1955-75) in the major leagues, leading his league in saves three times; Kerry (or Butch) would pitch and play first base in the low minors (1961-63).

Von looked like he might become the best athlete of the bunch. He was All-State in both basketball and baseball at Arnett High School, posting a 44-8 pitching record in his three years on the team. As a senior, he went 21-1 with 243 strikeouts and just 17 walks and 25 hits allowed in 117 innings—and also batted .545 with nine home runs.[62] Von turned down a basketball scholarship at Kansas and signed with the St. Louis Cardinals for a $50,000 bonus on May 23, 1957, four days before his high school graduation as valedictorian of his class. "It seemed almost as though he should report directly from high school to the Hall of Fame, skipping the National League altogether," recalled one reporter.[63]

At age 18, Von went straight to the parent team, joining brother Lindy on the Cardinals' staff. Lindy, 21, had gone 7-6 as a rookie in '56, and was on his way to a 15-9 sophomore season.

Von finally got into his first game on June 13, hurling four scoreless innings in relief against the Phillies. The right-hander with the smooth over-hand delivery was impressive, allowing just one bloop hit and no walks, and striking out four. Was he nervous? "Yes, walking up the line to the mound," he said, "but not while I was pitching. I've pitched lots before."[64]

Three days later, McDaniel again pitched four scoreless innings in relief, again surrendering but one hit and no walks, and fanning five—against the defending NL champion Brooklyn Dodgers. The buzz was already starting for the youngster the press dubbed "Mr. Vonderful."

On June 21, McDaniel made his first major league start, against the defending NL champion. All he did was toss a two-hit shutout—both hits of the infield variety—to beat Brooklyn, 2-0. Still no nerves? "That wasn't the time to be nervous or excited," he said. "I just thought about two things—bear down and keep the ball low."[65] Brooklyn's Elmer Valo, who had been in the major leagues since 1940, was impressed. "The control," said Valo. "And the poise. I've never seen anyone like him—he pitches like an old man. It has to be instinctive." Hall of Fame

---

62. Broeg, Bob. "Scout Predicts Birds' 4-H Kid Won't Have to be Farmed Out." *St. Louis Post-Dispatch*, May 28, 1957.

63. Herskowitz, Mickey. "Von McDaniel's Fans Pulling for Him at 3B." Unidentified clipping in National Baseball Library file, 1962.

64. Broeg, Bob. "Rookie's Debut is Balm in 8-1 Loss." *St. Louis Post-Dispatch*, June 14, 1957.

65. Broeg, Bob. "18-Year-Old Yields Only 2 Scratch Hits, is Master in Clutch." *St. Louis Post-Dispatch*, June 22, 1957.

teammate Pee Wee Reese agreed, saying "he can put the ball where he wants."[66]

On June 27, McDaniel beat the Phillies, though he finally gave up a run after starting his career with 19 straight scoreless innings. And on July 2, he defeated the Milwaukee Braves, giving him a 4–0 record and 1.71 ERA. "The catcher spots the glove and he hits it," said Braves future Hall of Famer Eddie Mathews. "He looks very good."[67]

The Cardinals had attracted only about 13,000 per game in attendance in 1956, but averaged 27,439 in McDaniel's first three home starts. He was called the biggest gate attraction since Hall of Famer Bob Feller.[68] Two hundred-twenty kids from Illinois were turned away at the July 2 game.[69]

McDaniel struggled a bit in his next three starts, taking two losses, but on July 28 came back with a real gem. He hurled a complete-game shutout to beat the Pirates, 4–0, allowing just one hit and no walks. Von required only 99 pitches, and was reported as the youngest man ever to pitch a one-hitter in the major leagues.[70]

On August 20, McDaniel pitched a complete game to beat the Giants, 3–2. He now sported a 7–3 record and 2.63 ERA. Von tossed another complete game his next time out, August 27 vs. the Pirates, but lost, 2–1. He pitched but three-and-a-third innings the rest of the year, finishing 7–5 with a 3.22 ERA. Despite his abbreviated season, it was one of the best ever for an 18-year-old. Since 1900, only Bob Feller had more wins at that age, going 9–7, 3.39 for the 1937 Indians. McDaniel negotiated a reported $2,500 raise to $8,500 for 1958.[71]

After the season, Von enrolled at Abilene (Texas) Christian College. "I went to college and I studied hard," he recalled. "I just didn't have time to keep in shape."[72]

The following spring McDaniel tried to do too much too soon, strained his arm, and developed a hitch in his delivery, bending his wrist backward behind his neck before releasing the ball.[73] He could throw naturally on the sidelines, or while working out in the infield, but reverted to the quirky delivery as soon as he reached the mound. "In succession, he lost his coordination, his control and his confidence," recalled long-time St. Louis

---

66. Mann, Jack. "The McDaniels: Faith and Control." *Newsday*, July 25, 1957, p. 20c.
67. Ibid.
68. "Von Biggest Gate Lure as Pitcher Since Bob Feller." *The Sporting News*, July 10, 1957.
69. "220 Kids Missed Seeing Von." *The Sporting News*, July 10, 1957.
70. "Von, 18, Believed Youngest to Hurl One-Hitter in Majors." *The Sporting News*, August 7, 1957.
71. Broeg, Bob. "Pay Hikes for McDaniels After 'Family' Negotiations." *St. Louis Post-Dispatch*, December 14, 1957.
72. Scarbrough, Jerry. "McDaniel's Comeback Try." Associated Press, July 9, 1963.
73. Isaacs, Stan. "Pathetic Von McDaniel… A Has-Been at 19." *Newsday*, March, 1959, p. 17c.

scribe Bob Broeg.[74] "It's kind of a mystery what happened to my brother," recalled Lindy. "In spring training in 1958, I could have caught my brother bare-handed."[75]

Once the regular season started, Von appeared in just two games for the Cardinals. On April 18, his 19th birthday, he faced five batters and all five got hits. On May 11, he gave up five walks in two innings before being yanked. Three days later, he was sent down to the AA Texas League, never to return to the bigs.[76] After coughing up 30 walks, 23 hits, and 29 earned runs in just 18 innings, McDaniel was demoted down to Class B. He fared no better there, posting a 9.75 ERA with 17 walks and 14 hits allowed in 12 innings, and by 1959 was all the way down to Class D. A newspaper headline that spring said, "Pathetic Von McDaniel.... A Has-Been at 19."[77] Ironically, McDaniel was born in the same month and year as Phil Niekro, who would pitch until 1987 on his way to the Hall of Fame.

In the lowest rung of pro baseball, McDaniel had a singular season in 1959. Although he seemed to be regaining his touch on the mound (13–5, 3.49), he began converting into a position-player, and wound up with 22 games at first base, 20 at pitcher, 19 at shortstop, and 16 in the outfield. Overall, McDaniel batted .313 with 10 homers and 71 RBI in 104 games. He would pitch only 46 more professional innings.

Over the next seven years, McDaniel played mostly third base, moving up as high as Triple-A before retiring in the spring of 1967. Over 878 minor league games, he had 83 home runs, 466 RBI, and a .254 batting average.

Sam McDowell—McDowell was one of the most feared pitchers in baseball from 1965–70. The 6'5" southpaw led the AL in strikeouts five times, amassing 1652 K's (and 700 walks) in those six seasons, almost 400 more whiffs than any other AL pitcher. Sudden Sam still holds the all-time record for most total strikeouts (2271) before age 30. McDowell also led the league in ERA in 1965 and in shutouts in '66, earned six All-Star selections, and was AL Pitcher of the Year in 1970.

Things went swiftly downhill from there, though. McDowell went just 32–42 from 1971-on, finishing with a mediocre 141–134 log, despite 2453 strikeouts (11th all-time, to that point) and a 3.17 ERA.

The reason for his downfall, in his words: "I was the biggest, most

---

74. Broeg, Bob. "Sir Galahad in Baseball Flannels." *St. Louis Post-Dispatch*, July 1, 1973, p. 2F.
75. Lustig, Dennis. "Whatever Happened to... Von McDaniel?" *Cleveland Plain Dealer*, July 10, 1972.
76. Associated Press. "McDaniel Surprise Card Cut." May 15, 1958.
77. Isaacs, Stan. "Pathetic Von McDaniel... A Has-Been at 19." *Newsday*, March, 1959, p. 17c.

hopeless, and most violent drunk in baseball."[78] Like Don Newcombe, McDowell overcame his alcoholism and became an outspoken role model for millions of other alcoholics.

Alex McKinnon—Delayed by a contract scandal and illness, McKinnon didn't reach the majors until he was almost 28, but he seemed to be improving each year. After batting .272 as a rookie in 1884, he improved to .294 and .301, and was at .340 (.365, using that year's rule of counting walks as hits) through July 4, 1887, lifting his career mark to .296. He complained of not feeling well after that morning's game, and died of typhoid fever 20 days later, aged 30.[79]

Sadie McMahon—John McMahon, better known as "Sadie" or "Matchie," joined the American Association at age 21, and soon became among the top pitchers in the junior circuit. In his first full season, 1890, McMahon led the league in complete games (55), innings (509), strikeouts (291), and wins, going 36–21. The next year he again was tops in complete games (53), innings (503), and victories, finishing 35–24.

Shifting to the stronger NL, Sadie was not as dominant, going 42–43 over the next two seasons, and earning a month-long suspension stemming from his drinking and carousing.[80] He rebounded to a 25–8 log in '94, backed by the legendary Orioles lineup (.343 team batting average). McMahon then missed almost a year due to what he called torn tendons in his shoulder,[81] won only 21 more big league games, and was out of the majors before he turned 30. His lifetime record was 173–127. He died in 1954, and was elected to the Delaware Sports Hall of Fame a quarter-century later.[82]

Minnie Minoso—Delayed by his color and language barrier, the black Cuban player Minnie Minoso finally got his chance to play regularly in the majors in 1951. He was 28, according to his published birthdate, November 29, 1922. Over the next decade, he was one of the top players in the AL, leading the league in hits, doubles, and slugging once each, in triples and steals three times apiece, and in being hit by pitch nine times, earning seven

---

78. Pietrusza, David, Matthew Silverman, and Michael Gershman, editors. *Baseball: The Biographical Encyclopedia*. Kingston, NY: Total Sports Illustrated, 2000, p. 746.
79. Smith, James D., III. "Alexander J. Mckinnon." *Nineteenth Century Stars*. Kansas City, MO: Society for American Baseball Research, 1989, p. 89.
80. Tiemann, Robert L. "John J. McMahon." *Nineteenth Century Stars*. Kansas City, MO: Society for American Baseball Research, 1989, p. 90.
81. Smith, Red. "Sore Arms and Such Never Bothered Guys Like 'Sadie' McMahon." Unidentified newspaper, March 28, 1943.
82. *The Sporting News*, June 9, 1979.

All-Star selections. He finished with 1963 hits, 186 homers, 1023 RBI, and a .298 average.

Many have campaigned for Minoso to be elected to the Hall of Fame, using the argument that, if we plugged in normal numbers for pre-age-28 seasons, Minnie would have, oh, about 3000 hits.

But in his 1994 autobiography, Minoso admitted that his actual birth-year was 1925. He said he had lied about his age in order to get a visa and qualify for the Cuban army. That jibes with the fact that his earliest documented pro baseball experience was in 1946, with the Negro leagues' New York Cubans. And it makes him 25 in his 1951 rookie season, severely undermining the Hall of Fame argument (not to mention costing him his claim as the oldest man to get a hit, when he singled in 1976).[83]

Minoso got decent support in BBWAA voting for the Hall, peaking at 90 votes in 1988, and still gets substantial consideration when his name comes up in veterans' committee voting, including nine of a possible 16 votes in 2012 and eight of 16 in '15, his two most recent tries.

Justin Morneau—A 2010 baserunning collision ended Morneau's reign as one of the AL's top sluggers. At 29, he had knocked in 470 runs in the previous four seasons.

After batting .319 with power in the minors, Morneau debuted with the Twins in 2003. In 2006, he had a 34–130–.321 season to win the AL MVP. Two years later, he went 23–129–.300 and finished second in the balloting.

Morneau was off to his best season in '10, with 18 homers, a .345 average, and a 1.055 OPS through 81 games, earning his fourth straight All-Star selection. But while trying to break up a double play on July 7, Morneau collided with Toronto second baseman John McDonald's knee, resulting in a concussion which ended his season and bothered him long after. He would never again be a productive player, a batting title with the Rockies in '14 notwithstanding.

Morneau had had at least one previous concussion, after being beaned by Seattle's Ron Villone on April 6, 2005. Morneau also suffered a vertebral stress fracture in 2009, discovered by a CT scan after he went through a season-ending 7-for-70 slump. In 2011, he was curtailed by a strained left wrist, a herniated disk fragment (leading to June 30 neck surgery), a jammed left shoulder (on an August 28 fielding attempt), and continued concussion symptoms. Over the next two years, Morneau had surgery on his left wrist, left knee, and right foot.

Morneau remained in the majors through 2016, but averaged just 11

---

83. Deane, Bill. *Baseball Myths*. Lanham, MD: Scarecrow Press, Inc., 2012, p. 170–72.

homers and 51 RBI per year after 2010. He finished with 235 homers and a .281 average.

Ed "Cannonball" Morris (c. 1888) won 114 games in his first three big league seasons. Library of Congress.

Ed Morris—Nicknamed "Cannonball," Morris debuted as a 21-year-old southpaw and proceeded to author three dominant seasons in the American Association. In 1884, he went 34–13, including a no-hitter, with 302 strikeouts for Columbus. Moving to Pittsburgh in '85, Morris was 39–24, completing all 63 of his games, and also topping the league in innings, shutouts, and strikeouts. And in '86, he was 41–20, leading the AA in wins and shutouts (12). In just three seasons, he had rolled up 1566 innings, a 114–57 record, 926 strikeouts, and a 2.33 ERA.

After Morris moved to the more-competitive National League in 1887, it was a different story. He pitched the next three seasons with Pittsburgh, going just 49–58 with 266 strikeouts in 968 innings. After a year in the Players' League, Cannonball's big league career was over at age 28. He finished 171–122.

Mark Mulder—For a five-year stretch (2001–05), Mulder was arguably the top left-handed pitcher in baseball, going 88–40. But due to a rotator cuff injury at age 28, he won just six games after that.

Mulder was the second overall pick in the 1998 draft, being signed by Oakland from Michigan State University. Characterized by "guile, poise and stubbornness" rather than pure stuff,[84] the 6'6" southpaw was on the

---

84. Kroichicvk, Ron. "Mulder's Confidence Makes up for Lack of 'Stuff.'" *San Francisco Chronicle*, June 3, 2000, p. E5.

A's within two years. After a lackluster rookie season ended by a herniated disk, Mulder blossomed in 2001 to go 21–8, winning his first of three Pitcher of the Month awards, leading the AL in wins and shutouts, and finishing second behind Roger Clemens in Cy Young Award voting. Mulder joined Tim Hudson and Barry Zito on Billy Beane's "Moneyball" staff; they enabled the A's to become the first team since 1900 to have three different 20-game winners under age 25 in consecutive seasons (2000–02). "I hope people realize how special these three guys are," said manager Art Howe. "Fifty years from now, people are going to be telling their grandkids, 'I was there when those three guys were teammates, and now they're all in the Hall of Fame.'"[85]

Mulder followed with marks of 19–7, 15–9, and 17–8, earning All-Star selections and leading the league in complete games in both 2003 and '04 (though the former season was ended by a stress fracture in his right femur). But his arm was already starting to bother him, and he went 0–4, 7.27 over his last seven starts of 2004. He was traded to St. Louis for three players, including pitcher Dan Haren, on December 19.

Mulder went 16–8 for the Cards in '05, but "I did it with smoke and mirrors," he says.[86] The smoke dissipated in 2006: he went 6–7 with a 7.14 ERA and missed two months with shoulder problems; on September 12 he had surgery to repair a partial tear of his rotator cuff. Mulder returned to the Cards in 2007 on a two-year, $13-million deal but, after three poor outings (0–3, 12.27), underwent a second operation on September 24. When he wasn't able to rebound in 2008 (0–0, 10.80), the Cardinals bought out his contract.

Mulder talked with the Brewers about a comeback, then announced his retirement in 2010 to concentrate on other things: his new wife and family, pursuing a pro golf career, and, later, a job as an ESPN analyst.

In the fall of 2013, Mulder experimented with a new delivery, and found that he could throw effectively and without pain. Impressed with what they saw, the Angels signed Mulder to a conditional contract and invited him to spring training in 2014, a veritable 36-year-old rookie. But Mulder suffered a torn Achilles tendon during agility drills on February 15, and his final comeback attempt was over. His lifetime big league record was 103–60 for a .632 percentage.

Thurman Munson—On August 2, 1979, I was one of 15,319 at Shea Stadium, watching a Phillies-Mets twi-night doubleheader. This was in an era when pretty much the only news sources were the 6:00 and 11:00 TV

---

85. Urban, Mychael. "Big Three Bummed About Breakup." MLB.com, December 19, 2004.
86. DiGiovanna, Mike. "Mark Mulder Makes Pitch to Renew Career with Angels." *Los Angeles Times*, February 11, 2014.

news, and the next day's newspaper. Philadelphia won the first game, 7–4, followed by a long rain delay. Soon after game two finally got underway, there was an announcement on the scoreboard: "—BULLETIN—YANKEE CATCHER THURMAN MUNSON WAS KILLED TODAY IN PLANE CRASH NEAR CANTON-OHIO."

Did you ever hear 15,319 people gasp?

Munson was one of the best and most respected players in the game. In nine full seasons, he had earned seven All-Star selections, three Gold Gloves, the 1970 Rookie of the Year Award, and the 1976 MVP, and captained the Yankees to two straight World Championships, batting .357 in post-season play.

Munson finished with 1558 hits and a .292 average. Some thought his premature death cost him Hall of Fame numbers. But, though Munson was just 32, it was an old 32. Over a decade behind the plate had taken a toll on his body; he'd had shoulder surgery in the previous off-season, and suffered through constant aches and pains. Munson was still hitting for average, but his power had dropped off drastically in the past two seasons: just six homers in 1978, and three in 97 games in '79. Furthermore, he was tired of the daily grind and the time away from home, and thinking about retirement. He took up flying just so he could spend time with his family between games. It's not likely that Munson would have added much more to his baseball résumé.

Munson was on the Hall of Fame ballot from 1981–95, peaking at 62 votes (15 percent) in his first try, when the tragedy was still fresh on voters' minds. He did even worse in veterans' committee voting, with a high of six votes out of 82 in 2007.

Steve Olin—On March 22, 1993, Olin was killed in a boating accident which also claimed the life of a pitching teammate, Tim Crews, and injured another, Bobby Ojeda. Olin was coming off an excellent season as the Indians' relief ace, posting an 8–5 record with 29 saves and a 2.34 ERA in '92. But his career mark at age 27 was just 16–19 with 48 saves

Tony Oliva—Chances are that Oliva will be recognized at Cooperstown eventually; otherwise, he would be in the first section of this book. Oliva got as much as 50 percent of the vote in the BBWAA balloting before his eligibility moved over to the Veterans' Committee. He has consistently exceeded 50 percent in 2003–present voting, missed by just one vote in his most recent try via the "Golden Era" committee (2015), and he is slated to get another shot in December 2021.

Oliva was an outstanding hitter whose numbers were disguised by the environment in which he played, and whose career was knocked off course by a crippling knee injury. In his first eight full seasons (1964–71), his finishes in the AL batting race were first, first, second, eighth, third, third, third, and first. Tony also topped the league at various times in runs, hits (five times), doubles (four times), and slugging. He was an All-Star in each of the eight seasons and was a perennial MVP candidate.

A knee injury cut short Oliva's '71 season, and limited him to 10 games in '72. It looked like his career was over at age 34. At that point, Oliva had a .313 career batting average over parts of 11 seasons, as compared to the .243 overall AL mark during that period.

The new designated hitter rule allowed Oliva to continue his career in 1973. Even though he could barely run or take the field, he could still hit. Basically playing on one leg, Oliva batted .277 over the next four years as the Twins' DH before retiring. Ironically, the new rule—while extending his career—may have sabotaged his Hall of Fame chances. Had Oliva been forced to retire four years earlier, while still at the top of his game, he might have gotten the treatment afforded to another Twins outfielder two decades later, Kirby Puckett.

Here's a comparison between Oliva and Puckett in some key areas:

MVP Voting—Oliva had finishes of second (twice), fourth, sixth, and tenth, amassing a total of 1.90 award shares. Puckett had finishes of second, third (twice), sixth, and seventh (three times), totaling 2.55 shares. Advantage: Puckett.

Black ink—As listed above, Oliva had a total of 14 league leaderships in important offensive categories. Puckett led in hits four times, RBI once, and batting once, a total of six. Advantage: Oliva.

All-Star selections—Oliva was an All-Star in each of his first eight full seasons. Puckett was an All-Star in each of his last 10 seasons. Advantage: Puckett.

Post-Season—Oliva helped the Twins to the 1965 AL title and the 1969–70 divisional titles, batting .314 in post-season play with 3 homers in 13 games. Puckett helped the Twins to the 1987 and 1991 world championships, hitting .309 with 5 homers in 24 games. Too close to call.

Batting—Oliva averaged 5.96 runs created per 27 outs, as compared to the league's 4.00, so he was 49 percent better than average. Puckett had 6.08 RC/27 to the league's 4.57, 33 percent better than average. Oliva had 238 adjusted batting wins, Puckett 216 in more games. Advantage: Oliva.

Baserunning—Oliva was 86-55 as a base-stealer; Puckett was 134-76, both mediocre (though Puckett had the advantage of turf). Puckett ground into a lot more double plays, but he was right-handed.

Of course, Oliva could only hobble during his DH years, which couldn't have helped his team much. Advantage: none.

Defense—Oliva, a right fielder, won a Gold Glove Award, and had 76 fielding runs, but led the AL in errors three times. Puckett, a center fielder, won six Gold Gloves while leading the league in putouts three times and assists twice, and amassing 137 fielding runs. Advantage: Puckett.

So, who was better? It looks pretty close to me. And yet, Kirby made it to Cooperstown before he turned 40, while Tony waits outside into his 80s.

Mel Parnell—Parnell's career was delayed by World War II, and shot down by a broken pitching arm, but for a six-year stretch he was one of the best pitchers in the majors. From 1948–53, Parnell went 109–56.

After posting a 16–9 record with a 1.59 ERA in the Mid-Atlantic League in 1942, Parnell spent 3½ years in the U.S. Army Air Corps. He returned in 1946 to go 13–4 with a league-leading 1.30 ERA in the Eastern League. Parnell was promoted to the Red Sox in '47, but after a shaky start was sent back to the minors for more seasoning. In his fourth game for Louisville of the American Association on July 28, Parnell took a line drive to his pitching hand. He missed the rest of the season with a broken finger.

Parnell made it back to the Sox in 1948. He pitched only sporadically in the first half of the season, but became the team's most reliable hurler in the pennant stretch, going 12–3 after July 7 to finish 15–8 with a 3.14 ERA—impressive, for a southpaw who pitched his home games in Fenway Park. He proved it was no fluke in 1949, going 25–7 and leading the AL in complete games (27), innings (295), wins, and ERA (2.77, though Mike Garcia is now credited with the title). Parnell finished fourth in AL MVP voting. After the season, he revealed he had been pitching with a sore elbow since a 12-inning game on May 7.[87]

Parnell followed with records of 18–10, 18–11, 12–12, and 21–8, shutting out the world champion Yankees four times in the latter season. But on April 24, 1954, Parnell's pitching forearm was fractured by a pitch from his former roommate, Mickey McDermott. Parnell didn't start another game until August, and was tentative when he did pitch. He finished the year 3–7.

Parnell wrenched his knee during spring training of 1955, was out until June, and was ineffective when he returned. He finished 2–3 with a 7.83 ERA.

After recovering from a severe ankle sprain on May 16, 1956, Parnell had one last hurrah. He tossed a no-hitter over the White Sox on July 14, and through August 23, he was 7–3 with a 2.70 ERA. But he never won

---

87. Associated Press. "Parnell Reveals 1949 Arm Injury." April 3, 1950.

another game, finishing 7–6, 3.77. His left elbow had begun bothering him again, and he was found to have a bone growth. Parnell started the 1957 season on the disabled list, then retired on July 10, after reaching his 10-year milestone to qualify for a pension. He finished his career 123–75 with a 3.50 ERA, and is still Boston's career victory leader among southpaws.

Johnny Pesky—Like his former teammate Dominic DiMaggio, Pesky has gotten support as a Hall of Fame candidate, despite missing three prime years due to military service. A good shortstop, Pesky also could swing the bat, leading the AL in hits in each of his first three seasons. But, as with DiMaggio, even if we pencil in normal seasons for 1943–45 (based on his averages in the surrounding seasons), Pesky's career totals are not quite Hall of Fame caliber: 1193 runs, 2075 hits, 22 homers, and a .314 average. He received just one vote in BBWAA elections, in 1960.

Rico Petrocelli—After four nondescript seasons, Petrocelli had a breakout year in 1969: 40 homers, a .297 batting average, and a .589 slugging percentage. At the time, only future Hall of Famers Ernie Banks and Arky Vaughan had ever posted a higher mark while playing shortstop.

Petrocelli never quite matched that performance, but he remained a productive player until he was beaned by Jim Slaton on September 15, 1974. That ended his season, and he suffered dizziness and balance problems the rest of his career, which concluded two years later at age 33.[88] Petrocelli finished with 210 homers and a .251 average, and received three votes in the 1982 Hall of Fame balloting.

Jimmy Piersall—Featured in the major motion picture *Fear Strikes Out*, Jimmy Piersall overcame mental illness to fashion a solid big league career. After exhibiting extremely erratic behavior in his rookie season of 1952—he later said he didn't remember any of it—the 22-year-old Piersall was institutionalized and treated with electroshock therapy.[89] He returned to complete a 17-year career with five teams, earning two All-Star selections and winning two Gold Gloves in center field. Overall, he batted .272 with 1604 hits, before embarking on a long broadcasting career. Piersall died in 2017.

Arlie Pond—At age 25, Erasmus Arlington Pond had a .648 winning percentage for his young pitching career. But another calling brought him halfway around the world, never to return to the majors.

---

88. James, Bill. *The Bill James Baseball Abstract 1985*. New York: Ballantine Books, 1985, p. 139.
89. Pietrusza, David, Matthew Silverman, and Michael Gershman, editors. *Baseball: The Biographical Encyclopedia*. Kingston, NY: Total Sports Illustrated, 2000, p. 890.

Pond attended Norwich University and the University of Vermont, for whom he pitched a no-hitter against Yale. After graduating, he remained in Burlington to earn his medical degree in 1895, then went on to the College of Physicians and Surgeons in Baltimore. There, Orioles manager Ned Hanlon convinced Pond to join his club for the summer. Pond appeared in just six games that year, also serving as the team doctor.

Pond joined the Baltimore Orioles' regular rotation the next two years, going 16–8 and 18–9 in 1896–97. But he hardly pitched in the first half of the 1898 season. On July 6, Pond tossed a five-hit shutout to beat the slugging Philadelphia Phillies. It proved to be the final game of his pro career.

The previous day, Pond had been appointed acting assistant surgeon of the U.S. Army, and he soon found himself stationed on the Philippine Islands. Thousands of American soldiers there had contracted tropical diseases during the Spanish-American War, and a subsequent guerrilla war added to the casualty count over the next four years. By then the island nation was an American colony and the U.S. government was determined to stop the spread of diseases like bubonic plague, cholera, smallpox, and leprosy there. Thus Dr. Pond remained in the Philippines under Governor General William Howard Taft. Pond became medical inspector for the Board of Health in 1903, and chief of the Southern Islands Hospital in 1906. He finally received his military discharge in 1919, but remained on the Philippines in private practice and business ventures, becoming a millionaire and a national hero. He died in 1930 in the same hospital in which he had saved countless lives.[90]

Bret Saberhagen—Another pitcher overworked in his youth, Saberhagen alternated great seasons with injury-riddled, ineffective ones. He debuted at age 19 in 1984, and won the Cy Young Award (20–6, 2.87) and World Series MVP the following year. Then came records of 7–12, 18–10, and 14–16, before his best season in '89. Saberhagen went 23–6, leading the AL in innings, complete games, wins, percentage, and ERA (2.16), earning his second Cy Young.

Saberhagen pitched through 2001, but never again hurled as many as 200 innings in a season. He finished 167–117 with a 3.34 ERA and 1016 days on the disabled list. Saberhagen won the 1998 Tony Conigliaro Award, and received seven votes in 2007 Hall of Fame balloting.

Johan Santana—Johan Santana won two unanimous Cy Young Awards and three ERA crowns, but is not likely ever to make the Hall of Fame.

---

90. Simon, Tom. "Arlington Pond: From Rutland to the Philippines." In *Green Mountain Boys of Summer*, p. 28–33.

Santana's weapons included a 95 mph fastball, a devastating 74 mph change-up, and a Gold Glove. After four seasons as a middle-reliever and spot-starter, the southpaw made the Twins' rotation at age 25 in 2004. Following a slow start, he proceeded to finish 20–6, leading the AL in strikeouts (265), ERA (2.61), and just about every analytic measure, earning unanimous Cy Young honors. He was just as good in 2005 and '06, completing a 17–0 streak in the former season, and receiving his second unanimous Cy Young in the latter one, after going 19–6 and topping the league in starts, innings, wins, strikeouts, and ERA. Traded to the Mets for four players in 2008, Santana signed a huge seven-year contract, and led the NL in starts, innings, and ERA. But he pitched in September on a torn meniscus in his left knee, requiring off-season surgery.

Santana's next two seasons were ended prematurely by surgery on his pitching arm: arthroscopic surgery to remove bone chips from his elbow in '09, and anterior capsule surgery on September 14, 2010, costing him the entire '11 season. Through age 31 in '10, the 10 most similar pitchers to Santana include only one Hall of Famer, Roy Halladay, though Max Scherzer is likely to make it two.

Johan returned to enjoy a good first half (6–4, 2.76) in 2012, including the Mets' first-ever no-hitter on June 1, but the 134-pitch outing was the beginning of the end. After June, Santana appeared in just five more games, losing all five with 43 hits and 33 earned runs allowed in 19 innings (increasing his career ERA from 3.06 to 3.20), before being shut down. His problems were said to be lower back inflammation and an ankle issue, and Santana didn't blame the Mets' manager, saying he argued to stay in games.

Though Santana's contract kicked around for several more years, he never pitched another pro inning. On April 2, 2013, he had a second shoulder surgery. The Mets bought out his contract at the end of the year, and he went to the Orioles and Blue Jays over the next two years. While trying to work his way back, he suffered a torn left Achilles tendon in June 2014, a toe infection, and shoulder tightness.

Santana finished 139–78 (.641) with 1988 strikeouts in 2026 innings. He went onto the Hall of Fame ballot in 2018, but received just 10 votes and was dropped.

Urban Shocker—Shocker went 60–28 with a 2.01 ERA in the minor leagues, 1913–16, before making it to the bigs at the relatively late age of 25. He died at 37 of a heart ailment. In between, he was one of the best pitchers in the game.

Even though he pitched the bulk of his career for a mediocre team (St. Louis Browns) in a great hitters' park, and insisted on a disproportionate amount of work against the Yankees, Shocker never had a losing season. He had four straight 20-win campaigns, including a league-leading 27 in 1921, and finished 187–117 (.615) with a 3.17 ERA. Shocker had excellent control and was a master of studying the hitters and pitching to their weaknesses. Even when his fastball and heart were failing him, he was one of the league's most effective hurlers in his last full season, going 18–6, 2.84 in 1927.

Shocker died more than seven years before the first Hall of Fame election. He received a total of just nine votes spread over five elections.

Urban Shocker (1924) never had a losing record in the majors. Library of Congress.

Wayne Simpson—Simpson electrified the baseball world in the first half of 1970, much like Vida Blue would the next year and Fernando Valenzuela would in 1981. At age 21, Simpson made his major league debut for Cincinnati on April 9, and pitched a two-hit shutout against Don Sutton and the Dodgers. Ten days later, he shut out Gaylord Perry and the Giants on one hit. At that point, Simpson had allowed just seven hits and one run (0.36 ERA) in 25 innings. After absorbing his first defeat, 3–1 to the Cardinals on April 24, he ran off 10 victories in a row. Through July 5, the Reds' 80th game, Simpson was 13–1 with a 2.27 ERA. In 18 starts (during which the Reds were 17–1), he tossed nine complete games, and allowed just 86 hits in 139 innings. He ranked tied for first in the NL in wins, first in percentage (.929), and second (by .02) in ERA.

Simpson faltered a bit the rest of that month, and then on July 31, "I threw a fastball inside to [Cubs slugger] Billy Williams and the whole shoulder seemed to give away. I finished the inning, but I couldn't raise my arm before the next inning started."[91] Simpson appeared in just two games, totaling 5+ innings, the rest of the year. He still finished second

---

91. Harmon, Pat. "Simpson Says He's Well, Will Pitch Again." *Cincinnati Post & Times-Star*, December 2, 1970, p. 33.

in the league in ERA and first in opposing batting average, but he was essentially through. Simpson went just 22–28 with a 4.89 ERA (highest in the majors during that period) after 1970, and his career was over at age 28.

In truth, Simpson's first-half performance of 1970 was far above anything his previous pro performances would have forecast. In 374 minor league innings, Simpson had gone 18–25 with a 4.11 ERA, striking out 285 batters, walking 259, and giving up 326 hits. After becoming the Reds' #1 draft pick in 1967, the erratic righty had led three different leagues in wild pitches, two in walks, and one in hit batsmen. He did show progress in the Puerto Rican Winter League in 1969–70, and many felt his 151 innings there led to his undoing the following summer.

Simpson eventually had several bypass operations due to circulatory problems in his arm, and still does not have full use of it.

Grady Sizemore—In Sizemore's first four full seasons (2005–08), he established himself as one of the better players in baseball, earning three All-Star selections and two Gold Gloves, and averaging 160 games, 116 runs, 41 doubles, 8 triples, 27 homers, and 29 steals per season. Through age 25, the two most similar players were Barry Bonds and Duke Snider. But Sizemore had a litany of injuries and surgeries thereafter, winding up his 10-year career with 150 homers and a .265 average.

Dave Stieb—Though never a 20-game winner, Stieb was regarded as one of the AL's top pitchers from 1980–90, earning seven All-Star selections. He topped the league in WAR three times, innings twice, and in ERA once, and tossed a no-hitter after several near-misses. Through age 32, the eight most-similar pitchers include four Hall of Famers.

But Stieb suffered shoulder and back injuries in '91, and won only 10 more games in the majors. He finished 176–137, 3.44, and got seven votes in the 2004 Hall of Fame election.

George Stone—In the first 28 seasons of the current American League, the batting title was won by a future Hall of Famer in 27 of them. The lone exception was George Stone.

It's not clear why Stone did not become a big league regular until he was nearly 29. He excelled in the minor leagues in the early 20th century, including a .406 average with 254 hits in the American Association in 1904. Stone finally got his shot with the St. Louis Browns the next year, and promptly led the AL in hits and total bases.

Stone had a fantastic season in 1906, leading the league in total bases, batting (.358), OBP (.417), and slugging (.501)—and remember, this was the

George Stone, shown near the end of his career (1910), was the only non–Hall of Famer to win an AL batting title before 1929. Library of Congress.

Deadball Era. He was regarded as a speedy runner and reliable fielder. Stone turned 30 late in the season.

But he was already thinking ahead toward life after the game. "I realize that each year I continue in base ball sets me that much further back in a business career," Stone told *The Sporting Life*. "I am still a young man and believe it should be the ambition of every young man to get in business for himself.... No, in a few years you will see me hustling for myself in my Nebraska home." Indeed, he would become a banker in Nebraska by 1912.[92]

Stone held out before the 1907 season, and his batting average dropped off nearly 40 points in each of the next two years. Slowed by illness and injuries, he was out of the majors after the 1910 season. He finished with a .301 average over 848 games.

Frank Tanana—Tanana was emerging as the best pitcher in baseball at age 24, but overwork turned him into a journeyman junkballer.

Tanana joined the Angels' staff at age 20 in 1974, and proceeded to win *The Sporting News*'s AL Rookie Pitcher of the Year honors. The following year, the southpaw went 16–9 with a 2.62 ERA for the last-place team, topping the league with 269 strikeouts—the only time between 1972 and 1979 that Nolan Ryan failed to lead the AL. Tanana led the league in fielding independent pitching. In 1976, Tanana went 19–10 with 261 K's and a 2.43 ERA, topping the AL in WHIP, and earning his first of three Player of the Month Awards in an eight-month span.

On July 3, 1977, Tanana celebrated his 24th birthday by pitching his 14th consecutive complete game. Seventy-four games into the season, he

---

92. Jones David, editor. *Deadball Stars of the American League*. Dulles, VA: Potomac Books, Inc., 2006, p. 787.

was 12–5 with six shutouts, 144 strikeouts, and a 1.89 ERA—a pace for a 26–11 mark with 13 shutouts and 315 K's. But his arm was spent, and he went just 3–4, 3.87 the rest of the way, not pitching after September 5. Tanana still managed to lead the AL in ERA, shutouts, and WAR in 1977, but his days as a dominant pitcher were over.

His fastball gone, Tanana relied on guile to remain in the majors through age 40 in 1993. He finished 240–236 with 2773 strikeouts and a 3.66 ERA. Tanana went on the Hall of Fame ballot in 1999, but failed to receive a vote.

Oscar Taveras—On October 26, 2014, the Cardinals lost one of their prized prospects when Oscar Taveras died in a drunk driving accident in his native Dominican Republic. The 22-year-old outfielder had debuted in the majors just 148 days before.

The Cardinals signed Taveras as a 16-year-old on November 15, 2008, and he moved up from Rookie ball to AAA over the next 5½ years. Oscar batted .319 lifetime in the minors, topping .300 in five straight seasons—including .371 in 2011, and .320 with 350 total bases in '12—before his big league call-up.

Taveras had just a .239/.278/.312 slash-line in his 80 major league games, but there is little doubt he had the makings of a star.

Virgil Trucks—In 1952, Trucks pitched two no-hitters and a one-hitter—and that was the *worst* season of his career.

After dominating in the minors—including a 418-strikeout season and several no-hitters—Trucks became a solid AL pitcher in the 1940s and '50s. Only twice did he lose more games than he won—including an inexplicable 5–19 record in that '52 season. More often, Trucks would have records like 14–8, 16–10, 14–9, 14–13, 13–8, and 13–8. His best years were 1949 (19–11), 1953 (20–10), and 1954 (19–12). Trucks led the league in strikeouts in '49, and in shutouts in '49 and '54, his two All-Star seasons. He finished 177–135; if not for the two years he missed in World War II service, he likely would have topped 200 wins, improving his chances of Hall of Fame consideration. Trucks did receive four votes in the 1964 election.

Mickey Vernon—In a checkered career, Vernon led the AL in doubles three times and batting twice, earning seven All-Star selections. Despite missing two entire seasons in military service, he amassed 2495 hits. With normal seasons plugged in for 1944–45, Mickey might have had about 2850, putting him in the top 20 all-time at the time of his retirement. Vernon was on the Hall of Fame ballot from 1966–80, peaking at 96 votes (25 percent) in his final try. He later got as many as 14 (of 82 in 2007) votes in veterans' balloting.

Zoilo Versalles—At age 25, Versalles was the best all-around shortstop in baseball. At 31, he was out of the major leagues for good.

The Cuban-born shortstop debuted in the majors at age 19 in 1959. By 1963, he was an All-Star, leading the AL in triples for the first of three straight years, and unseating Luis Aparicio for the Gold Glove Award.

Versalles put it all together in 1965, winning another Gold Glove, and leading the Twins to the AL pennant. His offense was unheard-of for a shortstop in that era. Versalles was tops in the AL in runs, doubles, triples, extra-base hits, and total bases; he also finished second in hits and third in stolen bases. He was the overwhelming choice as the AL's Most Valuable Player.

Few non-pitchers ever went on such a precipitous decline at such a young age. Within two years, Zoilo's batting average had dropped by 73 points and his slugging percentage by 180. He then lost his regular status, bounced around to five different big league teams over four seasons, and wound up in the Mexican League.

Versalles batted an aggregate .217 with no power after his MVP season. It is unclear what led to his rapid decline; there were problems with his back and his vision, but he never spent a day on the disabled list.

Eddie Waitkus—Delayed by World War II, Waitkus didn't become a big league regular until he was almost 27. He proceeded to top .290 in each of his first four full seasons, earning two All-Star selections. But Eddie's career took a bizarre and near-fatal turn in 1949. On June 15, he was summoned to the hotel room of a deranged 19-year-old fan, Ruth Steinhagen. Steinhagen pulled out a pistol and shot Waitkus, ending his season and almost his life. The incident may have inspired an event in Bernard Malamud's novel, *The Natural*.

Waitkus returned to complete a respectable 11-year career, batting .285 in 1140 games.

Dick Wakefield—As a rookie, Wakefield finished sixth in AL MVP voting. The following year, he finished fifth, even though he missed half the season in military service. He took a .326 career batting average into the service—but returned to hit a tepid .268 thereafter, collecting his last big league hit at age 28.

It sounds something like the stories of Johnny Beazley, Buddy Lewis, and Cecil Travis, but it's not. Wakefield was someone who excelled when the level of competition was the weakest, and fell back to earth when Johnny came marching home—and didn't really care one way or the other.

The son of big league catcher Howard Wakefield, Dick was a big, talented athlete, particularly good at hitting a baseball. After he batted .370 with nine homers in 26 games as a sophomore for the University of Michigan in 1941, Wakefield announced he would quit college to sign a pro baseball contract. This set off a bidding war for his services among 11 of the 16 major league teams. The Tigers won, paying some $52,000 plus a custom-built car to sign him, an unheard-of bonus for someone with no pro baseball experience.[93]

Wakefield batted .300 in 55 games for Winston-Salem in 1941, then won the Texas League MVP Award with Beaumont in '42 after leading the circuit in hits, doubles, and batting (.345). He joined the Tigers in 1943, by which time most of the star players were in military service.

Wakefield had a sensational rookie campaign, playing in all 155 games, leading the AL in hits (200) and doubles (38), and finishing second in total bases and batting (.316). A few days after the season ended, he was inducted into the Navy.

In an odd situation, a Navy order to down-size the cadet program allowed Wakefield and many others to secure a temporary discharge the following summer. He rejoined the Tigers six days later, on July 13, at which time they ranked seventh of eight teams with a 36–42 record. But sparked by Dick's heavy hitting, Detroit went 52–24 (plus two ties) the rest of the way, surging to within one game of the pennant-winning St. Louis Browns.[94] Wakefield wound up playing exactly half of the Tigers' 156 games. Had he maintained his pace for a full season, he would have led the AL in home runs, total bases, walks, batting (.355), on-base average (.464), and slugging (.576). As mentioned, despite his late start, he finished fifth in MVP voting, including a couple of first-place votes.

Wakefield returned to military service on November 30, 1944, and was honorably discharged on January 5, 1946. By then, writers were gushing at the prospect of an AL batting title race between Wakefield and Ted Williams, who hadn't played in the majors since 1942. The two players even made eight public wagers as to who would outdo whom in what category.[95]

Once the season started, it was clear that Wakefield wasn't anywhere near Williams's class. Ted hit his usual .342, while Dick slipped to .268. Marks of .283, .276, and .206 followed, with Wakefield missing more than 40 games each season. He insisted he was playing hard, but was the victim of injuries and lack of playing time.

Reading contemporary newspaper articles about Wakefield gives a pretty good picture of his personality, and clues to what went wrong with

---

93. Devine, Tommy. "What's with Wakefield?" Unidentified magazine article, 1949, p. 58–59.
94. *Ibid.*, p. 95.
95. Murphy, Bob. "Wakefield, Williams Slug it out with Words." *The Sporting News*, 1946.

his career. Among the adjectives used to describe him were cocky, controversial, flippant, happy-go-lucky, lackadaisical, laid-back, nonchalant, non-conforming, self-centered, temperamental, and tempestuous; the nouns included clown, enigma, prima donna, problem child, and spoiled brat. "He is not concerned with fielding or base-running," reported one article. "He considers those things plain nuisances and necessary evils."[96] By the second half of the 1940s, he didn't seem concerned with playing at all, complaining about the life of a ballplayer, and engaging in various disputes. He "apparently had cared little about playing baseball since he came back from the Navy," offered another sportswriter.[97]

Wakefield was traded to the Yankees on December 17, 1949, but got only two at bats in pinstripes before he was dealt to the White Sox. Wakefield demanded a raise and, when he didn't get it, refused to report. Commissioner Happy Chandler ordered him back to the Yankees, who didn't want him. They suspended Wakefield, then sent him to their Oakland farm team, where he played in 1950–51. He got a tryout as a catcher with the Indians in spring training, 1952, and two at bats with the Giants later that year. When they demoted him to the minors, he refused to go, and his pro career was over at 31.

Pete Ward—Fewer than 20 players have finished in the top 10 in MVP voting in both their rookie and sophomore seasons. Among them are Joe DiMaggio, Frank Robinson, Mike Piazza, Albert Pujols, and Mike Trout.

And Pete Ward.

Ward, a Canadian-born third baseman, started in the system of the Orioles, who already had a fellow named Brooks Robinson at the hot corner. After batting .321 in five minor league seasons, and getting just 21 at bats with the O's, Ward was traded to the White Sox in the Hoyt Wilhelm–Luis Aparicio swap on January 14, 1963. Playing in a poor hitters' park in a poor hitters' era, Ward posted a 22–84–.295 season, helping the Sox to second place in '63. He was second in the league in hits, doubles, and total bases, and fifth in batting, good for a ninth-place finish in MVP voting and *The Sporting News*'s Rookie Player of the Year award (he finished second in BBWAA voting, behind pitching teammate Gary Peters). In '64, Ward (23–94–.282) finished sixth in MVP balloting as the White Sox came within a game of dethroning the Yankees.

Prior to the 1965 season, Ward injured his neck in an auto accident on his way to an NHL game. Back problems followed, and Ward batted just .234 over his last six seasons before being released at age 33.

---

96. Salsinger, H. G. "Wakefield." Unidentified magazine article, p. 84.
97. Talbot, Gayle. "The Wakefield Awakening." *Baseball Digest*, January, 1950, p. 77.

Lefty Williams—A March 13, 1919, *Sporting News* article presciently said, "What ever Joe Jackson does Claude Williams will do." Two years later, the two would be among the eight players banned from baseball for their alleged roles in the 1919 "Black Sox Scandal." But, unlike Jackson, Williams could not become eligible for the Hall of Fame even if he were reinstated someday, because he did not play 10 years in the majors.

Claude "Lefty" Williams began his pro career at age 18 in 1911. He won two strikeout crowns and 82 games in the minors between 1912 and 1915. Included was his 1915 Pacific Coast League season, when he rolled up a 33–12 record, leading the league in wins and K's (294).

Claude "Lefty" Williams (1917) was the winningest AL left-handed pitcher over his last five seasons. Library of Congress.

Williams, who had pitched briefly with the Tigers in 1913–14, joined the White Sox for the 1916 season. He proceeded to post five straight seasons with a .600+ winning percentage: 13–7, 17–8, 6–4 (a season interrupted by wartime shipyard service), 23–11, and 22–14. No American League southpaw had more than his 81 wins during that period; the closest, Babe Ruth with 70, was no longer pitching.

Williams's career came to an abrupt halt when the scandal broke at the end of the 1920 season. Though he and the other seven were acquitted of conspiracy in 1921, the following day Commissioner Kenesaw Landis declared that none of them would ever again play organized baseball. Williams, 27, finished with an 82–48 record (.631) and 3.13 ERA.

Dontrelle Willis—At age 23, the "D-Train" had earned two All-Star selections, but he won only four games after his 26th birthday.

After going 27–5 with a 2.31 ERA in parts of four minor league seasons, Willis debuted in the majors at age 21 on May 9, 2003. The lefty with a herky-jerky motion quickly became a phenom, starting 9–1 for the Marlins and earning All-Star selection two months after his debut. He finished the season 14–6 with a 3.30 ERA and the NL Rookie of the Year Award, capping the year with three scoreless relief appearances in Miami's World Series victory.

Willis had a monster year in 2005. He went 22–10 with a 2.63 ERA for the otherwise sub-.500 Marlins, topping the NL in wins, complete games, and shutouts (5). He finished second behind Chris Carpenter in Cy Young Award voting, and won the Warren Spahn Award as the majors' top southpaw.

Willis was also an excellent hitter. In one stretch over 2003–04, including post-season, he had 10 straight hits. In 2005, Willis became the first pitcher since 1973 to bat seventh in the lineup. He hit .244 lifetime with six triples and nine homers in 389 at bats.

But D-Train's pitching went downhill after '05. He slipped to 12–12 and 10–15 the next two years before signing a lucrative contract with the Tigers. Willis then was a combined 4–15 between 2008 and 2011, shuffling from the Tigers to the Diamondbacks and Reds, then the systems of the Phillies, Orioles, Angels, and Giants. He had a drunk driving arrest in 2006, suffered two knee injuries in '08, and spent most of '09 on the DL with an anxiety disorder. D-Train's pro career ended in April 2014, and he finished with a 72–69 major league record.

Don Wilson—On September 28, 1974, Astros fireballer Don Wilson two-hit the Braves, 5–0, in what proved to be his final major league appearance. He retired the last 10 batters of the game, with only one hitting the ball out of the infield. Ninety-nine days later, Wilson was found in his garage, dead at 29 of monoxide poisoning, an apparent suicide.

Wilson showed flashes of brilliance during his nine-year career. As a rookie, he no-hit the Braves, 2–0, on June 18, 1967. On May 1, 1969, he did the same to the Reds, 4–0, en route to a 16-win season with 235 strikeouts. Wilson had his best year in 1971, going 16–10 with a 2.45 ERA, topping the NL in opposing batting average, and earning an All-Star selection. In his final month in the majors, on September 4, 1974, Wilson had a chance for a third no-no. He held the Reds hitless for eight innings, but manager Preston Gomez removed him for a pinch-hitter; reliever Mike Cosgrove gave up a hit and the Astros lost, 2–1.

Wilson finished 104–92 with a 3.15 ERA.

Jimmy Wood—Though he was 28 when baseball's first professional league was formed, Wood was a star in the first three seasons of the National Association. He batted .332 with speed and power for four teams from 1871–73. But he developed a leg abscess in the latter year and attempted to lance it himself with a pen-knife. A severe infection ensued, and he wound up losing the leg. Wood remained in baseball as a manager the next two years.[98]

Kerry Wood—As with teammate Mark Prior, Kerry Wood's arm and career were derailed by overuse at a young age.

On May 6, 1998, in just his fifth big league start, Wood matched the major league record of 20 strikeouts in a game, one which has been called the best ever pitched; besides the K's, he allowed just one scratch hit and zero walks. It was one of eight outings that year in which he threw at least 120 pitches at age 20. Despite missing the last month of the season due to a "dead arm," Wood was named NL Rookie of the Year on the strength of a 13–6 record and 233 K's in only 167 innings.

In Wood's first start the following spring training, he went down with a torn ulnar collateral ligament, requiring Tommy John surgery, and he missed the entire season. Cubs manager Jim Riggleman accepted blame for overusing the young pitcher, but Wood's physique and mechanics were also factors. He carried a lot of weight and threw across his body.

Wood came back with three straight strong campaigns in 2001–03, striking out 700 batters in 599 innings. Included were a league-leading 266 K's in '03, a year in which he also led the NL in total pitches (4,007), and finished second to Prior with 111 pitches per start.

But Wood started only 36 more games in the majors after that season, retiring on May 18, 2012, as an oft-injured bullpen man. He never won more than 14 games in a season, winding up 86–75, with a 3.67 ERA, and 839 days on the DL. He received two votes in 2018 Hall of Fame balloting.

David Wright—At age 27, Wright had earned five straight All-Star selections, two Silver Slugger Awards, and two Gold Gloves at third base. The 10 most similar players to Wright at that point include five Hall of Famers. But an injury early the next season set his career on a downward spiral.

On April 19, 2011, Wright got into a collision with the Astros' Carlos Lee. After playing in pain for the next four weeks, Wright was diagnosed with a stress fracture in his lower back, and missed more than two months. In 2015 he would be diagnosed with chronic spinal stenosis, a narrowing of the spinal canal.

Wright returned to have a couple more All-Star seasons in 2012–13, but his playing time and production began a steep decline thereafter. He wound up playing only 77 games after his 32nd birthday, walking out two years early on a lucrative contract, and finishing with 242 homers and a .296 average. He becomes eligible for the Hall of Fame in 2024.

---

98. Overfield, Joe. "Tragedies and Shortened Careers." *Total Baseball*, 1989.

Appendix B
Players Who Made the Hall of Fame Despite Careers Cut Short

Many players made it to Cooperstown despite their careers being delayed, interrupted, or prematurely ended. Following are 16 of the most notable cases:

Roy Campanella—On January 29, 1958, the Dodgers' three-time MVP suffered a broken neck in an auto accident, leaving him permanently paralyzed. At 36, Campy had just completed his tenth season with Brooklyn (not to mention a decade in the Negro leagues before that), ensuring Hall of Fame eligibility; he was elected in 1969. It's not likely that Campanella would have added much to his résumé even without the accident; he was clearly in decline (just 85 hits in 1956 and 80 in '57), and the Dodgers' 1958 move to Los Angeles from hitter-friendly Ebbets Field would not have reversed that trend.

Orlando Cepeda—As of his 27th birthday in 1964, Cepeda's career Triple Crown stats (221, 743, .310) were almost identical to Hank Aaron's (219, 743, .318) at the same age. But a serious knee problem cost Cepeda most of the 1965 season, and hampered him the rest of his career. He finished with roughly half of Aaron's career home run total, but enough credentials to earn Veterans' Committee selection in 1999.

Roberto Clemente—On September 30, 1972, Clemente smacked a long double against Jon Matlack for his 3000th career hit, becoming just the 11th player to reach that milestone. Nobody knew it would also be his final hit (though he was hinting at retirement). Three months later, Clemente was killed in a plane crash while on a mercy mission. The Hall of Fame's Board of Directors waived the five-year-wait rule for Clemente, and he received 393 of a possible 424 votes in a special election whose results were announced on March 20, 1973.

Mickey Cochrane—When Cochrane hit a game-tying solo home run off the Yankees' Bump Hadley in the third inning on May 25, 1937, nobody realized it would be the final official at bat of Mickey's career. At 34, the Tigers' catcher-manager was still near the top of his game. The homer had brought his season average over the .300 mark for the ninth time in his 13 big league seasons. Cochrane was regarded as the best all-around catcher in the sport, probably the best of all time.

Two innings later, Cochrane lay prostrate at Yankee Stadium's home plate, his skull fractured in three places. A Hadley fastball on a 3-1 count (3-2, by some sources) had sailed inside, crashing into Cochrane's temple with a sickening sound. "Good God Almighty," Mickey mumbled. "I lost the ball." He would battle for his life, slipping into and out of consciousness for some 10 days before recuperating. Except for a one-inning stint in a 1938 exhibition game, Mickey Cochrane would never play again.

The Tigers were battling the Yankees in the pennant race as the two teams began a crucial series on that fateful date. "This first game is all-important," said Cochrane. "If we can win it we'll take the series." He had respect for the opposing pitcher that day. "He has everything," Cochrane had once said of Hadley. "A fastball that buzzes by your chin, and a curve that has you breaking your back when you swing at it." When Cochrane poled a Hadley pitch into the right field stands, the score stood at 1-1. It was the same when Mickey batted two innings later. "I relaxed, thinking it would go by," Cochrane later said about the fateful pitch. "All of a sudden I lost sight of it.... I think I could have played four or five more years, but there's nothing that can be done about that now."

Mickey finished his career with a .320 lifetime average. He was inducted into the Hall of Fame in 1947, just the third catcher so honored.

Dizzy Dean—In a heavy-hitting era, Dean emerged as arguably the best pitcher in the game. After two solid seasons, Diz erupted for a 30-7 record at age 24 in 1934, earning the NL MVP Award. He followed with 28 and 24 wins the next two years, finishing second in MVP voting both times; before Barry Bonds, nobody had a higher percentage of MVP votes over a three-year span.

But things went swiftly downhill after Dean suffered a broken toe in the 1937 All-Star Game. Conventional wisdom is that Diz tried to come back too soon and, favoring his toe, injured his arm at age 27. He won only 17 more big league games.

Craig Wright makes a persuasive case that Dean's arm was already on the way out even before the toe injury, a victim of overuse at a young age. Diz was already complaining of soreness and pitching erratically. "The injury was a minor contributor at most in the emergence of Dean's shoulder problem, which had the classic symptoms of a rotator cuff injury," writes Wright. "It is far more likely that Dizzy was simply another case of a great young pitcher being pushed too hard, and breaking down in what was expected to be mid-career."[1]

Dean did pitch in parts of 12 seasons, earning 1953 Hall of Fame selection for his peak value—and his fame.

Dizzy's Daily Double

This book contains many references and comparisons to Dizzy Dean, he of the National League's last 30-win season in 1934. Dean's feat ultimately was made possible by two dubious decisions within a few hours, courtesy of NL President John Heydler (in his final season on the job). Before the game of June 27, 1934, a telegram from Heydler arrived, reversing the official scorer's decision in the June 23 game. Then Dean went out and "beat" the Dodgers that day—or, at least he was awarded the victory after the scorer consulted with Heydler.

There were no formal rules governing pitchers' wins and losses until 1950, but 1934 scorers almost invariably followed the same guidelines used today. Here are the details of the two games, neither of which would have resulted in a "W" for Dean under modern rules:

June 23: Bill Hallahan, having hurled the sixth inning and given up one run, was pinch-hit for by Pat Crawford in the bottom of the inning. Crawford's single capped a five-run rally that gave the Cards a 5–4 lead. Dean came in (in what today would be called a "save" situation) and shut down Brooklyn the rest of the way. The scorer gave the win to Hallahan, but in stepped Heydler. His telegram of the 27th read, "Dean pitched great ball during three innings to protect one-run lead and is winner. Hallahan pitched one inning rather poorly and did not stand to lose the game even had he continued." Huh?

June 27: Dean left the game with two out in the top of the ninth, two runners on base, a 7–7 score, and slugger Mel Ott up. Jim Mooney came in, retired Ott, and watched as Bill Delancey hit a homer in the bottom of the ninth to win it for the Cards, which under modern rules would give the win to Mooney. But Mike Haley, the same scorer who had been overruled earlier that day, gave the win to Dean and asked Heydler to review his decision. Heydler agreed.[2]

---

1. Deane, Bill. *Baseball Myths*. Latham, MD: Scarecrow Press, Inc., 2012, p. 74–75.
2. Simons, Herbert. "Did Dizzy Dean Win 30—or Only 28—in 1934?" *Baseball Digest*, October-November 1968, p. 81–84.

Ed Delahanty—On July 9, 1903, Ed Delahanty's mangled body was found at the bottom of Niagara Falls. He had last been seen alive a week earlier, when he was evicted from a train crossing the Niagara River, due to drunk and disorderly conduct. Thus ended the life and career of arguably the greatest slugger of the first 30 years of major league baseball.

Delahanty had played 16 years in the majors, 13 of them with the Philadelphia Phillies. He topped .400 in three seasons, had the NL's best slugging percentage four times, and hit four home runs in one 1896 game. After joining the American League at age 34 in 1902, Big Ed promptly led the fledgling circuit in doubles, batting (.376), OBP, and slugging. He was hitting .333 in 1903, and had hit safely in his last 16 games, going 26-for-62 (.419) with seven doubles.

Delahanty finished with a .346 lifetime batting average. He was elected to the Hall of Fame in 1945.

Ed Delahanty, shown early in his career (c. 1888), was better known for hitting the ball than picking it up. He batted .346 for his career, topping .400 three times. Library of Congress.

Lou Gehrig—After more than a decade as one of the game's most prodigious sluggers, Lou Gehrig had an off-year in 1938. People assumed it was the normal aging pattern of a 35-year-old athlete. But by the next spring, he could barely compete, forcing him to end his 2130-game playing streak and seek answers at the Mayo Clinic. The verdict: Larrupin' Lou had amyotrophic lateral sclerosis, and his career was over. Two years later, he would be dead of the ailment known ever since as Lou Gehrig's Disease.

Gehrig finished his career with 493 homers, 1995 RBI, and a slash line of .340/.447/.632. He was elected to the brand new Hall of Fame by a special decision of the BBWAA on December 7, 1939. Shortly after, Gehrig became the first player ever to have his uniform number retired.

Lou Gehrig (c. 1930) was "the Pride of the Yankees." Library of Congress.

Hank Greenberg—Greenberg's career was limited to just 1394 games, but he was one of baseball's best sluggers of all-time. Hank won the AL MVP Award after driving in 170 runs at age 24 in 1935. He then broke his wrist the following April, missing almost all of the heaviest-hitting season in AL history. Greenberg came back to knock in 183 runs in 1937, hit 58 homers in '38, and win his second MVP Award in '40.

Greenberg became the first major leaguer to be drafted during World War II (even before the country joined the fray), and nobody missed more playing time because of it. He joined the U.S. Army in May 1941, not to return to the majors until July 1945. Hank helped the Tigers to the world championship that year, led the league with 44 homers in '46, and retired to start a front-office career a year later. Until David Ortiz in 2015–16, nobody had ever hit more than Greenberg's 69 homers in his final two seasons. Hank was elected to the Hall in 1956.

Addie Joss—Joss was one of the game's best pitchers in the first decade of the 20th century. He debuted with a one-hitter on April 26, 1902, and later hurled two no-hitters, including a perfect game on October 2, 1908. Joss topped the AL in ERA in 1904 and '08, and in wins in '07. Through 1910, he had a 160–97 record (.623) with a 1.89 ERA, the second-lowest in baseball history.

But on the eve of his tenth season, Joss was stricken with tubercular meningitis, and he died suddenly on April 14, 1911, the day before his 31st birthday.

Joss was made ineligible for the Hall of Fame in 1946, when the rule requiring 10 seasons of playing time was added; Joss had only nine. But the

Hall's Board of Directors waived it to allow Joss's election by the Veterans' Committee in 1978.

Ralph Kiner—Kiner's major league career was delayed by three years of military service, and was ended at age 32 due to back problems. In between, he just made the 10-year minimum for Hall of Fame eligibility, averaging a record 37 home runs per season.

Kiner led or tied for the NL lead in homers in each of his first seven seasons, 1946–52. Battling chronic sciatica and seeing diminishing production and playing time, he retired just three years later, embarking on a long and colorful broadcasting career. Kiner was elected to the Hall with one vote to spare in 1975, his final try on the BBWAA ballot.

Addie Joss, shown here near the end of his career (1910), is the only man elected to the Hall of Fame as a player, without having played the requisite ten seasons. Library of Congress.

Sandy Koufax—Koufax went just 36–40 over his first six years, but was 129–47 with five ERA titles and three Cy Young Awards in his next six seasons before retiring at age 30 due to an arthritic pitching elbow. He became the youngest man ever elected to the Hall of Fame, receiving the honor in 1972, just 20 days after his 36th birthday.

Conventional wisdom says Koufax was a late bloomer, but his blooming was mostly the product of two environmental factors: his team's move to a great pitcher's park, Dodger Stadium, in 1962 (he had a 1.37 career ERA there, 3.38 elsewhere), and the expanded strike zone of 1963–68, which extended to the top of the batters' shoulders.

Kirby Puckett—Puckett's career came to an end on September 28, 1995, when he was beaned by Dennis Martinez, breaking his jaw. The following spring, Puckett was diagnosed with glaucoma—reportedly unrelated to the beaning—and was forced to retire at age 35. He finished with a .318 average and 2304 hits in 12 seasons, an average of 192 per year, and was elected to the Hall of Fame in 2001. He died five years later.

Jackie Robinson—Robinson was already 28 when he broke the long-standing color line in 1947, but still accomplished enough on the field to attain first-ballot Hall of Fame election in 1962. In 10 seasons, Robinson earned Rookie of the Year, an MVP, and six All-Star selections, helping the Dodgers to six NL pennants.

Amos Rusie—Rusie was a dominant pitcher, when he wasn't squabbling with management. At age 24 in 1896, Rusie already owned 198 big league victories and five NL strikeout titles, and was regarded as the biggest box-office draw in the majors. But he and Giants owner Andrew Freedman didn't see eye-to-eye: Freedman had fined Rusie $200 for various transgressions the year before, and now was offering his ace a 20 percent pay-cut (from $3,000 to $2,400) to conform with a salary cap implemented for '96. Rusie refused to sign anything unless his fines were refunded; they weren't and he didn't. Rusie sat out the entire season, and finally initiated a $5,000 lawsuit against the Giants, challenging the reserve clause. The other NL owners pooled their funds to settle the dispute out of court, and famous Amos was back on the mound in 1897–98. But another disagreement with the bitter Freedman led to Rusie's skipping the 1899 and 1900 seasons. Traded to Cincinnati for an unproven prospect named Christy Mathewson, Rusie just didn't have it any more. After having amassed 246 career victories by age 27, he had zero thereafter. He was elected to the Hall in 1977.

In his heyday, Amos Rusie (shown in 1895) was the biggest drawing card in the majors. Library of Congress.

Ted Williams—Nobody missed more playing time due to military service than Williams: he spent the entire 1943–45 campaigns in the U.S. Navy air corps, and returned to action with the Marines during the Korean Conflict, costing him most of the 1952–53 seasons. Plugging in normal numbers for the missing time, Williams might easily have become the all-time leader in runs (2392), RBI (2409), and walks (2713), winning two more Triple Crowns to add to the two he actually won. But then, if he hadn't missed those years, he probably would not have played until 1960, as he did. Williams was all set to retire after the 1954 season, until a fan pointed out that his career numbers would not rank very high at that point. He was elected to the Hall of Fame in 1966.

Ross Youngs—Youngs, a good but not great player, died tragically of a kidney ailment at age 30 in 1927. He made it to the Hall in 1972, at a time the Veterans' Committee was making a lot of questionable selections. Youngs had played in exactly 10 seasons, batting .322—but at a time when league averages were in the .280s and .290s. He led the NL in runs and doubles once each.

Ross Youngs, shown in 1920, batted .322 lifetime before his death at age 30. Library of Congress.

Bibliography

Books

Ankiel, Rick, and Tim Brown. *The Phenomenon: Pressure, the Yips, and the Pitch That Changed My Life*. New York: Public Affairs, 2017.
Appel, Marty. *Yesterday's Heroes*. New York: William Morrow, 1988.
Bissinger, Buzz. *Three Nights in August: Strategy, Heartbreak and Joy Inside the Mind of a Manager*. New York: Houghton Mifflin Company, 2006.
Bucek, Jeanine, editorial director. *The Baseball Encyclopedia*. New York: Macmillan, 1996.
Carter, Craig, editor. *Daguerreotypes*. St. Louis: The Sporting News Publishing Co., 1990.
Charlton, James, editor. *The Baseball Chronology*. New York: Macmillan Publishing Co., 1991.
Constitution and Playing Rules of the National League of Professional Base Ball Clubs. Chicago: A. G. Spalding & Brothers, 1877.
Deane, Bill. *Award Voting*. Kansas City, MO: Society for American Baseball Research, 1988.
Deane, Bill. *Baseball Myths*. Lanham, MD: Scarecrow Press, Inc., 2012.
Graczyk, Wayne. *Americans in Japan*. Self-published, 1986.
Gregory, Corinne Taylor. *Once There Was a Dam*. Beaver Dam, KY, self-published, 1982.
Gutman, Bill. *Fisk * Rose * Bonds * Cedeno*. New York: Grosset & Dunlap, Inc., 1974.
James, Bill. *The New Bill James Historical Baseball Abstract*. New York: Free Press, 2003.
James, Bill, and Rob Neyer. *The Neyer/James Guide to Pitchers*. New York: Fireside, 2004.
Johnson, Lloyd, and Miles Wolff, editors. *The Encyclopedia of Minor League Baseball*. Durham, NC: Baseball America, Inc., 1993.
Johnson, William H. *Hal Trosky, a Baseball Biography*. Jefferson, NC: McFarland & Co., Inc., Publishers, 2017.
Jones, David, editor. *Deadball Stars of the American League*. Dulles, Va.: Potomac Books, Inc., 2006.
Kahn, Roger. *The Era*. New York: Ticknor & Fields, 1993.
McLain, Denny, with Eli Zaret. *I Told You I Wasn't Perfect*. Chicago: Triumph Books, 2007.
Michelson, Court. *Michelson's Book of World Baseball Records*. Chicago: Adams Press, 1985.
Neft, David, Richard M. Cohen, and Michael L. Neft. *The Sports Encyclopedia: Baseball*. New York: St. Martin's Griffin, 2000.
Neft, David S., and Richard M. Cohen. *The World Series*. New York: St. Martin's Press, 1990.
Nowlin, Bill, and Clayton Trutor, editors. *Overcoming Adversity: Baseball's Tony Conigliaro Award*. Phoenix: Society for American Baseball Research, Inc., 2017.
Pietrusza, David, Matthew Silverman, and Michael Gershman, editors. *Baseball: The Biographical Encyclopedia*. Kingston, NY: Total Sports Illustrated, 2000.
Reichler, Joseph L., editor. *The Great All-Time Baseball Record Book*. New York: Macmillan Publishing Co., 1993.
Rice, Ed. *Baseball's First Indian*. Tidemark Press, 2003.
Schechter, Gabriel. *Unhittable!* Los Gatos, CA: Charles April Publications, 2002.

Simon, Tom, editor. *Deadball Stars of the National League*. Washington, D.C.: Brassey's, Inc., 2004.
Society for American Baseball Research. *Minor League Baseball Stars*. Manhattan, KS: Ag Press, Inc., 1984.
Thorn, John, Phil Birnbaum, and Bill Deane, editors. *Total Baseball*. Wilmington, DE: SPORT Media Publishing, Inc., 2004.
Tiemann, Robert L., and Mark Rucker, editors. *Nineteenth Century Stars*. Kansas City, MO: Society for American Baseball Research, 1989.
Wood, Gerald C. *Joe Wood: The Biography of a Baseball Legend*. Lincoln, NE: University of Nebraska Press, 2013.

Newspapers and Periodicals

Albany (N.Y.) Times-Union
American Magazine
Arizona Diamondbacks Media Guide
Arizona Republic
Baltimore Sun
Bangor Daily News
Baseball America
Baseball Digest
Baseball Magazine
Baseball Quarterly
Baseball Research Journal
Beacon (OH) Journal
The Bill James Baseball Abstract
Binghamton (N.Y.) Evening Press
Bison Tales
Black Sports
Boston Globe
Boston Herald American
Boston Sunday Post
Brooklyn Eagle
Brooklyn Times Union
California Angels Media Guide
Chicago Daily News
Chicago Sun-Times
Chicago Tribune
Chicago Tribune Magazine
Christian Science Monitor
Cincinnati Enquirer
Cincinnati Post
Cincinnati Post & Times-Star
The Citizen
Cleveland Plain Dealer
Cleveland Plain Dealer Magazine
Collier's
The Desert Sun
Detroit Free Press
Detroit News
East Valley Tribune
Elmira Advertiser
Fresno Bee
Guideposts
Hartford Courant
Herald-Banner
The Hill-Top
Houston Astros Media Guide
Information Please Sports Almanac
Inside Sports
Kaleidoscope
Kansas City Star
Kansas City Times
Look
Lorain (Ohio) Morning Journal
Los Angeles Herald Examiner
Los Angeles Times
Miami Marlins Media Guide
Milwaukee Brewers Media Guide
Nashville Sports Weekly
The National Pastime
The National Sports Daily
New York Clipper
New York Daily News
New York Herald Tribune
New York Journal
New York Post
New York Sunday News Magazine
New York Times
New York Times Magazine
New York Tribune
New York World Telegram
New York World Telegram-Star
New York Yankees Press, TV, Radio Guide
Newsday
Nine: A Journal of Baseball History and Social Policy Perspectives
Oneonta (N.Y.) Daily Star
Oriskany Falls (N.Y.) Sentinel
Palm Beach (Fla.) Post
Philadelphia Inquirer
Philadelphia North American
Philadelphia Public Ledger
Pittsburgh Press
Reach's Official Base Ball Guide
Rolling Stone
St. Louis Globe-Democrat
St. Louis Post-Dispatch
San Diego Union-Tribune

Bibliography

San Francisco Chronicle
San Francisco Examiner
Saturday Evening Post
Smithsonian
Spalding's Official Base Ball Guide
SPORT
Sportfolio
The Sporting Life
The Sporting News
The Sporting News Baseball Yearbook
Sports Collectors Digest
Sports Illustrated
Springfield (Mass.) Daily News
The Sunday Star
Tampa Times
TV Guide
USA TODAY
Utica (N. Y.) Daily Press
The Utica (N. Y.) Observer-Dispatch
Vice Sports
Washington Post
Washington Star
Wayne Independent (Honesdale, Penn.)

Press Services

American Association
American League Service Bureau
Associated Press
Cincinnati Reds
Cox News Service
Delta State University
Los Angeles Dodgers
St. Louis National Baseball Club
United Feature Syndicate
United Press International

Online Sources

Azcentralsports.com
BaseballsPast.com
BostonHerald.com
ESPN.com
MLB.com
SABR's BioProject
SI.com
Yahoo Sports

Telephone Interviews

Steve Busby, June 9, 2017
Dave "Boo" Ferriss, June 13, 2015
Carlos May, November 21, 2015
Wes Parker, May 17, 2020
Dickie Thon, November 20, 2017

Index

Numbers in **_bold italics_** indicate pages with illustrations

Aaron, Hank 28, 30, 41, 106, 118, 197, 198, 293
Abbott, Jim 219
Abreu, Jose 169
Affleck, Casey 254
Agganis, Harry 219–20
Alexander, Grover 164, 181
Allen, Johnny 182
Allen, Mel 82
Alomar, Roberto 85
Alou, Felipe 7, 29, 220
Alou, Jesus 220
Alou, Matty 220, 230
Alou, Moises 136, 220
Alston, Walter 54, 127, 128, 144, 178
Altuve, Jose 195
Anderson, Sparky 30, 77, 78
Andrews, Dr. James 137
Ankiel, Declan 10
Ankiel, Denise Turton 5, 10
Ankiel, Lory 10
Ankiel, Richard A. "Rick" 5–10, 269
Ankiel, Richard P. 5–6, 8, 10
Ankiel, Ryker 10
Anson, Cap 14, 86, 99, 262
Aparicio, Luis 287, 289
Appling, Luke 94
Arias, Maria 65
Ashburn, Richie 96
Autry, Gene 18

Baker, Dusty 136, 138
Baker, Frank "Home Run" 21, 49, 157
Baker, Gene 127
Baldwin, Charles "Lady" 220–21, ***221***
Bancroft, Dave 38
Bang, Ed 20
Banks, Ernie 83, 85, 130, 280
Barnes, Charles R. "Ross" 3, 10–15

Barnes, Joseph 11
Barnes, Mary Weller 11
Barrett, Charley 139
Barrow, Ed 175
Bartman, Steve 136
Baseball: Individual Strategy and Team Play 48
Bauer, Hank 165
Bavasi, Buzzie 187
Beane, Billy 276
Bearden, Gene 221–22
Beating the Odds: The Al Rosen Story 161
Beazley, Johnny 222–25, 287
Beazley, Terry Morton 224
Bechtel, George 241
Bedient, Hugh 212, 213
Bell, Buddy 168
Bell, Cool Papa 124
Belle, Albert J. (Joey) 225–26
Bench, Johnny 113, 255
Bender, Chief 46, 171, 209
Bender, Sheldon 107
Berger, Heine 163
Berra, Yogi 157–58
Betts, Mookie 55, 141
The Bill James Historical Baseball Abstract 237
Black Sox Scandal 233–34, 246, 259, 263, 290
Blades, Ray 223
Blair, Paul 226–27
Blanks, Larvell 78
Blass, Steve 2, 227, 266
Bloomer Girls 207
Blue, Vida 26, 43, 121, 228, 283
Bluege, Ossie 193, 194
Blyleven, Bert 23
Boggess, Dusty 143
Boggs, Wade 157

305

Index

Bond, Walt 189
Bonds, Barry 2, 89, 226, 284, 294
Bonham, Ernest "Tiny" 228–29
Boras, Scott 6
Bostock, Annie T. 15, 17
Bostock, Lyman W., Jr. 3, 15–19, 65
Bostock, Lyman W., Sr. 15
Bostock, Yuovene B. 16, 18, 19
Boudreau, Lou 85, 117–18
Bowens, Sam 233
Boyd, Jake 98–99
Bradley, Anna B.K. 22
Bradley, Anna "Nan" 22
Bradley, Norman 22
Bradley, William J. "Bill" 20–22, *20*
Bragan, Bobby 27
Branca, Ralph 126
Brett, George 17, 157
Bristol, Dave 107
Brock, Lou 30, 83
Broeg, Bob 271–72
Brouthers, Dan 100, 133–34
Brown, Willard 185
Browning, Tom 81
Bunning, Jim 205, 267
Burkett, Jesse 171, 172
Burleson, Rick 187
Burns, Britt 229
Burns, Tom 99
Busby, Betty 23
Busby, Jim 23
Busby, Marvin 23
Busby, Melissa 25
Busby, Michelle 25
Busby, Mike 23
Busby, Pam 27
Busby, Sara 27
Busby, Stephanie 25
Busby, Steven L. "Steve" 3, 23–28
Busby, Steven, Jr. 27
Busby, Susan 23
Busby, Terri 25
Bush, George H.W. 218
Byrne, Bobby 213, 214
Byrne, Tommy 96

Cabell, Enos 149, 150
Cabrera, Miguel 28, 41, 63, 198
Camilli, Dolf 140
Campanella, Roy 124, 125, 178, 293
Campaneris, Bert 16
Campanis, Al 53
Campbell, Jim 75
Carew, Rod 16, 18, 112, 266
Carey, Max 156
Carlton, Steve 23, 64, 104, 251
Carmichael, John P. 181

Carpenter, Chris 229, 291
Carter, Gary 158
Carty, Rico 2, 229–30
Caruthers, Bob 49, 230–31, *231*
Cavarretta, Phil 140
Cedeño, Cesar E. 28–34
Cedeño, Cora 29, 30, 32
Cedeño, Diogene 29
Cedeño, Juanita 29
Cedeño, Milagros 29
Cepeda, Orlando 121, 130, 198, 226, 293
Chambliss, Chris 149
Chance, Dean 231–32
Chandler, Happy 289
Chandler, Spud 232
Chapman, Barbara J. 34
Chapman, Everette 34
Chapman, Kathleen M.D. 36, 38
Chapman, Rae-Marie 38
Chapman, Raymond J. "Ray" 34–39, *35*, 161, 269
Charboneau, Joe 232–33
Chinea, Orlando 62
Cicotte, Ed 233–34, 261, 263
Clarke, Fred 141, 172, 193
Clarkson, John 87, 100, 246
Clayton, Royal 203
Clemens, Roger 2, 65, 79, 204, 205, 211, 276
Clemente, Roberto 30, 130, 189, 264, 293–94
Cobb, Ty 14, 35, 58, 100–01, *259*, 260, 261, 262
Cochrane, Mickey 294
Colavito, Rocky 167
Cole, King 234–35, *235*
Coleman, Jerry 41
Coleman, Joe 72
Collins, Eddie 36, 195, 260
Collins, Hubert "Hub" 235
Collins, Jimmy 20
Comiskey, Charles 263
Comiskey, J. Louis 140, 183–84, 224
Cone, David 150
Conigliaro, Anthony R. "Tony" 1, 39–44, 191, 228, 229, 236, 245, 259, 281
Conigliaro, Billy 39, 42, 43
Conigliaro, Ritchie 39
Conigliaro, Salvatore 39, 43–44
Conigliaro, Theresa 39
Conkling, Roscoe 11
Contreras, Jose 62
Coombs, Bobby 47
Coombs, John W. "Jack" 44–50, *45*, 210
Coombs, Mary E. 47
Cooper, Bill 107
Cooper, Mort 223, 224
Corcoran, Gertrude 52

Corcoran, Lawrence J. "Larry" 50–53, *51*
Corcoran, Michael 52
Cosgrove, Mike 291
Coveleski, Stan 87
Craig, Roger 146
Crane, Sam 14
Crawford, Pat 295
Crawford, Sam 49, 102
Creighton, Jim 235–36
Crews, Tim 277
Cronin, Joe 165, 194, 195
Cuccinello, Tony 111
Cuellar, Mike 26, 121

Dahlen, Bill 195
Daily, Hugh "One Arm" 236
Daley, Arthur 92
Dalkowski, Steve 236
Dallas 150
Daniel, Dan 92, 103, 225
Dark, Alvin 221
Davis, Carlyn 54
Davis, Carol 57
Davis, Chris 63
Davis, Eric 236–37
Davis, George 102, 172
Davis, Harry 172
Davis, Herman T. 53
Davis, Herman T. "Tommy," II 53–58, 144
Davis, Herman T., III 54
Davis, Lauren 54
Davis, Leslie 54
Davis, Shirley Johnson 54
Davis, Willie 53, 237
Dean, James 1
Dean, Jay "Dizzy" 7, 49, 119, 120, 121, 124, 165, 177, 237, 238–39, 294–95
Dean, Paul "Daffy" 223, 237–40
Deford, Frank 2
de la Cruz, Altagracia 30–31
Delahanty, Ed 20, 172, 296, *296*
Delancey, Bill 240, 295
Devlin, Jim 240–41, 295
Diaz, Loui 64
Dickey, Bill 94, 96, 223
DiMaggio, Dominic 241, 280
DiMaggio, Joe 30, 41, 89, 92, 95, 96, 100, 102, 195, 198, 200, 223, 241, 248, 289
Doerr, Bobby 40, 68, 83, 85, 94
Donlin, Turkey Mike 241–42, *241*
Doyle, Dennis 84–85
Drabowsky, Moe 40
Dravecky, Dave 2, 242
Dressen, Chuck 118
Drew, J.D. 6
Dropo, Walt 156
Drysdale, Don 55, 121

Duffy, Hugh 100, 172
Dunlap, Fred "Sure Shot" 242–43, *243*
Dunn, Jim 216
Durocher, Leo 30, 139, 143

Easter, Luke 243–44
Eisenhower, Dwight 128
Eisenreich, Jim 244–45
Elberfeld, Norman "Kid" 193
Ellis, Sammy 81
Ellsworth, Dick 105, 106
Embree, Red 68
Esasky, Nick 245
Evans, Billy 181

Fairly, Ron 55
Falls, Joe 72
Fear Strikes Out 280
Feller, Bob 22, 51, 68, 94, 106, 121, 163, 165, 183, 209, 233, 252, 271
Felsch, Oscar "Happy" 245–46, *245*
Ferguson, Bob 133
Ferguson, Charlie 58–61, *59*
Ferguson, Mary S. 60
Fernandez, José D. 61–65
Fernandez, Penelope Jo 65
Ferriss, David 69
Ferriss, David M. "Boo" 3, 66–70, 178, 258
Ferriss, Lellie 66
Ferriss, Margaret 69
Ferriss, Miriam I. 69, 70
Ferriss, William D. 66
Fidrych, Ann P. 75
Fidrych, Carol Ann 71
Fidrych, Jessica 75
Fidrych, Lorie Jean 71
Fidrych, Mark S. 70–76
Fidrych, Paul 71, 74
Fidrych, Paula 71
Fidrych, Virginia 71
Finley, Charlie 121, 228
Fishel, Bob 160
Fisk, Carlton 149
Fitzgerald, John "Honey Fitz" 212
Fleitz, David 173, 176
Flick, Elmer 97
Flynn, Jocko 246
Ford, Gerald 73, 218
Ford, Whitey 79, 150, 164–65, 267
Forsch, Ken 187
Fosse, Ray 246–47
Fowler, Bob 17
Foxx, Jimmie 200
Freedman, Andrew 299
Fresh Yankee 96–97
Frey, Lonny 139
Frick, Ford 117, 127, 263

Frisch, Frank 238
Furcal, Rafael 7

Gagne, Eric 136
Galvin, Pud 50
Garcia, Mike 279
Garciaparra, Nomar 2, 247–48
Garciaparra, Ramon 248
Garland, Wayne 248
Garner, Phil 189
Gehrig, Lou 93, 96, 158, 198, 199, 200, 255, 296, *297*
Giamatti, Bart 217, 233, 234
Gibson, Bob 64, 87, 107, 108, 119, 120, 150, 205
Gibson, Josh 124
Gibson, Kirk 206
Giles, Marcus 136, 137
Gillette, Gary 220
Gillick, Pat 29
Giselman, William 99
The Glory of Their Times 217
Glynn, Bill 158
The Godfather 40
Gomez, Lefty 79, 90, 182, 183
Gomez, Preston 291
Gonzalez, Mike 223
Gooden, Dwight "Doc" 121, 135, 249
Gordon, Joe 94, 167
Goslin, Goose 141
Graney, Jack 37
Greenberg, Hank 156–57, 165, 200, 297
Gregg, Vean 249–50, *249*
Grich, Bobby 187
Griffey, Ken, Jr. 28
Griffith, Clark 100, 102, 211
Gross, Milton 90
Grove, Lefty 163, 182, 183, 211
Gruzdis, Jimmy 153
Guerrero, Pedro 250
Guilfoile, Bill 234
Gullett, Buford 76
Gullett, Cathy H. 77
Gullett, Donald E. "Don" 76–80, 108, 121
Gullett, Donald, Jr. 77
Gullett, Lettie 76
Gullett, Tracy 77
Gutteridge, Don 111, 112

Hack, Stan 140
Hadley, Bump 294
Hahn, Frank "Noodles" 250–52
Haley, Mike 295
Hall, George 252
Halladay, Roy 282
Hallahan, Bill 295
Hamilton, Billy 49, 172

Hamilton, Jack 41
Hamilton, Josh 252–54
Hamilton, Tom 168
Handley, Gene 83
Hanlon, Ned 281
Harder, Mel 165
Haren, Dan 206, 276
Harper, Bryce 41
Harridge, Will 199
Harris, Bucky 194
Harvey, Ervin "Zaza" 254
Harwell, Ernie 73
Hawkins, Joan 18
Hawpe, Brad 137
Heath, Jeff 91
Heinbechner, Bruce 19
Helms, Tommy 31
Hendrix, Jimi 1
Henrich, Tommy 92
Herman, Billy 195, 266
Hernandez, Livan 62
Hernandez, Orlando "El Duque" 62
Herrmann, Ed 247
Hershberger, Willard 90, 254–55
Hershiser, Orel 204
Hertzel, Bob 146
Herzog, Whitey 27
Heydler, John 295
Hite, Mabel 242
Hobbs, Roy 233
Hoen, Dr. Thomas L. 94
Hogan, Jeff 71
Hogg, Bill 21
Holland, John 85
Holliday, James W. "Bug" 255
Hollocher, Charlie 255–57, *256*
Hornsby, Rogers 115
Houk, Ralph 72, 96
House, Tom 135
Howard, Bruce 117
Howard, Frank 55, 144
Howe, Art 276
Howsam, Bob 107
Howser, Dick 135
Hoy, William "Dummy" 257, *257*
Hoyt, LaMarr 258
Hubbell, Carl 23
Hubbs, Dorothy 82
Hubbs, Eulis 82
Hubbs, Gary 82
Hubbs, Keith 82
Hubbs, Kenneth D. "Ken" 1, 81–86
Hubbs, Kirk 82
Hubbs, Kraig 82
Hudson, Tim 276
Hughson, Tex 258
Hunter, Catfish 18, 25–26

Index

Hutchinson, Fred 42
Hutchison, Helen S. 86
Hutchison, the Rev. William 86
Hutchison, William F. "Bill" 86–88, 171
Hyland, Dr. Robert F. 240, 256

Irvin, Monte 30, 185
Irwin, Art 60

Jackson, Bo 259
Jackson, Joe 2, 233, 234, 248, 259–61, *259*, 290
Jackson, Reggie 17, 18, 149, 247
Jackson, Travis 195
Jalil, Abdul 18
James, Bill 3, 72, 147, 148, 157, 188, 233, 237, 247–48
Janvrin, Hal 215
Jenkins, Fergie 23, 25, 26, 64, 104
Jennings, Hugh 175
Jensen, Jackie 261
Jeter, Derek 6, 187, 204, 247–48
Jobe, Dr. Frank 27, 64, 79
Jocketty, Walt 6–7
John, Elton 73
John, Tommy 8, 64, 78, 292
Johnson, Ban 37
Johnson, Nick 220
Johnson, Randy 7, 63, 150, 203, 205
Johnson, Walter 52, 64, 106, 120, 165, 210–11, 212, 214
Jones, Sam 165
Joplin, Janis 1
Jordan, Pat 8
Joss, Addie 21–22, 65, 210, 297–98, *298*
Joyce, Bill 261

Kaat, Jim 26
Kahn, Roger 143, 144
Kaline, Al 28, 100–01, 102, 121
Kauff, Bennie 261–62, *262*
Kauffman, Ewing 28
Keefe, Tim 49, 87
Keeler, Willie 21, 58, 172
Keller, Charles E. "Charlie," II 89–97
Keller, Charles, III 91, 96
Keller, Donald L. "Don" 91, 96
Keller, Frank 89
Keller, Hal 89
Keller, Hugh 89
Keller, Martha Jean 91
Keller, Martha L.W. 91, 97
Kelley, Joe 172
Kelly, Don 158
Kelly, George 99
Kelly, Mary 99
Kelly, Father Thomas 162, 166

Keltner, Ken 154, 155
Kennedy, Bob 81, 84, 85
Kennedy, John F. 1, 212
Kerlan, Dr. Robert 56, 64
Kerr, Dickey 262–63
Kile, Darryl 7, 150, 264
Killefer, Bill 256–57
Kilroy, Matt 264, *264*
Kiner, Ralph 30, 156, 159, 298
King (Koenig), Charles F. "Silver" 264–65, *265*
King Kong 90
Kingman, Dave "Kong" 265
Kittle, Hub 146
Klein, Chuck 55
Kluszewski, Ted 30
Knoblauch, Chuck 266
Kosco, Andy 122
Koufax, Sandy 51, 104, 105, 106, 108, 119, 124, 150, 202, 298
Krause, Harry 266–67, *266*
Kuhn, Bowie 121, 197, 228
Kurkjian, Tim 136
Kusick, Joe 71

Lajoie, Napoleon "Nap" 172, 173–74, 175, 201, 210
Lambert, Dr. Claude 111
Lamon, Pam 32–33
Landis, Kenesaw M. 139, 262, 290
Lane, Frank "Trader" 167
Lange, Charles 98
Lange, Grace A.G. 99
Lange, Mary K. 98
Lange, Mona V. 99
Lange, Sarah G. 99
Lange, William A. "Bill" 97–100
Lange, William, Jr. 99
Lannin, Joe 215
Largent, Mr. & Mrs. Roy 181
Larkin, Frank "Terry" 267
LaRussa, Tony 5, 8, 9
Lary, Frank 267
Lasorda, Tommy 178
Latman, Barry 167
Lebovitz, Hal 165
Lee, Carlos 292
Lee, Spike 130
Lee, Thornton 194
Lemon, Bob 160, 165, 167
Lent, Cassidy 3
Leonard, Buck 124
Lewis, Carol Lee 103
Lewis, Frances O. 103
Lewis, John K. "Buddy" 100–04, 194, 287
Lewis, John K., Sr. 101
Lewis, John M. 103

Lewis, Kelly 103
Lincecum, Tim 205
Lindstrom, Fred 100–01, 102
Loes, Billy 178
Lolich, Mickey 119
Lombardi, Ernie 92, 254
Luque, Dolf 268
Lyons, Ted 183

Mack, Connie 45, 46, 48, 117, 199
Maddux, Greg 5, 7, 104, 136
Maglie, Sal 267–68
Malamud, Bernard 287
Maloney, Carolyn R.D. 105
Maloney, Earl 104, 109
Maloney, James W. "Jim" 77, 80, 104–09
Maloney, Jami 105
Maloney, Jason 105
Maloney, Jeanne 104
Maloney, Lyn 109
Maloney, Marjorie K. 104
Maloney, Sharon 105
Mancuso, Gus 223
Mantle, Mickey 28, 41, 96, 120, 164
Maranville, Rabbit 38
Marichal, Juan 55, 108, 119
Marquard, Rube 210
Martin, Billy 160
Martin, Pepper 240
Martinez, Dennis 298
Martinez, Pedro 63, 215
Mathews, Eddie 39, 41, 119, 157, 271
Mathewson, Christy 47, 52, 209, 212, 299
Matlack, Jon 293
Matthews, Gary 29
Mattick, Bobby 105
Mattingly, Don 268–69
Mauch, Gene 17
Maud Muller 1
Mauer, Joe 135
May, Carlos 3, 109–14
May, Elizabeth 111
May, Jacob 113
May, Lee 110, 111, 113
May, Luis 111
May, Margaret H. 110–11, 112
May, Mildred 110
May, Rosemary B. 113
May, Tommy 110
Mays, Carl 34, 36–38, 269, **269**
Mays, Willie 30, 55, 118, 146
Mazeroski, Bill "Maz" 84, 85
McCarthy, Joe 49
McCarver, Tim 5
McCormick, Jim 246
McCourt, Frank 130
McCovey, Willie 158

McDaniel, Kerry "Butch" 270
McDaniel, Lindy 270, 272
McDaniel, Max Von 269–72
McDermott, Mickey 279
McDonald, John 274
McDougald, Gil 165–66, 169
McDowell, Jack 136
McDowell, Sam 272–73
McGinnity, Joe 87
McGraw, John 48, 175
McGwire, Mark 7, 155
McHenry, Alice 114
McHenry, Austin B. 114–16
McHenry, Austin "Bush," Jr. 116
McHenry, Ethel 116
McHenry, Hannah M.J. 114
McHenry, Leone 116
McHenry, Dr. Oscar E. 114
McKechnie, Bill 254
McKeon, Jack 24
McKinnon, Alex 273
McLain, Betty 116
McLain, Dennis D. "Denny" 116–23
McLain, Dennis L. 118
McLain, Kristin 118, 122
McLain, Michelle 118
McLain, Sharon (Sharyn) A. Boudreau 117–18, 122, 123
McLain, Timothy "Tim" 116, 118
McLain, Timothy E. 118
McLain, Tom 116–17
McMahon, John "Sadie" 273
McMullen, John 151
McVey, Cal 12
Medwick, Joe 54–55, 94, 198
Melillo, Oscar 156
Mercer, Sid 74, 120
Merriwell, Frank 170
Merritt, Jim 81
Messersmith, Andy 26
Meyers, Chief 171
Miley, Mike 19
Minoso, Minnie 273–74
Mitchell, Kevin 161
Mitchell Report 8
Monroe, Marilyn 1
Mooney, Jim 295
Moore, Terry 224
Morales, Kendrys 62
Morgan, Joe 30, 148
Morneau, Justin 274–75
Morris, Ed "Cannonball" 275, **275**
Mulder, Mark 275–76
Mulleavy, Greg 177
Munro, Neil 3
Munson, Thurman 73, 158, 276–77
Murphy, Dale 149

Index

Murphy, Justin 246
Murray, Eddie 198
Murray, Jim 90
Murtaugh, Danny 82
Musial, Richard Kerr 263
Musial, Stan 30, 94, 224, 263
Myer, Buddy 101–02

Nagy, Mike 112
Naismith Basketball Hall of Fame 1, 53
The Natural 233, 287
Neagle, Denny 226
Neal, Bob 167
Negro League Baseball Hall of Fame 202
Nemec, David 255
Newcombe, Billie R. 129
Newcombe, Donald "Don" 123–31, 273
Newcombe, Donald, Jr. 129, 130
Newcombe, Evit 124
Newcombe, Freddie G. 124, 128
Newcombe, Gregory 124
Newcombe, Harold 124, 129
Newcombe, James R. 124
Newcombe, James "Roland," Jr. 124, 129
Newcombe, Kelly 129
Newcombe, Norman 124, 129
Newcombe, Sadie S. 124
Newcombe, Tony 129
Newhouser, Hal 68
Neyer, Rob 147
Nichols, Kid 87, 100, 172
Niekro, Phil 23, 272
Nineteenth Century Stars 231
Nixon, Richard 228
Nixon, Russ 32, 247
Nolan, Gary 81
North, Bill 247

O'Brien, Buck 211
Ojeda, Bobby 277
Olin, Steve 277
Oliva, Tony 2, 16, 277–79
O'Malley, Peter 130
O'Neil, Dr. Eugene E. 219–20
Ontiveros, Steve 229
Orr, David L. "Dave" 131–34, *132*
Orr, Emily 134
Orr, James 131
Orr, Rachel 131
Ortiz, David 204, 265, 297
Otis, Amos 28, 29, 246
O'Toole, Jim 81
Ott, Mel 39, 40, 100–01, 295
Owen, Mickey 93

Palmer, Arnold 65
Palmer, Jim 23, 74, 79, 104

Palmer, Pete 3, 210, 220
Parker, Wes 3, 56, 57, 107, 237
Parnell, Mel 258, 279–80
Patten, Gilbert 170
Paul, Gabe 79
Pearson, Ike 140
Peavy, Jake 205
Peckinpaugh, Roger 99
Pedroia, Dustin 63
Perini, Lou 225
Perry, Gaylord 23, 205, 283
Pesky, Johnny 224, 280
Peters, Gary 289
Petrocelli, Rico 280
Phelon, W.E. 14
Phelps, Frank 13
The Phenomenon: Pressure, the Yips, and the Pitch That Changed My Life 10
Piazza, Mike 248, 289
Piecoro, Nick 206
Pierce, Franklin 181
Piersall, Jimmy 280
Piniella, Lou 112
Pinson, Vada 105
Plank, Eddie 46
Pond, Erastus A. "Arlie" 280–81
Porter, Cole 217
Povich, Shirley 102
Powers, Mike "Doc" 170, 171
Preuss, Alex 218
Princess Diana 1
Prior, Amanda 138
Prior, Caitlyn 138
Prior, Heather 138
Prior, Jerry 135
Prior, Jerry, Jr. 135
Prior, Mark W. 134–38, 292
Prior, Matthew 138
Prior, Millie 135
Prior, Millie, Jr. 135
Pro Football Hall of Fame 1
Puckett, Kirby 268–69, 278–79, 298
Pujols, Albert 248, 289

Queen, Mel 81
Quirk (trainer) 214

Radbourn, Old Hoss 50
Ramirez, Manny 6, 269
Ramos, Pedro 40
Reach, A.J. 58, 61
Reagan, Ronald 151
Redmond, Mike 63
Reese, Pee Wee 270–71
Regalado, Rudy 158
Reichler, Joe 163–64
Reiser, George 139, 142

312 Index

Reiser, Harold P. "Pete" 1, 3, 53, 54, 138–45
Reiser, Patricia T.H. 141–42
Reiser, Sally Ann 141
Reiser, Shirley 142
Reiser, Stella B. 139, 142
Resurrection: The J.R. Richard Story 152
Reuss, Jerry 31
Reynolds, Craig 188, 190
Rice, Ed 175
Rice, Jim 198, 226
Richard, Carolyn 151
Richard, Clayton 145
Richard, Crystal 151
Richard, Eric 151
Richard, Grethan 152
Richard, James Rodney "J.R." 1, 145–52, 178, 190, 264
Richard, J.R., III 152
Richard, J.R., Jr. 152
Richard, Lizzie F. 145
Richard, Patrick 151
Richard, Paula 151
Richard, Zemphery V. 151
Richardson, Spec 31
Rickey, Branch 115, 116, 124, 125
Riggleman, Jim 292
Righetti, Dave 160
Rijo, Jose 81
Rikard, Cully 143
Ripken, Cal 187
Ritter, Larry 217
Rivera, Jim 158, 179
Rizzuto, Phil 94, 141
Roberts, Doug 218
Robinson, Brooks 289
Robinson, Eddie 111
Robinson, Frank 105, 198, 289
Robinson, Jackie 53, 124, 125, 130, 299
Robinson, Wilbert 58
Rodriguez, Alex 157, 187, 204, 248
Rogers, John 61
Rojas, Minnie 19
Rolfe, Red 95, 182
Rosar, Buddy 91
Rose, Pete 2, 30, 147–48, 233–34, 245, 246
Rosen, Albert L. "Al" 153–61, 189, 243
Rosen, Andy 155
Rosen, Evelyn S. 155
Rosen, Jerry 153
Rosen, Jim 155
Rosen, Louis 153
Rosen, Rita L. 155
Rosen, Rob 155
Rosen, Rose L. 153
Rosen, Terese Ann B. 155
Rothenberg, Matt 3
Roush, Edd 97

Rowe, Schoolboy 211
Ruane, Tom 3
Ruffing, Red 183
Ruiz, Chico 19
rules changes 11, 13, 86, 87, 88
Rusie, Amos 49, 87, 172, 210, 299, **299**
Russell, Bill 148
Ruth, Babe 37, 58, 96, 117, 198, 224, 290
Ryan, Nolan 23, 26, 51, 146, 148, 149, 150, 264

Saberhagen, Bret 281
Sain, Johnny 118, 119
Salsinger, H.G. 170
Sandberg, Ryne 85, 266
Santana, Johan 2, 281–82
Santo, Ron 83, 85–86
Sayers, Donald 124
Sayers, Gale 1
Scarbath, Jack 95
Scherzer, Max 282
Schilling, Curt 203
Schmidt, Mike 18, 157
Schoendienst, Red 83
Score, Ann 162
Score, Anna Mae 162
Score, David 166
Score, Helen 162
Score, Herbert A. 162
Score, Herbert J. "Herb" 1, 161, 162–69
Score, Judy 166
Score, Mary 166
Score, Nancy M. 166
Score, Susan 166
Scott, George 25
Scott, Mike 160
Scullen, the Rev. Dr. Willard 37
Scully, Vin 179
Seaver, Tom 23, 65, 146, 147
Selbach, Kip 98
Sewell, Joe 38, 195
Sheets, Larry 233
Shocker, Urban 282–83, **283**
Shor, Toots 95
Shotton, Burt 125
Silbar, Mert 119
similarity scores 2–3, 21, 28–29, 41, 52, 85, 87, 97, 104, 121, 133, 141, 150, 195, 198, 205, 212, 233, 252, 266, 269
Simmons, Al 143
Simmons, Ted 146
Simpson, Wayne 79, 283–84
Sinatra, Frank 73
Sizemore, Grady 284
Skowron, Bill "Moose" 179
Slapnicka, Cy 163, 198

Index

Slaton, Jim 280
Slaughter, Enos 140, 141
Smith, Al 166
Smith, Barbara 18
Smith, Bob 81
Smith, Chester 81
Smith, Leonard 18, 19
Smith, Ozzie 188
Smith, R.E. 135
Smith, Tal 160
Snider, Edwin "Duke" 30, 54, 55, 141, 143, 198, 284
Sockalexis, Andrew 174
Sockalexis, Frances P.S. 169–70
Sockalexis, Francis P. 169–70
Sockalexis, Louis F. (Lewis M.) 3, 169–76
Sommers, Pete 133
Sosa, Sammy 55
Soto, Mario 81
Southworth, Billy 223, 225
Spahn, Warren 87, 126, 182, 291
Spalding, Albert 11, 12, 15
Speaker, Tris 36, 100, 156, 165, 201, 212, 216, 260, 263
Spink, J.G. Taylor 49
Spooner, Carol P. 177
Spooner, Karen 177
Spooner, Karl B. 146, 176–80
Spooner, Karrie 177
Spooner, Kelley 177
Spooner, Kevin 177
Spooner, Kim 177
Spooner, Maurice 176, 179
Stahl, Jake 211
Standish, Burt 170
Stanton, Giancarlo 41
Stargell, Willie 146–47
Steinbrenner, George 159–60
Steinhagen, Ruth 287
Stengel, Casey 144
Stenzel, Jake 172
Stephens, Vern 224
Stewart, Jimmy 184
Stieb, Dave 284
Stirnweiss, George "Snuffy" 90
Stock, Wes 40
Stone, George 284–85, **285**
Storm, Hannah 226
Stovey, Harry 255
Strasburg, Stephen 135
Stratton, Dennis L. 183
Stratton, Ethel M. 183
Stratton, Leslie 181
Stratton, Monty F.P. 1, 181–85
Stratton, Monty, Jr. 183
Stratton, Roland 181
The Stratton Story 184, 222

Superstars 79
Sutton, Don 23, 26, 283
Swann (district attorney) 37

Taft, William Howard 281
Tanana, Frank 285–86
Tango, Tom 147, 165
Tanner, Chuck 112
Tatum, Ken 112
Taveras, Oscar 286
Taylor, John I. 209
Tebbetts, Birdie 160
Tebeau, Patsy 172, 261
Tener, John K. 58
Terry, Bill 101
Thomas, Frank 6
Thompson, Sam 55
Thon, Cecilia 186
Thon, Evangeline 185
Thon, Francis "Frankie" 185, 186–87
Thon, Fred, Jr. 185, 186
Thon, Fred, Sr. 185
Thon, Freddie 185
Thon, Freddie, Jr. 191
Thon, Kenneth 185
Thon, Maria S.R. "Sol" 186
Thon, Mariana 186
Thon, Richard "Dickie Joe" 186, 191
Thon, Richard W. "Dickie" 3, 44, 160, 185–92
Thon, Soleil M. 186
Thon, Vanessa 186
Thorn, John 235
Thornton, Andre 233
Tiant, Luis 26
Torre, Joe 118
Torrez, Mike 189
Totton, Lucy 207
Travis, Ada 192
Travis, Cecil A. 195
Travis, Cecil H. 192–98, 287
Travis, Helen H. 195
Travis, James 192
Travis, Mike 195
Travis, Rickey 195
Traynor, Pie 20, 21
Trojovsky, John 198–99
Trojovsky, Mary S. 198
Trosky, Hal, Jr. 199, 201
Trosky (Trojovsky), Harold A. "Hal" 158, 198–202
Trosky, James 199
Trosky, Lorraine E.G. 199
Trosky, Lynn 199
Trosky, Mary Kay 199
Trotsky, Leon 201
Trout, Mike 1, 28, 64, 248, 289

Index

Trucks, Virgil 286
Turner, Edward 18
Turner, Thomas 18
Turton, Richard 5

Umbricht, Jim 189
Uncle Tom's Cabin 99

Valenzuela, Fernando 283
Valo, Elmer 270
Vance, Dazzy 181, 182
Vaughan, Arky 158, 195, 196, 280
Veach, Bobby 214
Veeck, Bill 243
Verducci, Tom 6
Verlander, Justin 51, 127–28
Vernon, Mickey 157, 286
Versalles, Zoilo 287
Villone, Ron 274
Viña, Fernando 226
Vincent, Fay 234
Virdon, Bill 149, 150
Vitale, Dick 73
Vitt, Ossie 200
Volquez, Edinson 253

Waddell, Rube 210
Wagner, Honus 14, 58, 97, 195, 196
Waitkus, Eddie 287
Wakefield, Dick 287–89
Wakefield, Howard 287
Walker, Harry 30
Wallace, Bobby 172
Walls, Lee 128
Walsh, Ed 46, 210, 212
Walton, Bill 1
Wambsganss, Bill 215
Wantz, Dick 19
Ward, Pete 289
Warneke, Lon 223
Waterman, Guy 125
Webb, Alicia B. 204
Webb, Brandon T. 202–07
Webb, Mr. & Mrs. Philip 202
Webb, Reagan 204
Weiss, George 89–90
Weld, Ernie 130

White, Deacon 12
Whittier, John Greenleaf 1
Wilhelm, Hoyt 289
Wilkens, Lenny 53
Williams, Billy 83, 283
Williams, Claude "Lefty" 263, 290
Williams, Ted 89, 91, 93, 111, 156, 158, 195, 196, 230, 236, 288, 299–300
Willis, Dontrelle 290–91
Wills, Maury 55
Wilson, Don 147, 189–90, 291
Wilson, Hack 55
Wilson, Jimmie 140
Wilson, Owen 132–33
Wood, Gerald C. 213
Wood, Harley "Pete" 207, 217
Wood, Howard E. "Smoky Joe" 3, 121, 207–18, **208**
Wood, Jimmy 291–92
Wood, Joe, Jr. 214, 217
Wood, John F. 207
Wood, Kerry 135, 1'37, 292
Wood, Laura T. O'Shea 214, 217
Wood, Rebecca S. 207
Wood, Robert K. "Bob" 214, 217, 218
Wood, Stephen L. "Steve" 214, 217
Wood, Virginia 214
Wright, Craig 60, 157, 294–95
Wright, David 2, 292
Wright, Glenn 195
Wright, Harry 158
Wright, John 124
Wynn, Early 165, 267

Yastrzemski, Carl 40
York, Rudy 94
Young, Cy 25, 51, 63, 64, 65, 74, 79, 87, 120, 121, 127–28, 130, 136, 147, 148, 201, 202, 204, 205, 210, 227, 228, 229, 232, 249, 258, 276, 281, 282, 291, 298
Youngs, Ross 300, **300**
Yount, Robin 100–01

Zernial, Gus 111
Zito, Barry 276

www.ingramcontent.com/pod-product-compliance
Lightning Source LLC
Chambersburg PA
CBHW030324020526
44117CB00030B/1024